SCENES AND PERSONALITIES IN ANGLO-JEWRY
1800–2000

Parkes–Wiener Series on Jewish Studies

SERIES EDITORS: DAVID CESARANI AND TONY KUSHNER
ISSN 1368-5449

The field of Jewish Studies is one of the youngest, but fastest growing and most exciting areas of scholarship in the academic world today. Named after James Parkes and Alfred Wiener, this series aims to publish new research in the field and student materials for use in the seminar room, to disseminate the latest work of established scholars and to re-issue classic studies which are currently out of print.

The selection of publications will reflect the international character and diversity of Jewish Studies; it ranges over Jewish history from Abraham to modern Zionism, and Jewish culture from Moses to post-modernism. The series also reflect the inter-disciplinary approach inherent in Jewish Studies and at the cutting edge of contemporary scholarship, and provides an outlet for innovative work on the interface between Judaism and ethnicity, popular culture, gender, class, space and memory.

Other Books in the Series

Holocaust Literature: Schulz, Levi, Spiegelman and the Memory of the Offence
Gillian Banner
Remembering Cable Street: Fascism and Anti-Fascism in British Society
Edited by Tony Kushner and Nadia Valman
Sir Sidney Hamburger and Manchester Jewry: Religion, City and Community
Bill Williams
Anglo-Jewry in Changing Times: Studies in Diversity 1840–1914
Israel Finestein
Double Jeopardy: Gender and the Holocaust
Judith Tydor Baumel
Cultures of Ambivalence and Contempt: Studies in Jewish-on-Jewish Relations
Edited by Siân Jones, Tony Kushner and Sarah Pearce
Alfred Wiener and the Making of the Wiener Library
Ben Barkow
The Berlin Haskalah and German Religious Thought: Orphans of Knowledge
David Sorkin
Myths in Israeli Culture: Captives of a Dream
Nurith Gertz
The Jewish Immigrant in England 1870–1914, Third Edition
Lloyd P. Gartner
State and Society in Roman Galilee, A.D. 132–212, Second Edition
Martin Goodman
Disraeli's Jewishness
Edited by Todd M. Endelman and Tony Kushner
Claude Montefiore: His Life and Thought
Daniel R. Langton

SCENES AND PERSONALITIES
IN
ANGLO-JEWRY
1800–2000

ISRAEL FINESTEIN

VALLENTINE MITCHELL
LONDON • PORTLAND, OR

First published in 2002 in Great Britain by
VALLENTINE MITCHELL
Crown House, 47 Chase Side, Southgate
London N14 5BP

and in the United States of America by
VALLENTINE MITCHELL
c/o ISBS, 5824 N.E. Hassalo Street
Portland, Oregon 97213-3644

Website: www.vmbooks.com

British Library Cataloguing in Publication Data

Finestein, Israel
  Scenes and personalities in Anglo-Jewry, 1800–2000. –
  (Parkes–Wiener series on Jewish studies)
  1. Jews – Great Britain – History – 19th century 2. Jews –
  Great Britain – History – 20th century 3. Jews – Great
  Britain – Social conditions – 19th century 4. Jews – Great
  Britain – Social conditions – 20th century 5. Jews – Great
  Britain – Civilization
  I. Title
  941'.004924

ISBN 0-85303-443-5 (cloth)
ISBN 0-85303-442-7 (paper)
ISSN 1368–5449

Library of Congress Cataloging-in-Publication Data

Finestein, I.
  Scenes and personalities in Anglo-Jewry, 1800–2000 / Israel Finestine.
    p. cm. – (Parkes–Wiener series on Jewish studies, ISSN 1368-5449)
  Includes bibliographical references and index.
  ISBN 0-85303-443-5 (cloth) – ISBN 0-85303-442-7 (pbk.)
    1. Jews–Great Britain–Politics and government–19th century. 2. Jews–Great
  Britain–Politics and government–20th century. 3. Jewish leadership–Great Britain.
  I. Title. II. Series.

DS135.E5 F465 2002
941'.004924–dc21
                                                           2002026521

Typeset in 11/13pt Sabon by Vitaset, Paddock Wood, Kent
Printed in Great Britain by
MPG Books Ltd, Victoria Square, Bodmin, Cornwall

To the Memory of
Jeremiah Finestein 1878–1958
Rosa Finestein 1885–1963
Simon Oster 1895–1976
Bessie Oster 1893–1979

Contents

List of Illustrations

Albert Friedlander and F.S. Worms (eds), *Meir Gertner: An Anthology* (London: Jewish Book Council, 1978).

10. Miriam Moses being installed as the Mayor of Stepney (1932) from A. Shapiro and M. Shapiro (eds), *Jewish East End* (London: Springboard Education Trust, 1996). Second from right: Barnett (later Lord) Janner, Liberal MP for Whitechapel.

11. Rabbi Kopul Rosen (1914–62), from Cyril Domb (ed.), *Memoirs of Kopul Rosen* (Carmel College, 1970).

12. Rebecca Sieff addressing the 1945 Federation of Women Zionists Conference, from *Golden Jubilee Volume of the Federation of Women Zionists* (London: Federation of Women Zionists, 1978).

13. Sir Leon Simon (1881–1965), at c. the age of 35, from Barnett Litvinoff (ed.), *Letters and Papers of Chaim Weizmann*, Vol. 6 (Jerusalem: Israel Universities Press, 1974).

14. Lucien Wolf, the original caricature appeared in the *Daily Graphic*, reproduced from Stuart A. Cohen, *English Zionists and British Jews: The Communal Politics of Anglo-Jewry, 1895–1920* (Princeton, NJ: Princeton University Press, 1982).

15. Israel Zangwill, from a portrait in *Vanity Fair* (1897), courtesy of Mr Harry Schwab, London.

16. Professor Brodetsky in academic dress at the opening of the Weizmann Institute of Science, Rehovot, 1949. Reproduced from Selig Brodetsky, *Memoirs: From Ghetto to Israel* (London: Weidenfeld & Nicolson, 1960).

17. Dr Abraham Cohen, distinguished Jewish scholar, and Minister of the Birmingham Hebrew Congregation, 1913–49. President of the Board of Deputies of British Jews, 1949–55. Reproduced from A.N. Newman, *History of the Board of Deputies* (London: Board of Deputies of British Jews, 1960).

18. Rabbi Dr Lord Jakobovits (1921–99), Chief Rabbi of the United Hebrew Congregations of the Commonwealth, 1967–91. Reproduced from the memorial service brochure (1999).

Introduction

In August 1995 there was held at the Oxford Centre for Hebrew and Jewish Studies a conference of Jewish scholars and communal leaders, professional and lay, from Israel, Europe and America. Its theme was the changing nature and structure of Jewish communities since the Second World War. The first chapter in this book is based on my address thereat and was included in the conference volume, edited by Ilan Troen, Professor of Modern History at the Ben-Gurion University, and published in America in 1999.

The Institute for Jewish Policy Research, appropriately and with due acknowledgement, adopted therefrom as the title of its *Report on Representation of the Interests of the British Jewish Community* (2000), the term 'A Community of Communities'. The community bears the marks of its original degree of centralisation and the impact of successive transformations in composition and culture. Three reasons might be offered for this distinctive amalgam of disparate features in the communal system.

The first relates to the reactions of regional communities to the instinctive, paternalistic and somewhat self-indulgent monopoly inherent in the authority long exercised by the upper Jewish echelons of the capital. Adverse reactions, no less instinctive and often amounting to regional mirror-images of metropolitan self-confidence, began in earnest in the 1850s, gained in vigour as that century advanced, and proceeded far into the twentieth century – in the course of a series of changing issues, policy differences, and personal relationships.

The second reason is connected with the freedom which was natural in the traditionally voluntary community which was Anglo-Jewry. Social emancipation long preceded civil and political emancipation. The Re-Settlement in the seventeenth century introduced no ghetto. Not since the medieval period has there been anything in the nature of an official category of continental-style *rabbiner*; no compulsory Jewish taxation by State organs or at the instance of the State was imposed; no obligatory constitutional or fiscal patterns were ordained. Neither the United Synagogue Act of 1870, nor the Chief Rabbinate clauses in the United Synagogue's Deed of Foundation and Trust, changed the voluntary essence of the communal system, whatever strains or anomalies time brought about. The libertarianism of life in Britain could not but affect the Jewish communal system and its ever evolving 'politics' and patterns.

The third reason is inextricably associated with the open door policy on immigration from 1836, which was not seriously halted until the outbreak of war in 1914, despite the provisions of the Aliens Act of 1905. The variety of continental immigrant groups multiplied the types of Jewish opinion, culture and practice in a community whose numbers were exceeded by the new arrivals, increasingly so from 1881.

These factors lie behind major parts of the first chapter and deeply influenced the aspirations and policies considered in the second, which is a revised and expanded version of sections of my paper written in the 1950s at the invitation of the American Jewish Committee. That paper was concerned with English law in relation to Jewish religious education in Britain, a paper sought by the Committee for comparative purposes in connection with the American educational scene, where different principles applied. A summary of the paper was circulated by the Committee for in-house information within the Committee and its affiliates. The original paper has not before been published.

Chapters 13, 14 and 15 in this book, relating to the Board of Deputies in 1948–49, are included as reflecting the impressions at that time of a comparatively new and no doubt impressionable younger member of the Board. Their more historical and less personal interest rests in their demonstration of the continuity of the at times anxious issues which characteristically beset the Jewish community's elected representative body during most of the twentieth century; questions as to its *modus operandi*, the extent of its recognition as the community's elected spokesbody, its relations with outside power structures within the community, and its financial constraints.

Since this book was compiled there has been negotiated between the different major religious bodies represented at the Board an agreement which bids fair to ease the former state of tension which marred both their own relationships and the working of the Board. The 'Stanmore accords', as their agreement has somewhat imperially been called by their leaders at the Board, have the express approval of the Chief Rabbinate. The Union of Orthodox Hebrew Congregations continues its non-membership of the Board, while retaining its cooperation in certain practical fields, notably 'Jewish Defence'.

These developments, perhaps parochial in themselves, are part of a course of events of wider compass which have becalmed the 'ecclesiastical' scene, to which short reference is made in the latter part of the first chapter. Such progress has coincided with, and may not be wholly unrelated to, the further confident expansion of opportunities for Jewish studies at all levels, marked by a yet greater intensity of programme than heretofor. This proceeds under the diverse array of yet more auspices than before, including the continuing proliferation and planning of additional Jewish day schools. A feature of the expanded opportunities for Jewish study has been not only the increase in the number of women among the students but also among the instructors – often on themes traditionally associated with male, generally rabbinic, lecturers. And what a long and varied history rests behind the declaration in the Jewish Year Book for 2002 by the President of the Board of Deputies that all Jewish schools should be Zionist schools! She is Mrs Josephine Wagerman, the former notable headteacher of the J.F.S. Comprehensive School, and the first woman and the first schoolteacher to be elected President of the Board. Meanwhile, with whatever irony, the desirability or otherwise of additional 'faith schools', and of segregation of 'races', in education has attracted public debate in the wider society and in the Jewish Community.

The final two chapters are clearly a kind of addendum. But they are not extraneous to the subject matter of the book. They touch on major concerns within sections of the Jewish community, such as the nature of Jewish identity, the purposes of its retention and cultivation, and the rationale of communal priorities. The chapters bear upon matters referred to directly or indirectly in different parts of the book. I am grateful to the publishers who took kindly to my suggestion that they be incorporated.

In circles where those questions have attracted attention, such attention has been accompanied by heightened concern for Israel's security. The concern for her security and peace, which is not limited to these circles, has become an ever-more self-conscious element in communal thinking and action, including a greater sense of need for adequate pro-active and reactive responses in the sometimes difficult field of media reportage and comment. The voice of senior professionals, notably younger recruits, has been especially note-worthy in this area, as elsewhere in the developing communal system. An adequate system for recruitment and training for future leadership, lay as well as professional, remains an aspiration, to which current leadership gives signs of a serious readiness to respond. Criticism of Israel's performance in the face of organized terrorism has at times chosen the tone of hostility to Israel as such, challenging her legitimacy, and using language and imagery which have long been associated with avowed anti-Semitism. The spate of local anti-Jewish incidents has sharpened communal concerns; this anxiety is not allayed by the incidents' fluctuating occurrence. The central role of the (United) Joint Israel Appeal, notably after its succession to the responsibilities of Jewish Continuity, has been much enhanced by communal requirements which came in the wake of the events of 11 September 2001.

A degree of duplication within the volume is perhaps natural in view of the interrelated themes explored in these chapters. This has been reduced to the minimum consistent with retaining the pattern and purpose of each chapter.

Thanks are expressed for permission to reprint articles or illus-trations, where appropriate. Where it proved impracticable to contact relevant copyright holders, apologies are extended for any omissions.

My thanks go to Frank Cass and his team at Vallentine Mitchell, notably Sally Green and Georgina Clark-Mazo, for their cooperation and professional skills. My prime thanks, as ever, are to my wife for her unfailing support and encouragement throughout.

Israel Finestein
London
June 2002

1

The Changing Governance of Anglo-Jewry 1950–2000*

The Jewish scene in Britain has been marked by paradox upon paradox.[1] It continues to bear traces of this condition. The ever-growing participation of Jews in politics, in the arts and sciences, in commerce and industry, has long been accompanied by an ever-increasing communal self-analysis and personal introspection. Robust projections of a viable Jewish future have mingled with warnings of fragility and decline, without the regenerative immigrations from Eastern Europe and Central Europe which much affected the late nineteenth century and the first half of the twentieth. Tell-tale signs of erosion and revival, of wide indifference, and wide enthusiasm for Jewish knowledge, offer at times a bewilderingly chequered communal picture.

Never before has there been such a plethora of Jewish religious and cultural institutions, seminars, and courses, for all sections of Jewish life and opinion and at all levels of age and attainment, as today. The annual number and variety of Judaica currently published in Britain hugely exceed the productions of any earlier generation. Yet informed opinion has it that the Jewish community is largely a non-reading society, a feature regularly bemoaned by those active in the fields of publication, education (adult and otherwise), and communal planning.

---

*First published in S. Ilan Troen (ed.), *Jewish Centres and Peripheries: Europe between America and Israel Fifty years after World War II* (Piscataway, NJ: Transaction Publishers, 1999).

A reminder of what had come to be, well before the 1970s, an extensively recognized pressing desideratum may be seen in the independently declared objectives of Jewish cultural institutions founded in that decade. The Orthodox-based and latitudinarian Yakar Study Centre in London (1978) for example, aimed 'to promote Jewish culture and tradition'. The Spiro Institute for the Study of Jewish History and Culture (1978), aimed 'to provide self-awareness and strengthen Jewish identity'. The Association of Jewish Sixth Formers (1977) was concerned with 'promoting a positive Jewish identity among sixth-form students' at school. These and other religious and cultural bodies continue their operations with comparable aspirations, in many differing contexts of Jewish thinking and outlook. Yeshiva study has never been more widespread; increasing numbers of former yeshiva students are found in the professions (especially in law) and in business (especially in real estate).

In March 1977, the Board of Deputies of British Jews convened a conference on 'Jewish Life in Modern Britain'.[2] One of the principal sections was entitled 'The Challenge of Secularisation', a theme debated mainly between the then Chief Rabbi, Dr (later Lord) Jakobovits, and the notable historian and former Communist, Professor Chimen Abramsky, secularist son of a former leading dayan of the London Beth Din. The conference was the successor to the pioneer conference convened by the Board under the initiating guidance of Professor Moshe Davis of the Hebrew University in 1962.[3] It is noteworthy that on the earlier occasion the subject of the growing secularisation was not on the published agenda. Fifteen years later its contemporary relevance had brought it to centre stage. Gone was the inhibition against high-level controversial public discussions on the subject (with some exceptions on the religious 'far right'). Under Lord Jakobovits's successor, Rabbi Dr Sacks, the theme became a frequent issue for public debate with leading secularists, in which Dr Sacks, as Principal of Jews' College and later as Chief Rabbi, was a participant. Dr Sacks' declared objective in participation was to stimulate the pursuit of Jewish knowledge. The issue came to be debated largely in the course of examining the ingredients of Jewishness in the modern world, a question sharpened by the creation and survival of embattled Israel.

Towards the end of 1948, the then Archbishop of Canterbury, Dr Geoffrey Fisher, amicably, but no less seriously, addressed the

Council of Christians and Jews (formed in 1943), of which he and the Chief Rabbi were among the joint presidents, on the nature of being a Jew. The term, he commented, 'may mean a Jew by race and religion, but equally it is used of people who are Jews by race and have no religion at all'. Such questions had long been publicly debated in Britain. The events of the twentieth century, including the establishment of Israel and Israeli nationality and citizenship, added to them a degree of immediacy and greater practicality in some sections of public opinion. In the Jewish community there was evoked a large disparity of responses. The State of Israel and her wars contributed to a reduction of restraint in some quarters in the questioning of religious authority; to a keener sense of attachment to Judaism (in whatever form) in others; and simultaneously to both, on the part of some. In any event there was a heightening of the sense of polarization in the Jewish community, adding yet more strength to the sensing and enunciation of differentials between religious groupings on the 'right' and 'left'.

The deepening of Jewish integration into society at all levels rendered ever more acute the concern for the cultivation and retention of a transmissible, distinctively Jewish, identity. This common interest within the Jewish community often aroused highly contentious public discussion over how to meet these ideals. Central to the exchanges have been the character and meaning of Jewishness in the open western society of today. In an era of rapid scientific advance, philosophical speculation (academic and popular), and critical historical study, such issues inevitably gained prominence – all the greater for many by reason of the mounting publicity attached to frequent and sharp personal and organizational contention. The contentions attracted attention even in the absence of any general popular intrinsic interest in the themes.

The Jewish community is sometimes perceived from the outside as a cohesive body; by some, even as a kind of unitary organism. In truth it is more a community of communities. The communities of Scotland, Wales and Northern Ireland are not the only ones in the United Kingdom with their own distinctive histories and character. Ideology, personality, geography, organizational interests, local concerns, and the habits of history, give the whole a fissiparous, not to say at times an apparently 'fissile' character.

London Jewry, totalling 220,000 and comprising two-thirds of

3

the Jewish community in Britain, has, like the major provincial cities (notably Manchester, in terms of numbers) its 'far-right' inward-looking enclaves, as well as wide economic and social divisions. The Jews in the eastern regions of the metropolitan area, notably in the extensive borough of Redbridge, are separated from the yet larger concentrations of Jewish population in the northern and north-west regions of London by more than the considerable size of the capital. The sense of distance is accentuated by a residual touch of an old social gulf between 'west end' and 'east end'. While any generalization would be inaccurate, there are self-conscious differences between the business and professional categories of Jewish residence in the north-western suburbs, on the one hand, and some sections within the occupational structure of the Jewish population in the east, on the other hand.

In 1995, the then President of the United Synagogue reported to its Council that it had not proved possible to procure a suitable dayan for appointment to the London Beth Din (otherwise known as the Court of the Chief Rabbi) who would be willing to take up residence, as was desired, in the eastern region of the London Jewish community; this in spite of the size of the Jewish community of Redbridge alone (20,000), including a large United Synagogue population. The Ilford area of Redbridge has the third largest congregation in the United Synagogue. Redbridge houses the largest community centre in Anglo-Jewry (Sinclair House), a major Jewish primary school, and a Jewish secondary school (opened 1993), with room for considerable growth on its 17-acre site. Whatever the reasons for it, the president's statement was a telling announcement.

Viewed in a continental perspective, the geography of the Jewish community is comparatively compact. This circumstance and the survival of its old central and entrenched organizations may seem, from the outside, to reflect and even to foster a high degree of cohesion. Such assessment does indeed have some element of historical warrant.

The Chief Rabbinate can be traced to the eighteenth century. It arose out of the rabbinate of the Great Synagogue, destroyed in a German air raid in 1941, in the old City of London. It was the parent congregation of Britain's Ashkenazi community. The Chief Rabbi, by the founding deed of trust of the United Synagogue, became constitutionally the sole religious authority of that body, by far the largest grouping of synagogues. It now comprises 66 congregations in the London area, incorporating approximately 30,000 households. The Chief Rabbi is also acknowledged as the religious head of the bulk of congregations in the 80 provincial Jewish communities. No marriage may be performed in any synagogue under his jurisdiction without prior certification by his office. This secures a considerable degree of uniform practice regarding qualifications for marriage, including, when relevant, the requirements for conversion. These qualifications and the rigorous requirements are matters of continuing controversy within sections of the Jewish community.

The Board of Deputies of British Jews, whose title echoes its eighteenth-century provenance, is traceable to 1760. It is the Jewish community's elected representative body, now including representation from nearly 200 synagogues in London and beyond, of all blends of Judaism, as well as provincial representative councils and many bodies representing women's groups, youth, specifically Zionist bodies, and other non-synagogal groupings. The Union of Orthodox Hebrew Congregations, often referred to as the 'far right', withdrew its representation 25 years ago. The leaders of the Union objected to an alleged recognition by the Board of the legitimacy of the rabbinate or ministry of the Reform and Liberal congregations by the Board's then recent constitutional amendments. The amendments were in fact an acknowledgement of the existence of the religious authorities of what are usually called the 'Progressive Synagogues' represented on the Board, and whose opinions might be sought on matters relevant to their communities.

The year 2001 saw the 300th anniversary of the erection in the City of London of the oldest extant synagogue in Britain (it is still in use). This is the synagogue of the parent congregation of the Spanish and Portuguese Jewish community in Britain, dating back to the 1650s. For many generations, that community was the dominant section of Anglo-Jewry in terms of numbers, wealth and influence.

The antiquity of this and other Jewish institutions long endowed their leaders with a traditionally acknowledged eminence inside and beyond the Jewish community. This was reinforced by the social standing associated with their public aspirations and general philanthropy. Their highly self-conscious anglicization was joined to a sharply delineated class system within their own community. That system followed the social patterns prevailing in society as a whole, but the sense of class was much accentuated within Jewish society by acute consciousness of differences in the length of British residence. The social elevation enjoyed by the longer-resident families was accompanied by a tradition of *noblesse oblige,* in particular towards the Jewish poor, including the succession of Jewish immigrants.

These features long conditioned the Jewish social system and the communal structure. Some marks of the old attitudes endured into the mid-twentieth century, before making way for new categories of leadership whose oligarchic preferences may nevertheless not always have differed substantially from the ingrained style of the old. Virtually all were now 'of immigrant stock'.

The resistance of the outgoing system to change had long been diminishing. The rate of inter-marriage, the incidence of departure from the Jewish fold, the loss of interest in assuming office in an increasingly fractious Jewish community, and the new opportunities and challenges in society at large, had their effect. Around the turn of the century, the Chief Rabbi, Dr Hermann Adler (1839–1911), would publicly complain of the absence of an adequate response from members of the old families to the call of what he deemed to be their communal, indeed, their public, duty. He was a staunch opponent of political Zionism, and he had inherited an instinctive respect for the spirit of the Victorian Jewish leadership. Like Lucien Wolf (1857–1930), the arch-publicist of the old regime, Adler brooded with anxiety over the prospect of the Jews in the immigrant localities acquiring an extent of influence over the communal image and communal policy at large, commensurate with their proportionate numbers in the total Jewish community. If the old culture of deference was waning in the country as a whole, so too was the case within the Jewish community. During the years of the Eastern European Jewish immigration between 1881 and 1914, Anglo-Jewry grew from about 60,000 to close on 300,000.

Some twentieth-century successors of the generation of the emancipation, which was achieved in the mid-Victorian era, looked upon the attainment thereof not only as a culmination in Jewish history and as a model for Jewish communities in other lands, but also as reflecting a kind of contract between the Jewish community and British society. It was perceived as the outcome of a tacit understanding (and not always tacit in some Jewish quarters in the later nineteenth century), within which any notion of political Zionism was, virtually by definition, excluded. Harry Sacher (1881–1971), businessman, journalist and close kinsman by marriage of Simon (later Lord) Marks (1888–1964) and Israel (later Lord) Sieff (1889–1972), was, with the support of the *Jewish Chronicle*, the most vigorous protagonist against the idea of any 'contract' and against the suggestion of any such related attributed consequence of the emancipation.

A baleful element in the old Victorian-style leadership was the considerable and axiomatic extent of self-approval exhibited by the principal practitioners of the system, including some sections of the successive cadres of prominent figures engaged in synagogal management and Jewish social welfare. An inveterate belief in the self-evident wisdom of the prevailing communal governance was often accompanied in the upper echelons by an habitual and conscious disinterest in the promotion of Jewish higher learning, and by a contentment with what in reality was a minimalist approach to Jewish education for the young. The twentieth century, to which something of this outlook was bequeathed, long bore the effects.

Periodic revolts in the nineteenth century against the pluto-aristocratic system and its educational minimalism had generally been personal. They were sometimes expressions of middle-class aspirations to share more prominently in the management of the community. With the great immigration, there were fresh surges of sharper conflict. The issue of Zionism came ever more to the fore, together with arguments over the advancement of Jewish educational standards and movements for more broadly based forms of communal government. Within virtually all the areas of contention, the same rift line was revealed between the adversaries. These concerns came to be more acutely expressed in public disputes with the 'establishment', on the part of children of immigrants, who had enjoyed university education. Prominent among them were Selig Brodetsky (1888–1954), distinguished mathematician and later President of the Board of Deputies and for a short period President of the Hebrew University; Norman Bentwich (1883–1971), notable academic lawyer and Zionist publicist; and Harry Sacher.

The newer and older communities affected each other profoundly, notwithstanding frequent and distracting conflicts within their own respective ranks. The old protocol and formality, and the new and more popular enthusiasms, proved in time to be mutually infectious. Many of the more recently arrived families, encouraged by fashion and their own economic advancement, strove eagerly to enter into the society and habits of the longer established Jewish community. The burgeoning Jewish upper middle classes in the late nineteenth and in the following century, often made common cause with the older range of inherited communal leadership, which many of them entered by public estimation or through marriage. They formed a significant element in the constellation of major influence well into the mid-twentieth century.

Despite the growing two-way assimilation between old and new, sharp divisions remained between them and were often intensely and publicly argued. They were ideological and social. In the eyes of the largely foreign-born, yeshiva-trained rabbis who served some congregations in London and in the north of the country, the ministers of the United Synagogue were themselves inadequately educated Jewishly. The Talmud Torah centres favoured by those rabbis and by many of their congregants, purveyed a Jewish education of higher calibre in substance and the amount of time devoted to it, than that offered in the far less intense 'synagogue classes' attached to many of the congregations of the United Synagogue in the newer and more salubrious areas of residence in London. Nor was the Council of the United Synagogue, which long before the mid-century had a majority of members of post-1881 families, as compliant as hitherto with the policies and assumptions of its leaders; the residual impact of the old culture of deference was found more in the old procedures than in common outlook.

There also arose in the Jewish community an ever-growing sense of awareness of the diversity between the old central religious system and its counterparts at and near the respective ends of the religious spectrum; and between Jews who by instinct or policy sought or retained a Jewish religious affiliation or attachment, and those who through policy or indifference, detached themselves from any such involvement. Religious, educational and social institutions had proliferated in the wake of the immigration, all with their own respective sources of authority.

The growing 'pluralistic' nature of the Jewish community was much enhanced through the immigration of about 60,000 Jews from Central Europe between 1933 and 1945. There were later smaller immigrations from Hungary, and Sephardi immigrations from Iran, Iraq, Aden, India and North Africa. Many of the post-1933 newcomers were of middle-class origin and included a significant proportion of people of western secular learning and modern Jewish study, rabbinic and secular. This inflow strengthened each segment of the Jewish community within all strands of thought and communal action.

History, memory and habit, which had earlier been factors making for some degree of cohesion, were less effective in a community increasingly affected by preferences and traditions associated with a diversity of backgrounds. Theological issues arose in pointedly disputatious form with greater frequency and acerbity, in a community whose leaders had in former times prided themselves on being less interested in theology than in efficient communal administration and finance. Immigration had transformed the community in more ways than in size.

In reality, that pride was somewhat misplaced. The Reform secession of the 1840s and the emergence of the Jewish Religious Union (precursor of the Liberal Synagogue) at the turn of the century, had provoked highly charged communal controversy and mutual recriminations, which were revived in the 1920s. Adler's successor, Dr Joseph H. Hertz (1872–1946), who had assumed office in 1913, condemned what he called 'this new Hellenism' in scathing terms. Yet a degree of placidity tended to reassert itself. The few United Synagogue Ministers and lay leaders who had joined the Jewish Religious Union eventually withdrew at Adler's request. Claude Montefiore (1858–1938), principal founder and theological mentor of the Liberal Synagogue, continued to serve on Jewish religious education boards which expressly acknowledged Adler's authority. Israel Abrahams (1858–1924), Reader in Rabbinics at Cambridge and the foremost scholar within the Liberal movement, and Montefiore, were on many occasions cited by Hertz in his widely used commentary on the Pentateuch, almost always approvingly. There was a certain intellectual camaraderie between Hertz and Abrahams and Montefiore, despite their sharp doctrinal differences and Hertz's Zionism which the other two opposed.

The lay leadership of the United Synagogue privately deplored the caustic severity of Hertz's denunciatory language.[4] The Jewish community, long famous for the practicality of its institutional life and its comparative calm in matters 'ecclesiastical', has nevertheless displayed a hearty zest for 'ecclesiastical' argument. But these discords did not disturb the inclusivist 'broadchurchmanship' policy and ethos of the United Synagogue, which indeed most of its 'clerics' and laymen, consciously or otherwise, preferred.

Hertz defined what he called the Anglo-Jewish position in theology in phrases which became famous. It was, he declared in 1931, 'religious advance without loss of traditional Jewish values and without estrangement from the collective consciousness of the House of Israel'.[5] What did it mean? He did not define 'religious advance'. As I have suggested elsewhere, his language:

> has no meaning when it comes to application, save for the expedient 'umbrella' connotation often attached to it, which is probably how Hertz hoped it would be construed. The strengthening of the religious 'right' and the religious 'left' (especially) in the wake of the Central European immigration, made the definition ever more difficult to apply. Hertz made a virtue of necessity. The necessity was to retain so far as he could the unifying factors in the community. (His) memorable (phrasing) has little to do with theology ...'[6]

With Hitler's rise to power and the increasing signs of overt anti-Semitism on the home front, divisiveness was not to be encouraged. Hertz was a conservative traditionalist, not readily assimilable either into the forms of rabbinic conservatism in fashion on the 'right' today or into the Conservatism or the Masorti movement of today. He is paradoxically, and with some reason, claimed by both.

In addition to disputes between Orthodox and non-Orthodox, there are enduring strains within Orthodoxy. There are, for example, four *batei din* (one of them is that of the Sephardi community) within Orthodoxy in London, all of which espouse the same religious codes. This has resulted in the now long-standing existence of four separate and independent 'commissions' for the licensing and supervision of *kashrut* facilities in London. Intermittent efforts to rationalize the system have consistently failed, with respective loyalties intact, tempers frayed, duplicated expenses unreformed, and many puzzled by what seems to some an unholy rivalry. The larger provincial communities have their own respective *batei din*, which are neither constitutionally nor necessarily subject to the London Beth Din.

The Chief Rabbinate is an office of the highest prestige outside the Jewish community as well as exercising a unique degree of authority within. The rabbinate under its jurisdiction has in general been viewed as partaking of what is variously termed mainstream, centrist, or modern Orthodoxy. Many in that rabbinate would regard any epithet as an unnecessary and indeed undesirable derogation from their Orthodox attachment, and have had reservations about the present Chief Rabbi's past use of any such adjectival definition.

The Union of Orthodox Hebrew Congregations does not accept the Chief Rabbi's jurisdiction. The Union was founded in 1926 out of a group of like-minded congregations by the Hungarian-born Rabbi Dr Victor Schonfeld, 'to protect traditional Judaism'. He also pioneered the Orthodox Jewish day school movement in London outside the East End, an important educational system which retains its affinity with the Union. With its 53 congregations, large and small, encompassing about 6,000 families, it adopts a separatist stance and maintains a critical and often acerbic voice on communal affairs. At times its rabbinic leaders, by reason of their *halakhic* standing, exercise influence on rabbinic and lay attitudes outside their own ranks, including influence on some of the rabbinate of the United Synagogue and some rabbis in the provinces who are ostensibly within the jurisdiction of the Chief Rabbi. The Union, whose families are mainly resident in distinct localities in London and Manchester, has an ideological affinity with the northern Gateshead Yeshiva.

Associated with the Union are some disparate hasidic groups, of whom the best known are Lubavitch elements, with their evangelistic outreach programmes. Jewish businessmen of a kind who less than a generation ago would have avoided involvement with the Lubavitch movement, are now among its principal philanthropists. This is a significant commentary on changing attitudes and professed values in the communal scene.

Nor does the Chief Rabbi's jurisdiction extend to the Federation of Synagogues.[7] It was founded in 1887 out of synagogues and conventicles in the East End, largely of recent immigrant membership, by Sir Samuel Montagu (later Lord Swaythling, 1832–1911), then a prominent member of the United Synagogue and at the time a local Member of Parliament in the Liberal Party interest. The Federation membership, like the Union, looked upon the Chief Rabbinate and the United Synagogue as excessively 'modernist' in thought and practice. It now comprises 35 synagogues in the London area (no longer mainly in the East End). Nowadays the religious standards of members barely differ from many in the United Synagogue. The rabbinate of the Federation, headed by its own Beth Din, would repudiate with greater vehemence than their United Synagogue colleagues, any suggestion that their Orthodoxy requires any epithet.

The Reform Synagogues of Great Britain (RSGB) had its origin in the Reform secession of 1840.[8] The significantly named West London Synagogue of British Jews, which was then established, remains the principal synagogue of the movement and has a membership of 2,000. The standpoint of the RSGB is comparable to that of the more 'progressive' elements in American Conservatism. The organisation now comprises 40 synagogues in and outside London and has its own Beth Din. It shares with the Union of Liberal and Progressive Synagogues (ULPS) the rabbinic training seminar bearing the name of Rabbi Dr Leo Baeck (1873–1956), the prominent leader of German Jewry who settled in England after World War II.

The ULPS, centring on the original Liberal synagogue in London, was founded in 1902 by Lily Montagu (1873–1963) and Claude Montefiore. The Union now incorporates 28 synagogues in and beyond London. Its standpoint is comparable to that of the American Reform movement. An example of the diversity of and the bestriding by the 'Victorian' Jewish community well into the twentieth century is afforded by the fact that Lily Montagu was the daughter of the founder of the Federation of Synagogues, and an aunt of Ewen Montagu (1901–85), later President of the United Synagogue. He was the last of the descendants of the eighteenth-century London magnate and synagogal leader, Levi Barent Cohen, to hold high office in the United Synagogue.

The Masorti (or Conservative) movement was founded in Britain by Rabbi Dr Louis Jacobs in 1964.[9] It may be regarded as comparable to the right-wing element of American Conservatism. The establishment of its first congregation was accompanied by a declaration of aim, namely 'to found an Orthodox synagogue in the Anglo-Jewish tradition of tolerance with freedom for study and enquiry in harmony with modern scholarship'. These terms reflect issues which were in the forefront of what became known as the Jacobs Affair.

Rabbi Jacobs, a Rabbi of the United Synagogue, had been appointed a tutor at Jews' College by its president, the then Chief Rabbi, Rabbi Israel Brodie (1895–1979). Rabbi Jacobs was denied the office of Principal because of his religious and theological opinions, whereupon he sought to return to his rabbinic post. This was now declared closed to him because of his opinions which, in fact, he had made widely known prior to his appointment to the College. A large section of the membership of his former congregation followed him out of the United Synagogue to establish the New London Synagogue. In 1985, the seven congregations within the movement formed the Assembly of Masorti Synagogues.

The special character of the Jewish community of Britain is illustrated by the fact that the Chief Rabbi and the United Synagogue regarded themselves, in their unrelenting opposition to Rabbi Jacobs, as upholding the community's traditions, while he and his supporters likewise presented themselves at the time as doing likewise. The respective proportions of reason and faith in the approach to tradition and the interpretation of scripture had for some time lain dormant within the public domain of the Orthodox community. When such questions came sharply and suddenly to the fore within the Orthodox community, a new type of dispute emerged within Anglo-Jewish Orthodoxy. In 1984, the newly formed Masorti Synagogue in Edgware, a Jewishly populous area in the metropolitan north-west, declared that its aim was 'to advance the practice of traditional Judaism'. The language differed little from that used to define the purpose of the Union of Orthodox Hebrew Congregations 60 years before. But the substantive differences were wide. Times had changed. New criteria had evolved with which to assess values and judge tradition. Ten years before the 'Jacobs Affair', Rabbi Dr Alexander Altmann, who prior to his departure for Brandeis was Communal Rabbi of Manchester (where in 1953 he founded the Institute of Jewish Studies, which was later transferred to University College London), stated that 'the English Jew wishes to evaluate and judge the legacy of the past in the court of his own personal conscience'.[10] An increase in the questioning assertiveness precipitated and also sprang from the affair. The trend hardened the 'right'. The persistent questioners within the traditional fold were not likely to grow fewer.

Transformed attitudes to authority were not limited to religious movements. The old feature of the communal system, whereby rabbinic or ministerial leadership was generally subject to the weightier influence of their lay colleagues, had been in line with long standing English practice. It was also related to the old social gulf between the lay leaders and the 'clerical' incumbents, who were generally of a different 'class'. The impact of the immigrations, out of which new lay leaders emerged, meant the virtual abolition in time of any sense of class distinction between the occupants of the pulpit and of the synagogue wardens' box. The role, vocality, and influence of the rabbis and ministers were much enhanced, as were their *esprit de corps* and later their salary structure.

The process was encouraged by the conscious acceptance by synagogal lay leaders that the influence of the synagogue will not be determined by the statutory services alone but will, to a growing extent, depend on 'extra-synagogue' programmes and involvements in which the rabbi is looked to as the principal architect and guide. Such religious, cultural, and social programmes have never before achieved the frequency and intensity currently common. It has been in relation to these developments, or the prospect thereof, that synagogue building or structured adaptations have often now been designed to be or to include 'community centres for cultural, recreational and educational purposes'.[11] The immediate post-war structures tended to follow the earlier pattern of the 'big synagogue' where formality prevailed amid memories or hear-say of the Victorian legacy. The effect of examples in Israel, the new enthusiasm for informality, and the fashion of recruiting younger age groups into leadership at all levels, have influenced the spirit and image of 'lay leader' in wide sections of the community, in contrast to any period before the 1970s.

In 1918, Lionel de Rothschild, grandson of the first Jewish Member of Parliament and nephew of the first Jewish Peer, had been elected President of the United Synagogue, thus continuing the family tradition. The election was, for practical purposes, the decision of his immediate colleagues. Until the early 1960s, such elections were generally foregone conclusions, the Council (consisting of representatives of the constituent synagogues within the Union) adopting by acclamation in a formal election the Honorary Officers' nomination. Rothschild was a leading opponent of the Jewish national idea as set forth in political Zionism.

Throughout his tenure at the United Synagogue, the main influence therein was that of his kinsman and Vice-President, Sir Robert Waley Cohen (1877–1952),[12] the managing director of Shell Oil in London, who succeeded Rothschild on his death in 1942. Waley Cohen, who made no pretence to personal Orthodoxy, regarded his devotion to the development of the United Synagogue partly as an act of family *pietas*. His uncle, Lionel Louis Cohen, London banker and a leading member of the Conservative Party, had been its principal founder. Waley Cohen also, and crucially, contemplated his intense involvement in its growth, as a matter of communal prudence and civic responsibility.

Skilled in forward-planning, delegation, and the art of generally achieving his ends, he supervised its substantial extension numerically and geographically in the rapidly widening metropolitan residential area. He accepted with relish the organization's 'broad-churchmanship', and set his face against whatever he discerned as ideological extremism. He set much store by its centralized administration, seeking to exercise firm lay control in his not always easy alliance with the religious headship of the Chief Rabbi. Waley Cohen realized that notwithstanding all its English, indeed Anglican, characteristics, the destiny of that synagogal body was bound up with the Eastern European immigrants and their progeny.

At the heart of his policy there was an English-like paradox which accorded both with the diversity of elements in his personality and with the diverse nature of the Anglo-Jewish community – at once a parish and a world. He was heir to his family's synagogal patrimony in a new world of heightened orthodoxy, a growing liberal spirit, democratic instincts, conscious secularity, and political Zionism. In his own way he was out of touch with every one of these features. He played a notable role in the industrial and commercial development of Palestine during the British Mandatory period, but stood consistently firm in opposition to the idea of Jewish statehood.[13] In London, Waley Cohen sought to establish, where he could, friendly working relations with the rabbis and spokesmen of the immigrant community, much of which by his time had long merged into Anglo-Jewry.

He and his immediate colleagues publicly envisaged a nation-wide synagogal structure modelled and centred on the United Synagogue, with expanded, centrally guided arrangements for part-time Jewish education on the pattern of the Central Committee for Jewish Education. That Committee had operated from the mid-1920s, notably as an inspectorate and advisory body, under the auspices of the Jewish Memorial Council which had been created largely by Waley Cohen. However, the major provincial communities had no wish to tax themselves for wider purposes than their own. The Chief Rabbinate, despite its nation-wide role, attracted minimal financial support from outside the United Synagogue, and, like the London Beth Din, was and is maintained almost entirely by that body. Nor was the popularity of the clerical-collared ministry as deeply rooted or as long-lived in those communities as was the case in the United Synagogue as late as the 1950s. There was also the related question of the somewhat awkward relationship between the United Synagogue and the foreign-trained, talmudically learned 'Rav', the popularity of which type was a marked feature of Jewish life in the north of England. That cadre had little or nothing to do with Jews' College, the seminary for the United Synagogue-style ministry (founded in 1855).

The bane of competition for communal funds long endured. An indication of Waley Cohen's readiness to change the system is afforded by the following venture, albeit within its self-imposed limitations. It also demonstrates the impact of prevailing impediments to change. During World War II, the main Jewish educational bodies formed themselves into a 'Joint Emergency Committee'. Its purpose was to provide Jewish education to the many Jewish children who, as part of the national plan, were housed in localities away from the main urban centres, in anticipation of German air-raids. This degree of Jewish unity in action encouraged united action for the post-war provision of Jewish education on the children's return home. It was, in any case, becoming more widely recognized that in general the pre-war standards were no longer acceptable, least of all in the light of the Education Act of 1944 which *inter alia* held out the prospect of a better organized system of education in Jewish day schools and also in part-time Jewish education.

The nation-wide educational conference convened by Waley Cohen (acting with Dr Nathan Morris, the community's foremost educationalist at the time) heralded a new approach. Jewish education was to be free to all and financed through a tax on synagogue seat rentals. However, the resulting newly established London Board for Jewish Religious Education, in which the main partners were the United Synagogue and the Federation of Synagogues, did not survive their continuing differences. The Central Council for Jewish Religious Education, which also sprang from the Conference, was a vehicle for raising standards in provincial Jewish schools and synagogal classes, but it was soon without funds, and was reduced to limiting itself to the valiant services of one inspector for the country as a whole outside London, before it likewise ceased to exist.

The Conference, the London Board, and the Central Council were Orthodox bodies. The London Board became incorporated into the United Synagogue, the 'Federation part' of the Board having returned to the Federation synagogue classes and its Talmud Torah system. The residual task of inspection in the provinces was taken over by the Jewish Memorial Council. The Central Council, including its plans for the creation of a residential seminary for the training of teachers, could not survive competition for communal funds between itself, the London Board and Jews' College. The inadequate supply of Jewish teachers in number and calibre remained an inhibiting factor in regard to Waley Cohen's nation-wide aspiration, and continued as a limiting factor in regard to any significant expansion of the community's educational system.[14]

Waley Cohen's outlook and example continued to exercise much influence in the years immediately following his death. That influence steadily declined. With the growing impact of the creation of the State of Israel, and in the light of higher expectations in Jewish education and the rise of new types of leadership – all of which developments were interrelated – new priorities arose for serious public discussion.

Waley Cohen's approach was in some respects, and ironically, paralleled by that of Brodetsky, the Ukrainian-born President of the Board of Deputies from 1939 to 1949. He was the first of the new immigration to hold that office. He was the leading British Zionist (next to his mentor, Chaim Weizmann). His unopposed election as president followed the retirement of the prominent and explicit non-Zionist, Neville Laski. Anthony de Rothschild, Lionel's brother, decided, with whatever misgivings, not to challenge Brodetsky, since he had no confidence in his own success and viewed his candidacy as likely to be gratuitously divisive. Brodetsky, the first and so far the only academic to hold the office, was acutely conscious that his election represented the opening of a new era. Yet by a reverse and significant analogy with Waley Cohen, he retained an admiration for what he perceived as the special public-spiritedness of the old governing regime, and a respect for the practicality of its administration. He had a passionate sense of the significance of the Anglo-Jewish community in the Jewish world scene and of the importance of the Board of Deputies as its spokes-man, especially to the Mandatory Government in London.

The comparative attitudes of Waley Cohen – the prominent anti-Zionist and communal autocrat – and Brodetsky – the Zionist and by birth, temperament and policy a democrat – are of historical interest. Brodetsky resisted what he deemed undesirable efforts to turn the Board into what might appear to be an appendage of the English Zionist Federation. It was a concern which he shared with Waley Cohen and Laski. For him the independence and authority of the Board reflected a continuation of the spirit in which Sir Moses Montefiore (1783–1884), President of the Board for more than a generation, had long ago acted in support or attempted support of Jewish communities overseas, often with the explicit approval of the British Government and sometimes its public support. The Board traditionally denounced unilateral interventions by individuals or groups with the British Government, however 'eminent' their lineage or public status. In 1943 the Board, by a narrow majority, ended its treaty (1878) with the Anglo-Jewish Association, and the Joint Foreign Affairs Committee created thereunder. The AJA, a private body of 'prominent' Jews, had by then become the main spokesman for non-Zionist opinion, as distinct from the Board's call for a 'Jewish Commonwealth' as part of the post-war settlement.

Brodetsky rejected Laski's contention that it was politically unwise for him to occupy the headship of the Jewish Agency in London while serving as President of the Board. There were severe tensions between the British Government and the Jewish Agency; Laski considered that in making representations to the Government on behalf of the Agency, Brodetsky compromised his position as a spokesman for Anglo-Jewry in his role as President of the Board. Brodetsky was no less anxious than his critics to sustain the Board's representative character and independence, but saw no conflict of interest.

He believed that it was important that the Zionists should be perceived not as being somehow extraneous to the established Jewish community or as having 'captured' the Board, but, as was numerically reflected within the Board, as being by far the majority party within the Jewish community. This, he thought, would strengthen the force of the Board's representations to the Foreign Office in opposing, in particular, the Government's restrictions on Jewish immigration into Palestine.[15]

His form of enlightened insularity for the Board, while differing in philosophy and purpose from Laski's position, shared with the anti- and non-Zionists an historical recollection of the one-time unique status of the Board at the height of British power. This kind of self-regard, however altruistic, could not survive as the twentieth century advanced. New types and sources of communal power were rapidly in the making.

In 1917, Simon Marks was elected to the Board of Deputies.[16] His purpose was to identify himself with the Zionists who were seeking to undo the influence of the Board's then leaders opposed to Zionism. His presence was a considerable accretion of strength to the Zionists by reason of his growing influence within the Jewish community and outside, and his family's public support for Weizmann. In 1962, Sir Isaac Wolfson (1897–1975) succeeded Ewen Montagu as President of the United Synagogue.[17] Between those two dates one may observe the steady rise to major influence on communal affairs by men of new wealth and Zionist enthusiasm, little interested, if at all, in the outlooks of the earlier decades. Marks and Wolfson were sons of Polish immigrants. With their philanthropy came considerable communal influence, greatly enhanced by the major fund-raising for Israel with which they were successively associated and to which they introduced progressively greater organizational skill and power.

Wolfson's chairmanship of what became the Joint Israel Appeal may be said to have inaugurated a fresh epoch in the history of leadership within Anglo-Jewry. It was decisive in setting the compelling fashion for younger Jewish businessmen to associate themselves in practical ways with that organization. The Six-Day War yet further widened the fashion in business and in the professions, and it extended across religious 'divisions' within the Jewish community, as well as bridging London and provincial communities. By reason of the Appeal's success and its ubiquity within the community, as well as because of the power of its leaders outside the community as well as their prominence within, the men who directed the Appeal wielded a degree of influence in the community which extended beyond the ambit of fund-raising for Israel. They were not beyond acting as power brokers in communal life, generally with a self-confidence and a sense of 'cousinhood' no less strong than that of the now bygone natural cousinhood of the old families, in spite of their own differences over Israel's performance and other matters from time to time.

The deepening integration into British society and the rise to preeminence of American Jewry in the Diaspora progressively weakened the Anglo-Jewish sense of its own centrality in diaspora affairs. The old insularity was progressively dissolved. In the process, the Board of Deputies encountered new authority structures within the Jewish community. A sign of the changing scene was the Board's decision to join the World Jewish Congress in 1974 as its British affiliate. From the inception of the Congress in 1936, the Board had resisted Nahum Goldmann's blandishments to join. Its inhibition was partly connected with a deep-rooted concern over what was thought to be the likely hostile reaction by anti-Semites and Gentile critics on the score of the Board's association with an international political Jewish organization, especially 'sinister' by reason of its foreign headquarters and cross-frontier 'Jewish ends'. The Board's attitude also sprang in part from its enduring and zealous protection of its own particular access to government.

Its decision to become part of the Congress (albeit retaining its independence) reflected the special politics of amiability practised by Lord Fisher (1905–79), the then President of the Board and a popular figure in the London Labour Party. His favourable approach was assisted by the enhanced Jewish self-assurance following the Six-Day War. Somewhat ironically the decision was also related to an increased sense of the desirability of concerted Jewish action to meet the heightened vocal anti-Zionism and anti-Semitism on the part of enemies of Israel and from the political far right. The change was symptomatic of the impact both of the Six-Day War and the Yom Kippur War in strengthening the perception of the common fate of the Jewish people. Britain's accretion to the European Economic Community, as it was then called, and the value of potential European international action against racism, further relaxed, in their different ways, the old tensions which the prospect of affiliation to the Congress formerly aroused.

The extent of integration is perhaps dramatically demonstrated by the distribution of Jews on the benches of the House of Commons. In the General Election of 1 May 1997, of the twenty known Jews elected, 13 were Labour, 6 Conservative, and one a Liberal Democrat (*Jewish Chronicle*, 9 May 1997). In the previous election (1992), the comparable figures nation-wide were eight, 11 and one. The change was part of the nation-wide party-political swing. It is clear that in areas of substantial Jewish residence, Jewish votes followed the national patterns. In 1955, there was one Conservative Jewish member, namely, Sir Henry d'Avigdor Goldsmid, bullion broker, son of a past president of the Board and descendant of the first Jewish baronet. Some Jews, including Sir Trevor Chinn, support both major parties through the parties' respective 'Friends of Israel'. Michael (later Lord) Levy, Chairman of Jewish Care and a prominent businessman, is a major fund-raiser for the Labour party. Sir Stanley Kalms is a well-known supporter of the Conservatives. Jews are found in all the main political parties in Britain. All three main parties, including the Liberal Democrats, have their 'Friends of Israel'.

There is no party political unanimity in the Jewish population in general or within the cadres of communal leadership. Jews tend to vote as citizens who take into account candidates' attitudes to Jewish issues, with a diversity of conclusions. Although overall there is diversity in the patterns of Jewish political affiliation, party leaders are conscious of what is sometimes called 'the Jewish vote', especially in constituencies of high Jewish population, where the votes of Jews may make the difference. This consciousness is particularly sharp at a time of narrow majorities in the House of Commons. Respective party leaders are generally on cordial personal terms with the leading figures, elective or otherwise, in the Jewish community.

A corollary of the increasing complexity of communal administration (which accompanied the multiplication of fresh insights and

21

concerns, especially in education and social welfare) has been a growth in the diffusion of leadership. From the ranks of major benefactors have arisen schemes and responses to perceived needs. Many were prominent in national politics, business, or the professions, and often were in a personal sense interrelated in major fundraising and funding, notably for Israel-oriented causes. The newer personalities in the growing plurality of authority have been inclined to seek communal influence and implement their schemes through newly created or specially adapted organisations where they could make decisions as they saw fit – in social welfare, education, 'Jewish defence' – without representative machinery or democratic procedures. They had their own sources of public standing. Many in the old ruling families had been prominent in banking and finance. In the comparatively new commercial empires of retail distribution, industrial manufacture and property development, their successors in the exercise of independent power within the Jewish community have had their own comparable bases.

Their readiness for the exercise of authority in the Jewish community did not imply any eagerness to work through the older institutions. They preferred the mutual confidence and approbation of their working colleagues or trustees to any public or 'parliamentary-style' debate. They and the leaders of the Joint Israel Appeal (in many instances the same people) came to constitute echelons of authority parallel to the authority of the elected representative leaders who were and are themselves, constitutionally, the successors to the long-ago displaced dynastic hierarchies. These representatives have retained their constitutional voice and influence, principally through the Board. Between the representative leaders and the newer echelons, the responsible distribution of power requires consultative machinery, however informal, and personal understanding, however different the origins of their avenues of influence. This is recognized by all parties. They are not divided by any issues of substantive policy.

Peerages, knighthoods and other royal honours continue to be a source of pride, especially when indicating recognition of public service. Title continues to attract a certain amount of respect in the Jewish community, not excluding perhaps some sycophantic attention. But none of this conceals the fact that the earlier 'mystique' has drained away, as in the wider society. The former comparative remoteness and the hierarchical character of communal government have largely been replaced by an abrasive conviviality. It is note-worthy that the (1997) president of the United Synagogue is a one-time minister in the employ of that body and is himself the son of a late *hazan* of the United Synagogue; he is a lawyer by profession.

Communal leadership has ceased to be accepted as the natural consequence of birth or wealth. This does not mean that philan-thropy and name have lost their habitual attraction, but they have largely ceased to be in themselves passports to office or communal power unless accompanied by recognized commitment, proven talent and visible success, particularly outside the Jewish community.

A significant demonstration of the critical analysis of authority and its performance in Jewish life is found in the developments in Anglo-Jewish historiography since the 1970s. The series of studies from the mid-1950s by Vivian Lipman, in the areas of demography, occupational structure and immigration, were precursors of the wide array of studies by younger successors in these and other fields – aiming to make known 'how life was and is' and 'how people lived and live'. A greater frankness emerged in the examination of the socially vulnerable, the underprivileged and the less well-known, and in the probing of the attitudes and responses to them and their concerns on the part of those in office or prominent in Jewish society at different stages of Anglo-Jewish history, including the modern period. Historical studies have appeared on Jewish trade unions and working-class needs and opinions in Anglo-Jewry, maternal and child welfare in the Jewish community, hospital services for Jews, the self-help Jewish friendly societies, Jewish refugees fleeing persecution or when resident in Britain, and abuses (conscious or otherwise) of authority, as well as Jewish responses to anti-Semitism and the contradictions in the liberal culture in which British Jews have lived.

These types of enquiry are in line with the expansion of historical and sociological studies in the academic world generally. They are also in part a reaction to what is seen as the earlier, somewhat decorous, Jewish self-lauding and its related 'apologetic' histori-ography. To the newer craftsmen and women in the historical field, Jewish leaders, in whatever office or position of authority in Anglo-Jewry, are the potential subjects of a degree of close and exacting scrutiny and, if considered necessary, unabashed criticism not common (with some short-term exceptions) before the 1970s. It is a world away from the time when permission was first given to the *Jewish Chronicle* to attend and report meetings of the Board of Deputies (1853). It amounts to an overarching form of accountability and is the community's ultimate pragmatism.

Associated with the newer spirit of enquiry are the considerable growth in Anglo-Jewish genealogical studies, the newer techniques for seeking out, preserving and studying old and contemporary local and general communal archives, and the expansion of the study of the growth and in many instances the decline of provincial Jewish communities, large and small. The Jewish Historical Society of England (founded in 1893), the oldest learned society in Anglo-Jewry, is associated with such ventures, having, especially since the 1960s, progressively broadened its interest in the newer spirit. It was long associated in people's minds with the older school.

The Institute for Jewish Policy Research evolved out of the Institute of Jewish Affairs in 1994. The latter had been created in 1941 by the World Jewish Congress as its cultural arm. It unilaterally broke away from the Congress and set up the new body in partnership with the American Jewish Committee. The fourth Lord Rothschild became president of the new Institute and is a substantial benefactor of it, as he was of the old. The Institute for Jewish Policy Research is described as 'the Jewish Think Tank' and has endowed itself with a wider remit than its predecessor. It seeks to influence opinion and policy on issues affecting Jewish life by its research and consequential reports and proposals, and by promoting public and organizational debate thereon. Its aims include 'the strengthening of the cohesion of society and the self-identity of Jewish communities by shaping the social and political agenda'.

The Chairman of the Institute is a leading member of the Reform community and head of a substantial property development company in central London. His vice-president is a Labour Peer. They and many other members of the Executive Committee have not been personally involved with the Board of Deputies, with which the Institute cooperates, as did its predecessor. The leaders of the Institute constitute a core of initiative, authority and leadership, in the Jewish community, of considerable and growing weight.

The purpose of the Community Security Trust (1996) is to combat racism and anti-Semitism. It comprises an expansion of earlier arrangements under substantially the same (now larger) body of trustees and lay and professional managers. The organization, as in its previous form, works in association with, but is independent of, the Board. Its leading figure was and is Gerald Ronson, prominent industrialist and property developer. Under the new arrangements, the Board concerns itself with the political, legislative and public relations sides of 'Jewish defence', while the new Trust is active in the provision of physical security for the Jewish community, the rendering of related advice and training, and monitoring the community's enemies. Both bodies work in association with the police.

The Defence Committee of the Board dates back to 1936. With the development of greater sophistication and specialization to meet the contemporary advance of racism, the aforesaid two broad types of activity steadily emerged as distinct kinds of operations, and are now the respective responsibilities of the Board and the Trust. In respect of the Community Security Trust, the then Chief Commissioner of the Metropolitan Police, Sir Paul (now Lord) Condon, publicly stated in 1998 that in no country of which he was aware was there 'such a sophisticated, developed, and disciplined community-based security organization', a degree of commendation likewise expressed by his successor, Sir John Stevens. The increase in the number of anti-Semitic and anti-Zionist incidents, paramountly the terrorist explosions at the Israeli Embassy and at the headquarters of the Joint Israel Appeal in 1994, had greatly enlarged the importance of this field of communal service. Its importance has been progressively enhanced by later events, notably by those of 11 September 2001 in New York and what ensued. The President of the Board and the Chairman of its Defence Committee are among the trustees of the Community Security Trust, whose creation might be construed by some as resulting in a contraction of the Board 's powers. Both bodies acknowledge the imperative need for their harmonious cooperation. Unlike its predecessors, the Trust sought corporate representation on the Board, which was accorded.

Older 'challenges' to the Board were on issues of policy, such as the pace and extent of the emancipation campaign, attitudes to Reform, marriage and divorce law, reactions to street anti-Semitism, and responses to political Zionism. The modern 'challenges' are in practice concerned more directly with the exercise of influence.

There is no challenge to the Board's long-established constitutional authority. If there are organizations which exhibit a certain sliding tendency which brings them towards or into the realm of the Board's actual or potential agenda, this does not reflect an intention to replace the Board or to oust its authority. Nor indeed was that generally the aim of the earlier challengers.

There is now a series of standing *de facto* power structures, each with its own sphere of authority, public recognition, and specialization. The creation of the Central Council for Jewish Community Services (1993) seemed, for a time, to presage another such body. The Institute for Jewish Policy Research and the Community Security Trust more clearly illustrate the multi-pronged character of the change in the communal system, of which change the Joint Israel Appeal had itself long been a demonstration and of which the merger of the Joint Israel Appeal and Jewish Continuity (1996) is the latest and the most remarkable. The whole process is marked by enhanced professionalism in high-profile specialized areas of communal life, where major private funding and fund-raising are engaged in by the respective independent initiators. In such enterprises, 'parliamentary' procedures and the elected representative character of the Board are not at a premium. Nor has it proved easy for the Board to muster comparable finances.

The desirability of modernizing the Board's structure and its modes of operation is long-standing. There developed a growing realization that upon the necessary changes depended the future impact of the Board upon the mind of the Jewish community, and in the wider society as the effective representative body of the community. That realization prompted a series of attempted changes at the Board. They did not at first meet with the widest favour within the Board. No doubt in a democratic assembly one should not be surprised to find differences of opinion on what forms of accountability are acceptable, and on how far plenary debates and committee deliberations should extend. The notion of change at the Board was supported by the leading lights of the Joint Israel Appeal, and was given consistent public support by the *Jewish Chronicle*. In 1994, the leaders of the Board decided to appoint an outside management consultant to advise on restructuring the Board without prejudice to its democratic character. The resulting Chelms Report (1995) was accepted by the Board in 1996 with a view to its implementation in time for the new triennium commencing in 1997. The essence of the accepted changes is the enhancement of the action-oriented character of the Board, greater efficacy in its decision-making processes, maximization of the use of the experience and expertise of involved laymen as well as professionals, and closer and regular consultation with leaders of major communal organizations.

A marked feature in recent years has been the increasing number of younger members of the community who have sought membership of the Board. This has especially been the case on the part of the younger women. It is part of the steadily advancing role of women in communal life. A significant enhancement of that role sprang from the creation, in 1971, of the Women's Campaign for Soviet Jewry.[18] Most of the members were middle-class Jewish housewives. Their objective was to bring public pressure to bear upon governments and public opinion in the interests of Jews seeking emigration from the Soviet Union to Israel. Their initiative and the extent of their success (sometimes in the face of some Jewish opposition because of their, at times, 'unsociable' methods) gave considerable prestige to the enterprise of Jewish women in seeking wider influence in the counsels of the community.

The examples of independence of mind and of skills in public office set by Miriam Moses (a pioneer in Jewish social, especially youth, welfare), by Rebecca Sieff (wife of Lord Sieff), Elsie Janner (wife of Lord Janner, long a prominent Labour member of Parliament and from 1955 to 1964 President of the Board, and mother of Greville Janner, who was to follow his father in both capacities and to the peerage), all active members of the Board, and others, had long been eagerly followed in many fields of communal effort. Women have long held senior elective offices at the Board. The occupancy by women of the office of President of Representative Councils in provincial cities has become commonplace. Women have been accorded equal representation on synagogal boards of management in the United Synagogue, as well as a considerable increase of representation on the Council of that body. The Chief Rabbi initiated a review of the role of women in the community. A number of advances in women's rights have been achieved with his support. Some issues, including certain *halakhah*-related issues, remain controversial and outstanding.

Some critics have queried the representative character of the Board in that it rests principally upon synagogal representation, and may therefore not represent those who, while consciously Jewish, are unaffiliated. It is estimated that one Jew in three does not belong to a synagogue.[19] One does not know what proportion of these 'non-affiliated' are associated with Jewish non-synagogal bodies. Further, some synagogues are not affiliated to the Board. The Board acknow-ledges these currently built-in 'limitations', but does not regard them as constituting in practice a significant diminution of its representative character. It regards itself as a unique forum for communal expression in all its diversity, and as making for com-munal cohesion, a heightening of communal awareness, and effective responsible action. The Board has the ear of government and public bodies on all issues affecting Jewish interests. It is perceived by them at all levels as entitled to proceed as the com-munal spokesman. While the Board progressively seeks to broaden its representational base, it does so without prejudice to its continu-ing entitlement and duty to act as the communal spokesman.

An area of increasing interest to the Board is the cultivation of inter-group and inter-faith relations. In the pluralist society of modern Britain, there are common interests between the Jewish community and the newer and far larger Asian and Caribbean communities. They share a concern to uphold the rule of law and where necessary to strengthen legislation against harassment, incitement and discrimination. Those groups are themselves each divided along religious lines. Since the 1960s, the Board has increasingly been involved in developing relations and good understanding with the diverse bodies. The Zionist issue has at times contentiously obtruded into discussions. In the main the leaders of the ethnic bodies, as they tend to be called, favour the preservation of the relationship. It is noteworthy that a vice-president of the Board recently served as vice-chairman of the government-sponsored Commission for Racial Equality, albeit in his personal capacity. Since the much earlier creation of the Council of Christians and Jews in 1943, there has developed in wholly new circumstances a much more extensive network of inter-group and inter-faith organizations. The Board's special role and example in this increas-ingly important and sometimes difficult field is widely recognized.

The Central Council for Jewish Social Service was created in

1972 as a loose association of Jewish social service agencies. Its purpose was to encourage cooperation where possible, and avoid duplication. Its foundation was a recognition of the increasing need for the rationalization of communal welfare services. In 1985, following a series of efforts to promote a policy of coordination and a system for determining priorities in the welfare field, Stuart Young, the Chairman of the Council, published a seminal paper entitled 'The Case for Unity'. Young was a prominent London accountant and a leading figure in fund-raising for Israel. His paper was addressed to the heads of the country's Jewish social service agencies. He reported that on a 'conservative estimate' the 'overall shortfall' on the funding of the social services associated with the Central Council nation-wide 'will amount to four million pounds annually'.

Young, son of a Russian immigrant and soon to be appointed by Mrs Thatcher as Chairman of the British Broadcasting Corporation, observed that the reduction of statutory grants and services under the Conservative government inescapably enlarged the scope of the voluntary sectors, and accentuated the problems of communal funding. In a numerically declining Jewish community, with a progressive increase in the proportion of the aged and infirm and at a time of increasing specialization in services (especially in welfare and education), the still largely unregulated forms of communal fund-raising were self-evidently antiquated.

The significance of Young's study was rendered all the greater by the publication in that year of the awaited report by a communal committee headed by the London accountant, Bernard Garbacz, treasurer of the Jewish Educational Development Trust, on the facts of communal funding. He reported that 60 per cent of funds raised in the community were directed to Israel causes, and 12 per cent to Jewish education.

Young called urgently for 'some form of rationalization and ultimately joint fund-raising' for social welfare services. In 1985, there were in London alone 87 different Jewish agencies 'all looking to the same sources for their support'. His proposals caught a growing mood, though, as he foresaw, some entrenched interests remained cautious. But what had generally been regarded as a closed route was opened up for serious practical examination. The time was ripe for the shift in communal debate. A series of coordinating schemes and amalgamations were to follow, of which the most spectacular were the merger in 1990 between the Jewish Welfare Board (founded in 1859 as the London Jewish Board of Guardians) and the Jewish Blind Society (1819),[20] and the amalgamation in 1996 of Norwood Child Care and Ravenswood, a substantial charity concerned with the residential care of the disabled.

These debates and developments encouraged comparable thinking in regard to the provision of Jewish education. Indeed, the process had been initiated in that field before Young's paper, in which process Young had himself been a participant. The laymen principally involved in the process in education were in many instances, like Young, leading the way in welfare and prominently involved in fund-raising for Israel, largely through the Joint Israel Appeal. In 1971, the then Chief Rabbi, Dr (later Lord) Jakobovits, with the financial support of those elements in the communal leadership, founded the Jewish Educational Development Trust (JEDT).

The event had a threefold significance. First, it demonstrated the continuity and, with whatever irony,[21] the historical centrality in the communal leadership of the Chief Rabbinate. The allocation of funds raised through the JEDT was not limited to Orthodox educational institutions, nor were the sources of funds confined to the Orthodox. Second, it illustrated the growing degree of independence of the Chief Rabbinate. The JEDT was not an offshoot or appendage of the United Synagogue. Among the Trustees and Patrons of the JEDT were members of the Progressive synagogues. Third, it brought together in institutional form for Anglo-Jewish educational purposes the leading figures in Israel-funding and fund-raising in Anglo-Jewry. This represented a dismissal of the principle, so far as it might still have subsisted, that there was any proper competition between fund-raising for Israel and major fund-raising for local causes. It was to be some time before the full consequence was given shape.

The Jewish student body (founded in 1919 principally by graduates in Liverpool and Manchester, and now the Union of Jewish Students), had neither an office nor professional staff until the creation of the Hillel Foundation and Hillel House in London in 1954. These foundations were the work of men and women largely identified with the British 'chapter' of B'nai B'rith. They were businessmen and professional people, Orthodox and non-

Orthodox, and were motivated by their recognition of the potential value to the Jewish community of facilitating Jewish study and encouraging Jewish commitment on the part of Jewish students while at the universities. It was mainly from within the same circle that initial and critical support came for the establishment of the high-level Jewish boarding school, Carmel College (1948), on the initiative of Rabbi Kopul Rosen, formerly Principal Rabbi of the Federation of Synagogues, and for the Oxford Centre for Post-graduate Hebrew Studies (1972). Members of this circle were mostly uninvolved in communal elective office.

Jewish students have never been more vocal or influential, at all levels of communal life, than today. Throughout the century there have emerged from their ranks leading figures in all branches of communal, including Zionist, enterprise. Upon the student body rested a special responsibility during the 'campus wars' of the 1980s at times of overt Arab and Muslim hostility to Zionism and to Jews at the universities. There is in that sphere a continuing task of 'defence' and public relations, in connection with which the Union works closely with the Board of Deputies and the Community Security Trust; it is done without (as far as possible) any diminution in the pursuit of the original purpose and the continuing ethos of the Union and Hillel in respect of Jewish education on campus.

Yet a ceaseless theme in communal debate has been the perceived threat to the community from large-scale indifference, apparent detachment, and 'Jewish' ignorance among Jewish students. The proportion of Jewish students far exceeds the proportion of Jews in the general population. The number of Jewish students overall who identify themselves at university with Jewish student societies is barely one half of the total. It is commonly held that these circumstances are related less to the nature of university life than to levels of Jewish education (if any) while at school over wide sections of the Jewish community.

As to the field of Jewish youth generally, the Executive Director of the Association for Jewish Youth publicly referred, in February 1989, to the languishing youth service as 'the cinderella of the community'. The association, a century-old loose federation of the largest array of youth clubs and groups, found itself by 1995 bereft of adequate funds, and was obliged to cease independent operations. It became incorporated into the specialized welfare organization,

Norwood Child Care, whose tasks were now to extend beyond its original remit which was the care of handicapped and deprived Jewish children and their families, so as to include the former social and educational tasks of the Association, for which additional staff were to be employed.

The independence of the Association had been in peril for some years on account of its declining income and the reductions in statutory grants. In 1993, the Central Council for Jewish Community Services, within its then recently extended ambit, commissioned an enquiry by Sir Bernard Rix into the state of Jewish Youth Services and how 'their needs can be facilitated'. The Rix Report (1994) advised the creation of a 'new central youth body to address a programme of work' outlined in the Report, principally in the field of Jewish education, including research into needs, techniques, 'marketing' and funding. This was intended to be in the interests of Jewish youth generally, including the Association and other youth groupings. The Report strikingly commented that 'the community as a whole has to be persuaded to see in the Jewish youth services a major imperative for the vibrancy of Jewish life, commitment and identity in succeeding generations'. It would be 'a fundamental aim of the new body to seek to raise the profile of Jewish youth work among the community as a whole', which could enhance relevant fund-raising. It was ironic that in an affluent community accustomed to high levels of fund-raising it was necessary, as late as 1994, to make and emphasize these points.

Events overtook the Report. No central body came into being. The new Chairman of the Central Council announced that 'the Central Council had no specific part to play in the development of the youth services, since Norwood Ravenswood and Jewish Care (are) directly involved in the running of AJY and Sinclair House respectively'. It is noteworthy that the specifically Zionist youth organizations, especially the religious ones, suffered less than the more general clubs and groups, by reason of the level of support from Israel-oriented adult bodies.

The above-mentioned irony is all the greater against the background of the repeatedly and widely expressed acknowledgement of the practical importance of ensuring the lively future of the Jewish youth service in all its facets. Representatives of Jewish youth from all segments of the younger community have, since the 1960s, been more prominent in communal life than in any earlier period. Some of them successfully aspired to high elective office or have been invited into the highest communal counsels. A former professional activist in the religious youth service in his thirties was, in 1996, appointed to the key post of Executive Director of the merged Joint Israel Appeal–Jewish Continuity, after five years as the director of the Chief Rabbi's office. It will be to that new, merged body that youth agencies will increasingly turn for significant seed money or other substantial aid.

The new scale of communal responsibilities (making all allowance for inflation) may be measured by the published accounts of the Jewish Board of Guardians (as it then was) for the first nine months of 1953, which showed a deficit of £7,800. It was hoped by the Executive Committee that by the end of the year the deficit on that year would be less. Barely 40 years later, the annual income alone of Jewish Care (as it now was) for the year was £10,000,000. How to relate the growing assortment of ever-expanding communal requirements to one another was a ceaseless source of concern in which the degree of success in any one or other field might well depend on the influence of a particular protagonist, or the fundraising flair of particular individuals, or the 'emotional' pull of the projected cause.

The sources of funding for necessary Jewish causes was an increasingly prominent issue in public and private debate. The cost of meeting Anglo-Jewish welfare and educational needs was substantially increased by recurring bouts of inflation. The economic recessions of the mid-1970s and the late 1980s intensified the growing pressure in favour of securing a balance between outflowing resources and the retention of adequate resources for local needs. The ever-developing perception of new types of service and needs in education and welfare sharpened the increasing concern over the attainment of an acceptable distribution. During the five years before 1967 the Jewish Community contributed to Israel via the Joint Palestine Appeal (as it then was called) alone a combined total of eleven million sterling. In the succeeding five years, the total raised was treble that sum.

In 1990, the businessman, David (Lord) Young (brother of Stuart, by then deceased), shortly after leaving Mrs Thatcher's government, became, *inter alia,* Chairman of the Oxford Centre,

President of Jewish Care, and Chairman of the Central Council for Jewish Social Service. He held these offices upon the nomination of colleagues and by an acclamatory form of 'election'. He had formerly served as a creative president of British Ort. It was upon his request that the Central Council extended its scope of membership to include communal agencies outside the field of social welfare, and renamed itself the Central Council of Jewish Community Services. He rejected any suggestion that he intended that the Council should in effect seek to replace the Board of Deputies, but he expressly retained the right on the Council's behalf to take such action *vis-à-vis* government at any level, within the Council's terms, as might be thought necessary, where such action had not been taken by the Board, whether the Board was agreeable or not. He did not exclude joint action where appropriate. He acknowledged that the Council was not an elected or representative body in any formal way, and made no pretence that it was democratic. In its new form the Council attracted some new member bodies, including the Institute for Jewish Policy Research.

Lord Young retired from the Council in 1995. Thereafter, its lower public profile did not prejudice in principle the continuation of its programme, but its pioneer courses for the training of professional and lay leadership suffered suspension through lack of adequate funding and other operations were imperilled for the same reason. Throughout his tenure Lord Young was a leading advocate for coordination in communal funding (not necessarily an overall communal chest). His was a major contribution to the climate of opinion which facilitated the funding decisions of 1993–96. At the time of writing, the Central Council remains dangerously under-resourced. Its success in fostering the coordinating spirit in communal thinking and practice has paradoxically set limits to its own viability.*

The notion of a 'community chest' or any combined overall communal financial appeal was alien to the community's historical development. The community's standing within British society had been conditioned in part by the self-imposed principle and voluntary practice of Jewish self-help. That is to say the Jews 'were not to fall on the rates'. Largely, the Jews 'would look after their own'.

---

*Since this was written the Central Council has dissolved itself.

The governing classes in the different sections of the Jewish community developed their own networks for the relief of poverty and the provision of education. The separate identities of the resultant charitable foundations were assiduously retained. Charitable fund-raising events came to form a large part of Jewish institutional and fashionable social life. Separate funding became an ingrained feature of communal life. With the onset of Zionism, the idea that any such appeals should be linked with Zionist fund-raising was anathema to most of the leading figures in communal life, as was Zionism.

From the 1950s, those who saw in the Zionist impulse and in the impact of Israel a significant means of strengthening the survival capacity of Jewish consciousness and identity in the Diaspora grew in number and voice. Further, Israel's cause was seen by them as a likely beneficiary of a secure and viable diaspora Jewish life. Many advocates of these views specifically rejected the imputation of any secularist philosophy on their part. A significant example was and is the Zionist Federation Educational Trust (founded in 1953), now called the Scopus Educational Trust. It declared its objective to be 'to provide a first class education in Jewish studies and the Hebrew language'. The Trust encompasses 15 primary Jewish day schools in London and five in major provincial cities. Its school in Edgware, opened in 1956, was located in premises which formerly housed the local congregation of the United Synagogue, which sold the property to the Trust.

The transaction indicated the United Synagogue's attachment to Jewish day school education and the Zionist cause – in contrast to its traditional opposition to both. Within its own remit the United Synagogue (1997) has five secondary and primary Jewish day schools, the former including the large JFS (founded in 1958), successor in name to the famous Jews' Free School of the old East End. The ZFE Trust in 1956 also declared that the education provided in its schools would be within a 'traditional Jewish framework'. At the time of the Edgware purchase the Trust, as required by the United Synagogue, accepted the Chief Rabbi's religious authority and curricular supervision in the school, a stipulation extended to all its schools.

In 1957, in a public speech at the annual conference of the English Zionist Federation, the then Israeli Ambassador in Britain, Eliahu Elath, observed that 'a solid background of Jewish and

Hebrew cultural education in this country must lay the foundation for a more general desire for a personal and active fulfilment of Zionism and so bring more of your young people to individual identification with the life of Israel'. While recounting the need to support Israel by widening financial aid, investment and *aliya,* his speech was in line with the growing communal feeling in favour of a fuller and reciprocal employment of identification with Israel as a means of strengthening Jewish life in Britain. If some major funders harboured an old concern that Israel's interests might suffer from any serious deflection of funds to local needs, they could not fail later to note the increasing realization expressed by spokesmen of the Government of Israel and the Jewish Agency, especially after the Six-Day War, that the hoped-for regenerative effect of the Zionist movement extended to the Diaspora; such effect would be ill-served by a system of inadequate local funding, quite apart from the beneficial impact on *aliya* which might reasonably be expected to accrue from a robust communal Jewish inner life.

In the Lucien Wolf Memorial Lecture for 1953, Redcliffe Salaman, scientist and Zionist, declared, 'I sincerely believe that Anglo-Jewry cannot survive indefinitely on its philanthropic achievements alone'. It was a reminder of what he regarded as the likely consequences of the continued neglect of Jewish cultural endowment and inadequate funding of Jewish education.[22] There had begun to develop an acute awareness of the then perceived numerical decline. In 1956, the tercentenary of the resettlement of the Jews in England was celebrated. Among the lectures occasioned by the event was that of Dr Abraham Cohen, President of the Board of Deputies and former Senior Minister of the Birmingham Hebrew Congregation, the only minister to have occupied the presidency. In his address on the then structure of Anglo-Jewry, Cohen commented:

> Anglo-Jewry has reached its numerical peak and a decline is bound to set in. The demographic data points unmistakably to that conclusion. But a new factor will be operative, which will offset the worst consequences of diminishing numbers, and that is the impact of the State of Israel. Its beneficial influence is even now discernible.'[23]

This amalgam of anxiety and hope, which became so characteristic of Anglo-Jewry, was further advanced by the volume of pioneering studies edited by Professor Maurice Freedman and published in London in 1955 entitled *Minority in Britain: Social Studies of the Anglo-Jewish Community.* In his Autumn Address in 1984 to the rabbis and ministers within the Chief Rabbi's juris-diction, Victor Lucas, the then President of the United Synagogue, regretfully observed that 'there is a pessimism hovering over our community' and that 'in some cases it comes from our preoccupa-tion with numbers'. By that time the point in the messages of Salaman, Cohen, Freedman and others had become familiar (though not necessarily with any conscious attribution) in the common parlance of all who sought any major role in communal affairs. The ever-falling birth rate outside the 'far right' of the community was not thought likely to be 'offset' by the high birth rate of the 'far right'. Notwithstanding that continuing high rate, the annual death rate in the community as a whole was soon to exceed the overall birth rate.

The extent of the changes which were but pending at the time of Elath's address might be measured by Sir Trevor Chinn's later rhetoric at the 'Dialogue', convened in Jerusalem in June 1994 by the President of Israel, with Diaspora leaders. Sir Trevor, industrialist and like his father before him a dominant figure in the policy and operations of the Joint Israel Appeal, declared that Jews committed to Israel 'no longer identify themselves as defined by the World Zionist Organisation'. He added, 'We must set out new national priorities, we must reach out to the unaffiliated to the help of Jewish people who see no value in belonging to our communities, we must create links of education, culture, language.' This carefully chosen presentation was infused with ideas and couched in terms largely unfamiliar to lay leaders in Anglo-Jewry of an earlier generation. It was a new strand of Zionism, concerned with the means for the cultivation of an informed and transmissible Jewish awareness. It seemed to imply that the success of Zionism in the creation of the State of Israel may not, in a secular world, be in itself a facilitator or an encouragement to that end. In advocating visits to Israel as part of an educational process, Sir Trevor described them as 'seminal expansions that can change lives Jewishly'.[24]

In 1965, the Board of Deputies set up what is now its Community Research Unit. This was in the wake of a climate for self-enquiry engendered by the Board's Conference in 1962 and the publication of its proceedings. There followed a progressively widening enquiry into facts and trends in the communal scene, the reports on which made a major contribution to the availability of material necessary for planning in a variety of fields.[25] The community entered upon a more intense age of Reports in the mid-1980s commissioned by major communal organizations.

Reports have ranged respectively over welfare, education, the youth service, organisational structure, demographic and occupational distribution (especially in the outer metropolitan suburbs), population trends, social and religious attitudes and much else. The outburst of research marked the growing partnership between lay leadership and Jewish academics – social scientists, demographers, statisticians – in contrast to an earlier epoch of some academic detachment (with notable exceptions) from the organized Jewish community. It also revealed the growing appreciation throughout the communal leadership of a responsibility to meet, by pro-action and reaction, the plainly evident need for change.[26] There was no substitute for disciplined research and expert assessments.

In the autumn of 1992, two reports were published of special interest. One was by a committee headed by Fred Worms and commissioned by the JEDT on the state of Jewish education, and the other by a committee headed by Sir Stanley Kalms commissioned by the United Synagogue on the condition of that organization. The Worms Report was significantly entitled 'Securing Our Future'. Fred Worms, an accountant and entrepreneur, was an early and vocal advocate of the rationalization of fund-raising, particularly with a view to establishing the priority of Jewish education, even at the 'expense' of funds for Israel. The Report called for a 'national council' for the funding and supervision of educational facilities, Orthodox and non-Orthodox, and for the determination of priorities, adequate funding for the training and remuneration of teachers, and a higher degree of professionalism in all facets of educational supervision and administration.

The findings of the committee were seized on by the Chief Rabbi, who welcomed the whole of the Report as further demonstrating the urgency of his own call in his installation address in 1991 for action to ensure Jewish continuity. In his published response, he pointedly commented that 'economic crisis is forcing the community to decide its priorities', in the face of the confirmed low level of educational attainment, the serious decline in numbers receiving any form of Jewish education, and the growing losses in terms of affiliated or identifiable Jews. By the time of the publication of the Worms report, the Chief Rabbi was on the way to creating the expectedly ameliorative organization which he called 'Jewish Continuity'.

The Worms Report, like the Young Report in its own sphere, sharpened awareness of the shortcomings in the prevailing system. It contributed much to the innovative spirit which was, in effect, dissolving the residues of the Victorian legacy and, in particular, undoing the remnants of a besetting complacency. The Chief Rabbi was optimistically envisaged as the head of the proposed 'national council' by whatever name it might operate. Time was to decide differently. Meanwhile, it was noteworthy that the Worms Committee included a prominent rabbi of the Reform community.

The Kalms Report was equally significantly entitled 'A Time for Change'. The circumstances which led the lay heads of the United Synagogue to set up the committee further illustrate the extent of the changes within the community, especially as seen in the operation of leadership within that synagogal body. It was the first time that the United Synagogue had countenanced an 'outside' enquiry. It found itself in unaccustomed serious financial straits. Its membership was shown to be consistently falling. The decline in numbers was only in part due to natural decrease. There was a fall both in absolute terms and also relative to other synagogal bodies. There was a loss of United Synagogue members to synagogues to the 'right' and the 'left' of the United Synagogue. There was also some transfer of 'allegiance' to other synagogal bodies by children of former members of the United Synagogue.

The 'rightward' move (which was and is visible within the present membership of the United Synagogue), reflected a turning (not limited to any one Jewish group – and as a modern trend, not limited to the Jewish fold) to metaphysical philosophies, special forms of piety, more intense study, and a preference for the more participatory and informal forms of religious service. The lax attitude to Jewish observance on the part of the lay leaders of the United Synagogue in the 1950s became unacceptable. That circumstance is at least in part a reaction to the secession of 1964.

On the part of some members of the United Synagogue their response to the Jacobs Affair was to find in the 'rightward' tendency within the United Synagogue a reason for leaving that body for Masorti or Reform. There was on their part a certain weariness with traditional forms of Jewish religious practice, accentuated by an advance in scientific styles of thinking in a somewhat more sophisticated community. The 'Zionization' of the Progressive synagogal groups had also lifted for some what might otherwise have been a barrier to affiliation.[27]

These developments, in their diverse ways, were part of the background to the increasingly severe financial plight of the United Synagogue; a state of affairs which reached crisis point following a series of controversial extensions of commitment and loss-creating decisions, at a time of inflation and economic recession. Sir Stanley Kalms, prominent industrialist, former Chairman of Jews' College and of the JEDT, and a past honorary officer of the United Synagogue, had been an influential sponsor of the 'candidature' of Rabbi Dr Jonathan Sacks for the Office of Chief Rabbi. He was later to express sharp disenchantment with the new incumbent because of what he considered the Chief Rabbi's over-zealous involvement with the Orthodox outlook.

The adoption by the Council of the United Synagogue of most of the Kalms Report was followed by some consequential changes, each of which was without precedent in the United Synagogue and had been outside any realistic contemplation until the late 1980s. In addition to the inevitable economies, the Council of the United Synagogue under the new constitution was substantially reduced in size. A greater degree of independence was accorded to the constituent synagogues in regard to their local expenditure and synagogal development, and the number of women representatives on the Council from the synagogues was substantially increased (though not to the level urged by the new honorary officers). The former bench of honorary officers had resigned and in their place were elected honorary officers who were largely Sir Stanley's fellow committee members and coadjutors. There soon followed the newly prescribed reduction in the number of elected honorary officers from nine to three (the president and two vice-presidents), the remainder being nominated directly by those three from the body of the Council. This combination of wider democracy, and tighter constitutionally provided central control, represented, within the context of the United Synagogue, the growing communal fashion for structural 'streamlining', and for the selection of men of proven talent for particular departmental headships, without the uncertain recourse to serious ballot.

In his immediate published response to the Kalms proposals, the Chief Rabbi observed that the failure of the United Synagogue to attract, had a 'significance' which was 'less financial than spiritual'. The Chief Rabbi sought to remedy the weakness by stressing the nature of the United Synagogue as 'inclusivist', and by reminding the synagogues themselves of the importance of enlarging their religious and cultural programmes beyond the synagogal services proper. His book, *Community of Faith,* published to mark the 125th anniversary of the United Synagogue, was a presentation of a communal philosophy of inclusivism. The Chief Rabbi hoped that this old-new open-to-all (Jews) policy, by a religious institution which was governed religiously by the *halakha* as interpreted by him, would dispose of or ease what he termed 'the crisis of identity' from which he declared the United Synagogue had suffered 'in recent years'.

In 1993, the Chief Rabbi, in reference to the conclusions of the Worms Report, strikingly delineated a 'polarization' in Jewish education. 'For some', he observed,

> still only a minority, their education is becoming more intense. For others it is becoming less substantial year by year. Ironically, while the numbers attending Jewish day schools have grown, so too have the numbers receiving no education or little Jewish education. The Jewish community is beginning to divide less between Orthodoxy and others, or between the religious and the secular, but between those who know and those who do not.[28]

He contemplated,

> a single body – to promote, strategize and resource all those many activities in our community which create Jewish continuity – to aim at a complete transformation of Anglo-Jewish attitudes so that Continuity moves from last to first place in our communal agenda.

The most prolific area of communal planning had long been occupied by the concern encapsulated in the title of the Chief Rabbi's book, *Will We Have Jewish Grandchildren* (1994). The report of the Institute for Jewish Policy Research (1996) was relied on by him as yet further reinforcing the 'urgency' of the matter, notably the indication that 36 per cent of the Jewish community was unaffiliated and that the rate of intermarriage was in the region of 44 per cent. The community's priorities 'had to change' he declared at the Board of Deputies in March 1996, 'in order to spend as much on strengthening Jewish identity as (is) spent on Israel and welfare'. His formulation had become yet more dramatic and specific than his original call for 'Jewish continuity' or his public launching of 'Jewish Continuity' as an organization in May 1993.

The readiness of the Joint Israel Appeal in 1994 to contribute, as such, directly – and substantially – to Jewish Continuity was a major event in the community's history. It heralded a partnership of an unprecedented nature. Yet the general anxiety to stem the tide of assimilation served to arouse a sharpening discord over proposed procedures to achieve that end. The Chief Rabbi, as the president and effective head of the movement and organization which he had summoned into being, encountered mounting difficulties in holding an acceptable balance between conflicting groups. Those on the religious 'left' whose Judaism was self-evidently 'legitimate' to themselves, were faced by bodies and individuals who deemed such 'legitimacy' as spurious. Those on the religious 'left' were concerned about the proportionate extent of allocations from Jewish Continuity to institutions of the 'right'. Objection was taken in some ranks on the 'right' (more particularly the 'far right') to the Chief Rabbi's involvement in the financing of Progressive educational establishments. Efforts to assuage critics by declarations from the Chief Rabbi as to his attachment to 'Torah-true Judaism', and his attitudes to those who rejected his interpretation of *Torah min Hashamaim,* evoked no less severe criticism from the 'left'. No language or structure under the direction of the Chief Rabbi could satisfy one party without antagonizing another. The inclusivism of the United Synagogue did not subdue or contain the communal contention.

The Chief Rabbi declared his readiness to hand over to laymen the task of determining a revised structure for Jewish Continuity and relieving him of any responsibility for the distribution of funds raised under its banner. In the event, nothing less than the merger of the Joint Israel Appeal and Jewish Continuity was deemed sufficient to ensure the harmony of interests between those two bodies, and indirectly to enhance sufficiently the prospect of an acceptable distribution of funds with immunity for the Chief Rabbi from criticism in respect thereof. The essence of the scheme, agreed upon in 1996, was that there would be unified fund-raising by the one body created through the merger, the funds being raised directly and expressly for British Jewry as well as for Israel.

Israel had, so to speak, come of age, and so had the British Jewish community. Long gone was the time when the United Synagogue sought to exclude Zionism from its synagogues as being 'political' and extraneous to Judaism. The decisions of the Joint Israel Appeal in 1994 to enter into partnership with Jewish Continuity, and later to enter the merger, reflect the final virtual consensus that the needs of Israel and of the Diaspora are complementary. These events in Anglo-Jewry had a wider significance than domestic only.

There is a further dimension to the developments. Some have perceived, in the Chief Rabbi's departure from any strategic control of the funds, a modern sign of the 'anomaly' of the Chief Rabbinate in a community where its jurisdiction holds sway over a segment only, albeit by far the largest and containing the greater part of the Jewish community. They comment that this 'anomaly' dates from the birth of the Reform movement in Britain, to be followed by separations and independence from the Chief Rabbi's headship in the long intervening years, on the 'right' and on the 'left'. Among the rabbinate of the United Synagogue and of a number of provincial congregations, there has been from the 1960s a 'rightward' move-ment in the approach to scripture and *halakha* which was not common in an earlier generation. Indeed, there is evidence that some of the congregations positively prefer the more *hasidic* incumbents.

Those who uphold the traditional status of the Chief Rabbinate point to the long and unique history of the office, its rootedness in the British scene (and in British society at many levels), and the weight of numbers who come within its jurisdiction. It is *sui juris* as a Jewish office and as a British office. Its supporters observe the extent of cohesion, sense of community and distinctive identity that it has afforded Anglo-Jewry, in spite of occasional turmoil. It is clear to observers that its role requires a considerable degree of effort, tact and forbearance on its part and on all sides. Never before has this question been as extensively discussed in public and in the corridors as today. Ironically the passing (August 1996) of Rabbi Gryn (see note 26), a prominent proponent of communal harmony despite and because of major religious differences, was followed by acts of omission and commission and responses thereto, all of which accentuated tension between religious 'right' and 'left' and within the Orthodox community. At the time of writing, the consequences, if any, for the communal system or its 'ecclesiastical' structure cannot with certainty be discerned.

Beginning in the eighteenth century, the historical role of the rabbi as ultimate arbiter in disputes over communal policy was progressively attenuated in the Jewish world. In Britain, that attenuation was all the more marked because of the long-standing erastian character of national life, especially in England. The Chief Rabbi's transfer of his authority to laymen in the matter of the financial resources of Jewish Continuity may be seen as in line with that characteristic of Anglo-Jewry. Professor Leslie Wagner, former Chairman of Jewish Continuity's Allocation Committee before the merger, had significantly observed that it was important 'to guard against the religious communities setting up their own bodies outside the new single organization'. Allocation arrangements within the new body were planned to be so directed as to obviate any need, it was hoped, for any such departure from the scheme. To the extent that such arrangements and the policy decisions relating thereto are in lay hands, and are not seen as introducing contentious religious issues, the Chief Rabbi's withdrawal in this matter need imply neither infringement of nor derogation from his communal role. Yet the withdrawal, even if unilaterally decided on by him, had an enforced character about it which perhaps may, paradoxically, impinge adversely upon the status of the office which had given birth to the original scheme. This may depend on the wider circumstances of the office's operations and the reactions thereto.

The new body, like the old Joint Israel Appeal, has cross-community support and again, like its predecessor, is led at all levels by men and women from across the Orthodox and non-Orthodox spectrum. It envisages itself as a facilitator (not as a founder or executant of plans) for the expansion of Jewish educational facilities (formal and informal, day school and part time) and for the development of the highest standards of professionalism in all departments, educational and administrative. The merger came about because it was necessary, if religious differences were not to disrupt any overall system for educational funding.

But, not all issues were or could yet be resolved. What is the essence of the 'Israel experience' which it is intended to include in education provision? What is the Jewishness which it is intended thereby to stimulate? What facets of Israel's performance are to be brought to bear upon Jewish education? A crucial factor in these respects, and in developments in education generally, will be the emergence (starts have in the past periodically been made or attempted) of adequate facilities for the recruitment, training and remuneration of Jewish teachers in Jewish subjects, as will in particular be required in the Jewish school system, for the considerable expansion of which there are major schemes promoted through private benefactions.

Questions may also be raised as to the forms of public accountability (if any) of the directors and governors of the new body in respect of the massive sums at their expected disposal, as well as methods to ensure the continued attractiveness into its management on the part of new, younger recruits from business and the professions. The creation of acceptable machinery for determining priorities remains a communal prospect and aspiration – not only in the sphere of education – yet to be realized. How far and over what time-span the latest developments will affect the impact of Jewish education on such phenomena as the extent of indifference, the degree of secularization, the rate of intermarriage, and the pace of *aliya,* are questions for the future. Meanwhile, in recent years the communal system has moved with unparalleled rapidity along fresh paths and towards new horizons.

In the distinctive, indigenous communal system of Anglo-Jewry a many-sided process of change has been in progress for half a century. The contrasts between the 1940s and the 1990s in styles and objectives reflect in microcosm the major transformations affecting the Jewish world – the changing Israel–Diaspora relationship, the new (old) meaning of Zionism, the changing patterns of Jewish leadership, the yearning for answers concerning Jewish identity and purpose. It was inevitable that in the long aftermath of Emancipation and the Holocaust, Jews should be thrown back upon their sources. It was characteristic that in Anglo-Jewry a significant catalyst towards the moulding of revised communal structures should be the combination of financial stringency and the consequential pressure for rationalization and priority choices. The stages in the process have characteristically been by way of responses fashioned by pragmatic assessments of what the times required and by estimates of what could be delivered at successive stages, given some measured institutional novelty or revision. Throughout, the assessments and responses were advanced by, and in themselves considerably promoted, the rise of professionalism in all aspects of the communal service, as well as the ever closer mutual dependence of talented, professional and gifted laymen (elected or otherwise) in every major field of communal endeavour.

NOTES

1. On the statistical and demographic fronts and generally, see Marlena Schmool, 'British Jewry: Prospects and Problems', in S. Ilan Troen (ed.), *Jewish Centres and Peripheries* (1999), pp. 227–52; her 'A Century of British Jewish Statistics' in S.W. Massil (ed.), *Jewish Year Book, 1996* (London: Vallentine Mitchell), pp. ix–xvii, and Marlena Schmool and Frances Cohen, *A Profile of British Jewry* (Board of Deputies, 1998). In this article I have used the term 'Anglo-Jewry' to denote the Jews of the United Kingdom.
2. Proceedings published in V.D. Lipman and Sonia Lipman (eds), *Jewish Life in Britain 1962–77* (New York: K.G. Saur, 1981).
3. Proceedings published in Julius Gould and Shaul Esh (eds), *Jewish Life in Modern Britain* (London: Routledge, 1964).
4. The author recalls being shown by the late Cecil Roth a letter to him from Waley Cohen expressing angry surprise over Hertz's addresses on the subject. Waley Cohen had believed the object was to attract Jewish ex-servicemen into synagogal affiliation, an aim which in the event he did not consider they were likely to achieve by their substance and tone. The addresses, delivered in 1925–26, were published under the title *The New Paths*, and were republished in 1927 in Hertz's *Affirmations of Judaism* (Oxford: Oxford University Press). In his preface to the latter volume, Hertz referred to the 'welcome' accorded to *The New Paths*. He entertained no doubt about the utility and importance of the work in what he called 'the religious unrest of the age'.
5. *Sermons, Addresses and Studies*, Vol. 1 (London: Soncino Press, 1938), p. 258.
6. 'Profile of a Community: Anglo-Jewry since 1933', *Jewish Quarterly* (London), Vol. 30, No. 4 (1983), p. 24. For illustrative exchanges on Hertz's position from today's diverse standpoints, see *Jewish Chronicle*, from 27 May 1994 to 10 July 1994 inclusive.
7. Geoffrey Alderman, *The Federation of Synagogues 1887–1987* (London: Federation of Synagogues, 1987). For a robust presentation of the Federation's case against merger, see interview with its senior dayan, Rabbi Israel J. Lichtenstein, *Jewish Chronicle*, 17 January 1997.
8. A.J. Kershen and J. Romain, *Tradition and Change: A History of British Reform*

Judaism, 1840–1994 (London: Vallentine Mitchell, 1995).

9. Louis Jacobs, *Helping with Inquiries: An Autobiography* (London: Vallentine Mitchell, 1989).

10. Rabbi Dr Alexander Altmann, 'The Task before Anglo-Jewry', *Jewish Affairs*, Vol. 9 (January 1954), pp. 28–30 (courtesy, Library of London School of Jewish Studies).

11. Among the priorities announced by the then President of the United Synagogue, Victor Lucas, in 1984, on behalf of its newly elected leadership, were 'the recruitment of a new generation of (younger) leaders to administer synagogal affairs' and the 'furtherance of practical steps to adapt synagogue buildings as genuine community centres for cultural, recreational and educational purposes', *Jewish Chronicle*, 28 September 1984. The two tasks were complementary, and recognized the increasingly communitarian character of the Jewish community, with less emphasis on old-style paternalism, and the 'sanctity' of precedent. 'We are getting people in their 30s and 40s taking up leadership roles', declared Seymour Saideman, the President of the United Synagogue in 1996, *Jewish Chronicle*, 7 June 1996. The trend was noticeable in many areas of Jewish communal life.

12. Israel Finestein, 'Cambridge Contrasts: Waley Cohen and Brodetsky', in William Frankel and Harvey Miller (eds), *Gown and Tallith* (London: Harvey Miller Publishers, 1989), pp. 47–51; Robert Henriques, *Sir Robert Waley Cohen* (London: Secker & Warburg, 1996); A.N. Newman, *The United Synagogue 1870–1970* (London: Routledge, 1977); S.S. Levin (ed.), *A Century of Jewish Life, 1870–1970* (London: United Synagogue, 1970).

13. Waley Cohen and his second cousin, Lionel Cohen (later Lord Cohen of Walmer, a leading English judge) retired from office at the Board of Deputies in protest against the substance and style of the Zionist influence thereat.

14. For a revealing, if highly personal, account of the Central Council by a zealous provincial leader and a Treasurer of the Council, see Armin Krausz, *Sheffield Jewry: Commentary on a Community* (Bar-Ilan, Ramat Gan: Naor Publications, 1980), pp. 150–9.

15. Gideon Shimoni, 'Selig Brodetsky and the Ascendancy of Zionism in Anglo-Jewry 1939–45', *Jewish Journal of Sociology*, Vol. 22, No. 2; Stuart A. Cohen, 'Another View of Brodetsky's Role and Achievements', *Jewish Journal of Sociology*, Vol. 24, No. 1 (1982); Israel Finestein, 'Comments' on foregoing papers, *Jewish Journal of Sociology*, Vol. 24, No. 2 (1982); Gideon Shimoni, 'The Non-Zionists in Anglo-Jewry 1937–48', *Jewish Journal of Sociology*, Vol. 28, No. 2 (1986); Selig Brodetsky, *Memoirs: From Ghetto to Israel* (London: Weidenfeld, 1960).

16. Paul Bookbinder, *Simon Marks* (London: Weidenfeld, 1993); Israel Sieff, *Memoirs* (London: Weidenfeld, 1970).

17. Montagu's retirement from office was preceded by the Council's rejection of his nominee as Treasurer of the United Synagogue. That rejection evidenced changes in the balance of power within that body and was perceived by some as having comparable implications within the communal system generally.

18. Daphne Gerlis, *The Wonderful Women in Black: The Story of the Women's*

Campaign for Soviet Jewry (London: Minerva Press, 1956).

19. 'Key Findings': see Note 26.

20. The new combined body, known as Jewish Care, has since 1990 incorporated a number of other Jewish welfare agencies. In 1995, Jewish Care raised £10,000,000 to support its work, rivalling in terms of income (and mounting thereafter) the hitherto pinnacle achievement of income by the Joint Israel Appeal. The weight of influence in communal affairs on the part of the leaders of an organization disposing of that kind of annual charitable income is bound to be significant.

21. Geoffrey Alderman, 'The British Chief Rabbinate: A Most Peculiar Practice', *European Judaism*, Vol. 23, No. 2 (1995), pp. 45–58. For some aspects of the Chief Rabbi's role relating to the Board of Deputies and generally, and attitudes to such a role, see Abba Bornstein and Bernard Homa, *Tell it in Gath* (London: A. Bornstein and B. Homa, 1972), and Sidney Frosh, President of the United Synagogue 1987–92, in *Hamesilah* (London: United Synagogue, Pesach, 1985).

22. In the 1950s a concerted effort was made under influential auspices to raise substantial sums for the endowment of higher Jewish studies, and for youth education. The proposals were intended to mark the tercentenary of the resettlement of the Jews in England. The principal personalities heading the Appeal were Sir Isaac Wolfson and Lord Cohen of Walmer. The Appeal fell far short of target. The tertiary education plans were not proceeded with. The money raised was transferred to the Jewish Youth Fund (established in 1937 to help promote religious education among the young, and to assist leisure time facilities and social welfare among them). The episode paralleled remarkably the effort made in the 1920s, under no less influential auspices, to raise funds by communal appeal for like purposes. The leading figures in that Appeal – designed as part of the Jewish memorial following World War I – were Sir Robert Waley Cohen and Chaim Weizmann. The Appeal fell far short of target. The tertiary educational plans were not proceeded with. The monies raised were committed to the Jewish Memorial Council (established 1919) for use in assistance to Jewish youth educational facilities. Since the 1970s, a number of personal or corporate Jewish benefactions have made possible a series of endowments for Hebrew and Jewish studies at certain universities. While this reflects changing attitudes and has been widely welcomed, there has remained some criticism over the unplanned nature of these developments and what is regarded in some quarters as a falling short by the Jewish community of opportunities and needs. For example, see exchanges between Dr David Aberbach and Jeremy Leigh, in the *Jewish Chronicle*, 16 January 1987 and 17 July 1987, and between Dr Aberbach, David Lewis and Rabbi Jonathan Magonet, *Jewish Chronicle*, 30 August 1996, 13 September 1996 and 27 September 1996. For a directory of centres of teaching in Jewish studies (but not necessarily in respect of Jewish students) see Sharman Kadish, *The Teaching of Jewish Civilization in British and Irish Universities and other Institutions of Higher Learning* (Jerusalem: International Centre for University Teaching of Jewish Civilization, 1990).

23. Abraham Cohen, *Three Centuries of Anglo-Jewish History* (Cambridge: Jewish Historical Society of England, 1961), p. 183. The prevailing spirit in some quarters in the 1950s may be gathered from the memoirs of the then Chief Rabbi, Israel Brodie, in his address to the British Mizrachi Conference in November 1953 published in his *The Strength of my Heart* (London: Living Books, 1969), pp. 369–75:

> Not a single penny of Jewish Agency Funds should be spent (in Britain) on Jewish education. When we speak (in Britain) of Jewish education, we mean religious Jewish education. I am opposed to the diversion of any money collected under Zionist auspices being granted or loaned to any Jewish school. (p. 369)

24. Proceedings, Shalom Eilati (ed.), *The Tribes of Israel Together: A Dialogue with the President of Israel* (Jerusalem: Beit Hanassi), p. 83. See also, Israel Finestein, 'An Approach to a New Emphasis', in Moshe Davis (ed.), *Zionism in Transition* (New York: Arno, 1980).

25. In addition to regular and statistical reports published by the Community Research Unit of the Board of Deputies and the periodic reports published by the Institute of Jewish Affairs and its successor on communal life, opinions and prospects, there were special studies of selected areas, including: B.A. Kosmin and N. Grizzard, *Jews in an Inner London Borough (Hackney)* (London: Board of Deputies, 1975); B.A. Kosmin, B. Bant and N. Grizzard, *Steel City Jews: Sheffield* (London: Board of Deputies, 1976); N. Grizzard and P. Raisman, 'Inner City Jews in Leeds', *Jewish Journal of Sociology*, Vol. 22 (1980), pp. 22–33; B.A. Kosmin and C. Levy, *Work and Employment: Redbridge* (London: Board of Deputies, 1981).

26. The statistical and geographic study by Stanley Waterman and Barry Kosmin published by the Board of Deputies in 1986, entitled *British Jewry in the 80s*, and the report prepared by the Institute for Jewish Policy Research in association with the Community Research Unit of the Board and the City of London University ten years later, had much impact on the Jewish reading public in terms of sharpening the already acute concern over the pace and degree of contraction and erosion amidst counter-signs of the deepening and widening Jewish religious and cultural interests. In 1996 the Institute published 'Key Findings' of the later report, which were presented by Stephen Miller, Marlena Schmool and Anthony Lerman and published by the Institute under that title.

27. From the 1960s, the senior minister of the principal Reform synagogue was Rabbi Hugo Gryn (1930–96), a survivor of Auschwitz, prominent spokesman in every branch of Zionist effort and an influential advocate of Jewish day school education, including in particular the new day school enterprises of his own movement.

28. During the 25 years from the mid-1950s the number of Jewish day schools in Britain trebled to about 60, and the number of pupils trebled. But this total did not include more than about one-quarter of the Jewish school-age

population; and there were insufficient Jewish secondary school places. Remedial plans were under way in the 1970s and wider plans are being promoted. In part-time Jewish education, hours are severely limited, the standard of facilities have generally not been high, and the recruitment and training of teachers continued to suffer the consequences of earlier neglect in the provision of resources. At any one time a third of Jewish children of school age were found not to be in receipt of Jewish education. These matters were and are at the centre of attention in the 'revivalist' spirit which gained ground. Stuart Young in his Report (1978) to the JEDT on the then supply of teachers and the facilities for their recruitment, training and remuneration, had warned of the likely results of investing inadequate resources in these fields. Well-made schemes continued to labour under the impact of the pressure on communal resources. See Jacob Braude, 'Jewish Education in Britain', in Lipman and Lipman (eds), *Jewish Life in Britain 1962–77*, pp. 119–29.

SELECT BIBLIOGRAPHY
Exclusive of items mentioned in text or Notes.

Alderman, Geoffrey, *The Jewish Community in British Politics* (Oxford: Clarendon Press; New York: Oxford University Press, 1983).
—— *London Jewry and London Politics 1889–1986* (London, New York: Routledge, 1989).
—— *Modern British Jewry* (Oxford: Clarendon Press; New York: Oxford University Press, 1992).
—— *Troubled Eden: An Anatomy of British Jewry* (New York: Basic Books, 1970).
—— *The Cousinhood* (New York: Macmillan, 1971).
Bentwich, Norman, 'The Social Transformation of Anglo-Jewry 1883–1960', *Jewish Journal of Sociology*, Vol. 2 (1960), pp. 16–24.
Black, E.C., *The Social Politics of Anglo-Jewry 1880–1920* (Oxford: Blackwell, 1989).
Bolchover, Richard, *British Jewry and the Holocaust* (Cambridge: Cambridge University Press, 1893).
Cesarani, David (ed.), *The Making of Modern Anglo-Jewry* (Oxford: B. Blackwell, 1990), including 'The Transformation of Communal Authority in Anglo-Jewry 1914–40', by him.
—— *The Jewish Chronicle and Anglo-Jewry 1841–1991* (Cambridge: Cambridge University Press, 1994).
Collins, K.E., *Second City Jewry: The Jews of Glasgow 1790–1919* (Glasgow: Jewish Archives, 1990).
Cooper H. and P. Morrison, *A Sense of Belonging: Dilemmas of British Jewish Identity* (London: Weidenfeld and Nicolson, 1991).
Endelman, Todd M., *Radical Assimilation in English Jewish History, 1656–1945* (Bloomington, IN: University Press, 1990).
Finestein, Israel, 'The Estrangement of the Anglo-Jewish Intellectuals', *Jewish Quarterly*, Vols 3–4 (1984), pp. 46–52.

—— 'Changes in Authority in Anglo-Jewry since the 1930s', *Jewish Quarterly*, Vol. 2 (1985), pp. 33–6.

Jakobovits, Rabbi Immanuel (Lord), *If Only My People: Zionism in My Life* (London: Weidenfeld, 1984).

Kosmin, B.A., 'The Face of Jewish Suburbia', *Jewish Chronicle*, 14 and 21 July 1978.

—— 'Localism and Pluralism in British Jewry 1900–80', *Transactions of the Jewish Historical Society of England*, Vol. 28 (1984), pp. 111–25.

Krausz, Ernest, *Leeds Jewry: Its History and Social Structure* (Cambridge: Jewish Historical Society of England, 1963).

Kushner, Tony (ed.), *The Jewish Heritage in British History: Englishness and Jewishness* (London: Frank Cass, 1992).

Lipman, V.D., *The History of the Jews in Britain since 1858* (Leicester: Leicester University Press, 1990).

Olsover, L., *The Jewish Communities of North-East England, 1755–1980* (Gateshead: Ashley Mark, 1980).

Pollins, Harold, *Economic History of The Jews in England* (Rutherford, NJ: Fairleigh Dickenson University Press, 1982).

Rubinstein, W.D., *History of the Jews in the English-Speaking World: Great Britain* (Basingstoke: Macmillans, 1996).

Sacks, Chief Rabbi Dr, J.E., 'Religion and National Identity: British Jewry and the State of Israel', in E. Don-Yehiya (ed.), *Israel and Diaspora Jewry* (Ramat Gan: Bar-Ilan University Press, 1991), pp. 53–60.

—— *One People? Tradition, Modernity, and Jewish Unity* (London: Littman Library, 1993).

Shatzkes, Pamela, *Holocaust and Rescue: Impotent or Indifferent? Anglo-Jewry, 1938–1945* (Basingstoke: Palgrave Publishers, 2002).

Taylor, Derek (ed.), *Jewish Education* (in the United Kingdom) 3 Vols (London: JEDT, 1981–84).

Wasserstein, Bernard, *Britain and the Jews of Europe, 1939–45* (Oxford: London Institute of Jewish Affairs, 1979).

Williams, Bill, 'The Anti-semitism of Tolerance', in A. Kidd and K. Roberts (eds), *City, Class and Culture* (Manchester: Manchester University Press, 1985), pp. 74–102.

Worms, F.S., *A Life in Three Cities, Frankfurt, London, and Jerusalem*, Part 2 'Business' and Part 4 'Communal Involvement' (London: Peter Halban, 1996).

2

Anglo-Jewish Attitudes to Jewish Day-School Education 1850–1950

This chapter concerns both the era of Jewish civil emancipation and its long aftermath. Among the themes which vividly illustrate the transformations within Anglo-Jewry were the changing approaches to the desirability or otherwise of Jewish day-school education. This is not a history of Anglo-Jewish education but an examination of attitudes. The changes reflected generational differences in outlook, aspirations and priorities. Fashions and opportunities in the wider developing society played their part in changing opinions.

Influential elements in the lay leadership, for all their Jewish commitment and habits of philanthropy, evinced a consistent complacency towards Jewish educational standards. The prime targets were perceived to be the anglicization of immigrants and their families; resistance to Christian conversionist efforts; the encouragement of manual skills among impoverished youth; and the curbing of pauperization and street begging.

It was accepted that the Jewish 'charity' day-schools, later known as the Jewish 'voluntary schools', were necessary in the areas of immigrant residence. They were seen not only as Jewish educational establishments but also as significant anglicizing agents. In the 1850s, contentions arose over the idea of providing Jewish day-school education in other localities and/or for children of the middle classes. These disputes did not readily subside.

Complacency extended to the recruitment and training of an adequate supply of competent teachers. These pages do no more than touch upon that important aspect of the communal scene.

Reliance on the flow of immigrants to make up teacher numbers offered no assurance of competence. Nor was the remuneration or status accorded to the teacher likely to encourage many prospective candidates of calibre. Schemes for improvement in teaching skills were hesitant in inception and of limited appeal. Financial constraints were, in practice, a persistent major consideration.

It was not until around the middle of the twentieth century that the 'paramountcy' of the question of teachers began to be communally recognized in earnest. This recognition came in response to the pressure of the self-evident needs in Jewish schools and classes, and the relentless publicity in the Jewish press and elsewhere on this subject by Jewish educationists such as Nathan Morris and Edward Conway and by communal analysts like the businessman and religious Zionist, Jacob Braude. A further factor in bringing about the new perspectives was the realization that any successful expanded system of Jewish day-school education would ultimately depend on the availability of more teachers trained for the teaching of Jewish and general studies. While there can be no doubt that there were some excellent teachers in the earlier epoch at the Jews' Free School and elsewhere, the overall picture gave far less ground for optimism.

NATIONAL BACKGROUND

The State had been a late-comer to education.[1] This was deemed the natural province of the religious authorities. Education was neither compulsory nor of uniform or consistent standard. Towards the end of the eighteenth century and in the early part of the nineteenth, the energy and enthusiasm of Nonconformist groups and of the Evangelical wing of the Church of England infused into religious and social life an extra practical impulse. One indication was their encouragement of the provision of more schools and classes for the education of the poor. A pioneer association in the building of additional voluntary schools was the British and Foreign Schools Society, established in 1811 by the principal Nonconformist bodies. Within months there was created, under the patronage of the Church of England, the National Society for Promoting the Education of the Poor in the Principles of the Established Church. By 1850, there were approximately 17,000 Church schools, and 1,500 schools linked to the Nonconformists. In the first 70 years of that century, the number of Roman Catholic schools rose from three to 350.

The first grant from the public purse for popular education was famously made in 1833. It was in the sum of £20,000 and was limited to the Anglican and Nonconformist schools. This fell far short of the demands of educational reformers. In 1825, Henry Brougham, later Lord Chancellor, had published his *Practical Observations upon the Education of the People,* advocating a policy of national popular education, with particular emphasis on instruction in reading and writing. It was a trend-setter in this field among political radicals. In 1827, it was followed by the setting up, with his crucial support, of the Society for the Diffusion of Useful Knowledge. Before the passage of the Bill in 1833, which authorized the making of the grants-in-aid to schools, John Roebuck had in vain sought to persuade the House of Commons to devise 'means for the universal and national education of the whole people'. His proposal had the backing of utilitarians, radicals and secularists.

While Church spokesmen and the Nonconformists were opposed to the secular ethos of Roebuck's motion, they were also uneasy about one another's relation to State aid in education. The former were disturbed by the prospect of State support for the teaching of 'dissenting' principles. Nonconformists and their political allies were disturbed by the idea of State intervention in aid of Church schools. An important influence in favour of some measure of State aid were the proposals which, in 1833, emerged as the Factory Act which prohibited the employment of children under nine. Although there were many evasions of its provisions, the widespread 'release' of children under that age from the factories added to the pressure for State intervention in support of education.

An Education Committee of the Privy Council was established to determine allocations from the central fund, which in 1849 was raised to £30,000. An Inspectorate was soon appointed in respect of schools benefiting from State aid.[2] The sense of competition between National Society schools and those of the Nonconformists was accentuated by the fact that in many areas the sole available school was one of the former, where the only religious education would be Anglican. In 1850, public expenditure on schools reached £125,000, and continued to rise, exceeding £800,000 in the 1860s.

JEWISH APPLICATIONS AND DIVERSITY

The first application for financial aid for Jewish schools was made in 1847, by the Board of Deputies of British Jews. In that year, Roman Catholic schools were for the first time accorded a State grant. The Board urged the Jewish case on the ground of civic equality. It was further encouraged to do so by the Acts of 1845 and 1846, which respectively opened municipal office to professing Jews and gave legal recognition to Jewish religious, educational and charitable endowments. The Education Committee of the Privy Council in the event proved chary of supporting the advancement of non-Christian indoctrination by grants to Jewish schools.[3]

In 1852, the Government was presented by the Board with a particular application relating to the Manchester Jews' School. The case was considered to have special merit. It was to become a test case. That school, founded in 1838, had 60 pupils by the date of the application. Its own request to the Education Committee elicited the reply that the Committee's terms of reference did not extend to assisting Jewish schools. The reply was deemed especially unreasonable in the light of the movement in that city to establish a series of free schools which were to be aided by a special local rate (to which local Jews would, with other rate-payers, perforce contribute), but would not include a Jewish school as long as the Education Committee retained its stand. The general tuition at the local Jewish school had been commended by the Government's inspectors.

The special circumstances of Manchester,[4] allied to the advancing tide of liberal emancipatory opinion and the personal support of Lord John Russell (Prime Minister between 1846 and 1852), greatly helped the Board in its long negotiations with the Education Committee. A model trust deed was drafted on the Board's behalf as the standard basis upon which Jewish schools would operate if aid were granted. In the deed as finally adopted, State aid was to be conditional upon aided Jewish schools being opened to non-Jewish children. The Manchester Jews' School had long been open to non-Jewish pupils, although it was rare for such to enrol. The Board, under pressure from some Jewish schools and the restrictive example of many Christian denominational schools, had sought, unavailingly, to exclude this requirement.

The Board was soon to change its mind on this subject, which at the time was a matter of controversy within the Jewish community. Sir David Salomons, a member of the Orthodox community and (later Sir) John Simon of the Reform Synagogue were prominent exponents of the condition stipulated by the Education Committee.[5]

Another of the agreed provisions in the deed was that at Jewish schools the sole religious instruction was to be Jewish, with the right of withdrawal during such instructions on the part of non-Jewish children. Religious education was to be under the superintendence of the Chief Rabbi or of a person appointed for this purpose by the School Committee. The Board had originally sought to limit this authority to the Chief Rabbi. Neither the Education Committee of the Privy Council nor the principal Jewish emancipationists nor most of the Governors of the Jews' Free School favoured any such limitation.

There were at this date five Jewish voluntary schools in London, with a total attendance of approximately 2000 children, more than one-half of whom were enrolled at the Jews' Free School in Whitechapel (founded in 1817). The remaining centres were the Westminster Jews' Free School (1820); the Jews' Infants School (1841); the West Metropolitan School (1849), attached to the Reform Synagogue; and a cluster of schools around the Sephardi Synagogue, dating back to the seventeenth and eighteenth centuries and which, in 1850, had 250 children in attendance.[6]

OPPOSITION

A revealing and much cited episode in the history of the non-charitable Jewish schools is offered by the fate of the Jews' College School which was founded by the Chief Rabbi, Nathan Marcus Adler, in 1855. This school was instituted concurrently with and as a potential 'feeder' for Jews' College, which was created to be the training seminary for the Jewish Ministry. The Chief Rabbi's publicly declared object in regard to the school was to create 'a public day school for the sons of our middle ranks'. Such a school, he wrote in a public letter in 1852,

> is urgently required, especially in London, where there are good educational institutions for our poorer brethren, but none for those of the classes above them. Attendance in the public schools of the general community subjects our sons to this disadvantage, that they are not only deprived of one school-day in the week – Saturday – but are necessarily left unprovided with sound religious instruction.

His aim was to furnish the pupils with 'an efficient general education, such for example as that afforded by the City of London School, together with sound religious instruction'.[7] The charge for each day pupil was £10 a year.

Influential opposition soon manifested itself against the idea of the school. Salomons supported the seminary plan, but in a letter to Adler castigated the proposed day school as 'unadvisable and unnecessary'.[8] Salomons deemed it to be 'unnecessary' in view of the well-established Jewish private schools which by this time were a significant feature in the structure of the Jewish community. Adler realized the worth of those schools, but appreciated likewise that their fees rendered them almost exclusively the preserve of the affluent. His school was to cater for the *middle* ranks who, while anxious to fight shy of the eleemosynary establishments, might be reluctant or unable to meet the expense of the older private establishments.

It was in regard to the 'inadvisability' of Adler's school that the opinion of the influential Salomons is especially instructive. The historian of Jews' College writes: 'In particular, objection was taken to what seemed a move in the direction of segregation at a time at which many of the leading Jews were striving towards some measure of assimilation in political, civil and social matters.[9]

Faced with the competition of the existing Jewish private schools and the growing resistance of Jewish parents who attached much importance to the social benefits which might accrue from an education at, say, the City of London School or University College School, Adler persisted with his venture amid mounting difficulties. An important factor in the future of his school, situated though it was in Finsbury Square, a comparatively new area of Jewish residence, was the continuing migration of Jewish families to the west and west-central regions of the metropolis. Their places were taken mostly by lower middle-class families and Adler was obliged to reduce the fees of the school to six guineas a year.

The school was finally closed in 1879. The immediate cause of the closure was financial, but the essential consideration was the indifference or opposition to such an establishment on the part of those sections of the Jewish community whom it was the Chief Rabbi's purpose to serve through the school. At no time did the attendance at the school reach 100. The fate of Adler's school was a sign of the times.

EDUCATION ACT 1870

As the metropolitan Jewish community expanded numerically and geographically, the size and number of the Jewish voluntary schools grew. In the 1860s, Jewish schools were founded in Bayswater, Stepney and south of the Thames (in the Borough), and a second Jews' Infants School was opened. By the end of the century, the number of children in the Jewish schools approached 8,000, of whom 3,500 were at the Jews' Free School.

By 1850, there were six Jewish schools in the Provinces. The largest were in Liverpool, Manchester and Birmingham, with a total roll of approximately 220. In Hull, Bristol and Leeds the total was nearly 60. By the end of the century, the expanded three former schools had a total roll of nearly 3,000.

Side by side with the voluntary schools there was, from the early 1860s, an increase in the number of Jewish and other private schools for families able to afford the fees, not counting the so-called Public Schools for the upper echelons of society. The availability of schools for the mass of the people, like their standards and motivations, depended on individual founders and the respective denominational bodies or local churches. There was no national pattern in the distribution of schools, some areas, especially rural, often being without any school.

The rapidly increasing population and governmental economies stemmed the pace of educational growth. Education was not always free for poor families, and the proportion of children in receipt of education steadily fell. A telling event was the formation in Manchester in 1864 of an alliance between secularist groups and Christian religious denominations in order to set up the Manchester Education Society to assist poor parents to pay school charges. In 1868, the Liberal victory in the General Election, and the growing conviction that in the emerging age of competitive imperial powers it was necessary to advance popular education, thrust education into the forefront of the legislative programme. The expanded electorate, following the electoral reform of 1867, gave urgency in any event to the need for a more robust approach to the wider provision of education.

W.E. Forster, the head of the Liberal Government's Education Department, was impressed by the official revelation that barely one half of the children of England were in receipt of education, and that education was grossly and unevenly distributed and widely inconsistent in standards. The Radical wing of the Liberal party pressed for a system of free, compulsory and unsectarian education. The proposal was vigorously presented by the Birmingham League, established in 1869 under the direction of Joseph Chamberlain, a leading Nonconformist whose interest in the subject was in part influenced by his eagerness to deflect State aid from denominational religious instruction. His group was content to receive less from the State rather than see public funds sustain Anglican indoctrination. Forster, brother-in-law of Matthew Arnold, the widely noted advocate of educational reform, and himself a Quaker industrialist, was unlikely wholly to share that view but was not indifferent to the general educational argument.

The Government's prime object, as defined by Forster, was 'to bring elementary education within the reach of every English home'. He was agreeable to excluding the provision of local rates for denominational teaching but was not averse to increasing the State's grant to the denominational schools. On the religious question generally, his ambition was to secure a compromise which might attract both Church and Dissent. In introducing his Bill in 1870, he told the House of Commons that 'on the speedy provision of elementary education depends our industrial prosperity, the safe working of our constitutional system and our national power'. He added:

Civilised communities throughout the world are massing themselves together, each mass being measured by its force; and if we are to hold

59

our position among men of our own race or among the nations of the world, we must make up for the smallness of our numbers by increasing the intellectual force of the individual.

'It was plain', wrote an insightful historian of the Victorian age, 'that the vast deficiencies in elementary education could now only be made good by public effort, by schools tax-aided and rate-provided.'[10] The pragmatic and limited educational motivations of the politicians were no less plain, however grand the broader context and the prospect of national, even imperial, advantage.

The main feature of the Act of 1870 was that it required the creation of locally elected School Boards who were to establish schools – Board Schools – where necessary in their areas out of local rates. The Government was empowered to assist these schools out of general taxation. Forster's Education Department greatly increased its support for the denominational schools, whose numbers soon doubled. They were outside the system of Board Schools and outside rate-aid.

The Board of Deputies gave close attention to the proposed measure throughout its passage. It was especially involved in consultations leading to 'conscience clauses' in the Bill. Section 14(2) of the Act of 1870 – famous for the Cowper-Temple clause from the name of its mover in the House of Commons – laid down that in the Board Schools 'no religious catechism or religious formulary distinctive of any particular denomination should be taught'. Section 7(2) permitted the withdrawal of children from religious instruction on grounds of conscience. This provision was related to the fact that the Act envisaged religious 'undenominational' instruction in the schools in the form of Bible reading, which would consist of 'undenominational' Christian instruction, or would include such. This arrangement was viewed as unacceptable to Jewish conscience, and Jewish children availed themselves of Section 7(2). The Act was followed by the creation of large numbers of Board Schools throughout the country.

The Board of Deputies' interventions had been especially prompted by the avowed activities of the Christian conversionists, notably the London Society for Promoting Christianity Among the Jews. The Board had written to Forster expressing its apprehensions.[11] Advocating the amending clause in the original Bill, the

Board had stated: 'It is believed that nothing short of such a provision as this will secure that perfect freedom from proselytizing efforts which it is understood to be one of the main designs of the Bill to afford.' The particular 'necessity' which the Board successfully urged on Forster was 'a time conscience clause' which:

> shall provide that the religious instruction (including the reading of the Bible) if any, in Elementary Schools, shall take place at a fixed time, either before or after the secular instruction, and that the parent of every child attending such schools be informed of the hours appointed for such religious instruction.

A further request of the Board was that:

> the children of persons professing the Jewish religion as well as of every other religious denomination, may be exempt from attendance at Elementary Schools on Saturdays or such other days as the parents may conscientiously desire to observe as sacred, without forfeiting thereby any of the benefits or advantages of the Schools.

These requests, which had been submitted by the Board after consultation with the Chief Rabbi, were incorporated in amendments moved to the Bill in the House of Commons by Sir John Simon, with whom the Board worked in harmony on these and related issues. In welcoming the Act in its final form, the Board declared its belief 'that it will afford to Jewish children residing in those parts of the country where no Jewish schools exist, facilities not hitherto possessed for acquiring a good secular elementary education, without the risk of having their religious training tampered with.'[12] Where was that training and Jewish education in general to be made available, and in what form and whence the teachers?

Later legislation gave sharper form to these questions. In 1876, Parliament required 'education committees' to be locally appointed for the purpose of encouraging parents to ensure their children's attendance at school. Parents could be made liable for their wilful involvement in any non-attendance. In 1881, elementary education became compulsory for children between the ages of five and ten, later rising to 12. In 1891, elementary education at the municipal schools became free. In 1918, the age limit was raised to fourteen.

FASHIONS, ASPIRATIONS AND REALITY

On the celebration of Queen Victoria's diamond jubilee in 1897, the *Jewish Chronicle*, on 18 June, sought to define the key differentiating factor between the Jewish community of that time and that of the age of her accession. 'English Jews', wrote the editor, 'are (now) able to go in and out among other Englishmen without feeling or arousing any estrangement on account of race or religion'. There has been, he added, an increase in 'the community of feeling between Jews and Christians'. Among the features listed to explain such developments was that Jew and Christian came together 'in childhood' and shared common interests in books, public events and sport. The editorial was not only a portrayal of what were noted as facts but was also an invocation to sustain and advance the process. 'It must be our constant effort', concluded the editor, 'to anglicise our community'.

The editor was Asher Myers, a notable synagogal leader in London and prominent supporter of movements for the advancement of Jewish culture in Britain. Like many of his associates he regarded the Jewish 'foreigners' in their midst as – themselves or their children – prospective Englishmen, provided in particular that any self-isolation on their part would be subject to erosion by an English education. The overwhelming Victorian aspiration conjured up the word 'anglicization' should not, as it was felt, be allowed to be misjudged in the public mind by the standing charge of unremitting foreignness levelled against some sections of Jewish society. Such charges were not confined to East End Jews.

Considerations of personal social status became mingled with the belief that the standing of all Jews was somehow bound up with visible serious anglicizing efforts. Nowhere were enlightened self-interest and altruism simultaneously more in evidence than in the debates over the highly lauded benefits of 'mixing' in schools. The Education Act of 1870 intensified the long-standing dispute. If Salomons was the lay father of the 'mixing' body of opinion, Hermann Adler became its premier 'spiritual' exponent.[13] Attendance at the Jewish voluntary schools was deemed appropriate, indeed natural, where financial circumstances precluded an alternative or where the parents or Jewish welfare agencies thought it of value in assisting children the better to become assimilated into the

English Jewish community, or the better to become equipped for some kind of gainful employment.

Critics of plans for additional Jewish voluntary schools did not limit their hostility to such plans for 'newer' regions. On 13 February 1870, Benjamin Louis Cohen, brother of the principal founder of the United Synagogue, disclosed at a public meeting held at the Stepney Jewish Schools (and fully reported in the *Jewish Chronicle*) that he and Marcus Adler (President and principal founder of the Schools and Nathan Adler's son) had sought to raise funds for the erection of an extra school building in that vicinity. They had, he declared, met with opposition from 'a distinguished member of the community' who categorized the denominational schools as 'opposed to the spirit of the age'. Despite the opposition, the additional school accommodation was provided.

There had long been a stream of middle-class Jewish opinion which ran counter to the assumptions, and failed to share the apprehensions, of the 'distinguished' opposition. A vocal member of this body of opinion was Henry Keeling, synagogue warden, member of the Board of Deputies, and popular personality in the City of London. 'I have always considered', he observed in the *Jewish Chronicle*, on 23 July 1869, 'that the successful termination of the struggle for the attainment of civil and religious liberty was to secure us in the exclusive right of upholding our institutions distinct from those of other creeds.' On that principle, he concluded that Jewish parents need entertain no inhibition in sending their children to Jewish schools.

Keeling's views were reinforced by anxiety lest Jewish children at general schools be drawn to what might be the prevailing Christianity. He thought it was impossible to place Jewish and Christian children together in schools without running a significant risk of the exercise of Christian influence, even if unwittingly. Some polemicists who did not decry the 'mixing' in good private day schools or in the prestigious public day schools (in all of which Jews won honours), warned nevertheless of 'dangers'. In a long and ringing editorial on 10 August 1869, the *Jewish Chronicle* spoke of the importance of Jewish instruction at home or elsewhere by parent or teacher, 'to counteract' potential effects resulting from Jewish attendance at non-Jewish schools. The editor doubted whether such was made available in many cases. These warnings were against the background outlined in that journal on 21 September 1866 by 'H', probably Michael Henry, soon to become editor. 'In the education of the Jew of the upper classes', he then wrote, 'the language and literature of his race are strangely disregarded – and insufficient time (is given) to (Jewish) religious education'.

Striking evidence of the seeming indifference generally within the Jewish community towards the provision of Jewish education is found in the number and nature of the appeals by the Jewish Association for the Diffusion of Religious Knowledge. Founded in 1860, its main purpose was to sustain the Jewish classes held in those Board schools where there were large numbers of Jewish children. In its annual report (1882), the Committee declared that it had become 'a matter of grave consideration whether this Institution shall any longer be carried on, [thereby] allowing [through] the community's indifference the large number of Jewish pupils of Board Schools to grow up as pagans destitute of 'religious instruction' (p. 9). The coming increase in the number of pupils was not met by any commensurate inflow of resources. The Association was, in 1894, succeeded by the Jewish Religious Education Board, which was to labour under like limitations.[14]

On 14 May 1869, when the prospect of Forster's Bill had increasingly concentrated many Jewish minds, Aaron Levy Green, the influential Minister of the Central Synagogue in London, had contributed a characteristically well-informed article to the *Jewish Chronicle* (under his regular pseudonym 'Nemo'). He pronounced himself 'glad' to encourage Jewish children to attend 'general schools' in cases where they 'learn religion at home ... There is no kosher grammar'. Where it was necessary to counter 'the neglect of Judaism at home', it was 'essential' to sustain the free Jewish schools.

Levy was in close contact with powerful communal figures. Some of them were leading members of his congregation, who favoured attendance at general schools for their own children and those of the middle classes in any event, for reasons other than Jewishly educational. Following the availability of elementary education for all, they doubted the wisdom or the need for expenditure on the provision of more Jewish day schools.

A vocal proponent of Jewish day-school education was Arthur Cohen, President of the Board of Deputies (1880–95), Liberal politician and the senior commercial barrister of his day. He was

President of the Borough Jewish Schools. The Schools had been founded expressly for children of the poorer and middle-class families south of the Thames. In June 1883, at the triennial dinner in aid of the Schools, he declared that Jewish children 'could not, would not and should not go to the Board Schools'. His reason was that 'it was necessary that they should be educated as Jewish children'.[15] This statement, from such a source, was widely reported in the Jewish and general press and aroused much controversy in Cohen's immediate circle and elsewhere. Cohen took great pride in the fact that of the 158 children at the Borough Schools, 103 were girls, and that the Government's grant had been increased by more than five per cent annually during the preceding three years. One Jewish critic, taking Cohen to task for his exuberant language, commented that Cohen's view that Jewish parents would not send their children to schools unless Hebrew and Judaism were taught, must presumably be taken to refer to 'Jewish parents of the poorer classes'. Jewish parents of the 'middle and upper classes', argued the critic, 'tend in a different direction'. The Jewish community should trust the Board Schools in the Borough to give their children a sound secular education, while relying upon Sunday and evening classes for their Hebrew and Jewish instruction.[16]

In Jewish areas special facilities for Jewish education were instituted by the London School Board in schools which were largely Jewish in composition. This involved the provision of Jewish instruction on the school premises during school hours or thereafter by teachers on the staff of the respective schools. Such arrangements, which were retained by the London County Council after its incorporation of the work of the London School Board, were not in strict accordance with the law but were in practice discretionary to the School Board or County Council. 'In one or two London Board Schools', wrote Sidney Webb approvingly in 1904,

> by a convenient evasion to which no one objects, the creed expounded is not that of Christianity at all ... and Jewish teachers are deliberately selected in order that they may expound the Jewish Bible to Jewish children, for whose convenience the whole school is closed on the Jewish Festivals.[17]

For decades, schools in the Jewish centres of population exhibited in such ways many features of Jewish schools. These practices were not confined to the more obviously Jewish areas of London. As early as 1896, Jewish residents in Kensington asked the London School Board for facilities for instruction in the Jewish faith at schools in the district. The Board replied that in all schools where there were sufficient Jewish pupils to form a class, arrangements would be made.[18]

'The tolerant London School Board', wrote Miss Henrietta Adler in respect of the 1890s,

> was keen in drawing in these intelligent (Jewish) children into its own schools. At first the parents were unwilling as they were desirous that the pupils should obtain Jewish religious instruction (which was available in the Jewish schools, together with the ordinary secular curriculum). The London School Board determined however to make their own schools attractive and acceptable to Jewish parents and children.[19]

The Board appointed Jewish headteachers and teachers to some of its schools in Jewish districts. This, further observed Miss Adler, 'paved the way for a greater willingness on the part of parents and children to take advantage of the municipal schools'.[19] Many Jewish managers were appointed to Board Schools, and there were notable Jewish members of the London School Board, including Claude Montefiore.

The Jewishness of some Board Schools did not pass unchallenged. Criticism of the trend was expressed with some vehemence before 1914 by publicists who detected in this situation grounds for further attacks on the unrestricted entry of alien, that is Jewish, immigrants. 'Schools in certain districts', wrote Sir William Evans-Gordon, a prominent restrictionist and a local Conservative Member of Parliament, in 1903, 'are being converted into Hebrew seminaries.'[20]

The 'rapidity' of this process was demonstrated by him on the basis of some schools which eight or ten years before had been occupied predominantly by Gentiles and which by 1903 were almost entirely Jewish. 'Sixteen Board Schools' he wrote 'have been practically Judaised'. They are 'conducted' as 'Jewish Schools'. He referred to schools where arrangements had been made for Jewish religious instruction to be given to the Jewish pupils.

> The Jewish community maintains schools which are admirably conducted and provide education for great numbers of pupils. But these by no means fulfil all the requirements ... In the Christian Street

Board School in Whitechapel, a fine building opened in 1901, out of 927 pupils only 15 are Christians ... The children in the foreign quarters of the East End are far more numerous than would be the case if the inhabitants were English. As a consequence, a greater number of schools have to be built (involving) extensive destruction of house property and ... further displacement of population.

A significant acknowledgement of the increasing tendency of Jewish parents to send their children to the Board Schools instead of to the Jewish schools was implied in the Chief Rabbi's proposal in 1895 that the Jewish community should seek legislative permission to provide Jewish denominational teaching to Jewish children in the Board Schools *during school hours*. This proposal would have required an amendment to the Act of 1870. Adler was unable to persuade the Jewish Religious Education Board to agree that the necessary approach should be made to the Government. He had the support of Claude Montefiore, who a few years later was to found the Liberal Synagogue, but Adler was opposed by the Orthodox Jew, Samuel Montagu (later Lord Swaythling), the anglicized banker and the protagonist of the religious opinions of the Orthodox Russo-Polish immigrants. Montagu declared that not only had the Jewish community not sufficient teachers to implement such a plan – more than an additional 200 would have been necessary in London alone – but if the Jews were to press for denominational teaching in the Board Schools they would find themselves in alliance with the 'Church Party', to whom, he declared, most Jews were in general opposed.

Concern about any extension of the Jewish day-school system had long rested on interrelated grounds of ideology and expediency. The ideological argument was based on the assumption that whatever helped to integrate the Jews into the texture of the nation without radically undoing their religious identity was good, and that the segregation into Jewish schools had undesirable implications of separateness. The practical grounds had been characteristically set out by Aaron Asher Green, Minister of the recently formed Hampstead Synagogue (1892) in 1899. 'The more [Christian and Jewish boys] combined, the more would Jewish boys be able to enter into open competition with everyone else'. The strength of this proposition was by no means self-evident.

He condemned the creation of 'any institutions which would

make Christian boys think there was any difference between Jewish boys and themselves'. Yet surely the differentials were already amply indicated by the different arrangements made in general schools for the religious instruction of Jews. Indeed the London School Board had already issued its regulations (adopted by the London County Council) for the closure of schools for Jewish festivals and early closing on winter Fridays where 50 per cent of the pupils were Jewish, as was the case in many instances. It is significant that Green took the opportunity in the same address of dissociating himself by parallel argument from the then current effort to found a Jewish hospital in London.

On the same occasion Haham Moses Gaster, the religious head of the Sephardi community, expressed a contrary sense of priorities from that of Green. Gaster described 'the position of the [Jewish] community' as 'gradually becoming more and more insecure and unstable'. He emphasized his belief that Jewish schools had a special role to play in its resuscitation. Their exchanges attracted much attention. Although the contentious public debate long continued, the Green–Gaster exchanges were its high point. No one failed to note that the encounter between these two protagonists was between a non-Zionist and Zionist, between a spokesman for the then established Adlerian system of thought and an 'outsider' who on broad policy had the support of many influential 'East European' Orthodox rabbis in London and beyond – and of a significant number of Jewish university students and graduates, often of recent immigrant parentage.

Whatever the nature of the communal or wider debate, the reality of Jewish concentration in the general schools in areas of populous Jewish residence had its own, if long-term, telling effect in weakening old inhibitions. This did not mean that there was anything like a consistent or uniform change of attitude. In all sections there remained reservations of varying degrees of intensity. The slowly widening acceptability of Jewish day-school education was part of a wider shift of instinct and opinion. There was progressively less concern felt among Jews over the need to ensure overt demonstration of their membership of, and attachment to, the general society.

Yet the continuing departure of Jewish families from older areas of residence caused the proportion of Jewish children attending Jewish schools in London to fall. By 1900, the number of Jewish children at Board Schools exceeded the total at Jewish schools. In the newer areas of Jewish residence, resort was had to the limited forms of Jewish education provided in part-time synagogal classes, while the newer immigrants living in the older regions might avail themselves either of the *chedarim* or of the more intense Talmud Torah centres after school hours, whether attending Board School or Jewish school by day.[21]

1902–1914

In the generation which followed the Education Act of 1870, the denominational schools in general were faced with strong competition from the Board Schools. The newer and superior accommodation and equipment often available at the latter establishments challenged the denominational centres. The Voluntary Schools needed a fresh impetus of public support. The denominations were not alone. The view was gaining ground in many lay quarters that their existence, by adding variety and choice in the country's educational life, was desirable. Many would have subscribed to the expressions of Dr M.J. Wilson, then Archdeacon of Manchester and former Headmaster of Clifton College. In 1894 he wrote:

> Regarding secular education alone, it is of the highest interest of the nation to retain – under favourable conditions – Voluntary Schools, as enlisting the work and influence of educated and religious people, interested in children; as productive of originality in school management and educational progress; and as a security against deadly uniformity and loss of freedom and individuality in the nation.[22]

By the end of the century, the issue was less whether further significant public aid should be forthcoming to the Voluntary Schools than upon what terms. The Education Act of 1902, introduced by Arthur Balfour's Conservative Government, abolished the School Boards; placed elementary education into the hands of the local municipal authorities direct; added to their responsibilities the crucial provision under the Act of secondary education; and transferred to them control over denominational schools (of which there were more than 14,000) in return for the public maintenance of the schools, other than the fabric of the buildings.[23]

Lord Rothschild, the lay head of Anglo-Jewry and the dominating benefactor of the Jews' Free School (which he and his family had for more than 50 years made their special concern) unavailingly resisted the application of this measure to London, to which it was extended in 1903. Rothschild was mindful of the advantages of rate-aid that now fell to the Jewish schools as to the other denominational schools, but he was willing to substitute himself as the supplier of the necessary funds for the Jews' Free School in order to retain control. In fact, the Acts of 1902 and 1903 maintained the existing arrangements as far as religious teaching was concerned. 'The nine large Jewish schools (forming one per cent of the total number of schoolchildren in London) will inculcate their own faith and observe their own Festivals'.[24]

In secular education and in general discipline and the provision of equipment, the Local Education Authority – in London, that was the London Country Council – was now charged with responsibility. While the appointment of teachers was left to the managers of the Voluntary Schools – that is those who formerly were in control – the Local Education Authority had the right under the new dispensation to disallow an appointment on educational grounds. The managers of the school, however, had the right to dismiss teachers if their failings were in respect of their capacity as a teacher of religion. The Local Education Authority had no power to erect new Voluntary Schools or to contribute to the cost of building repairs, alterations or improvements. Such work remained dependant solely on voluntary subscriptions from the denominations. The financial responsibility of the Local Education Authority included the cost of denominational instruction in the Voluntary Schools.[25]

Jewish educationists welcomed the easing in the financial strain under which the religious bodies had laboured. 'Now that their financial strain has been relaxed', wrote L.G. Bowman, the headmaster of the Jews' Free School,

> and their powers and responsibilities of management curtailed, they can and no doubt will direct their attention to the improvement of religious instruction. In the case of the Jewish community, there is an additional ground for regarding the present an opportune time to overhaul the organization and conditions of religious teaching. The pressure of the Jewish problem has within the last decade or two revivified the Jewish consciousness; the feeling of racial solidarity has

70

not within living memory been so strong or so widespread as today. In these circumstances we may look for an attempt to infuse into our children something of the spirit which is animating Jews all over the world. And there can be no better medium than through the Bible and religion lessons. There can be no denying the existence of a widespread doubt as to the value and effectiveness of the religious teaching provided in the old Voluntary Schools.[26]

In his installation address as Chief Rabbi in April 1913, Dr J.H. Hertz declared: 'Today the great majority of Jewish boys and girls in their adolescent period – in fact nearly all our youth in the secondary schools – are left without any religious guidance'. There was, he said, 'a crying need for improvement'.[27] In a vigorous public speech at the Conference of Anglo-Jewish Preachers in 1925, Hertz, not for the first time, spoke critically of certain attitudes to 'our denominational schools'. While observing that 'few dispute the necessity for social work' there were 'some English Jews' who 'utterly fail to grasp the importance of (those schools). Their attitude is quite different from that of the English Catholic, Anglican or Wesleyan towards his church school ... They ... speak of the undesirability of (what they call) herding ...'[28] Hertz's language revealed his long-standing impatience with opinions which continued to prevail in some quarters. It also reflected his continuing concern at the overall levels and uneven distribution of Jewish education.

In 1910, Rabbi Dr Victor Schonfeld presented to the Jewish community his idea of a Jewish secondary school in London. This was within a few months of his arrival in England to assume his appointment as Rabbi of the North London *Beth Hamidrash*, the founder-institution of the Union of Orthodox Hebrew Congregations. This Hungarian-born, charismatic rabbi was deeply imbued with the tradition of Samson Raphael Hirsch of Frankfurt and infused with the desire to see in Anglo-Jewry a viable, impeccably Orthodox *kehilla*, perhaps in cooperation with, but outside the framework of, the 'established' community.

Schonfeld envisaged the proposed school as, in the long run, the first of a possible network of such schools, elementary and secondary, from which would be drawn the future membership of the intended Union. It was also viewed as a source for cadres of men and women who would enter Anglo-Jewry's synagogal and institutional life generally and make an important difference in stemming what he believed to be the steady erosion of whole segments of the community. 'It is the nightmare of the Anglo-Jews', he stated in 1926 at a meeting convened to raise funds for his projected school,

> to be considered foreign. Those who insist that Jewish boys and girls must receive their secular education in a non-Jewish environment are advocating – knowingly or unknowingly – complete assimilation. The lukewarm, soulless, hymn-singing Judaism taught in one or two hours weekly cannot produce conscientious Jews.

To some, this castigation seemed unduly harsh and provocative. Possibly that was its intention. To others, it seems a plain statement of the reality, an opinion not confined to Schonfeld's entourage. Soon after his death in 1929 at the age of 49 – in the year in which his School was opened in Finsbury Park, North London – his son, Rabbi Dr Solomon Schonfeld, assumed his father's rabbinic position and took charge of the school and the plans for its eventual replications. Despite their inward-lookingness Jewishly, as well as the disciplined detachment from political Zionism under Solomon Schonfeld, the success of the schools and their cumulative impact rendered them an important herald of, and a significant contributor to, considerable transformations in conventional outlook.

INTER-WAR YEARS AND EDUCATION ACT 1944

In the spirit of reconstruction which followed World War I, concern over the deficiencies in the Jewish educational system grew. In 1919, it became a regular refrain in the editorial columns of the *Jewish Chronicle*. The concern was shared by groups ranging from secular Zionists, such as the editor, Leopold Greenberg, to Jewish educationists of all hues of Jewish opinion. The conception of additional Jewish day schools broadened its appeal. Prominent among Orthodox lay educationalists who supported Greenberg's pleas was Augustus Kahn, warden of the St John's Wood United Synagogue, an admirer of Schonfeld's initiative, and a leading personality in the Union of Hebrew and Religion Classes, which administered the network of part-time classes attached to metropolitan synagogues. His views carried added weight by reason of his distinction as an Inspector of Schools for the Board of Education.

With each year it was increasingly clear that such communal educational advances as had been made fell well short of needs. In its fourth Annual Report (1926) the Central Committee for Jewish Education, accountable to the Jewish Memorial Council (whose leaders were mainly antipathetic to any extension of Jewish day-school education) acknowledged this reality. The available financial resources, therein wrote the Director, Herbert Adler, were wholly inadequate. The Committee could not meet demands made upon it for books, class inspections, or additional classes. In particular, no satisfactory basis was provided for the recruitment, training and remuneration of teachers. Training courses lacked a sufficient supply of students. No bursaries were affordable. Reforms devised in 1932 in the system of recruiting, training and examining prospective teachers did not improve the intake or overall standards. In his report for 1938–39, Adler observed that in the Provinces only one-half of Jewish children were in receipt of Jewish education, and little more in London.

The worst apprehensions were confirmed in 1939–40 by the revelations of the general state of Jewish education on the part of Jewish children sent from urban areas as part of the national wartime evacuation of children. The shock of this discovery was similar to that sustained at the national level following the widespread enquiries which preceded the educational legislation of the 1870s.

The spirit and provisions of the Education Act of 1944 reduced the weight of the critics' case against the idea and operation of Jewish day-school education. The Act fostered the fashionability of such education, and presented the Jewish community with the prospect of significant tangible support for the extension of its system of denominational schools. To secure adequate communal funding to qualify such schools (existing or projected) for receipt of governmental aid became an important target for Jewish individuals or organizations concerned in this field, or who were moved by the legislation to become so engaged.

Such aspirations were in tune with Zionist motivation, whether religious or secular. They also fed the ambitions of prominent Jewish educationists and others to make a major and lasting difference to remedy the by then much-canvassed inadequacies in the educational system.

A characteristic Zionist-linked presentation of Jewish educational requirements was that of Dr Joseph Heller, notable Jewish educationist and Zionist publicist. In his *Jewish Education: Tasks and Methods* (1945), published by the English Zionist Federation's Education Department, he wrote:

> The Hebrew child must learn Hebrew not merely as the language of the Holy Scriptures and of the prayer-book; he must learn it as a living, spoken national language with an old and many-sided literature, capable of satisfying a wide range of cultural, literary and aesthetic interests. Jewish history must be presented not only as a history of a religious community, but as the history of a people which has struggled for its national existence and striven to conserve its individuality in most difficult social, economic and political conditions ... (pp. 13–14).

For a decade after World War II, public debate over the legitimacy and respective merits of 'Zionist' schools and 'religious' (by which at that time was meant 'Orthodox') schools was an intermittent but increasingly marked element in communal life. What was at issue was less the idea of Jewish day schools than under whose authority and auspices they were to be established and conducted. Upon that issue depended the distinctive ethos of the school.[29]

This did not mean that all were persuaded. Some retained pedagogic reservations. Some considered school influence less effective in many instances than that of home. Some were concerned over the possible disruption of family life which might result from the emergence of different standards of religious observance and/or Jewish attachment on the part of children from those to which their parents were accustomed. There was also the echo of the once influential doubts, to which, in 1953, Dr Redcliffe Salaman, scientist and Zionist, gave eloquent expression. With reference to the expansion of the Jewish Secondary Schools Movement under Rabbi Dr Solomon Schonfeld (which then included three schools within the purview of the London County Council), Salaman said:

> It is a policy with a definite separatist inspiration and before any judgement can be reached as to its effect, it remains to be seen how its students react when later they find themselves in the hurly-burly

of national life. We are apt to forget that the Jewish youth brought up in a non-Jewish environment has a certain conditioning to undergo, a certain strain to withstand. To postpone these experiences until early manhood is an experiment that is not without serious risk to the individual and perhaps to the community.[30]

But the strength of the opposition had been outmatched by the enthusiasm and philanthropy of those to whom Jewish day-school education had come to be seen as necessary to communal viability. The opposition had largely lost its confidence and its effective leadership. Those families who sought to avail themselves of the perceived benefits of the great public or independent schools, residential or otherwise, could turn to the possibility of Jewish Houses thereat and/or, with school consent, periodic visits by outside Jewish teachers was attractive.

To the extent that later generations of former East End families preferred not to send their children to Jewish schools, this was generally not part of any considered philosophy. Sometimes to some extent it reflected a consciousness of some element of social elevation. It was also in part connected with a belief or surmise as to the superiority of the general education provided in the Board (later Council) Schools, before the later records of academic successes at Jewish schools recast opinions. Parental attitudes in such circles tended to be more pragmatic than philosophic; and so far as there remained some inhibition, this was not necessarily shared by their teenage children.

During the twentieth century, steadily but unremittingly, the norms and methods common in the public relations of the preceding age became antiquated for increasing numbers of Jews. War service, military and civil, in the new century, reinforced by the long-term effects of national education and the wider opportunities in business and employment at all levels, contributed to the progressive waning of old tradition-bound inhibitions. In widening circles of intellectual opinion there was a heightened sense both of the need for, and the inherent value of, deeper Jewish education. Such sentiments were in part a long-term off-shoot of the nineteenth-century European *haskalah* which had its limited but expanding reflection in Britain. It was often allied to, and in many instances was the product of, Zionist stimulus and the attraction of involvement in a perceived Hebrew revival, however limited in numbers.

The reactions of Anglo-Jewish Orthodoxy to what was seen as religious laxity in the leadership of the Jewish community were much taken up with the declining educational standards and the falling numbers of those receiving Jewish education. Between the East End Rabbis and their provincial counterparts on the one hand and significant exponents of the Zionist-related Hebrew revivalism on the other hand – despite their differences – there were some common aspirations. Prominent among them was the aspiration for greater attention to be given to Jewish day-school education, springing from their belief in its saving quality for the viability of the Jewish community.

Cecil Roth, writing in 1967 on 'The Haskalah in England', in reference to that movement in England in earlier centuries, applied the term 'to the movement for the revitalization and modernization of Hebrew culture in general'.[31] The Anglo-Jewish, Zionist-inspired *maskilim* of the first half of the twentieth century and later were fired by such enthusiasm. They preached Zionism and modern Hebrew culture as an antidote to the Jewish educational ills of the community as well as a form of general Jewish awakening to the sights, sounds and prospects of a restored and rejuvenated Jewish national home. Sir Leon Simon was a regular and prestigious protagonist. 'Unless the sense of belonging to the Jewish people is present', he wrote, 'the teaching of Judaism as a religious and ethical system, without any reference to the concrete realities of the Jewish present, can produce only a sort of hot-house Judaism with no strong roots'. Simon added:

> it should be regarded as an important function of Jewish education to secure that every Jewish child has some knowledge of Hebrew as a living language, knows in outline what Jews have done and are doing for the rebuilding of their National Home in Palestine and, most important of all, feels that these things are matters of vital concern to himself or herself. At the present time, when new horizons are opening out before our people, I believe that this is the most urgent of all the reforms of which our educational system stands in need.[32]

A highly significant feature of the Education Act of 1944 was that thereby it was rendered permissible for Jewish children at secondary or elementary schools to receive Jewish teaching during school hours – on school premises for the former. 'Withdrawal classes' for Jewish children during school hours became an established, widespread feature of the Jewish educational system. At the nation-wide Jewish education conference in London held in November 1945, much hope was expressed in the wider opportunities which this offered for the provision of Hebrew and religious education to pupils who might otherwise be bereft of any such provision wholly, or in large part. But it was clear that the major hope on the part of the Jewish educationists rested with the prospect of an expanded system of Jewish day-school facilities. Jewish instruction during school hours and within a Jewish ambience was increasingly seen as the major desideratum of the post-war age.

Different rationales came together to advance the idea and its realization. One such was echoed by R.A. Butler, President of the Board of Education, in his address on 10 January 1944, at a specially convened meeting of the Board of Deputies on the implications of the proposed education legislation. He related the Jewish provisions of the measure to the Holocaust. 'Never', he observed, 'has there been such a time in the history of the Jews, never such a diaspora, and never such suffering in their history.' He added: 'Therefore it is more than ever important that the Jews should concentrate their energies on bringing up their children and young people in the tradition of Hebraism.'[33]

The Act of 1944 was long heralded by the promptings of leaders of all denominations and the exhortations of prominent educationists. A common theme was that 'the basis of good citizenship is character, and a man's character depends upon his beliefs'.[34] A classic presentation of the case for educational reform from a humanist point of view came from Sir Richard Livingstone, then President of Corpus Christi College, Oxford, in 1943, in his *Education For a World Adrift*, pp. x–xi. 'In an age of social change and in a society like our own', he wrote,

> where opportunity has hitherto not been equal, the problem of equal opportunity demands to be solved and rightly fills the mind. But (it may) make us so concerned with providing schools that we do not consider what is to be taught inside them ... What are we to teach? ... What sort of human beings should (education) produce? ... Knowledge is important; still more so is the power to use it; but most important of all is what a man believes, what he thinks good and bad, whether he has clear values and standards and is prepared to live by them.

This approach was gaining ground in the then teaching profession, especially in the secondary schools.[35]

The Education Act of 1944 was avowedly directed to enhancing the influence of religion upon the minds of schoolchildren – all schoolchildren – subject to the by then traditional and continuing conscience clauses. Children at secondary schools who were withdrawn from attendance at religious instruction were to be allowed their own denominational instruction on the school premises in school hours by teachers appointed and paid by the denomination. Parents of Jewish children in elementary (primary) schools became entitled to have them withdrawn to alternative accommodation, if available nearby, for Hebrew and Jewish religious instruction during the scripture periods.

NEW STYLE COMMUNAL PLANNING

In the 1940s, the prospective extent of the viability of the Jewish community had become a regular, and was to prove a continuing, topic of debate and analysis. Among the most relevant issues were the nature and limits of the impact of the Jewish educational system, a subject which attracted the closest scrutiny. Erosive assimilation (in the modern open society) and its child and companion, indifferentism, heightened the concern of many communal activists on all sides of communal life. While the issues were usually presented as 'religious', concern was not necessarily limited to 'religionists'.

To the Jewish emancipationists in the nineteenth century, the Synagogue was seen as the central factor in Jewish institutional life. The secure synagogal establishment viewed itself, not wholly without some justification, as custodian of the community's future. Critics of that establishment saw at the time that the future rested at least as much, and probably more, on the Jewish home and classroom. In the next century that view prevailed. This attitude was one of the major contributions of the Eastern European immigration, and was reinforced in the twentieth century by the Central European immigration.

By stages, in the twentieth century the Jewish community, sometimes slowly and at times amid institutional controversy, moved towards an era when the centrality of Jewish education in the communal programme became settled policy.

Writing in 1944, Dr Nathan Morris, then Director of the Joint Emergency Committee for Jewish Religious Education, described 'the majority of adults of the present generation [of Anglo-Jewry] as the products and victims of a system of Jewish education from which they carried away so little as makes hardly a difference to their religious, cultural or social life'. In the two decades before 1939, standards and attendances at educational centres had steadily fallen. 'It borders on the absurd', he added, 'to expect [Judaism and Jewish history] to be taught to any purpose in classes where 90 per cent of the pupils leave at the age of 13 ... The present structure of Jewish education is old-fashioned and obsolete.'[36]

Central to Morris' vision of a re-structured future was the combination of educational forces (of which the war-time Joint Emergency Committee was to prove an exemplar and an encouragement), adequately financed, and resting upon the provision of Jewish education during school hours, including an expanded range of Jewish day schools. Among the sources of inspiration for change, he saw the study of 'recent and contemporary Jewish history ... (teaching) the great adventure of (Zionism), and ... (affording) access of our children to the original sources of Jewish knowledge ...'[37] He interpreted some of his findings as indicating to him 'an ominous decline in the quality and standard of the whole Jewish education in the country, which is becoming overwhelmingly rudimentary and insubstantial'. Morris described 'the wave of enthusiasm for *Ivrit beIvrit*' in the 1920s as an expression in some quarters of 'a new faith and hope in the future of Judaism and Jewish education'.[38]

In December 1946, Dr Isidore Fishman, Nathan Morris' senior colleague, described recent changes in education in the Jewish community as 'revolutionary'. This, he observed, was 'the logical outcome of the successful attempts' made to meet war-time exigencies by the Joint Emergency Committee, in which had been united the largest Jewish educational bodies. 'Perhaps', he added, (the JEC's) greatest achievement 'was in making (the community) education conscious.'[39]

Many events in the 1940s contributed to and exemplified the continuing 'revolution'. These events included the enduring creation of the Jewish Youth Study Groups movement in the secondary schools (1942); the scheme devised in 1944 by the Association for Jewish Youth (AJY) for 'the inculcation of Judaism' into its many associated youth clubs;[40] the expansion of Jewish youth movements, Zionist and non-Zionist, secular and religious, including Habonim, Bnai Akiva, and Bachad, in which bodies Central European 'refugee' elements played significant roles;[41] and the emergence of the Hebrew correspondence course, conceived by Nathan Morris, which fructified in 1950 in the volume entitled *Hebrew for All*, edited by Harold Levy, national inspector for the Central Council for Jewish Religious Education. This course proved a forerunner of a proliferation of classes and courses at many levels in Hebrew language and literature.

The nation-wide Jewish education conference in London in November 1945, of which Morris was the main educational architect, was the first of its kind. Not all its fruits were lasting, but the event deepened the mood for radical change, recognized the importance of community planning, and made clear the need to match new priorities with commensurate finance. In the wake and spirit of the conference, the United Synagogue instituted a levy on seat rentals for the advancement of Jewish education.

In 1945, Morris had no illusions about the remaining parental reservations towards the Jewish day-school idea. In a careful statement entitled 'The Jewish Day-School and the Reconstruction of Jewish Education',[42] he reminded the community of the historic role of the old Voluntary Schools. In the last year before the War the proportion of Jewish children known to be in receipt of Jewish education in London was less than one-half, and hardly ever reached that proportion during the whole of the inter-war period. The number of girls in such receipt in 1938 was absolutely and relatively smaller than ten years earlier. 'The great majority of pupils (boys and girls)', he added, 'namely all except those at the Voluntary Schools, are in receipt of that instruction at the "wrong end of the day".' Acknowledging the continuing move of Jewish families away from the old East End and in reference to the then proposed central Jewish 'high school' in London, he solemnly asked:

> Will the parents prove capable of some sacrifice ... of social ambition and personal prejudice and send their children to such a school and

enable it to become what it might and should become – the highest
expression of Jewish educational life in this country?

Morris's question, which was asked almost as much in anguish
as in hope, was soon overtaken by events. In May 1946, he reported[43]
that 'the community was showing a new interest in the Jewish day
schools'. Only seven of them survived the war, with a total roll of
under 1,000, which represented one child in 16 of school age in the
Jewish community, compared with 14 schools (excluding private
schools) before 1939 which had a total roll of 4,900, representing
one child in four. The New Education Act and the scheme eventually
prepared thereunder in 1952 in conjunction with the Ministry of
Education by the trustees of the former Jewish Voluntary Schools
held out high expectations for viability, standards and example.
Their resources were to be pooled. The plans of the London
County Council for the building of a series of large comprehensive
secondary schools in London was to include the large high school
envisaged by the Jewish Voluntary Schools' trustees. Certain
objections were lodged against the trustees' scheme by Rabbi Dr
Schonfeld but were, after lengthy negotiations, withdrawn on the
basis of agreed principles for the allocation of trust funds.

Under the scheme there arose the JFS Comprehensive Secondary
School in Camden Town. It was opened in 1958, not only as the
successor to the Jews' Free School but as a major marker for the
progressive, modern development of Jewish day-school education,
secondary and primary, which came to be seen in the later decades
of the twentieth century on the 'left' and 'right' of the community
as a principal and possibly decisive agency for Jewish renewal then
and later.

PUBLIC SCHOOLS, JEWISH HOUSES, JEWISH PUBLIC SCHOOLS

For most of the Jewish families who preferred to send their children
to Public Schools, the preference was inherited and instinctive.
There was in many cases a long-standing assumption as to an
identity (and as to the naturalness of and need for such identity) in
social outlook and behaviour between themselves and those of comparable wealth and social status in society. A virtually compelling

aspiration for them was the prospective endowment of their children with a Public School background. Class consciousness[44] was allied to a genuine conviction as to the high standards of education and character-building in those establishments, including the almost equally prestigious, non-residential Public Schools. At the various levels of the Jewish upper middle classes, fashion was an over-whelming inducement. New wealth tended to adopt the educational patterns of the old.

Lionel Louis Cohen, principal founder of the United Synagogue in 1870 and prominent Conservative politician, firmly believed that it was in the Public Schools that those English Jews who might by tradition be expected to accept senior office in the Jewish com-munity (and indeed less senior responsible posts) would be best trained. It would assist them to combine devoted Jewish attachment (including Orthodoxy) and active participation in British public life at whatever levels. This banker, kinsman of the Rothschilds and the leading member of the second most famous family in the Jewish community, was, in this belief, thinking paramountly of his own extensive family circle. But these considerations equally extended to other members of, and aspirants to, the various levels of 'com-manding heights' in synagogal life and related spheres.

To Cohen and his colleagues a vital element for the achievement of the hoped-for combination was the creation of Jewish Houses in the Public Schools. On his initiative, the first Jewish House at a Public Schools was instituted in 1878 at Clifton College.[45] Clifton was one of the newest of the Public Schools (1862) and was without the markedly exclusive traditions and habits of the ancient founda-tions. It quickly gained a notable reputation under its first head-master, the Reverend Dr John Perceval, future headmaster of Rugby. Perceval later declared that in Cohen's early approaches, he had acted on behalf of 'some leading member of the Jewish community'. Clifton became virtually the regular Public School for many socially and communally notable Jewish families. Among its students were Albert Henry Jessel, Cohen's nephew and ward and later Queen's Counsel and Vice-President of the United Synagogue, and Sir Robert Waley Cohen, another nephew who became the dominant figure in the United Synagogue for a generation in the following century. Clifton's example was in various forms adopted for a time else-where, the first to follow the model being Harrow in 1880.

In the closing years of the nineteenth century the attendance of Jewish pupils at Public Schools where no facilities existed for Jewish worship, instruction or observance, was much discussed in the Jewish press and in many a Jewish educational forum. On 12 May 1902, at the inaugural conference of the Union of Jewish Women, the Chief Rabbi, Dr Hermann Adler, spoke anxiously. 'I confess', he stated,

> that nothing fills me with graver misgivings as to the future of Judaism in this country than that there is an increasing number of parents who do not hesitate to send their sons to non-Jewish boarding schools and houses where Jewish home worship is altogether lacking.

He defined this 'indifferentism' as 'an act of grave disloyalty'.

On 15 November 1895 there appeared in the *Jewish Chronicle* an informed, but somewhat over-generalized, letter concerned with facilities for the education of Jewish girls. This had become a frequent theme of communal discussion, especially in relation to the attendance of Jewish girls at non-Jewish boarding schools, from the point of view of their Jewish attachment. The correspondent referred to 'four classes among the Jews'. They were the 'upper 10,000'; a wealthy middle class; a larger lower middle class; and the mass of 'hard-working craftsmen' and others. The first segment was described as being content to engage private tutors for their daughters. Members of the last section availed themselves of the Jewish 'charitable schools' or the Board Schools. The middle two sections, observed the correspondent, sent their daughters to Jewish boarding schools. The correspondence was initiated by a letter which deplored what was thought to be the growing tendency of Jewish parents to send their daughters to Christian boarding schools, where the fees might reach £100 a year and where it was expected they would meet 'the better classes'. The notion was expressed in the correspondence that such schools might exert a desirable 'moral' influence, without being necessarily 'a Christian influence'.

The correspondence[46] is of historical interest in indicating both the apprehension lest the mingling of classes might prove detrimental to social standards and standing; and the appreciation in some Jewish quarters that there was greater opportunity for social intercourse with the 'better classes' in non-Jewish schools than in Jewish.

Especially as far as boys were concerned, the 'upper-class' Victorian Jewish view that a Public School education was useful for their future exercise of higher social and communal responsibility survived far into the next century. In the *Jewish Chronicle*, on 31 August 1923, the Reverend Vivian Simmons, the Minister of the Reform community, examined the issue frankly. 'If the question were asked', he commented, 'which aspect of the problem of religious education among us Jews in England is the more pressing, that of Jewish children attending elementary schools or that of children at the Public Schools, the answer is by no means easy'. While elementary school education was that of 'a very large majority', the [product of the] Public School 'plays or ought to play a more important part, moves in a larger circle, and is of far more consequence as an individual, ... if the higher education does succeed in developing character and enlarging capacity'.

In a crucial acknowledgement, Simmons reminded his readers that the number of Jews at the Public Schools who 'receive little or no religious education is increasing to an alarming extent'. It was also clear that there were Jewish pupils at Public Schools who 'conformed entirely to the prevailing religious routine, including attendance at chapel and house prayers, [and] the New Testament with its dogmatic teaching ...'[47]

It was against this background that in 1923, the Jewish Memorial Council, of which Waley Cohen was Chairman, appointed a committee 'to consider the problems presented by Jewish boys and girls attending residential Public Schools ...' The committee reported in 1926 that most members were opposed 'at the present time' to the creation of a Jewish Public School. 'Apart from the fact', added the committee,

> that the sentiment of the country is at present opposed to such an idea, it would be an unsound plan for Jewish boys to be thus deprived of the advantages of attending the great Public Schools whose strong character and traditions play such an important part in the educational system of the country.

Influencing the majority of the committee was a desire to avoid an accentuation of Jewish self-segregation. The committee also found some indication of 'an absence of any great enthusiasm on the part of the (Jewish) community for the establishment of a Jewish Public

School'. The committee was of the view that even if more Jewish Houses were established, 'there would still remain large and increasing numbers of Jewish children whose parents would wish them to go to Public Schools but would not desire to send them to a Jewish House'.

The arguments which the committee had considered were many and were starkly summarized by Simmons as follows:

> It is urged that boys (and girls) who always eat at the same table and generally live together in one atmosphere are debarred from the full influence of Public School life; that the Jewish atmosphere predominates, and that they do not rub shoulders sufficiently with boys and girls of different types. Formal religion it is felt plays so small a part in the school life of the average child, that segregation in a special house based upon religious distinctions is an unnatural one. There do not exist special houses for Presbyterian or Baptist pupils, while an observant Roman Catholic does not send his son or daughter to a school based on Church of England principles, because there are Roman Catholic schools available. Again, it is contended that Jewish tendencies which are not desirable, specifically Jewish faults which Public School life should help to eradicate, are rather accentuated than otherwise by the Jewish house system; while the privileges that the observance of Jewish holidays requires is not a good thing for the Jewish boys and girls themselves in relation to their school-fellows. There is the further objection that Jewish boys in a Jewish house are taught and required to observe religious practices which in many cases the boys do not see in their own homes; or, to put it another way, conformity to one type of Judaism is forced upon them.

Following its assessment of the outlook on these matters of numbers of Jewish parents, the committee was driven to lay particular emphasis upon the provision of Jewish religious instruction *from outside*. 'It became clear to the Committee', said the Report,

> that although some of the parents whose children attend chapel are entirely devoid of any Jewish loyalty and are anxious that their children should not be known as Jews, this represents a small minority, and many of the parents who now allow their boys to go to chapel do so more or less in desperation as an alternative to allowing their school lives to be spent without any religious influence and would much prefer that their boys should be provided with Jewish religious guidance and instruction.

Most of the headmasters interviewed by the committee indicated that they would welcome the organization by Jewish parents of facilities for Jewish worship and instruction.

Upon the committee's recommendation, the Council adopted the practice, where possible and with headmasters' approval, of engaging Jewish tutors to provide Jewish instruction on the school premises, generally during the hours of chapel and religious instruction and/or other times convenient to the schools and pupils.[48] By 1950, such classes were held in thirteen Public Schools (the tuition paid for by parents), with a total attendance in excess of 100 pupils. The eagerness of some Jewish parents to secure for their children the perceived benefits of Public School education at the price of their attending chapel reinforced the reluctance of some headmasters to sanction a breach in the Christian character and discipline of their schools. There were more Jewish boarders at Public Schools where no Jewish facilities existed than the total of those where some Jewish provision was made. The Council made persistent efforts to render the availability of facilities more widely known and to dissolve the indifference (and occasionally the hostility) of parents.

The annual report of the Jewish Memorial Council in 1955 described the reports of its inspector, Albert Polack, as 'confirming the great value of the Jewish Religion Class in the religious education of the Jewish pupil'. Perhaps the major value of the tutorials was, by virtue of their existence, their encouragement of the consciousness of Jewish identity. But the inevitably limited extent of the education was apparent, as the inspector was the first to acknowledge. It amounted to one or two hours, ranging over Bible, 'religion' and Jewish history in a school without a Jewish House and without opportunities for Jewish home life, observance of dietary laws and where, as in most cases, the spirit of the school was institutionally and by habit Christian.

The character of the Jewish educational facilities at some Public Schools has been enhanced and the Jewish *esprit de corps* much enlarged, but for parents who sought a Public School education for their children combined with the continuing influence in school years of Jewish home life, the non-residential Public Schools have had a distinct attraction. One cannot ascertain how many parents were motivated by this consideration[49] in applying to such schools, and how many were influenced by the differential in fees or by the greater difficulty in gaining entry into the great boarding Public Schools.

A Jewish Public School had long been beyond the horizon. It came into view, like much else, as a realistic target in the course of the progressive emancipation of the Jewish community from its deeply engrained Victorian habits of mind. This emancipation was to a considerable degree a long-term result of the Eastern European pre-1914 immigration and the intake from Central Europe after 1930. It was a continuing, self-propelling process under the initiating weight of the many operative factors to which reference has been made. Among those diverse factors, the rise of political and religious Zionism as a cause and effect of this new kind of Anglo-Jewish emancipation proved to be increasingly significant. However much the nineteenth-century heritage retained its hold on the imagination and pride of sections of the community, the old substance and style lost authority. The exposure of their practical limitations and the incongruities of the old ideals projected new agendas.

The foundation of the first and only Jewish Public School in Britain by Rabbi Kopul Rosen in 1948 exemplified, if somewhat dramatically, the progress of the attitudinal transformation. It also demonstrated the efficacy of personal initiatives in respect of an idea whose time was thought to have come. Hertz had not been averse to the idea of such a school. In July 1924, at a much publicized nation-wide conference in Leeds on Jewish Education, he sharply rebuked those Jewish parents to whom 'the very idea of a Jewish school is an abhorrence, and even a Jewish House an absurdity'.[50] Next year, he informed the Anglo-Jewish Preachers' Conference that the question why he had not set about establishing a Jewish Public School 'was not infrequently asked' and that 'various educational experts within and without the community have indeed recommended' such a course. He went on:

> The objections that are strenuously urged against it are mostly based on the assumption of Jewish inferiority and will not bear a moment's examination ... The time is not yet, but it is sure to come, when we shall have a Jewish Public School worthy of the community.[51]

In strife with the lay leadership of the United Synagogue, including the key figure of Waley Cohen, Hertz was not minded to add this contentious issue to their differences. Financial pressure on the Jewish educational system was mounting, as soon were the financial requirements of Jewish relief at home and abroad. In the 1940s, beset by worsening ill-health and in sharp public discord with the lay leadership on the Zionist question, Hertz did not press the matter. Towards the end of his life much store was set by many on the intended large central metropolitan comprehensive Jewish day school.

During the post-war Jewish educational planning, the matter of a Jewish Public School aroused in some quarters a more practical communal debate than hitherto. A series of exchanges in the *Jewish Monthly* (the organ of the Anglo-Jewish Association) in the summer of 1947 reflected a changing mood. One writer pointedly contrasted the absence of such an establishment with the number and standing of the Public Schools founded and funded by the Roman Catholic and Nonconformist communities. Rosen shared the enthusiasm for more positive and more deeply rooted forms of Jewish education.

His energy and enterprise were supported by the philanthropy of a group of businessmen who were active Zionists, mostly religious Zionists, and not prominently, if at all, involved with any of the major established communal institutions. Carmel College (in Newbury, moving later to Wallingford) opened with 25 pupils. Within a few years the number rose to 200 and continued to increase. Fees were high. Some free places were introduced. A girls' wing was established. The College achieved considerable scholastic and athletic success. At an early stage a preparatory section was added.

The College was conducted as an Orthodox establishment with Rosen as its head. Something of the spirit which lay behind the setting up and management of the College emerged in this article in the College magazine in mid-1954.[52] 'At present', he wrote,

> our community witnesses the growth of a generation not of Jews but of non-Christians of Jewish parentage ... filled with an unexpressed resentment that they are different ... The authentic Jew can and will mingle with his Christian neighbour with confidence and dignity; the ignorant Jew is ill-at-ease within himself ... Is it not wiser to teach a child why he is a Jew so that by his knowledge he may grow to understand that difference is not to be confused with inferiority? ... Those who criticize the ideological basis of Jewish schools are

becoming fewer [and] in time (they) will come to accept them as a normal manifestation of Anglo-Jewish life.[53]

Whether or not his sharply pejorative portrayals persuaded the hitherto unpersuaded, his language caught both the directness of his personality and the challenge held out by his innovation. The College found favour in a wide array of opinion across disparate sections of Anglo-Jewry. Its eventual closure was not seen as a reflection upon its founder or his successors as heads of the College. Costs had mounted. Inflation of fees was a discouragement. His original supporters were not always enamoured of his at times personalized methods of administration. Some thought it wiser to retire than engage in continued dispute. In particular, for recruitment to posts in business or the professions, the attendance at a residential school steadily declined in significance and was less enviable as an emblem. Those wealthy enough to follow high fashion and/or pursue the prestige associated with the nation's older Public Schools continued to seek a way thereto.

The closure did not reflect a disenchantment of the Jewish community with the idea of the Jewish day school, albeit in some quarters with some ambivalence. That theme forms a major part of the subject-matter of the preceding chapter.

NOTES

1. In general see J.W. Adamson, *English Education 1789–1902* (1930) and S.J. Curtis, *History of Education in Great Britain* (1967).
2. In 1846 the Committee's influential Secretary, Sir James Kay-Shuttleworth, instituted a State-aided pupil–teacher system as a contribution to the supply of competent teachers.
3. The medieval idea of an identity between citizenship and membership of the national church lingered long after the passing of the medieval world and beyond the Reformation, however many practical inroads were made into it. As non-Anglican Christians entered more and more into the life of the State, the old idea came to relate to Christianity and enhanced in some minds the anxiety to limit the role therein of non-Christians. The suggestion that State aid might be forthcoming for the teaching of Judaism aroused much sensitivity.
4. Bill Williams, *The Making of Manchester Jewry 1740–1875* (1976), pp. 207–8.
5. Simon expounded his views more fully in 1880 when approached by a Jewish group which was considering the creation of a Jewish 'middle-class school' in North London. He agreed to join the committee on the firm condition that:

'[such schools] ... will be open to ... all denominations alike ... This will not prevent the fullest instruction in Hebrew and the Jewish religion which I hold to be paramount ... It must be obvious that whilst we Jews claim admission to all Public Schools, we cannot fairly withhold it from any of a different faith who might desire admission to ours ... It probably will be that not a single Christian parent will send his child to a school which is essentially Jewish, but it is incumbent upon us all the same to be careful in maintaining the principle which I have indicated and avoiding even the appearance of exclusiveness.

(*Jewish Chronicle*, 23 July 1880)

6. V.D. Lipman, *Social History of the Jews in England 1850–1950* (1960), pp. 45–9, 146–7, and *passim*; and A.M. Hyamson, *The Sephardim of England* (1951), pp. 94–5, 386–7.

7. Isidore Harris (ed.), *Jews' College Jubilee Volume* (1906), pp. vii–viii.

8. A.M. Hyamson, *Jews' College, London, 1855–1955* (1955), pp. 21–2.

9. *Ibid.* Adler's plan was foreshadowed by the proposal presented by John Braham, optician and synagogal leader of Bristol, in the *Voice of Jacob*, on 17 February 1843, for a ministerial and teachers' training College with a Jewish day school attached, on which in the event no action was taken: Israel Finestein, *Jewish Society in Victorian England* (1933), p. 256.

10. G.M. Young, *Portrait of an Age* (1936), p. 116.

11. Letter to Forster from J.M. Montefiore, Acting President, 28 March 1870: Board's Half-Yearly Report, Spring 1870, pp. 12–13.

12. Half-Yearly Report, Autumn, 1870, pp. 9–10.

13. On Nathan Adler's retirement in 1880 Hermann became his father's Deputy, succeeding to the office of Chief Rabbi in 1891 following his father's death. Hermann Adler, for long the senior preacher in the community, carried yet greater weight from 1880, not least in the debate on the Board Schools. For him and many others, an implication of the emancipation was not only the civic duty to support those schools by the natural payment of rates and taxes but also by encouraging attendance thereat. He was especially concerned to encourage attendance in areas outside London where there were no Jewish schools.

14. In 1904, the JREB launched a wide appeal for funds. Among those heading the appeal were the Chief Rabbi and Claude Montefiore, Vice-President. The Board sought to provide Jewish education for considerably more than 10,000 children attending London County Council Schools and non-Jewish Voluntary Schools. 'A very large proportion of that number', declared the appeal, 'have no other Jewish education.' The Board appealed for £16,000 to meet current responsibilities and to be able to extend the number of its classes, and avoid being driven to close some. The Board announced that its annual income had never exceeded £5,000. The appeal raised a total of £9,400: *Jewish Chronicle*, 13 January 1905.

15. *Jewish Chronicle*, 22 June 1883 and *Jewish World*, same date.

16. *Jewish World*, 29 June 1883. This tone of complacent optimism was characteristic of the time in many sections of influential command opinion. Another warning note of a different kind was struck in the annual report of the Jews'

Free School for 1885–86. While acknowledging that it was 'desirable' that 'a portion of our poor should ... send their children to the Board Schools (so long as provision is made for their religious education)', the report added: 'but it would be wrong if the wealthy Jews were to thrust the whole of the work of (secular) education on to the local rates. The London School Board rate is already somewhat a heavy one. How deplorable if the Londoner could show that his burden were augmented by the influx of foreign children.' In 1880 only 71 per cent of the available accommodation at the Jewish schools (nation-wide) was in use (Privy Council's Education Report as summarized in the Jewish press in October 1880).

17. Sidney Webb, *London Education* (1904). He added: 'It would seem, speaking generally, as if the few Jewish schools are of good average efficiency'. He thought that the same tribute could be paid to only about 20 of the approximately 300 Anglican schools in London. In his *A Headmaster Looks Back* (1946), Charles F. Nathan (not a Jew) refers to the Liverpool Jewish School, of which he was headmaster from 1909 to 1923, as being in 1909 'the best staffed school in my opinion in the city of Liverpool'.

18. Athelston Riley and others, *The Religious Question in Public Relations* (1911), p. 283.

19. Henrietta Adler, 'Looking Back', *Jewish Monthly* (September 1947), p. 34.

20. W. Evans-Gordon, *The Alien Invasion* (1903), pp. 33–7.

21. V.D. Lipman, see note 6.

22. M.J. Wilson, *Voluntary Schools and State Education* (1894).

23. For the difficult negotiations between the interested parties from the points of view of the senior civil servant involved and the Archbishop of Canterbury respectively, see B.M. Allen, *Sir Robert Morant* (1934) and G.K.A. Bell, *Randall Davidson* (1938).

24. Sidney Webb, see note 17.

25. Some Local Education Authorities resisted this interpretation of the legislation. The issue was finally decided against them by the House of Lords in *R.V. West Riding of Yorkshire County Council* in 1907. An increase by the Board of Education (as the Education Committee had by now become) in the total of its grant for Jewish schools was followed by the formation, in 1897, of the Jewish Voluntary Schools Association for the purpose of allocating that lump sum to the schools in such proportions as its governing body might decide. The Association survived the Act of 1902 under which wholly different financial arrangements were made. It continued to operate as a consultative body between the schools and as the spokesman of the schools in matters concerning them as a body. In 1921, the Jewish Voluntary Schools in London (at the prompting of the Central Committee for Jewish Education, a department of the newly created Jewish War Memorial Council) created their own Association whose objects were analogous to the older Association, which had lapsed during World War I. The new body included in its remit the arranging under the Central Committee of independent inspections of the schools and the allocation between the schools of Jewish communal grants from the Synagogues, notably from the United Synagogue.

26. L.J. Bowman, 'The Code of Instruction', in A.M. Hyamson (ed.), *Jewish Literary Annual* (1906). These sentiments sprang in part from Bowman's realization of the strength and influence of opinion in sections of the immigrant community restless with misgivings over educational standards which seemed to satisfy the more anglicized families and the communal leadership: see C. Russell and H.S. Lewis, *The Jew in London* (1900), pp. 214–25. Those sections tended to centre round the Federation of Synagogues and congregations of comparable outlook in immigrant areas generally in London and the provinces.

27. *Sermons, Addresses and Studies*, Vol. 1 (1938), p. 9.

28. *Ibid.*, pp. 141–2, and Vol. 2, pp. 140–1.

29. Typical exchanges appeared in the *Jewish Chronicle* as late as August–September 1956 between 'Zionist' and 'Jewish' educationists. Somewhat comparable differences existed within the Orthodox fold, which sometimes related to emphasis rather than principle. The chairman of the Zionist Federation's day-school committee was Dr I.S. Fox, an Orthodox Jew, son of the Russian-born Rabbi J.S. Fox, founder in Liverpool of the Hebrew high-grade school where modern Hebrew was taught as a living language. The different emphases are illustrated in the contrasts between, for example, Solomon Schonfeld, *Jewish Religious Education: A Guide and Handbook* (1943), chaps ix–xi, and 'Hebrew Day Schools', in *Gates of Zion* (London: Central Synagogue Council of Zionist Federation, 1950).

30. Lucien Wolf Memorial Lecture, 1953, pub. 1954.

31. H.J. Zimmels, J. Rabbinowitz and I. Finestein (eds), *Essays Presented to Chief Rabbi Israel Brodie* (1967), p. 365.

32. *Willesden Synagogue Review* (April 1945), pp. 14–15.

33. *Jewish Chronicles*, 14 January 1944.

34. *Times* editorial, 17 February 1940. The editor castigated the 'common idea' that 'religious education must be considered as altogether the affair of the Churches'. He added:

> The truth is … that religion must form the very basis of any education worth the name (and) yet in some of the schools provided by the State there is no religious teaching, and in some of the secondary schools it is supplied for junior pupils only and dropped as a subject comparatively unimportant when they reach the upper forms.

> Among those who contributed to the lengthy and seminal correspondence in the wake of this widely publicized editorial (it was soon separately printed for public sale and within two weeks had sold 400,000 copies) was the Chief Rabbi Dr Hertz, who rejoiced in this influential support for the idea of religious teaching in the schools.

35. Bruce Truscott, *Redbrick and These Days* (1945), p. 162.

36. *Jewish Education, 1944, and After*, JEC Educational Publication, No. 51 (1944), pp. 4, 5, 7.

37. *Ibid.*, p. 12.

38. *Ibid.*, pp. 41, 43.

39. *Willesden Synagogue Review*, pp. 5–6. The raising of the school-leaving age in 1947 from 14 to 15 gave the Jewish community, under the Act of 1944, access to a significantly larger proportion of children of school age, all the more significant bearing in mind that more than 40 per cent of Jewish Children of school age in London alone attended neither Synagogue classes nor Talmud Torahs. Many Jewish parents did not avail themselves of the right to withdraw their children as allowed by the Act, as was revealed by the survey carried out in 1953 by the Education Committee of the Board of Deputies.

40. The AJY scheme had in its day a special interest in that it was reasonably taken to mark that movement's recognition that the anglicization, which had for so long been among its conscious prime objectives, needed to be balanced by a heightened cultivation of attachment to the Jewish heritage. It was directed particularly at 'detached' youth. Judaism as a path towards ending confusion over identity seemed to be a central part of the purpose of the exercise.

41. Morris, Fishman and their colleagues were genuinely encouraged by the fact that, in Morris' words, 'considerable numbers of young people have joined together on purely educational grounds and for serious educational purposes' (see note 36, p. 6). While warning against overrating this, he referred to these developments as 'symptoms of an … inner conviction of the need for a regenerated and revitalised system of Jewish education'. He laid special emphasis on the Jewish Youth Study Groups movement as well as on the educational programmes of the specifically Zionist-inspired bodies.

42. Joint Emergency Committee for Jewish Religious Education in Great Britain, Educational Publications, No. 55.

43. Report on Communal Conference on the Reconstruction of Jewish Education in Great Britain, Central Council for Jewish Religious Education in the United Kingdom, p. 21.

44. Mark Grosseck, product of a South London Board School and an ironic and somewhat amused spectator, wrote that Board School products 'lacked that tone, that poise, that touch of finesse, that impalpable something which instantly reveals the English gentleman (or gentle boy), his uniqueness, his breeding … [A Board School pupil] could never be mistaken for a scholar of those establishments', M. Grosseck, *First Movement* (1937), p. 31. For a serious appraisal in the mid twentieth century, see J.F. Wolfenden, *The Public Schools Today* (1949).

45. E.M. Oakley, *Clifton College 1862–89*, with historical introduction by J.M. Wilson. See also, Albert I. Polack, 'Clifton and Anglo-Jewry', in N.G.L. Hammond (ed.), *Centenary Essays on Clifton College* (1962), pp. 51–71.

46. *Jewish Chronicle*, November–December 1895.

47. Per Joseph Polack, Jewish housemaster at Clifton, in his report to the special committee of 1923, published separately by the Jewish Memorial Council.

48. Alexander Rosenzeig, *The Jewish Memorial Council: A History 1919–1999* (1998), chap. 14.

49. The possibility of integrating the influences of home and school was held, among others, by Frederick Walker, High Master of the Manchester Grammar School (1859–76) and of St Paul's School in London (1876–1905), to be

among the greatest merits of the non-residential Public School. This influential figure, a devout Anglican, sought to broaden the bounds of the two Public Schools over which he had charge, to include pupils who were neither Anglican nor Christian. The City of London School and University College School, both connected in their history with the emancipation movement, were likewise open to Jews. Herbert (later Lord) Samuel, who was a pupil at the latter (1883–88) wrote that:

> Orthodox Jewish families of that generation seldom sent their children to the residential Public Schools on account of the difficulty of providing religious teaching and of maintaining the special observances ... If I missed the influences that are breathed in with the atmosphere of the ancient schools I had at all events the benefits of a modern curriculum, such as they at that time had hardly begun to offer.
> *Memoirs* (1945), p. 4.

Middle-class families able to afford the fees had the option of the private (often boarding) proprietary Jewish schools. They varied in standards but the best were of a high order. The best known in London were that of H.N. Solomon in Edmonton and that of Leopold Neumegen in Highgate (founded there in 1799 by Hyman Hurwitz), which moved to Kew in 1842. Many of their pupils achieved notable roles in Jewish and general public life.

50. Hertz, *Sermons, Addresses and Studies*, Vol. 2 (1938), p. 27.
51. *Ibid.*, p. 142.
52. Reprinted in Cyril Domb (ed.), *Memoirs of Kopul Rosen* (1970), pp. 231–5. See, among Rosen's successors, Jeremy Rosen, 'Carmel in Crisis', *Jewish Chronicle*, 14 March 1975, and Philip Skelker, 'Thriving on a Diet of Soccer and *siddur*', *ibid.*, 1 November 1985.
53. In this article and generally, Rabbi Rosen was especially concerned about the practice of sending Jewish children to Church schools. If one motive was the parental eagerness to secure for their child a private school education, another reason might have been the absence in the area of any other school. There were also areas where there were insufficient easily accessible school places outside the Church schools. Attendance or otherwise at religious worship and instruction would depend on the trust deed of the school and decisions of headmasters. When Arnold Page (formerly tutor in Greek to Claude Montefiore and later Dean of Peterborough) was a curate in Bishopsgate in the heart of Jewish London towards the end of the nineteenth century, he was moved by the advice of William Rogers, the local Rector, to arrange with the Chief Rabbi facilities for the Jewish religious instructions of Jewish children in Church schools in the area (Lucy Cohen, *Some Recollections of C.G. Montefiore* (1940), p. 38). There were a few cases where a Church school, because of its location, came to have a preponderantly Jewish composition. This happened in St John's Schools in Cheetham, Manchester, where Jewish children had received Jewish instruction from visiting teachers. By 1926, as many as 80 per cent of the pupils were Jewish. The managers felt unable to conduct the schools further as an Anglican establishment and the schools were

closed, the pupils being transferred to the Manchester Jewish School in Manchester or the municipal schools (I.W. Slotki, *Jewish Education in Manchester and Salford* (1928)).

SELECT BIBLIOGRAPHY

Baum, J. and Baum, B., *Life of H.N. Solomon*, Jewish Research Group, Edmonton Hundred Historical Society: New Series, No. 43 (1981).

Bentwich, N., 'Refugee Influences', *Jewish Monthly*, Vol. 9 (1947), pp. 24–9.

Black, Gerry, *History of Jews' Free School, London, since 1732* (1998).

Braude, Jacob, 'Jewish Day Schools', *Jewish Chronicle*, 26 February 1954.

—— 'Survey of Jewish Schools: Teachers, Paramount Problem', *Jewish Chronicle*, 30 July 1973.

Cassell, Curtis, 'West Metropolitan Jewish School, 1845–97', *Transactions of the Jewish Historical Society*, Vol. 19 (1960), pp. 115–28.

Cohen, Michael, 'Lessons to be learned: Jewish Day School Movement', *Jewish Chronicle*, 13 July 1984.

Conway, Edward, 'The Training of Teachers', in Derek Taylor (ed.), *Jewish Education* (Jewish Educational Development Trust, 1981–82), pp. 9–13, 17–19.

—— 'Revolution in Jewish Education', in Derek Taylor (ed.), *Jewish Education* (Jewish Educational Trust, 1983–84), pp. 12–14.

Fishman, Isidore, 'Jewish Education in Great Britain in 1945', *Jewish Forum* (November 1945), pp. 60–66.

Gertner, Levi, 'Day School Education Sponsored by the Zionist Federation (over 25 years)', *Zionist Year Book* (1974), pp. 338–42.

Gould, Julius and Esh, Saul (eds), *Jewish Life in Modern Britain* (1964) [incl. 'Jewish Education in Great Britain', by Isidore Fishman and Harold Levy, pp. 67–85].

Greenberg, Suzanne K., 'Anglicisation and the Education of Jewish Immigrant Children in East End', in A. Rapoport-Albert and S.J. Zipperstein (eds), *Jewish History: Essays in Honour of Chimen Abramsky* (1998).

Newman, A.N. (ed.), *Provincial Jewry in Victorian England* (1975).

Osborne, Irving, 'The Education of Jewish Immigrants in Tower Hamlets, 1870–1914', in A.N. Newman (ed.), *The Jews in the East End, 1840–1939* (1981), pp. 163–72.

Short, G., *Responding to Diversity? Initial Investigation into Multicultural Education in Jewish Schools in the UK* (London: Institute of Jewish Policy Research, 2002).

Stanton, W.W. (headmaster of Hasmonean Boys Schools – part of the Jewish Secondary School Movement – from 1945 to 1980), 'A Headmaster Looks Back', in Derek Taylor (ed.), *Jewish Education* (1981–82), pp. 24–6.

Steinberg, Bernard, 'Anglo-Jewry and the 1944 Education Act', *Jewish Journal of Sociology*, Vol. 31, No. 2 (1989), pp. 81–108.

Valins, O., Kosmin, B. and Goldberg, J., *Future of Jewish Schooling* (London: Institute of Jewish Policy Research, 2001).

Webber, Alan, 'A Perspective on Jewish Education', *Jewish Year Book* (2001), pp. 17–22.

3

The Estrangement of Anglo-Jewish Intellectuals*

The term intellectual is a comprehensive one. It includes, but is not limited to, academics, novelists and dramatists. It often covers members of professions and a certain class of journalist. It may denote that substantial section of society composed of people who value the things of the mind.

Many members of these groups are hard-headed men of the world, with a high regard for the practical. The Jewish community has much to gain by attracting the interests and energies of its academics and intellectuals to the management of communal affairs in all departments and at all levels. Some are so engaged, but the phenomenon of the elusive Jewish academic remains a communal issue which merits responsible consideration.

To call a person an 'intellectual' is sometimes intended as a compliment. But sometimes it has been used as a convenient term of mild derision. There is an age-old tension between the study and the market place. It is at least as old as the Reformation when clerics ceased to hold the monopoly of office and when politics became increasingly the province of merchant and adventurer, in addition to the prince.

Book-learning and research do not ensure intelligence or judgement. Nor does their lack necessarily preclude them. But a genuine and deep interest in the humanities is wrongly thought by some to reflect and nourish a detachment from reality. Even the

---

*This chapter is substantially the text of the author's address to the Institute of Jewish Affairs on 12 October 1983 and was published in *Jewish Quarterly*, Vol. 31, Nos 3–4 (1984).

science researcher sometimes suffers this silent calumny. The professional man or woman is less likely to be so regarded. Yet likewise they will at times take care not to be mistaken for people with much time to read books outside their special field. This caution may be professional prudence. It may also be related to the notion that books – while they may be an endearing social grace – connote the taking of shelter from the gritty gusts of life.

Such features have been markedly present in Anglo-Jewish society. It is a paradox. No section of the human family has attached to study and knowledge the same importance as the Jews. Few societies have been as well able as Anglo-Jewry to endow and sustain institutions of higher learning and the attendant publications, and to provide a responsible degree of patronage for study at all levels – able, that is, in terms of finance and organization, if the necessary understanding and will were there.

The Jewish communal leaders who emerged in England during the emancipation were in the main gifted persons, with a talent for administration and public relations. They had a passion to be seen to perform good works, and a profound and axiomatic belief in the standards and social methods of the upper middle classes of their day. The relative openness of English society since the Resettlement in the seventeenth century and a reliance upon Jewish scholars from abroad, had not been inducements towards the cultivation of Jewish study on these shores. Communal leaders in the nineteenth century inherited and cultivated a certain detachment from the speculative, and retained an instinct for the pragmatic.

Their public and private success was considerable. It disinclined them from seriously questioning the viability of the communal system or the balance in society which they and their fathers had secured. Only slowly did they realize that the success of the emancipation put the system in jeopardy. New opportunities drew their successors away from the old idea that the continuity of communal service was a family commitment. In any case the weakening of authority in every sphere, and the rise of scientific materialism and the secularist outlook, raised acute questions as to whether in good conscience they could retain such commitment any longer.

Meanwhile, the system of rule by the old families died hard. The practical advantages of paternalistic government accorded with the perceived needs of the day and with the habits of class-conscious

English society. 'Another constant in the character of England', wrote Professor Ernest Barker, 'is the vogue of the amateur ... England is the home of professions ... But England is also anti-professional. She has always cultivated an amateur quality.'[1] Jewish leaders took on the stamp of the skilled English amateur and the outlook of English practicality, with its deference to ancient institutions, if they were thought to work. Serious Jewish study somehow became associated with the 'foreigner'. An unconscious sense of minimalism prevailed in Jewish education.[2]

Those who rebelled against this limited philosophy early in the twentieth century were associated by the adherents of that philosophy with so-called presumptuous immigrants and, what was worse, with what was deemed to be the unrealizable fantasy known as political Zionism. When Augustus Kahn, Leon Simon, Norman Bentwich and Harry Sacher were young men, there was an intertwining between polemics over Zionism and the almost equally divisive issues about the rightful locale of power in communal government. The impact of the great immigration strengthened the hands of such new claimants to authority, but many years elapsed before they gained the day.

Throughout these debates, the leaders of the new forces were often intellectuals – young academics, men of letters, and independent-minded journalists frequently with university training. The careers of Israel Zangwill and Selig Brodetsky can only be fully understood against this background. It is noteworthy that in the early part of the century there was a modern-style alliance in support of the movement for Jewish day-school education for the middle classes, between those elements and sections of the 'right-wing' Orthodox rabbinate, in opposition to the established communal policy at that time.

There was a striking consistency through the new century. In 1901, in one of his farewell letters in the *Jewish Chronicle* before leaving for America, Solomon Schechter stirred the placid waters of English Jewry by words whose relevance was not confined to his day: 'If there was ever a time', he wrote, 'when the revival of Hebrew learning meant the very existence of Judaism, it is this ... ignorance is on the increase among our better situated classes. The Jew will ... have to rediscover himself'.[3] His references to the indifference of the lay leadership were not forgotten. For his presidential address to the Union of Jewish Literary Societies in 1905 (published in the *Jewish Literary Annual*, 1906), Lucien Woolf chose as his subject 'Anglo-Jewish literary ability'. He expounded the view that while the opportunities in England for higher learning and the outlets for literary talent had been well employed by individual Jews, there were serious limitations on literary production through lack of endowment or patronage. Joseph Hertz continued the challenge to these failings and inhibitions.

In 1928, Selig Brodetsky and Herbert Loewe collaborated to produce papers on 'The Intellectual Level of Anglo-Jewish Life'. Their enquiries revealed, as had long been supposed, a disengagement on the part of wide segments of the lay leadership from any personal interest in Jewish study. The rupture between the leadership and Jewish academics continued to be much commented on. In 1947, Cecil Roth described the 'supporters of intellectual and literary endeavour in Anglo-Jewry' as 'a neglected and by now almost obsolete genius'.[4] There were some individual and organizational stimulators and patrons of Jewish learning, especially in the postwar years of communal introspection and of concern for the promotion of instruments for the community's survival capacity. The series of publications by the British Section of the World Jewish Congress in the 1950s entitled the 'Popular Jewish Library' was an important example. In more recent times, the Littman Library of Jewish Civilization has given immense impetus to research and publication. But there remained in the minds of academics certain convictions as to the philistinism implicit in what appeared to them to be the scale of communal priorities. Their fears were generally unallayed notwithstanding the expanded operations of Jews' College, the Leo Baeck College, the Society for Jewish Study, the Institute of Jewish Studies and the Jewish Historical Society.

Many of the modern writers who were Jews touched upon Jewish themes as from the outside. It is as though Jewish academics and *littérateurs*, while making sensitive sketches of the Jewish community, did so from a high vantage point; and noting complacent materialism below, did no more than wring their hands or shake their heads over the folly of it. There were of course exceptions who wrote from within. They highlight the same conditions.

In February 1946, the editor of the *Jewish Academy*, the periodical of the Inter-University Jewish Federation, wrote as follows:

The qualifications for leading positions in Anglo-Jewish organizations seem to be business ability and success in material spheres ... A knowledge of business methods has replaced the knowledge of Jewish history and Jewish philosophy. The success of Jewish organizations headed by such leaders is measured by the smooth running of their machinery rather than by the values which such organizations ostensibly represent.

If that statement has a touch of the intemperance of youth, it represented assumptions and sentiments commonly held in Jewish academic life at all levels.

The strictures in that typical passage have become far less applicable since it was written. There has been in progress in many quarters considerable discussion over future trends – how to retain the interest of the younger age group in distinctive Jewish life, how to strengthen the ties between central agencies and disparate congregations, how to define and meet Jewish educational needs for today, and how to define the relations between Israel and the Diaspora in order to maximize their mutual effects. These are among the subjects which open fields of enquiry and actions to which academics had and have realistic contributions to make.

The businessman is expected to be able to give quick decisions, to set in motion practical logistical studies, to be at home in large-scale administration, and to prudently delegate without abdication of authority. Everyone acknowledges that these are important qualities. The attributed skills of the academic are the facility to analyse, formulate and present; the talent and habit of objectively examining issues; the capacity to set trends and give a lead by propounding new ideas or refurbishing old ones in changing circumstances.

All these respective qualities are needed in the hierarchy of communal leadership. It is by no means the case that these sets of aptitudes are bound to be divided. They can be found in one person. Academics may evince the businessman's qualities as readily as the busy chairman of companies who for his part may equally well show skills which are usually associated with the academy.

However, the tension has persisted. There developed a pervasive idea among academics that in Anglo-Jewry a premium was placed on organization and public relations, and that this all too readily becomes a substitute for original thinking. It is not an entirely just appraisal but was a recognizable portrait. But if the above respective talents cannot neatly be categorized as between groups, there is a sufficient degree of reality in the classification to justify it being taken note of.

Academics tend to be highly sensitive to the manner in which their particular skills are responded to. After all, those skills are part of their stock-in-trade, of whose standing and repute they are professionally and personally conscious. Unless there is some common perception as to how their experience and expertise can be effectively deployed in the communal arena, there remains an inhibition against their use, which becomes an inhibition shared by all. Think tanks, brains trusts, and advisory committees can easily become talk shops to salve the consciences of laymen who want to be seen to be searching for the best advice. If academics are to be encouraged to apply their minds to major practical communal questions, there has in some way to be forged a genuine interplay between the process of analysis and the process of decision-making.

Academics are by temperament and policy averse to being organized, used, or quoted for purposes not intended by them. In 1970, Charles Leibman posed the following question in the general context of authority in contemporary Jewish life: 'Are the contributions of academics indeed welcome, or are intellectuals wanted as window dressing? Is the status of intellectuals a function of Jewish esteem for scholarship or Jewish esteem for those who have made their mark in the Gentile world?'[5] It would be especially foolhardy to overlook these apt questions in the Anglo-Jewish community.

In no other section of the Jewish community has the impact of modern trends been more marked than among the academics. Some of them have shown a superiority complex towards the interests and style of the lay leadership. There are instances where such superiority complex is wholly misplaced.

It has sometimes been accompanied, with equal force, by an inferiority complex on the part of academics. This arises from one or both of the following factors. The first is the self-acknowledged substantial ignorance of matters Jewish, combined in some cases with an utter loss of interest in Judaism in any form. Such a state of mind can be especially inhibiting when it is joined to a true inability to adopt any intellectual commitment likely to prove acceptable to the religious right, left or centre. An interest in Judaism, unless well informed, will probably fall short of establishing any honest attachment to any school of thought.

The second source of a sense of inferiority concerns the scale and influence of fund-raising, and the authority which fund-raising expertise or large-scale fund-raising can wield over the character and the machinery of organized Jewish life.

The pervasive fund-raising to which Anglo-Jewry has become accustomed since the mid 1950s, if not earlier, is on a scale formerly unknown, even allowing for inflation. This was especially so in respect of Israel-linked causes. The fund-raising, in particular for Israel, created its own hierarchy, in which influence and eminence were bound to be measured in terms of one's role in the elaborate effort. The resulting power and prestige can hardly be limited in practice to the confines of fund-raising.

The emergence from the 1950s of a compact body of major fund-raisers for Israel produced a powerful source of communal authority. There was little which these men and women could not bring about in the Jewish community, should they set their minds to it. And there were few areas of communal life in which their support was not likely to be the key to success, if it could be procured.

These circumstances strengthened the assumption of many onlooking Jewish intellectuals as to what they apprehend may be an irretrievable condition, as they see it, of Anglo-Jewish governance. In their eyes, that condition has a double nature. First, they detect an a-cultural ambience of thought and priority. Second, they have the feeling that wealth is a substantial and possibly decisive factor in the retention and transmission of authority. Such sentiments can amount to an almost unshakable deterrent against personal involvement.

Some years ago, Nicholas Kochan carried out a private survey, by correspondence and interview, of a selected number of Jewish intellectuals of diverse attitudes. He was concerned to explain what, with forgivable exaggeration, he called the 'mass abstension' of Jewish academics from communal affairs. His report appeared in the *Jewish Quarterly* in the summer of 1978. There was much force in his tentative conclusion that 'the key to the non-participation of academics ... may be the low level of Jewish culture in general'. He noted the vicious circle in that if cultural poverty deters them, 'they themselves are at least partly to be blamed'. Whatever the reasons, he rightly declared that 'the situation calls for soul-searching on the part of communal leaders and academics alike'.

Some significant initiatives were taken. The creation of the Academic Study Group on Israel and the Middle East in 1978 was one such example. The Centre for Contemporary Studies from time to time assembled selected Jewish academics and prominent laymen to consider a range of contemporary issues. The Israel-Diaspora Trust became engaged in convening Jewish intellectuals and lay personalities to examine current Jewish questions. All such efforts gave an opportunity for the expression of an *esprit de corps* on the part of Jewish academics in the field of communal thought and action, while at the same time piercing their comparative isolation and facilitating the interplay of ideas for policy between respective segments of the community.

In 1962, the Institute of Contemporary Jewry of the Hebrew University, acting under the auspices of the Board of Deputies, held a conference in London of Jewish academics and organizational leaders to examine the structure, social composition and religious and ideological trends within Anglo-Jewry, as well as the role of the social scientist. In 1977, the Board convened a successor conference on these and related topics. These occasions were valuable exercises in bridge-building between academics and laymen in the study of the present and to some extent in preparing for the future.[6]

The Institute of Jewish Affairs (IJA) had a long tradition, carried over from the enterprise of the British Section of the World Jewish Congress, of assembling leading academics and lay leaders to consider communal trends and prospective policies. Its Policy Planning Group was a standing committee directed to such ends. The IJA has been converted into the Institute for Jewish Policy Research.

Whatever the undoubted value of all such efforts, there remains in some circles a sense of estrangement. There is no escape from the need to examine further the nature of such sense or allegation.

Since the 1930s, the number of Jewish students has far exceeded the Jewish ratio in the population. The proportion has steadily increased. The proportion of University teachers of all grades who are Jews has increased, and if anything, has exceeded, relative to the total of university teachers, the proportion of Jewish students in the population. The total number of such academics at Universities, as best as one can judge, is not far short of 2000.

A tiny fragment of them became proponents of the New Left. Many are committed Jews and Jewesses of varying degrees of connection. Many are puzzled or indifferent spectators. Such indifference is often outward only, and does not mean an inner freedom from unease – unease over the adjustment, or lack of it, between different traditions and concerns, as well as over Gentile reactions, rarely spoken, to the nature of such adjustment or lack of it. There is often a certain malaise consisting either of a despair over finding a rationale for distinctive Jewish survival (other than the unsolicited pressure of anti-Semitism), or of a troubled indifference to the task.

It would be a mistake to think in terms of any fixed numbers of Jewish academics, even if that were precisely ascertainable. There is a regular intake of young graduates and researchers. The situation is one of flux, with probably an ever-rising total. The above-mentioned malaise accompanies the student body from whom in due course the academics are recruited. It is part of the self-imposed, continuing task of the Bnai Brith Hillel Foundation and the Union of Jewish Students to provide antidotes and stimuli at those levels of the academic community.

The reactions of the academics to life have much in common with those of the Jewish community as a whole. There are the same divergencies, with the same range of attitudes and assumptions. It is all too easy to talk of estrangement while ignoring the fact that these cadres of well-read opinion frequently face the same predicaments and labour under the same recollections as the Jewish community generally.

Their views about Israel, Judaism, assimilation and public relations belong to the times in which they live and are not the specialized product of academic life.

In a materialistic and highly competitive society, they endure the same pressures making for conformity and/or advancement as obtain in the wider world. To the extent that secularity is often the context in which the Jew is spoken of, such definitions are applicable in like measure within and beyond the academy. To the extent that there has been a return to metaphysical and meta-historical philosophies and traditional forms of thought and practice, such are likewise found within the academy.

Significantly there is among the academics as among Jews at large a growing sense of the essential unity of the Jewish people. 'The essential unity of the Jewish people', wrote Professor Morris Ginsberg in the *Jewish Journal of Sociology*, in July 1964, 'is due not only to the fact that Jews have a sense of solidarity, but to the objective interdependence of the different communities which does not depend entirely on their own volition.' It was, added that doyen of the academic community, 'a point of fundamental importance'. The distance which Ginsberg had travelled from the strong Jewish nuances of his youth gave his ultimate refusal to be detached from his people and their cares a notable quality.

The unalterableness of the interdependence and the accompanying strength of the sense of Jewish distinctiveness, are weighty matters. In the absence of a conscious, strenuous and persistent effort to contract out and disappear Jewishly – which are difficult objectives to achieve – the influence of those matters goes deep. The acute self-consciousness which these phenomena and considerations bring in their wake is often sharper in the University 'cloister' or laboratory than in the world outside.

One reason is that scholarship abhors unexplained differences. The self-esteem of scholars requires the assumption that differentials call for explanation, and that, given time and effort, explanations can be found. Jewish survival, international Jewish kinship, Jewish cohesion and identity, have about them an element of improbability, bordering some might say upon mystery. They are features which those trained in academic discipline are prone to want to demythologize.

Another factor making for sharp self-consciousness is that nowhere is there a keener encounter between cultures and systems of thought than at the universities. It is unlikely that Jewish academics, least of all those concerned with the social sciences, would not, at least privately if not also publicly, feel drawn as a matter of intellectual self-respect, perhaps even curiosity, to ponder upon and even analyse these elements with the skills and equipment which are the tools of their profession.

The sense of legacy has been greatly heightened in our generation. Furthermore, at a time when the decomposition of old authority is daily proclaimed and social and racial turmoil are ever more evident, scholar and layman alike tend to look back to origins in order, the more readily, to sustain or analyse familiar or inherited values. How far modernity has corroded those values and thereby impinged upon Jewish cohesion and distinctiveness and identity, touches upon questions towards which indifference is unreasonable, anti-intellectual and in the end dangerous to self-esteem.

It is most doubtful whether indifference is anything as widespread among Jewish intellectuals as is sometimes supposed. Responses may, from the point of view of interested communal observers, appear negative. Even alienation is remote from indifference.

Self-consciousness is likely to be all the sharper by reason of the fact that in the academic world in particular an intelligent response of some kind is probably expected. In its absence, or if the artificialities of concealment or by-pass are indulged in, this is in itself a form of response likely to be noted in any event. The common room is one of the most searching places in the world, and not necessarily by way of actual direct enquiry.

Intellectuals, as a by-product of their vocational interests and/or of their predisposition to analyse from general principles, are often in the business of social criticism. Intellectuals sometimes tend to stand aside from institutions of authority or establishment. Their inclination is to subject them to critical scrutiny in terms of their utility, their representative character, and their approximation in impulse and action to standards of fairness and need measured by general principles of justice and reason.[7]

Within Jewish society such tendencies may operate with greater natural vigour because of the nature and composition of that society. In society at large intellectual pursuits long ago ceased to be confined within any ecclesiastical framework. This development was part and parcel of what was thought of as an emancipation from inhibitive authority. Within Jewish society, which is still defined in many respects by reference to religion, such departures evoke virtually unavoidable tensions. Furthermore, in a Jewish society in which large areas of public life, including the religious domain, have traditionally been and to some extent remain subject to forms of bureaucracy, the intellectual groups of whom we speak will not readily or easily respond to efforts to counter a degree of detachment. Nor should one overlook a natural Jewish fractiousness on their part.

Yet there probably never was a riper time for many years for the taking of measures to draw Jewish intellectuals closer to the inner life of the Anglo-Jewish community, in terms of consultation, honorary office, or professional occupancy. In some of the very factors making for tension there is the potentiality for its creative resolution. There has been a mounting and anxious awareness among the lay leadership and within the Jewish community generally of the proportion of academics who, consciously or by default, remove themselves from positions of influence in communal life. There is an increasing concern over the elusive academic. There have been repeated public references to the disenchantment in Jewish academic circles with the Jewish community, its system and organs of government, its outlook and apparent goals. There is at the same time a rising conviction that the expertise and ideas of the academics have a useful and needful role to play in communal affairs.

There is a continuing modern reappraisal of the nature and machinery of communal government. Associated with it is the current preoccupation with questions of training and recruitment for leadership, honorary and professional, centrally and locally and in all spheres.[8]

There are issues which 30 years ago were little heard of. They are part of the ever-growing communal self-analysis and the anxious study of the community's future prospects. Whatever else is required of leadership, it must have a perception of trends and the capacity to assess needs. At times of rapid change, new kinds of need arise and new tests of authority come into being. The old deference goes. Old bases of prestige are questioned. Everywhere leadership is under new styles of scrutiny. In such circumstances the detachment of academics inexorably becomes highly anomalous and particularly untimely.

Some of these factors can both deter academics and at the same time incline and even drive them to reflect upon the nature of Jewishness and its ties. An especially powerful factor in this connection was the Lebanese War of 1982. It sharpened the impact of all the elements to which reference has been made, and graphically illustrated their effect. The effect on opinion of that war and its associated events dramatically demonstrated the objective interdependence of the Jewish people of which Ginsberg had spoken. An interrelated factor was the realism of which Maurice Freedman gave a noteworthy reminder in 1974. 'We all recall a time', observed Professor Freedman, 'when Israel was a prominent part in the furnishings of [the liberal imagination] ... those days are gone ... the normalization now realized in Israel ... makes Israel far too much like a developed country to allow it to continue to be worthy of sentimental investment.'[9]

Hobson's choice was thrust upon Jewish analysts, formulators and publicists. There could be no disinterest. Questions arose concerning Jewish purpose and Jewish pride, which aroused the curious and startled the uncommitted by their apparently sudden pertinence. Nowhere was the inability to be disinterested more strongly felt than in the academic community. An interest in the nature of the relationship with Israel was heightened where it existed, and aroused where it slumbered.

There was a variety of reactions among Jews, ranging from the political left to diverse Zionist positions. Many of the hitherto seemingly disinterested who were silent felt no less that they had, at least in private, to come to terms with (the at times) involuntariness of mutual Jewish involvement. It was not so much that a new realism was born, as that the awareness of actuality was accentuated. Sentiments went beyond the hurt sustained by the unfairness of the attempted equation between Zionism and racism. No longer did opinion, whether Jewish or Gentile, appear influenced by older factors tending towards understanding and sympathy for the Zionist cause. Jewish statehood had in a sense gone beyond Zionism. It had come of age, and so to speak was at bay.

The practical, emotional and intellectual questions posed by the new scene, and indeed the philosophical and religious questions, were many. Even a dissociation or an attempted dissociation from that scene required some examination of the relationships under review. Implicit in all the questions is the challenge of a new era. It is not surprising that the World Zionist Organisation has encouraged the growth of seminars of Jewish academics. The published description of the 'two basic purposes' of the project is most significant:

> One stemmed from the awareness that the ideological underpinning of the Zionist idea and the Zionist deed had not kept up with the changes and the reality of the post-state era. The other was part of a broader attempt to contend with the imbalance which had developed in the make-up of the leadership and activist potential of the Zionist movement, which by and large did not reach the academic and intellectual sectors of Jewry.[10]

There is a connection between those observations on the one hand and signs of the contemporary revolt against the dominance of scientific materialism on the other hand. No connection may appear at first sight. But in the Jewish context, the search for identity and the concomitant interest in 'roots' and inheritance quickly alight upon attitudes and aspirations far older than Herzl. The secular Jew, or the Jew who is so by default of being distinctively anything else, lives on the capital of the tradition which he rejects or ignores. Anti-Semitism and ethnicity apart, he needs that tradition if he is to test his own assessment of the constituent elements of Jewishness, whatever they may be.

The Jewish academics who, by the passage of generations or through choice or indifference, are remote from any awareness of or attachment to Jewish sources and learning, are not necessarily free from predicament. They are also likely to appreciate that one result of that remoteness is that it derogates from their right to judge and, what is more important, from their capacity to do so. It is as though they are about to be lost to a civilization to which the world insists on attaching them, and from which they are themselves loath or unable to cast themselves asunder. There is a remarkable quality about many a vanishing Jew. Even in his negativism, there is often detectable the feeling for a lost vision, the sense of a moral ascendancy gone astray.

In connection with the project to which I have referred there was convened in Jerusalem in July 1982 an international conference of Jewish academics. In a striking address, Professor Ephraim Katzir declared that following the creation of the State, the second stage in the realization of what he termed 'the Zionist ideal' was 'the creation of a model type of society'. To define and clarify it was, he said, the object of the conference. He was not indulging in a euphoric utopianism. His address was concerned with nothing less than the ethical and moral foundations of the State of Israel and of Jewish distinctiveness.[11]

Anglo-Jewry has a like task within its own compass, and its academics have a like responsibility. There is a clear case for serious and sustained efforts to be made to get behind the inhibitions. The community needs its academics, just as they need the community. The time is ripe. Academic isolation would now partake of a warrantless egocentricity. The beginning of bridge-building is the awareness of mutual need and an appreciation of respective attitudes.

In 1963, an assembly of Jewish intellectuals was convened in London by the British Section of the World Jewish Congress to consider 'The Identity of the Jewish Intellectual'. It was chaired by Israel Sieff, who consistently encouraged the study of the questions posed in this paper and the collaboration of academics and laymen therein. In his introductory address, he stated:

> We have to be careful to discard scepticism as the sole guide, for it may be on occasions a corroding and dissolving element of man's faith in intellect ... Our past is always with us and it is on the fundamental values of our tradition that the fate of Jewry must depend.

He spoke not in terms of pseudo-prophecy but in the language of a practical assessment of the world as he saw it and the Jewish role therein. Jewish learning was at the root of it. Despite the many changes in mood and emphasis, the transcript of the proceedings of that conference reveals not so much an estrangement as predicaments, not so much a detachment as an anxious concern. They are a continuing state of mind. The communal leadership would do well to strengthen and multiply the dialogues, define common interests, and encourage involvement.

NOTES

1. Ernest Barker (ed.), *The Character of England* (London, 1947), p. 565.
2. For the leadership's general outlook, see Chapters 1 and 6 hereof, and Israel Finestein, 'Profile of a Community', *The Jewish Quarterly*, Vol. 30, No. 4 (Spring–Summer, 1983), p. 18.
3. S. Schechter, *Studies in Judaism* (London, 1908), 2nd series, chap. 8.
4. Cecil Roth, 'Literary Patrons in Anglo-Jewry', *Jewish Monthly* (September, 1947), p. 13.
5. C.S. Liebman, 'Dimensions of Authority in the Contemporary Jewish Community', *Jewish Journal of Sociology* (June), 1970.
6. The proceedings were published in 1964 (eds Julius Gould and Shaul Esh) and 1981 (eds V.D. Lipman and Sonia Lipman), respectively. The creation of the Association of Orthodox Jewish Scientists, Graduates and Professionals was in its own way in indication of commitment to the common good and against isolation.
7. There have been many signs in the United Kingdom since 1945 of the

recognition by government of the public benefits which accrue from attaching academics to the machinery of government. Frank Beeley, Professor of Politics at Aberdeen, has been prominent in pressing for a greater say by the country's leading social scientists in national policy-making. They are, he declared, 'anxious to defend themselves against imputations of impracticality and lack of realism … They want to demonstrate their usefulness.' Mr Bruce George, MP, one of his supporters, stated: 'There is a lot of hostility among parliamentarians who are dismissive of academics, and many academics are contemptuous of politicians.' He hoped the new movement would 'help to bridge the unbridgable', *The Times*, 2 April 1984.

8. The papers and proceedings at the impressive conference on 'The Future Leadership of British Jewry', held in London on 23 March 1980 under the auspices of the Institute of Jewish Affairs, were a valuable contribution to the examination of these questions.

9. M. Freedman, 'Great Britain', in Moshe Davis (ed.), *The Yom Kippur War: Israel and the Jewish People* (1974), pp. 163–4.

10. G. Wigoder (ed.) *Towards a Zionist Renaissance* (1982), p. 5.

11. *Ibid.*, p. 11.

4

Israel Jacobs (1775–1853), Bethel Jacobs (1812–69) and the Jewish Community of Hull*

The increasing number of Jews who entered Britain in the second half of the eighteenth century was reflected in the creation or expansion of provincial centres. Hull, as a thriving port and market town, was an attraction for itinerant tradesmen, and in due course a likely place in which to settle for them.

Hull was not only (next to London) the major point of arrival into England from the Continent, but was also rapidly developing as an important outlet to the Baltic and elsewhere for the manufacturing produce of the Midlands and the North. It progressively grew in population, estimated in 1805 to be 29,500. By 1851, that figure had more than doubled. The canals enhanced the value of the Humber to foreign trade both ways. In particular, the completion in 1816 of the trans-Pennine canal widened the area for which Hull was the most convenient port.

In 1815, there arrived in Hull the first steam packet to sail up the Humber, a herald of cheaper and quicker access to and from the Continent, which expanded both local business life and the pace of immigration into and through Hull. The building of three great docks in the city (1778, 1809 and 1829) demonstrated and facilitated her continuous rise in manufacture and trade, both coastal and export.

---

*Based on the author's paper 'The Jews in Hull between 1766 and 1880', in *Transactions of the Jewish Historical Society of England*, Vol. 35 (2000).

In some respects, Hull Jewry classically illustrates the history of provincial Anglo-Jewry. In certain ways there were also some analogies in structure and inner-tensions with the far larger and more complex community of London. Yet throughout, the Hull Jewish community had and has its own distinctive historical, geographical and social contexts.

The French Wars greatly impeded immigration. At the outbreak of war in 1793 there were probably about 40 Jewish souls, increasing to perhaps 60 by 1815. With the conclusion of the Wars in 1815, the local Jewish community grew. There was a significant increase in immigration in general into England. In July 1840, the new Hull–Selby railway linked Hull to the main lines of England, and in particular to London.

By 1780, the six or seven resident Jewish families were a group large enough to provide a regular *minyan* and sustain a regular place of worship. The first synagogue was opened towards the end of that year in Posterngate, off Market Place. The premises were a disused Roman Catholic chapel which had been sacked by a mob in 1780 in a local extension of the Gordon Riots. The site was rented from Father Howard, the Roman Catholic minister acting on behalf of his community, who found alternative premises almost immediately. The shattered building was rebuilt as a small synagogue, described in 1798 as 'neat and convenient'. Between 20 and 30 people resorted there for worship by that date.

The synagogue was in use until 1826. From 1809 there was a second congregation, comprising members of a secessionist group headed by Joseph Lyon, pawnbroker, later of High Street. The new body met in premises in Parade Row on a site later incorporated into the Junction (later Prince's) Dock, which was opened in 1829. The personal differences behind the secession persisted. Lyon died in 1812 in his fifty-seventh year. Lyon's wife was Rose, daughter of Abraham Ralph of Barnstaple, who died in 1805 after more than 40 years in business in that town, mainly as silversmith. Lyon's synagogue became the premier of the two, largely because Lyon had maintained a minister, at his own expense. Samuel Simon (sometimes Simons), the first Jewish minister in Hull, was sometimes referred to as 'rabbi'.

Lyon's defection from Posterngate and his attraction of members was a serious blow to the finances and administration of the older establishment. After his death in 1812, time healed the earlier controversies and the two congregations drew together. Both groups had always made use of the one Jewish cemetery. Lyon was one of the last to be buried there. Simon was *shochet* and *mohel*. He would not have confined his services in those capacities to the families of his own congregation. Around 1812, there was need for a new burial ground, and in May of that year trustees were nominated to find and secure new premises for a joint congregation as well as a burial site. On 5 June 1812, the trustees took a lease of a piece of ground facing the new extension of Hessle Road. In 1819, the freehold was purchased in the names of George Alexander, John Symons, Bethel Jacobs, Ephraim Jacobs and Barnard Barnard. That site continued in use until 1858, and from the start was used by both congregations.

Land for a new synagogue was found in 1825 at 7 Robinson Row and purchased freehold for the two congregations, which in 1826 amalgamated to form the Hull Hebrew Congregation. My niece, Dr Ann Bennett, has drawn my attention to a record in the Sun Fire Insurance archives that Lyon had insured his original house and shop in Blackfriargate in 1798 for £999. The insurance was transferred to his premises in High Street to which he moved later that year. His widow, Rose, continued the pawnbroking business.

Joseph Lyon, who lived in Hull for at least 20 years, acquired local fame. John Symons, whose parents knew him, wrote in his recollections that leading families in Hull had such confidence in Lyon's integrity that they would leave with him their valuables when they travelled out of town. How far this was an insurance or some other form of commercial transaction I cannot say. The description of him in the local press on his death that he was 'greatly respected' appears to have been intended as more than a formal goodwill tribute.

Progress on the construction of the new synagogue and its opening in 1826 were extensively reported in the local press. The Great Synagogue in London contributed £15 towards the cost of building, on the application for aid from Solomon Meyer and Israel Jacobs, but not before the honorary officers of the Great Synagogue were assured that the building work had begun. The effusive thanks of Meyer and Jacobs are recorded in the minutes of the Great Synagogue's Committee for 18 June 1827.

The amalgamation of 1826 was largely the work of Solomon Meyer (1766–1863) and Israel Jacobs (1773–1853), the lay heads of the older and newer synagogues, respectively. Meyer's career was characteristic of many of the early members of the local Jewish community. He was long a member of the Great Synagogue in London whose register records him as coming from Brod (Brody) and as living in Sheffield by June 1822, and thereafter in Hull. He was a travelling salesman and probably familiar with other towns in the north. He continued to register additions to his family at the Great Synagogue. His wife, Sarah, died in April 1828 and was buried in that synagogue's cemetery. He developed a business as merchant and factor in Sheffield and Hull. He and Jacobs each laid a foundation stone, paying into congregational funds £3 10s and £1 11s 6d, respectively, to mark the honour. Meyer died in Hull and was buried in the new Jewish cemetery in Hedon Road.

Israel Jacobs had lived in Hull at least since 1801. He dealt in clocks and watches and quickly established himself as jeweller, goldsmith and silversmith. By 1822, he had a branch in the fashionable Long Room Street in Scarborough, where he was referred to as 'gentleman Jacobs of Scarborough'. In his later years he lived there for most of the time. He succeeded Meyer as president of the Hull Synagogue. His wife, Sarah Barnett (1770–1853), predeceased him by a few months. Their son, Bethel (1812–69), married Esther (1810–76), daughter of Joseph Lyon. Israel Jacobs died in Scarborough on Erev Rosh Hashannah and was buried in the Hessle Road cemetery in Hull. He had become a venerable figure whose personal authority proved to be an inherited family trait in the local scene and beyond.

The principal collaborator of Meyer and Jacobs in and after 1826 was George Alexander, who served intermittently as president between 1832 and 1851. He was born in Hull in 1791, son of Shimshon Ben Zender, known as Sampson Alexander, a sealing-wax and pen-maker, who died in Hull in 1824 aged 79. His widow, Sarah, died there in 1830 and like him was buried in the Hessle Road cemetery. The Alexanders were members of the namesake family in Portsea. George Alexander was a silversmith, jeweller, and dealer in foreign coin. His son-in-law, Elias Hart, a jeweller, alternated with him as president in the 1830s and 1840s. Alexander was succeeded as president by Bethel Jacobs in 1851, and in 1859 was appointed

Rosh Hakohol, the first of three so appointed in Hull. He continued his active association with the management of the synagogue until his death in 1865 in his seventy-fifth year. The fact of his Hull birth is prominently recorded on his tombstone. His local dynasty continued through his granddaughter, Miriam Hart, who in 1854 married Solomon Cohen (1827–1907), a Sheffield-born clothier who had settled in Hull in 1850, after employment in the clothing industry in Manchester. His father, Lazarus, had been a clothes dealer in Sheffield. From 1856, Solomon was prominent in synagogal life and was soon a rising figure in the local municipality. He was elected president of the synagogue in 1868, and later combined congregational duties with holding office as Town Councillor, Guardian of the Poor, Chairman and Trustee of the Hull School Board and Chairman of the Hull and Goole Sanitary Committee. Alderman Cohen's youngest son, Dr George Alexander Cohen of Harringay, became, in 1907, the first Jew in England to be appointed coroner. The elder Cohen was the first Jewish Alderman in Hull.

In 1832, the Jews of Hull entered into fuller public view in a curious episode. James Acland was a political agitator who, at a time of pressure, in many parts of the country, for parliamentary reform, attracted increasing local attention in Hull in 1831 over his attacks in print and speech against real or imagined local abuses of power in the city. It was a part of the widespread campaigning for municipal reform which was linked with movements for the abolition of abuses in the parliamentary electoral system. In 1832, there began in Hull the hearing of evidence by a parliamentary commission on the conduct of the unreformed corporation. Acland aroused some popular passion and gained sufficient support to be elected a church-warden of the Holy Trinity Church, the extensive local parish church. Between August 1831 and July 1833, he published the *Hull Portfolio*, a weekly, in which he listed, with details, the targets of his criticisms. He seemed to have fallen from grace, and in August 1832 was convicted of criminal libel and was sentenced to a term of imprisonment, but not before he had brought into his net of attack the leaders of the local Jewish community.

Acland's fire was concentrated on the imposition of a *shechitah* tax on kosher meat. He seems to have equated the powers exercised by the rulers of the synagogue with those vested in the unreformed, close corporation of Hull. On 15 January 1832, in his weekly, in a long article entitled 'Jews' Beef', and signed 'Philo', he wrote that the tax bore heavily on poor Jews since their religion forbade them from resorting to untaxed meat, presumably from non-kosher butchers or from any dealer in kosher meat who avoided the tax burden through the use of an unauthorized *shochet*. He had been especially severe on the city corporation on account of the tolls which it had imposed or permitted; the Jewish meat tax seems to have fallen into a like category in the critic's estimation.

At that time, the only retail supplier of kosher meat in Hull was one Robert Hepple, a Christian whose shop in Market Place had a separated kosher section, the meat there being distinguished by appropriate Hebrew words. 'Poor Jews', proclaimed Philo, 'loudly declare against this offensive tax'. He cited one local Jew – he appears to have consulted only one, with the initial purpose of discovering the meaning of the Hebrew – as telling him that the local Jews were governed by a 'vestry' who, knowing well that the Jews were under the necessity of buying the marked meat, have set on it a tax of one penny per pound in spite of the fact that their 'priest' (who acted as *shochet*) had a regular salary paid out of the synagogal seat rentals of a guinea per annum each. Hepple was said to charge an extra penny per pound for himself.

Acland and his informant either knew nothing about, or took no notice of, the use made of the *shechitah* tax towards synagogal expenditure on Jewish education or the relief of Jewish indigents. Yet it is to be noted that such tax was the subject of periodic complaint within the Jewish community at large, especially when increases were imposed. It was thought that some profit remained therefrom in synagogal general funds. On 28 May 1847, the *Jewish Chronicle* bemoaned 'the unjust increase of this – to a certain extent – unavoidable tax by the congregational boards who derive an annual profit from it.' Pressures on congregational funds (with in some cases the temptation to seek to retain a reserve for contingencies) was a recurring feature, and the Hull Jewish community was no exception. The community continued to use the services of a local non-Jewish butcher. From time to time the synagogue refused to permit a Jew to open a local butcher shop in competition. In the 1860s, there were for a period two non-Jewish butcher shops serving the Jewish community.

As was his practice, Acland appended the names and occupations

117

of those under attack: George Alexander, President, silversmith; Israel Jacobs and Elias Hart, silversmiths; Isaac Daniels, hawker; Solomon Meyer, 'late pawnbroker'; and Abraham Hassan, described simply as 'Turk'. Acland demonstrated his impartiality by adding an editorial note condemning clergymen of all denominations, Christians and Jews, for their alleged sin of covetousness. Neither the congregation nor any of those named appear to have made any public response to him, It was said of him that he was the means of removing 'some local abuses' in the public life of Hull. Abraham Hassan, who may or may not have had some quality of provenance or appearance to endow him with the appellation of 'Turk', was a Hebrew teacher.

Before Nathan Marcus Adler became Chief Rabbi in 1845, the nearest authorized *shochet* to Hull, was S. Newman in Leeds.[1] It is clear from the synagogal minutes that Simon had received Adler's 'permission' to practise as a *shochet*. The context makes it plain that by that word was meant official 'authorization'. This appears to have occurred shortly after Adler's appointment. It is equally certain that Simon performed this role long before that date. In May 1863, Bethel Jacobs exchanged letters with Adler as to the need of the then local Reader and *shochet*, Ephraim Cohen, to receive training in the porging of hindquarters. Until 1860, Simon continued as the regular porger, assisted latterly by the *shochet*, one Rosenbaum. At the congregation's cost, Adler was willing to arrange for Cohen to be trained in London. It was agreed to allow Cohen to undertake the course provided that the congregation's expense was limited to £5. I have not discovered whether Cohen took the course. It is significant that Simeon Mosely, a prominent member, expressed the view that 'many members would not take hindquarters even if porged', presumably because of considerations of *kashrut*. It is also of interest that in 1863, one of the non-Jewish butchers in whose premises kosher meat was sold was replaced for tampering with seals on the kosher meat.

The pace of immigration quickened in the 1830s, especially after the enactment of free entry in 1836. The steamboat soon became a daily and cheap form of transport from continental ports. Most of the new arrivals set out from Hamburg, some from or through Holland. Most of the newcomers were from Germany or Russian Poland. Only a small proportion stayed in Hull, the others moving to London, other centres in the north, or westwards to Leeds, Bradford and Lancashire. In many cases, the objective was Liverpool, with the intention of leaving for the United States. By 1835, the Hull Jewish community comprised about 200 souls. The official register of immigrants for 1838 shows 229 arrivals for that year in Hull, among whom were between 80 and 90 Jews, of whom most settled in Hull. In addition, about ten had arrived first in Goole and had then moved to Hull. Of the 80 or 90, about 20 were described as 'merchants' (a variegated designation), 12 as 'pedlars' and ten as 'tailors'. There were some 'capmakers' and 'shoemakers'. Nearly all appeared to be single, or at least unaccompanied on arrival. Among the ten who arrived at Goole for Hull were Jacob Abrahams and Raphael David, both from Prussia and respectively tailor and hatter; Levin Isaac, described as 'rabbi' from Poland who intended to travel to Hull *en route* for America via London; Joseph Rosenberg, a 'saddler' from Poland, who expressly declared an intention to live in Hull, as did Moses Ehrenberg, silversmith. The arrivals at Goole included four wives who intended to join their husbands in Hull, three of whom were described as 'tailors' and one as a 'joiner'.

The number of Jewish names in the local directories – business and residential – doubled between 1842 and 1846. So too did the number of Jewish destitute. From about 1840, there was chronic poverty in about one quarter of the local Jewish population, including for this purpose transmigrant temporary Jewish residents. After the Continental upheavals of 1848–49, the rate of arrivals was greatly accelerated.

Side by side with the working jewellers and travelling salesmen (some of whom developed their own retail or wholesale businesses) and the capmakers and other manual workers (self-employed or otherwise), there were in Hull from the 1840s a number of substantial Jewish business houses. Israel Jacobs' son, Bethel, in addition to his large and fashionable shop at 7 Whitefriargate, had by the early 1840s a factory or workshop in the nearby Post Office Buildings and conducted an extensive business in silverware, watches and jewellery in Hull and district, and, by order, from London and Paris.

Abraham Barnett (1810–1901) at 49 Waterworks Street and later ('and Son') in Carr Lane, developed his business in clocks, fancy goods and antiques, to which expanding business his son, Barnet, succeeded. The elder Barnett was an early resident in the then socially exclusive Coltman Street, where he died. Abraham's daughter married (later Sir) Joseph Joel Duveen, a travelling salesman of enterprise who arrived in Hull from Holland in 1867 and who in due course entered into partnership with his brother-in-law. Barnet Barnett, among other roles in municipal and Jewish life in Hull, was President of the local branch of the Anglo-Jewish Association before settling in London. Duveen greatly developed the antiques business and later opened his soon famous premises in New York and in London's Oxford Street. His eldest son, Joseph (later Lord Duveen), who was born in Hull in 1869, achieved fame and fortune as the pre-eminent international art dealer of his age and was a notable philanthropist.

In 1826, the full trade description of each of George Alexander, Hart Jacob, Israel Jacobs and Julia Symons was 'goldsmith, silversmith, watch and clockmaker and jeweller'. Of the four bullion dealers in Hull at that time, two were George Alexander and Julia Symons, which may have meant no more than that they each operated a bureau de change for gold and silver coin.

Julia, daughter of S. Levy of Portsmouth, was the widow of Moses Symons, a native of Portsmouth, who died in 1823. Symons was a founder member of the Humber Lodge of Freemasons, and was in business as clock- and watchmaker, jeweller and coin dealer. Julia succeeded to the business, and in the *Hull Advertiser* on 12 August 1825 announced its continuation and asked for 'a continuance of the [public's] favours for the support [of herself] and four orphans'. She headed the family firm until 1872. It was continued after her death by her son, John, who had assisted her in the management.

John Symons (1823–1907), who was a pupil at the Hull Grammar School, began his commercial career in 1840 when he entered temporary service as a clerk in the local steamship company of Joseph Sanderson, and was first elected to the Town Council in 1863. He rose to the rank of Alderman and in 1890 was appointed, the first Jew, to be the town's Sheriff. He took special pride in his election in 1871 as a member of the Royal Irish Academy on the nomination of its President, Lord Talbot de Malahide. Symons was prominent in municipal and local Jewish congregational life for more than a generation, and his writings as antiquary and local historian were widely read locally. His contention was that there was a Jewish community in Hull in the seventeenth century, but Lucien Wolf rejected the suggestion (as did Cecil Roth later). In good conscience Symons had based himself on false 'recollections' and forgeries. Lengthy exchanges between the protagonists appeared in the *Jewish Chronicle* in April 1888 and February 1898.

In the second quarter of the nineteenth century, Isaac Lyon, described as a surgeon, lived at 24 Bishop Lane. It is tempting to think of him as related to Joseph Lyon. A contemporary was L.J. Levison, dentist, of Mason Street. They addressed the Hull Literary and Philosophical Society in the 1830s, forerunners to the series of Jews later to do so.

In 1824, Marcus Bibero was brought to Hull by his father, an immigrant pedlar from Cracow. The family (sometimes Bibro) was soon part of the synagogue membership. Marcus Bibero became a leading swimmer of world class, and by his advocacy significantly contributed to the successful movement for the municipal provision of swimming baths in Britain. Bibero, who died in 1910, was a Zionist who rallied to Herzl.

In the late 1850s, there began to enter into local communal prominence Lewis Holt (1826–1903), the German-born son of the *chazan* of Kempen in the Rhineland. He had arrived in Hull in 1847. A clock- and watchmaker, he became a travelling 'jeweller' and rose in affluence and communal influence. He lived in Porter Street and from 1872 conducted his jewellery business from premises in Midland Street. In the 1890s, he became the third member of the congregation to be accorded the title *Rosh Hakohol*. His son, Albert, continued the close connection with the synagogue. The Holt family moved to London, with branches in South Africa.

In the Hessle Road Cemetery in or about 1822, there was buried Barnard Barnard whose stone describes him as the son of 'the Rev. Rabbi Barnad of Portsea', who was sometimes known as Alexander Barnard (*d.* 1818). The families Barnard (sometimes 'Barnad') came to Hull from Portsea and Chatham and were probably interrelated. Barnard Barnard, a registered navy agent, was a coin dealer at 7 Queen Street in partnership with Moses Symons from at least 1816 until 1822. Moses Symons was likewise a registered navy agent. Lewis Lazarus of Portsea, President of the Portsmouth Synagogue and a fellow-agent, was executor both of Barnard Barnard and of

Symons.[2] In 1926, there died in Hull Birman Issachar Barnard, aged 85. He was a founding member of the Hull Western Synagogue and its Treasurer. His triple namesake lived in Chatham in the 1830s.

Ellis Davidson (1828–78), pioneer in the teaching of techniques for art study, was born in Hull. I believe his father was Abraham Davidson, surgeon chiropodist of 28 King Street in Hull in the 1830s. The family moved to London in 1838. Davidson's regular lectures to working-class audiences were regarded by the Jewish Board of Guardians in London as helpful in the promotion of apprenticeship schemes and interests outside the familiar over-crowded ranks of employment. He married Catherine, daughter of David Levy of Oxford Street, and lived in Maida Vale: *Jewish Chronicle*, 15 March 1878, and *Jewish World* of same date.

Harris Lebus (1852–1907) was long famous for his original styles of furniture and as the proprietor in London of one of the largest furniture factories in the world, with a labour force of nearly 4000. This entrepreneur was born in Hull, the son of Lewis Lebus, who arrived in Hull from Breslau in 1840. The family left Hull when Harris was a child. He was a pupil of the Jews' Free School and began business as a cabinet maker by the age of twenty.[3]

It was common for members of the synagogue to have business or family connections outside Hull. Some members lived outside Hull, or lived both in Hull and elsewhere. Hull was the Jewish religious centre for a large area, ranging from York and Scarborough to Boston and Louth in Lincolnshire across the Humber, from where Jewish families came for the High Festivals or on special family occasions. Circumcisions would be performed by the Hull *mohel*.

Of the 126 marriages in Hull between 1838 and 1870, 40 per cent of the bridegrooms were jewellers (of whatever grade or standing) and 14 per cent tailors. The proportions for the last 20 years or so of the century are in reverse, with the proportion of tailors higher, and also with an increase in the number of cabinet makers. These changes reflect the comparatively large influx of Eastern European Jews after 1881. Of the fathers of brides and bridegrooms in marriages between 1838 and 1870, of those classi-fied by trade in the marriage register, 44 were 'general dealers', 19 were 'merchants' and nine were 'travellers'. This total of 72 constitutes 40 per cent of those classified by trade. The meanings of those three categories sometimes merged into one another. The preponderant use of this description reflected in many instances the 'hawker' of the early century who had advanced economically. One detects through the century the broad changes of pattern in the local community's occupational structure. The appointment of Victor Dumoulin (1836–1921) of the mercantile firm of Gosschalk and Dumoulin (later Sheriff and Chairman of the local Chamber of Commerce and father of another Sheriff) as Turkish Vice-Consul in Hull in 1870, and later Consul for Austria, is a reminder of the Continental trading connections of a segment of the local Jewish community by that time.

In 1848, the synagogue had about 65 members, of whom eight were *ba'ale batim* (householders, or privileged members). There were in addition many resident non-members, including speedy transmigrants and short-term residents. On 'census Sabbath', namely 29 March 1851, 74 people were in attendance at the synagogue in the morning. This was nearly twice the normal attendance. By 1860, the membership stood at ninety. In the 1850s, the average number of births per year in the Hull Jewish community was 14 and the deaths five. In that decade, the number of members increased by 30. Between 1859 and 1860, the number fell from 91 to 80. By 1864, the total was 84. In 1870, the synagogue had 112 members, out of a far larger total Jewish population. The number of *ba'ale batim* in 1860 was 13, and that proportion was retained. The average intake of recent immigrants into membership was a small segment of the number of arrivals, most of whom in any event did not stay in Hull.[4] Most of the arrivals, whether they took up residence or not, remained in the category of 'strangers', some of whom would no doubt become members in time, but there was a constant (if changing) body of non-members (many in need of support, as were some members). They constituted a substantial local feature. The additional services at Festivals were more particularly intended for them, but pressure on the seating capacity in the synagogue obliged some members to resort to them.

The community was rapidly outgrowing the synagogue premises, as was seen from the start to be likely. The religious census-returns of 1851 show the total seating to be 95, of which seats 35 were classified as free. Furthermore, there were regular complaints that the premises were not wind and weatherproof. The building work of 1826 was found to have been defective. The pressing task of enlarging – in effect rebuilding – the synagogue was undertaken in 1851–52.

The new building was consecrated in September 1852, the foundation stone being laid by Israel Jacobs on 26 May. As in 1826, Simon composed a special prayer for the opening, and again the events were widely reported. Many Christians attended the consecration. It had been expected to hold the ceremony before Rosh Hashanah and it was hoped that the Chief Rabbi would attend. It would have been his first visit to a provincial community. The uncertainty of the date on which the building would be ready changed the plan. The ceremony took place shortly before Succoth at a time when Dr Adler was unable to be present, and he sent his regrets. He first visited Hull in 1869, accompanied by his son, Rabbi Dr Hermann Adler.

The movement for a new building, and the construction of it, had been under the charge of Bethel Jacobs, who by this time was a dominating influence in all matters appertaining to the congregation. The *Jewish Chronicle* described the new synagogue as being conducted on what the editor described as 'the strictly orthodox principles' of the old. A general appeal to the Anglo-Jewish community was made by way of a long, explanatory 'advertisement' in March 1851 in that newspaper, in which the burdens of the relief of the poor and the prospective cost of the building work were emphasized. Although the response to the appeal (including local contributions) was described as 'good', it was necessary to raise £600 on mortgage to finance the completion of the operation. There remained outstanding at the time some of the indebtedness incurred over the building of the old synagogue. The discharge of the latest borrowing remained a drain on congregational finances for some years.

The building committee under Jacobs' chairmanship took great care in the planning of the work, selecting from separate tenders for the different parts of the overall design of the architect. The synagogue was closely hemmed in and light came through the large glazed ceiling. The *Hull Packet* classified the internal architecture as of 'Grecian style'. The seating was of oak, and there was accommodation for 200 men and 80 ladies. A contemporary visitor described it as follows:

Interiorly it is a neat apartment lighted from the top, having a gallery along three of its sides for the female portion of the congregation. In the centre of the building is a raised platform, called the *behmah*, or reader's-stand. At the east end, beneath a handsome portico, is a kind of safe or tabernacle, called the 'holy ark' ... Above the ark is a semicircular window filled with stained glass, and one of the compartments represents the two tables of stone, having the Decalogue inscribed thereon in Hebrew characters. In front of the ark hangs the 'perpetual lamp', which was presented by Mr Simeon Mosely, as a memorial of his wife, Jesse, who died in 1852. Before the ark hangs a handsome silk veil or curtain, to which is attached a circular piece of velvet bearing a Hebrew inscription, wrought in silver thread, purporting that the veil was the gift of Mr Bethel Jacobs. The Minister delivers his discourses from a lectern on the platform of the ark.[5]

My uncle remembered the synagogue well and spoke of it, whether through pietistic nostalgia or otherwise, in tones of admiring respect. Services were held on Friday nights, Sabbath mornings and evenings, and on Monday and Thursday mornings.

Such was the rapidity of increase in the number of Jews in Hull, mainly through immigration, that the enlarged premises did not succeed, as had been hoped, in meeting requirements. The practice of holding additional services on the High Festivals in a hall outside the synagogue was resumed in the 1850s. On 18 April 1859, it was decided to alter the synagogue so as to make room for more seats for poor members at the charge of six pence. This did not relieve the wants of non-members, who outnumbered the total of members of all categories.

'No town of similar size in the kingdom', wrote the *Jewish Chronicle* on 8 September 1871, 'has a larger number of foreign Jews direct from foreign climes ...' For the High Festivals in 1875, the *Jewish World* reported that as many as 500 people attended the additional services in the hall of the Mechanics' Institute. By the mid-1870s, local adverse comment on the limited nature of the accommodation in Robinson Row grew into a regular feature of communal life and progressively increased in acidity. Procrastination was in practice encouraged by the feuds which characterized the congregation in the 1870s even more markedly than in previous years.

On his visit to Hull in May 1875, Hermann Adler urged in firm language the need for larger premises. There had already been opened in School Street a new small synagogue, or more accurately a *chevrah*, which was used principally by 'foreign Jews'. But that did not deal with the problem forcefully posed by Adler. The desire for larger premises was further fostered by the widening acknowledgement that Robinson Row was no longer in an area favoured by fashion.

Relief of the Jewish poor was never far from the centre of deliberations among the successive cadres of Jewish leadership in Hull. From the 1830s, the immigrant poor outnumbered the resident poor, and in due course expanded the ranks of the latter only to be replaced by the arrival of successive waves of immigrants. Often the number of immigrants who settled in Hull was outnumbered by those who came to Hull as transmigrants on their way elsewhere in Britain or to America. All these categories were in receipt of aid to some degree or other from private donations and/or limited sums from authorized congregational monies.

In 1847, there was formed in Hull the Society for the Relief of Distressed Foreigners. It was a non-denominational body controlled by a group of foreign merchants in Hull.[6] It was financed by voluntary contributions and seems to have been a pioneer in the provinces. No doubt some Jewish arrivals derived some relief from this body, but the Jewish community did not regard itself as relieved to any extent of the responsibility of assisting the Jewish immigrants, whether they were in Hull short-term or long-term.

In 1848, at a time of heightened immigration, there was established under the auspices of the synagogue a charity called the Gemilous Chasadim Philanthropic Society, as an instrument for the distribution of relief on some organized basis. In the following year, the Meshivas Nephesh Society was set up,[7] which was by its nature a Friendly Society. It attracted many members and provided sick benefits and other forms of contingent assistance. There was also founded the Malbish Arumim Society for the supply of clothes to 'poor children' in the local Jewish community. From time to time in the 1850s – more frequently than previously – the funds of the congregation were drawn on to help immigrants to travel on, or sometimes to return to, the Continent, or were used to meet some special circumstances. In addition, the constitution authorized the president to disburse a fixed sum each year on the relief of the poor.

There were occasions when the committee or the honorary officers invited members of the synagogue to form a special fund to assist a particular family.

From the late 1830s, the synagogue bought *matzah* for distribution among poor members. In 1859, 200 lbs of *matzah* and 20 lbs of *matzah* meal were bought for this purpose, and the quantities increased annually. Frequenters of any private *minyan* and persons who had not attended synagogue for a month before Pesach were excluded.

In 1861, encouraged by Philip Bender's advocacy, the Ladies' Hebrew Benevolent Society was created. It was governed by a group of ladies who undertook to visit the sick and contribute to a fund for medical services in confinement and at other times of need. For its members it was a Friendly Society; for non-paying beneficiaries it was a charity. Its benefits were limited to Jews of at least three months residence in Hull. The Society also founded a loan fund, insisting on inspection and enquiry before allocations or loans were advanced. Such provisions reflected the growing concern to avoid pauperization and encourage realistic self-help.

The synagogal organization of charity was mainly in the interests of members of the synagogue or resident Jews. Relief of the short-term resident, or the 'birds of passage', was often still left to individual or fortuitous charity, usually without regard to principles of self-help or the danger of pauperization. In 1880, the Hull Jewish Board of Guardians came into being, which amalgamated or took over several sets of commitment. It assisted the Jewish poor in Hull regardless of membership or length of residence. It was soon called on to aid larger numbers both of residents, new arrivals and transmigrants than Hull had ever known, while at the same time seeking to do so on an organized and realistically controlled basis.

Typical of the efforts made outside the Synagogue in the difficult times of the 1870s to succour 'the strangers', was the creation in January 1870, with the express public approval of the Chief Rabbi, of the Hull Hebrew Holy Institute, with the specific object of extending aid to them. It was inaugurated at a public dinner under the chairmanship of John Symons, attended by about 200 people. The *Jewish Chronicle* reported that after dinner, 'dancing commenced which was kept up with spirit until the early hours'. During the severe weather of November 1869, a special meeting of the synagogue was called, under Solomon Cohen's chairmanship, to solicit funds to relieve the needs of the Jewish poor, Cohen heading the subscription list. In 1872, the Jewish Soup Kitchen was opened, under the chairmanship of Israel Goldman, a glazier, for the provision of food for Sabbaths and Festivals to poor Jewish immigrants, to be followed by 1873 by the emergence of a further society directed to supply provision for Sabbaths and Festivals for 'strangers'.

An example of self-help on the part of the poorer elements in the Jewish community was the creation of the Hull Hebrew Mutual Benefit Society in the 1870s. It was a precursor of the expanding Jewish Friendly Society movement of the later decades of the century among the growing immigrant population.

The Hull Jewish community was the first in the provinces to contribute to Jews' College, probably done on Bethel Jacobs' advice. In reply to the Chief Rabbi's appeal, Jacobs wrote on 14 April 1852, as president of the congregation, that a general meeting had unanimously decided to send ten guineas to Adler's projected scheme. He added that 'the very heavy responsibility involved in the rebuilding of the synagogue and the establishment of the local Jewish school' precluded a larger donation. Jacobs expressed his regret at the absence of individual donations, for which Adler had also asked. But he sent him certain names and wrote that those gentlemen would no doubt respond to 'direct application' from the Chief Rabbi. Jacobs himself sent two guineas.

The Hull community received many requests for financial help and had great difficulty in meeting them. In November 1858, the general meeting refused to contribute to the fund for the commemoration of the admission of Jews to Parliament. The reason given was 'the large debt owed to the congregation'. This may be a misprint for 'owed by the congregation', but it could equally refer to the extent of arrears in seat rentals owed to the synagogue which was a constant source of anxiety to the committee. In April 1859, an appeal for assistance towards the building of a synagogue in Swansea was refused. In 1865, the sum of two guineas was sent towards the fund for the proposed synagogue in Sunderland – perhaps out of some sense of closeness to a sister community in the north. In April 1864, a similar request from Southampton had been refused, as was the request for aid from the Leeds congregation in 1863 in the relief of local Jewish poverty. In reply to these and similar requests, the synagogue referred to its own 'heavy liabilities'. Individuals did respond to many of these appeals, notably Bethel Jacobs, Mosely and Alexander. On some occasions, such as when Adler asked for aid for the poor Jews in Palestine in July 1854 or for Moroccan Jewry in January 1860, local collections were made. Early in that decade Joel Farbstein, later president, moved that the synagogue as such should never donate to any appeal from its funds. This counsel of despair was not accepted.

In the 1850s, members (apart from the much higher-rated *ba'ale batim*) paid an annual seat-rental which averaged about 10 shillings for each member. In 1862, income stood at £300, of which all, save the £4 10s surplus on the school account, was from seat rentals and offerings. The annual expenditure was £400. The loans contracted in 1852 and 1858 for the building-work on the synagogue and the purchase of the new cemetery had not yet been fully repaid. Near the end of 1861, a special meeting of the committee was called to consider ways and means of meeting the obligations. Only three members attended and no decisions were taken. To resolve the situation, extra efforts were made to collect rental arrears and certain charges were increased, one of which was the minimum marriage fee which was fixed in February 1864 at one and a half guineas. Seat rentals were progressively increased, fixed in 1874 in a range from £7 10s to £1 6s per annum. The fee for a wife's seat in the gallery was one guinea. There was an increasing number of cases in which, because of hardship, proportions of rentals and other charges were waived.

The Hull community was one of those which in advertisements for officials warned that applicants who attended 'for trial' or interview must pay their own expenses. The community faced difficulty in efforts to make provision for pensions for retired officials or to provide benefits in case of prolonged illness. In 1856, the congregation entered the newly formed scheme under Adler's presidency for the creation of a benefit society for the 'clergy'. And yet, on 6 August 1880, after the death of the greatly esteemed minister, Abraham Elzas, the *Jewish Chronicle* reported that his widow and children were 'quite destitute'. John Symons took a lead in raising a 'small fund' for them.

Until about 1850, Samuel Simon was the local religious factotum. For a short time Jacob Kirschbaum, talmudist and recent arrival from Cracow, was *shochet*, before leaving for Cheltenham (and later for the London Board of Shechita). When Philip Bender was appointed,[8] it was principally as second reader (hazan) and teacher. The added appointment was a burden on communal funds. In due course an additional teacher was also engaged. When Ephraim Cohen[9] was appointed in 1860, first as *shochet*, at a salary of £78 per annum, there was an appeal for voluntary donations to help pay him. Jacobs and Mosely (as was often the case) opened the list (£5 each) and a total of £22 was raised. When Elkan Epstein was appointed hazan and teacher in April 1864, his salary was £130 per annum, half of which was, on the committee's decision, to be paid from congregational funds, the remainder to come, it was hoped, from voluntary subscriptions. Immediately on this appointment, £42 was collected through such contributions, and the remainder for the first year had to be painstakingly found.

This chronic shortage of congregational funds probably reached its acutest point in July 1865, when the president felt obliged to inform the general meeting that for the time being there was no money with which to pay the teachers. I assume that the teachers' salaries were a first charge on such school fees as were paid. I take the president's announcement to mean that the synagogue at that moment lacked the means to supplement the income, such as it was, from the school fees. It is difficult to believe that the necessary supplement did not come before long from the private purses of the communal leadership. When Ephraim Cohen's weekly wage was raised in April 1863 by five shillings to £2, it was on condition that circumcision fees would be paid to him by parents (whether members or not) and not by the synagogue. If parents were too poor to pay, it is likely that the president would in his discretion pay him from synagogal funds.

The absence of Hull Jewry from the group of communities which participated in the election to the Chief Rabbinate in 1844 did not reflect any sense of independence from that office. Its influence was felt through the continuous and deep respect on the part of the succession of local Jewish leaders for the parent congregation of the Ashkenazi community in Britain. There was a readiness to abide by the discretion of the lay heads of the Great Synagogue, whose influence over the electoral conference would, it was rightly thought, be decisive.

During Solomon Hirschell's long term in office (1802–42) it was less his personal role than the fact that he was the religious head of the Great Synagogue which gave him that rank likewise over the comparatively distant community of Hull. The emergence of an Anglo-Jewish press in 1841 helped to draw the provincial Jewish communities into a greater consciousness of common Anglo-Jewish interests. The publicity it gave to debates over the criteria which might be applied in finding a successor to the outgoing Chief Rabbi would undoubtedly have been noted in Hull. Adler, especially after his post-appointment questionnaire to all Orthodox congregations in the United Kingdom and the Empire, and his subsequent publication of guidance for the direction of their congregational and educational work, acquired a visible personal role and an aura of personal authority which added significantly to the earlier accepted status of the office.

When Adler informed the Hull Hebrew Congregation of his intention to visit Hull in 1862, the local leadership was exceedingly embarrassed by the then vacancy in the offices of reader and preacher. It was felt to be unsuitable to welcome the Chief Rabbi without, in particular, a hazan for the occasion. Accordingly, Adler was invited to postpone his visit – even though he was planning a tour of Jewish communities in the North East. The tour took place, but did not include Hull. This was not the first time that a projected visit by Adler to that community did not materialize.

In November 1859, confusion and discord arose at the general meeting of the congregation over the sequence of certain portions of the liturgy. It was characteristically decided to place the difficulties before Adler. On his next visit to London, Bethel Jacobs did so in person and brought back written replies. There was no servility on the part of the congregation. When Adler had called on the community in November 1862 to raise funds for the relief of the Lancashire cotton operatives who had been rendered unemployed by the American Civil War, the Hull Hebrew Congregation responded by raising subscriptions for operatives in Hull, who as far as I know had not been as affected by the cutting off of cotton supplies to England. Local patriotism, it seems, took precedence over the Chief Rabbinical request.

The laws of the congregation, at least from the 1830s, were modelled on those of the Great Synagogue. It was governed by the president and the treasurer. There were usually two vice-presidents and a committee of seven, who, like president and treasurer, were elected by the annual general meeting of members. Past presidents and treasurers were members of the committee. Each synagogal member became entitled to vote, and not only the *ba'ale batim*. The latter alone were entitled to stand for election. The right to vote was extended to members by 1850.

The general meeting elected officers and committee from a list of nominations made partly by the outgoing committee and partly by the synagogal members at the general meeting. The effort by Bethel Jacobs in the committee in the late 1850s to limit the number of nominations made by the general meeting failed by one vote. There was some reluctance on the part of members of the committee to appear to want to limit the rights of members. Furthermore, hopeful canvassing for nomination and for office was thought to be a likely attraction to membership and thus be of benefit to revenue. Nominations from the floor were made on the day of the election and were the occasion for much disorder at meetings.

In 1853, the non-privileged members had been given the right to elect their own 'delegate' to the committee. Even in this limited form of representation, the election of one of their own number to the committee was seen as a major concession on the part of the *ba'ale batim* and the older leadership.[10] It was a modest act of prudence on their part in the face of mounting tension between themselves and the general body of members. The newer members often felt restive under the tight control of the English-speaking, middle-class, anglicized oligarchy.

General meetings were held quarterly. In addition, special meetings were called from time to time to consider the state of the school or to examine some particularly difficult communal dispute. Attendance varied according to the excitement of the time. Apart from elections, the business of the ordinary general meetings (in addition to receiving the committee's report and recommendations, especially in respect of any breaches of the rules of the congregation), would be (where necessary) to approve the appointment of officiants and officials on the committee's recommendation; to settle arrangements for Festivals (including the provision of additional services and the drawing of lots for the posts of *Chasan Torah* and *Chasan Bereshis* [*sic*]); and the airing of members' grievances, notably 'unfair' allocations of seats or *mitzvoth*.

In April 1859, Jacobs secured the appointment of a special committee to advise on such changes to the laws as may be necessary to limit the occasions for disputes. After a series of weekly meetings, some of which lasted hours, the special committee made no recommendations, presumably through lack of agreement. However, on 5 June 1859, the committee accepted a recommendation by the special group that no one was to be entitled to vote at general meetings who had not paid his seat rental for the preceding twelve months. In practice this would reduce the influence of perhaps the least well-off members. It was not a remedy for conciliation.

In April 1860, the rules were amended to increase from three to five guineas the fine for refusing the office of president if elected, and from two to three guineas the penalty for refusing the post of treasurer. If the object of those provisions was in part financial, the changes probably also reflected some concern at the unreadiness to accept the onerous tasks of the senior officers in facing the apparently habitual fractiousness of the congregation. Perhaps similar considerations lay behind the imposition earlier that year of a fine of one shilling (later raised to 1s 6d) for each absence by any member from committee meetings, unless he was out of town.

The laws of the congregation required the committee to meet monthly. This was the practice, but they met more often when circumstances required. Feelings in committee were often strongly expressed, no less than at general meetings. Not even the personal authority of Bethel Jacobs, Alexander and Mosely was always able to quell frayed tempers. Disorder was not confined to general meetings. Among the many matters which formed the committee's regular business were applications for increases of salary by synagogal officials; applications for permission to marry in the synagogue; the whole or partial writing-off of arrears in hard cases; and the prior allocation of Festival *mitzvoth*. This last point could provoke much heat. It also fell to the committee to consider allegations of favouritism in the president's allotment of and charging for seats.

One matter which occupied much time was the hearing of disputes between members of the synagogue. Such attempted adjudication was deemed by the committee to be a highly important responsibility – the object being to avoid, if possible, litigation in the Courts. One especially time-consuming episode arose from a member's allegation in 1858 that another member had slandered him. The careful minutes speak of 'depositions' and 'cross-examination'. Witnesses on both sides were heard. There is no sign that any of this was under oath, and it is unlikely to have been so. It was the committee's practice to seek a compromise and if possible an apology where appropriate, and in general to act as conciliators. It seems that the committee's decisions or guidance were generally accepted, but not always.

In the 1860s, Mosely several times sought to give up the presidency, but was persuaded to stay on. In 1863, he told his colleagues that his having to attend Court as a witness concerning a charge of assault in synagogue – having initiated it while president – was more than his self-respect could bear. He was a Town Councillor in the 1860s. A minute in the records of the Hull Watch Committee in October 1873, that ten shillings had been received from the synagogue for the attendance of two constables at the synagogue, perhaps tells a story. For some months in 1863 and 1864, Jacobs and Mosely felt it necessary to absent themselves from synagogal meetings because of persistent disorder.

How is one to explain the chronic fractiousness? The question was often asked at the time. Business rivalry may have played its part, especially in overcrowded trades. There was certainly much social distance and some personal tension between the longer-established well-to-do families and the various grades of more recent immigrants. There was also a contentious 'racial' self-consciousness between the respective groups and grades of immigrant.

One correspondent in the *Jewish Chronicle*, on 31 May 1872, signing himself J.F. of Hull – probably Joel Farbstein (1809–88) of William Street, the Polish-born local 'corn-doctor' (his term) or chiropodist and former President – referred to the dissensions in the northern Jewish communities generally. He welcomed the editorial demand for what he called 'eminent English lecturers' (by which he meant English-trained preachers). In the northern communities, he added, there was usually in each congregation 'a party or clique' in opposition to those in office. 'Circumstances', he commented, 'not character, is at fault'. 'Social difficulties', observed the editor, 'are in the way of harmony'. In May and June 1872, the journal urged the formation of groups of communities in respective regions, each group with a perambulating English preacher, who might give cohesion to disparate elements by weaving several communities into a larger whole. One such group, it was suggested, might be Hull, Sheffield and Nottingham. It is difficult to see how any such system would have touched any of the major causes or the habit of acrimony in Hull. A frequent visitor to Hull, writing on 28 June 1878 about the 'racial groupings' in Hull Jewry, observed that 'the Germans' look down on and mistrust 'the Russians', and the 'English' think 'they are superior to all foreigners'. He added significantly: 'the English portion ... seldom attend the synagogue'.

Sharp contests for office or committee, and heavy canvassing, proceeded in the 1850s with an enthusiasm which led the *Jewish Chronicle* to comment admiringly on the keenness of interest shown by the Jews of Hull in the conduct of their public affairs. This euphemism wore increasingly thin as acrimony advanced as a feature of local communal life. In 1853–54, at the time of unrest in some sections of Anglo-Jewry over the exclusion from the Board of Deputies of four Reformers elected to it by Orthodox synagogues, the dispute was especially acute in Hull. It seemed to bring forward in Hull some resentments of long standing.

The first representative of the Hull congregation on the Board was Solomon Meyer's son, Meyer Meyer (1814–80), a London merchant living in Sion House in Clapton (adjoining the comparatively new residential area of Stamford Hill), and later of Gordon Square. Meyer had been unanimously elected by the congregation in 1852. While knowing of the strong local feeling in favour of exclusion, he voted in favour of admitting the four to the Board, which was evenly divided on the issue. The division was resolved by the casting vote of the president, Sir Moses Montefiore, against division.[11]

The committee of the Hull synagogue, in an anxious debate on the question, voted by five votes to three in support of exclusion and by notice in the Jewish press repudiated Meyer's action. The majority stated their view that members of Reform were 'not qualified' to represent Orthodox congregations. Meyer publicly responded to the public announcement of the committee's vote by asserting his right to act in accordance with his conscience. He did not regard membership of the Reform Synagogue as a departure from the Jewish community; nor did he treat the fact that the Board deemed the Chief Rabbi to be its religious authority to be a justification for excluding a properly elected Deputy from serving on the Board.[12] He did not resign, as did Sir David Salomons, in a like position in regard to the New Synagogue in London. Had he offered his resignation it would probably have been accepted by the committee and the majority of the general meeting in Hull (unlike the reaction of the New Synagogue).[13]

For some time, Meyer's example was long cited in local communal debate with contentious approval or dismay. The preferred attachment of the synagogue to the jurisdiction of the Chief Rabbi had, however marginally, come under debate. Related to it locally was the continuing and sharper questioning of anything resembling patrician highhandedness. The Meyer affair had not been forgotten when a separate, but not wholly dissimilar, issue arose in 1856 to disturb the already uneven tenor of congregational life.

A small, dissenting congregation arose which sought to place itself under the religious guidance of Rabbi Solomon Schiller-Szinessy of Manchester. This short-lived secession of mainly Jews of recent arrival was as much personal as doctrinal, if doctrinal at all. That rabbi's estrangement from the Old Hebrew Congregation in Manchester and his acceptance of the ministry of the newly formed Manchester Reform Synagogue did not deter the seceders from the adoption of his religious headship, a status which he sought to confirm by assuming the title of Chief Rabbi of his two congregations, namely Manchester Reform and the new group in Hull. These events, with their wider implications for the communal structure and the status of Dr Adler, aroused the anxiety and the heightened anger of Bethel Jacobs, then president of his congregation.[14] Whatever the wider perspective, the dispute locally had more to do with a reaction against local oligarchic communal control.

The synagogal minute book of the early 1860s is good evidence of the inner turmoil. In 1863 and 1864, there is a record of the succession of prominent figures who declined to accept nomination for office. While Farbstein appears to have changed his mind about accepting nomination as president, it would seem he was elected before he had announced his change of mind. Some thought he was not properly a candidate. That was the opinion of a long-standing critic, Lewis Marks (1816–96), silversmith of 31 Waterworks Streets, who aspired to that office. With his friends, he did not regard Farbstein as president. Marks had been treasurer and expected the reversion. He said he was ready to give way only to certain named people, including Jacobs and Mosely. They repeated their intention not to stand. The minutes record that 'Mr Jacobs and some other members left the meeting' and that 'only a few voted'. At the outset of the meeting, 55 attended. The minutes were signed as correct by Farbstein as 'President'. It was later contended that in any event, among those who voted were some who, because of arrears, were not entitled to vote.

On 3 March 1865, the *Hull Packet* scathingly referred to the ongoing quarrel over whether Farbstein was legally elected to office. This largely personal dispute lay behind the grievous controversy a few months later over the manner of burial of a child (still-born?) and the later disinterment of the body (under the auspices of Marks, a relative) and its reburial in Sheffield. The lengthy Court proceedings which followed these events attracted wide publicity.

The editor commented as follows:

> Years ago, when the Jews of Hull were but a scanty and needy band, the representative men ... were really what they appeared, the leaders ... and the supporters of their humbler brethren ... But as steamers multiplied ... the ranks of the Jews in our town became more and more crowded by foreigners, who were less needy and more independent than the humble Jews who had so long meekly bowed the head to the half-dozen resident representative Hebrews who had always sat in the high places of the synagogue. Years ago the revolt began. First there was a whisper of disaffection; then open resistance ...

This over-dramatic and generalized language ignored the many cross-currents of opinion within local Jewish opinion. The *Packet* questionably suggested that the 'old ruling representative Jews' backed Marks. There is little doubt that most members favoured Farbstein. But the editor had touched on a feature of local Jewish life whose underlying role in communal debate was to become yet more marked. Such a feature was not limited to Hull, but it was rifer there than elsewhere because of the sharper local pressure of immigration in relation to the numbers of the longer resident, and the different traditions with which they were respectively familiar.

One practice in the synagogue which was thought irksome by some, I think rightly, was the long *misheberach* required by many of those who were accorded *mitsvoth* on Sabbaths and Festivals. The protracted blessings which accompanied the individual donations announced on those occasions were conducive to impatience, indiscipline and frayed tempers. On his visit to Hull in 1875, Adler urged their abridgement, describing the prolix procedure as 'almost unendurable'. The honorary officers were loath to interfere with a useful source of synagogal revenue.

Enhancing the effects of such combinations of circumstances and motives, there was in some quarters a sense of alienation from the London-oriented congregation of Hull. The Chief Rabbi's regulations for the conduct of services were received in Hull in 1847 as by other congregations within his jurisdiction. Whether formally adopted or not, they were certainly a powerful source of guidance. While these provisions, which urged the cultivation of solemnity, may not in this fractious community have been implemented in practice, the regulations, together with the laws of the congregation, gave some religious and constitutional sanction for adherence to the entrenched forms of leadership. In the age of large immigration and different incoming traditions, this made for friction, disaffection, 'personalities' and unrest.

There were several instances (of the kind painfully spoken of by Mosely) in the 1860s and 1870s when scuffles and assaults in the synagogue led parties to be summoned before the Hull Stipendiary Magistrates.[15] The usual result of conviction was for one or both parties to be bound over to keep the peace. Squabbles over seating arrangements (in a synagogue of only limited capacity for the numbers who sometimes attended) were among the causes for disturbance. In spite of reports in the local and Jewish press of the Court proceedings, and notwithstanding pleas by the Chief Rabbi, the Secretary of the Board of Deputies and the Magistrates, there seemed to have been an incorrigibility within some elements of the local community in the proclivity to disorder.

The cause of the emergence of another separate *minyan* in 1858 was neither doctrinal nor related to seating arrangements. It sprang from personal antipathies which were aggravated by the president's refusal to allow one of the disaffected group to be called up to the reading of the Torah on the anniversary of the death of his parent in accordance with recognized practice. The proffered reason for this exclusion was that the member on the comparable occasion in the previous year had failed to 'make an offering' to the synagogue in accordance with equally recognized practice. The exclusion was regarded as an affront to those who cared about decent synagogal behaviour. The instigators of the separate *minyan* were Jacob Alper, a Polish immigrant of 1846 and a travelling 'jeweller', and George Tickton, a working jeweller and, it seems, a gentleman of known irascible temperament.

The *minyan* met in the home of Jacob Friedman, Tickton's father-in-law. Despite being sent copies of the laws to remind them of the penalties attached to the holding of a separate *minyan*, the 'secession' continued. The threat of fines did not deter. The *minyan* now met in Tickton's home. As a warning at large, the committee sent a copy of the relevant laws, setting out the penalties, to every member of the synagogue. In December 1858, Alper appeared before the committee and recounted his personal complaint. He found no support. The *minyan* had procured a Torah Scroll (for use during their services) which appears to have been the property of the synagogue. Its retention was especially galling to the committee. Later that month, despite Bethel Jacobs' suggestion that the recalcitrant members should be given a further warning, the committee decided to withdraw membership and its rights from the offenders.

This was a substantial sanction, since membership included the right to send children to the school. Membership also freed members from liability to pay certain levies borne by non-members, including at that time an extra charge for the purchase of meat and poultry, and a special fee (£5, unless the president agreed a lesser sum) for burial in the higher and therefore more favoured ground. Expulsion from membership also involved a degree of social ostracism. It was decided that any person who buys meat or poultry for any of the seceders should be fined £1.

The committee viewed a separate *minyan* not only as hurtful to congregational pride and by definition wrong as a breach of authority, but also as a threat to congregational finances, the upkeep of education and poor relief, maintenance of the fabric of the premises and the discharge of the congregational indebtedness.

The committee demanded not only an end of the separation, but also, on the part of the leaders of it, written applications for renewal of membership. The quarrel smouldered for more than a year before the separatists returned to the fold. Some of them were to hold high office in the synagogue. Alper rose far in 'respectability', and by his death in 1896 had been elected president of the congregation seven times and was the second member to be appointed Rosh Hakohol.

The first published contemporary reference to a Jewish school in Hull to the best of my knowledge is in William White's *Hull Directory* for 1838. It is clear that Jewish schooling existed before that date, probably in a room attached to the synagogue of 1826, and in any event there was also available private tuition. Samuel Simon was the first teacher. Among his private pupils was Bethel Jacobs. Another private teacher was Abraham Hassan. The school of 1838 was a free school, catering for the Jewish education of the poor. With the expansion of the local community in the 1840s, there was felt to be a pressing need for extra accommodation and for a teacher in addition to Simon. An important part of the rebuilding of the synagogue premises in 1852 was the provision of such additional space. It took the form of a large school-room over the porch and was described in the local press as incorporated into the design for 'the better instruction of the poor scholars'. It was commended by the *Jewish Chronicle* as a 'capacious room'. In October 1852, the *Jewish Chronicle* reported that 40 children were taught there without charge (or at a nominal rate), paid for by the Hull 'Hebrew Education Society'. The Board of Deputies' returns indicate that in that year there were 15 boys and 14 girls in attendance, with two teachers. These varying calculations reflect in part the varying attendances, perhaps especially in the girls' section.

The education was under the control of the committee which called itself the Hull Hebrew Educational Society. Its membership coincided largely with the ruling body of the synagogue, whose constitutional connection with the society was at that time vague. The school was limited to the children of members. During the disputes of 1858–59, the children of the 'disfranchised' members were discharged from the school.

Teaching at the school was an integral part of the minister's task. Philip Bender, who was appointed in 1850, had soon urged the need for more accommodation and additional staff, and called for the school to be placed directly under the synagogue's authority. This last request was granted in June 1859, whereby issues came more readily within the ultimate purview of the general meeting of members. It was part of the response of the older leadership to the advance of a more self-conscious 'democratic' spirit – not confined to the Hull scene, Jewish or otherwise.

It was also laid down that as long as there was only one teacher, 25 children at most should be accommodated in the school. This reflected a desire for more effective tuition, which was part of Bender's aspiration, even though such policy could deprive other children of education in the school. It was hoped that the new policy would stimulate the search for and the appointment of additional staff. In reality, the restriction to 25 children was not adhered to. Limited congregational finances was one of the reasons for confining the school to one teacher – and he the minister. In an expanding community, the policy was from the start unrealistic and invidious. Early in 1860, there were 39 children in one class in the one room, including 25 boys and 14 girls, with one teacher. It was not until the end of that year that an assistant teacher was appointed and a second class formed.

In the reorganization of June 1859, it was stipulated that the minimum payment per child was to be three pence per week and that, subject to this minimum, the school committee should be entitled to arrange charges with the parents. In that year, it was decided that school arrears were to be considered, like the five shillings circumcision fee, as part of synagogal arrears and, as with synagogal arrears, the committee should have the right to write them off or negotiate reductions in special cases.

These changes reflected Bender's thinking and enterprise. The school committee had confidence in his judgement. In 1860 the committee, as a complimentary gesture, voted £5 for the school (presumably from synagogal funds) to be expended at Bender's discretion, and in 1861 bought library tickets from congregational funds for Bender's personal use.

The continuing pressure of expanding numbers had led Bender to propose – as a desperate measure – that while the boys should continue to be taught daily, the girls should attend during separate hours twice weekly, Monday and Friday. The proposal was not particularly attractive. It was adopted for a short time, but did not prove to offer any remedy, and in any case was rightly felt to be discriminatory. It was decided in August 1861 that no boy under the age of five, nor any girl under the age of six, should be admitted. In 1863, there were 35 boys, It was decided that if at least 12 girls attended, Wednesday afternoons would be devoted to their education. The incipient movement for a separate school for girls gained strength.

A separate girls' school was indeed established in that year, but it attracted few pupils and lapsed. On his visit to Hull in 1869, the Chief Rabbi called for its restoration, and in 1872, Adler's request was met by the setting up of the desired school. Mrs B.S. Jacobs, Bethel Jacobs' daughter-in-law, had been the principal mover and was president, following the example of Mrs Bethel Jacobs who had played the leading role in the scheme of 1863. In the 1870s, among the honorary teachers were young ladies of the Jacobs and Mosely families. From a roll of 11 girls at the start, the total by 1890 exceeded 130. The school had by then been placed under government inspection, and by the end of the century 200 girls were in attendance.

Meanwhile, the boys' school in the synagogue had undergone reorganization. From 1862, free pupils were now to meet for tuition at a separate time. The minimum age for entry to the school was fixed at six. For boys aged over ten the charge was to be a minimum of six pence per week. Girls over the age of ten were to pay one shilling. Hours of tuition were extended to five and a half each day, from 9 am, except that on Friday and Sunday tuition was limited to three hours. For girls whose parents wanted them to have Hebrew instruction only, special hours were appointed at a reduced fee. A school fund was set up, by voluntary subscriptions from members of the synagogue, to pay the fees in respect of the poor, but it was decided that even the poorest were to contribute at least a penny per week per child.

There was emphasis on the children's cleanliness. Teachers were authorized to inform the president at short notice of any case falling short of an acceptable standard of cleanliness and he was empowered to send a child home for the day in a proper case. The visitors committee was expected to attend at least weekly.

The succession of teachers after Simon's formal retirement largely comprised the procession of 'ministers' to the congregation. Standards of teaching varied and were often inconsequential to the appointments. Sometimes those who taught would have been appointed principally as *hazanim* (under whatever title) or as *hazanim*-preachers (whether called readers or ministers). Sometimes the search would be mainly for a teacher (or an assistant teacher) who would be required to perform other 'ministerial' role(s), such as the reading of the Torah or the conduct of the additional High Holidays services. The *shochet* or *mohel* (whatever other roles he might assume) might also be expected to teach or assist in the school.

In the early 1850s, Benjamin Jacobs was a short-term assistant reader and teacher. Ephraim Cohen came to Hull from Leeds in October 1860 after an 11-years' ministry in Leeds where, according to the *Jewish Chronicle* at the time of his move, he had 'furthered Hebrew education among the youth'. He was reader and *shochet* as well as a teacher, and later became the 'minister', including preaching in his remit. In the school he was assisted by one Smith, described as a Hebrew teacher. Henry Davis Marks, Meyer Elkin and Elkan Epstein served successively as ministers. There was some local pride concerning Epstein in his capacity as reader, in that he was once a cantorial pupil of the celebrated hazan and composer, Salomon Sulzer of Vienna. He was appointed in April 1864 at an annual salary of £130. Characteristic short-term appointments in the school were those of one Lindner (who came to Hull from Bristol) in the mid-1850s; Rosenbaum, who was *shochet* and *mohel* between 1858 and 1861 at 25s per week (as well as in receipt of a special payment for Yom Kippur services); and one Goldschmidt, who served as hazan and occasional preacher in the early 1860s. Their role in the school seems to have been markedly incidental to their 'ministerial' duties.

From the beginning, the Jewish school provided both Hebrew and secular teaching. The Board of Deputies' Educational Return of 1853 indicates that the subjects taught at the school were 'the elements of Hebrew, English and arithmetic'. From reports of the annual public examinations – sometimes bi-annual – this description appears too narrow. Probably the curriculum was extended and applied fitfully, with its scope and effect depending on the number of teachers available from time to time and their knowledge and methods. Certainly, ten years after the Board's report, the subjects included Bible, Hebrew grammar, 'the catechism', geography and arithmetic.

Teachers found much difficulty in handling a group of forty children of different ages and standards with only spasmodic assistance. In Abraham Jacobs, who came to Hull in 1866, the school acquired a teacher of Bender's capacity. Jacobs' appointment followed the recommendation by Moses Angel, head of the Jews' Free School in London. At a special general meeting of the synagogue in May 1864, convened to consider the state of the school, the uppermost idea was that, given the right teacher, standards would significantly improve. It was at that meeting that it was decided to elicit a recommendation from Angel.

There seems to have been little thought given to the benefit that might accrue from having more than one class, reflecting different levels of age, attainment and capacity. Special importance was attached to ensuring the effective teaching of fluent English and a knowledge of English grammar. The committee turned to Angel for help in finding a teacher well equipped to teach in those fields and who would also be a teacher of Hebrew and religion. Under Abraham Jacobs, standards appeared to improve. Discipline in school certainly did.

It is difficult to assess the Jewish and general education standards achieved in the school over the years. There were periodic inspections by individuals from London, including Simeon Singer, by prominent provincial ministerial figures, including George Emanuel of Birmingham, and sometimes by senior lay members of the congregation. Inspections usually consisted of, or included, the public examinations of pupils. Generally the reports spoke well of the standards of performance, but how far this reflected the generality of standards among the pupils as a whole is not clear. In 1863, a synagogue choir was recruited from the boys' school, with adults added. Henri Hartog, member of the synagogue and a music teacher, initiated the plan and undertook the training.

The establishment of municipal schools following the Education Act of 1870 drew a number of pupils away from Jewish schools. Concern over standards at the Jewish boys' school led a group of local Jews to open a boys' school outside the synagogue premises in 1871, offering a wider curriculum and aiming to instil a higher appreciation of the Jewish content of the schooling. The curriculum included not only Hebrew reading and religious knowledge, but translation of the Bible and prayers, and Hebrew writing.

In 1871, Abraham Elzas, then of Leeds, was appointed minister and teacher in Hull and became the superintendent of the local Jewish schools. This Dutch-born scholar arrived in England in 1867 at the age of 32. His translation of several books of the Bible in the 1870s and his notes thereon attracted wide attention among Jews and Christians. His annotated translation of the Minor Prophets (so called) was described by the *Jewish Chronicle* on 6 June 1873 as 'marking the commencement of a new period in the hitherto sluggish flow of Anglo-Jewish literary interest'. Each of his works was the subject of lengthy comment in the local press. Under his superintendence the Jewish schools advanced, but the draw of the new, and soon free, 'Board' schools affected the numbers who attended.

Abraham Elzas' tenure as minister, teacher and supervisor of the schools and classes gave him in practice freer rein than was enjoyed by his predecessors in the sphere of education. In addition to teaching in the boys' school, he taught Hebrew studies (on Sundays) in the girls' school: in charge of the latter school was Miss Jones, a Christian lady. He had more time and opportunity to deploy his pedagogic skills and enthusiasm than was formerly made available, and over a wider range of pupils. This state of affairs was facilitated by the presence of the series of incumbents in communal posts during his time: David Rosenthal who was *shochet*, *mohel*, assistant hazan and occasional preacher in the early 1870s; one B. Grossbaum, who was teacher and assistant hazan in the mid-1870s, as well as performing ministerial duties both for the Robinson Row congrgation and at the School Street Synagogue on its inception; and in particular Jacob Furst, the Vilna-trained, Courland-born *hazan* who served (mainly as reader) from 1870 until he left for Middlesborough in 1878, moving to Edinburgh in 1879.

By the time Hermann Adler visited Hull over the weekend of 21 May 1875, there was one Jewish boys' school. It was housed in West Street with about 45 pupils. The girls' school was housed in the vestry room adjoining the synagogue with about 35 pupils. Adler conducted a 'lengthy and severe' examination in the boys' school in 'Hebrew subjects', the three Rs, English grammar, history and geography. He pronounced himself 'satisfied'. He also carried out an examination in the girls' school. Again, the answer to the question as to the standards of Jewish knowledge reached by the boys and girls remains elusive.

Parents were expected to provide their children with the necessary books. Occasionally, private gifts of books were made for children's use at the schools. Adler allotted a grant from his fund raised for such purposes and undertook to ensure that Bibles would be sent by the Jewish Association for the Diffusion of Religious Knowledge. The problem of providing adequately qualified teachers was not resolved. Ill-health compelled Elzas to retire in 1876, and in 1880 he died in Hull.

Herman Bush, 'jeweller' and watch-maker, was the honorary secretary of the synagogue. He had an enthusiasm for education, especially vocational training. In 1878, he effected a significant improvement. The more advanced or gifted pupils were to be given the opportunity of more serious study, instead of being retained at standards of the less able or keen. In 1873, 'religious discourses' to children after the Sabbath morning services had been introduced. Later, David Fay, the minister, opened a 'congregational Sabbath school' in the synagogue. Fay, a former pupil and teacher at the Jews' Free School in London and a graduate of University College London and Jews' College, left Hull in 1883 to become minister at the Central Synagogue in succession to A.L. Green. In addition, private 'religious classes' were inaugurated by Louis Grouse, a former student of Jews' College. These developments may be said to herald the age of the 'synagogue-classes' system of Jewish education in Hull and the private *heder* forms of instruction for those who wished it, which systems succeeded to the variety of heirs to the school where Samuel Simon was once the teacher. The Jewish girls' school continued in Hull far into the twentieth century, and the present writer's sister was a pupil there under the long-lived and locally celebrated headteacher, Miss Annie Sheinrog.

In 1833, 650 Christians in Hull signed the national petition in favour of the current Jewish Emancipation Bill, organized by Barnard Van Oven. It was also signed by 28 Hull Jews. The general political tone in Hull reflected the strength of the Nonconformists in the life and commerce of the city and the growing local preference for parliamentary reform and free trade. This political atmosphere was favourable to the Jewish cause. After the Reform Act of 1832, the Members of Parliament elected in Hull were often protagonists of the successive emancipation bills and sometimes in the van of the movement. Notable among them were the prominent free trader, Sir William Hutt, MP for 42 years, first for Hull (1832–41) and then for Gateshead; Colonel T.P. Thompson, a Benthamite

1. Alexander Altmann (1906–87), Alice Holz Studios; from *Institute of Jewish Studies, 1954–94* (London: University College, 1994).

2. L.L. Bakstansky (far right) outside the London office of the World Zionist Organization, 77 Great Russell Street, in 1945. His two companions are (from the right) Professor Namier and Moshe Sharett. Taken from, Julia Namier, *Lewis Namier* (Oxford: OUP, 1971).

3. (Right) Isaiah Berlin (1909–97), with Professor Albert Neuberger at the Meeting of the British Friends of the Hebrew University in 1978, from *The Jewish Chronicle*, 1978.

4. Rabbi Hugo Gryn (1930–96). From Anne Kershen and Jonathan Romain, *Tradition and Change: A History of Reform Judaism in Britain, 1840–1995* (London: Vallentine Mitchell, 1995).

5. Armin Krausz, from Armin Krausz, *Sheffield Jewry* (1980).

6. V.D. Lipman (1921–90), from *Transactions of the Jewish Historical Society of England*, 31 (1990).

7. Lilian Montagu (1873–1963), a founder of the Liberal Synagogue and prominent social worker. Photograph from *The Jewish Chronicle*, reproduced from Chaim Bermant, *The Cousinhood* (1971).

8. Sir Moses Montefiore, illustration from 1878, reproduced from Moshe Davis, *Sir Moses Montefiore: American Jewry Ideal* (Cincinnati, OH: American Jewish Archives, 1985).

9. Levi Gertner (1908–76), Jewish educationalist and prolific organizer of Hebrew seminars, and from 1954 Director of the Zionist Day School Movement. Reproduced from Rabbi Dr Albert Friedlander and F.S. Worms (eds), *Meir Gertner: An Anthology* (London: Jewish Book Council, 1978).

10. Miriam Moses being installed as the Mayor of Stepney, 1932, from A. Shapiro and M. Shapiro (eds), *Jewish East End* (London: Springboard Education Trust, 1996). Second from right: Barnett (later Lord) Janner, Liberal MP for Whitechapel.

12. Rebecca Sieff addressing the 1945 Federation of Women Zionists Conference, from *Golden Jubilee Volume of the Federation of Women Zionists* (London: Federation of Women Zionists, 1978).

11. Rabbi Kopul Rosen (1914–62), from Cyril Domb (ed.), *Memoirs of Kopul Rosen* (Carmel College, 1970).

13. Sir Leon Simon (1881–1965), at the age of 35, from Barnett Litvinoff (ed.), *Letters and Papers of Chaim Wiezmann*, Vol. 6 (Jerusalem: Israel Universities Press, 1974).

14. Lucien Wolf. The original caricature appeared in the *Daily Graphic*; reproduced from Stuart A. Cohen, *English Zionists and British Jews: The Communal Politics of Anglo-Jewry, 1895–1920* (Princeton, NJ: Princeton University Press, 1982).

15. Israel Zangwill, from a portrait in *Vanity Fair* (1897), courtesy of Mr Harry Schwab, London.

16. Professor Brodetsky in academic dress at the opening of the Weizmann Institute of Science, Rehovot, 1949. Reproduced from Selig Brodetsky, *Memoirs: From Ghetto to Israel* (London: Weidenfeld & Nicolson, 1960).

17. Dr Abraham Cohen, distinguished Jewish scholar, and Minister of the Birmingham Hebrew Congregation, 1913–49. President of the Board of Deputies of British Jews, 1949–55. Reproduced from A.N. Newman, *History of the Board of Deputies* (London: Board of Deputies of British Jews, 1960).

1921 - 1999

18. Rabbi Dr Lord Jakobovits (1921–99), Chief Rabbi of the United Hebrew Congregations of the Commonwealth, 1967–91. Reproduced from the memorial service brochure (1999).

Radical, who sat for Hull from 1835 to 1837;[16] his son, Alderman Thomas Thompson, Mayor of Hull in 1841 and 1857, who was appointed Austrian Vice-Consul in Hull on the recommendation of his friend, Lionel de Rothschild; Matthew Talbot Baines, son of the influential owner of the liberal *Leeds Mercury*, who was the Recorder of Hull and then an MP for Hull (1847–52); and James Clay, son of a merchant family in the City of London and a life-long friend of Disraeli, notwithstanding political differences. Bethel Jacobs was one of the electors who signed the request to Baines in 1847 to accept nomination. Baines and Clay were among the Christians who contributed to the cost of rebuilding the synagogue in 1852.

After the establishment in the 1830s of the Hull Reform Association, Hull was one of the centres of reformist activity. The Anglican vote was divided on the issue. When Daniel O'Connell visited Hull in April 1836, he was officially greeted by the mayor amidst a tumultuous welcome – a marked difference from the attitude of a section of the populace in 1780. When the Corn Laws were repealed in 1846, church bells rang and the shops were closed as for a festival. Richard Cobden and John Bright had long been local heroes, whose visits to Hull were received with popular acclamation.

The considerable involvement of Jews in the municipal life of Hull in the twentieth century began with the election of Henry Feldman (1855–1910), woollen merchant and a founder member of the Western Synagogue, as mayor in 1906, the first Jew to hold that office in Hull. He was twice re-elected. Feldman was in the tradition of Aldermen Solomon Cohen and John Symons in the closing decades of the nineteenth century, who themselves followed in the paths set in the generation of Bethel Jacobs. In politics Feldman was a Unionist. Although prejudice was alive and from time to time overt, it was not the principal current of local opinion. More common and much to the fore were outward signs of harmonious relations between Jews and Christians in Jacobs' lifetime; that social image was transmitted, and it formed part of the background to the later local scene.

Feldman's father, Aaron, a 'jeweller', served, like Henry later, as president of the synagogue. He married in Hull in 1853, and was the son of a 'trader' whose wife was Rachel Harris. Rachel's father,

Nathan Harris, had been born in Lithuania. He was a talmudical scholar of high repute, popularly known in Hull as Reb Nahum, and the centre of informal talmudic study circles successively over a generation. He died in his mid-eighties in 1880. This grandfather of Henry Feldman represented, and was a progenitor of, a tradition in that city of a coterie of informal adult (though not always exclusively adult) talmudic study. It preceded the influx of Eastern European Jews from 1881, but was thereafter strengthened by the greater number of interested persons, and the enthusiasm which developed under the influence of men of considerable yeshivah training (such as Reb Nahum), who had made their way to Hull. This practice was not in the mainstream of the life of the local Jewish community, but it was in its time a significant leaven to Jewish education among the albeit limited number of participants and made a contribution to the consciousness, within the local Jewish community generally, of the *mores* and spirit which had been a marked feature of the European communities from which most of them had sprung. Yiddish was the usual language of communication in the coterie(s). Israel Levy (London-born son of Reb Aron, a member of Solomon Hirschell's Beth Din and former Secretary of Jews' College) was the minister of the Hull Hebrew Congregation from 1881, and thereafter of the Western Synagogue. He was likely to have been, in both successive offices, a senior participant in such talmudic circles. This did not preclude his delivering notable English sermons.

The evangelical wing of the Anglican Church was strong in Hull, indirectly stimulated by the growth in numbers and enthusiasm of the Nonconformists. In 1820, Hull had both the second-largest Methodist chapel and the largest parish church in the country. The true founder of the evangelical fervour in the city was Joseph Milner, who died in 1797. As headmaster of the Hull Grammar School, an historian of the Church and in particular as a highly popular preacher, he contributed greatly to the atmosphere in which the conversionist spirit grew. His main ally was his friend Sir William Wilberforce, the city's most eminent figure and a Member of Parliament for Hull. In 1810, a local committee of the newly formed London Society for the Promotion of Christianity among the Jews was formed, with Wilberforce as vice-president. His fellow-Member of Parliament for Hull, Thomas Thompson, a leading local banker, joined the group, which within a year had twenty-five subscribers.

Those Jews in Hull who were active in the city's public life, while welcoming the Judeophile stance of such local personalities, did not conceal their concern over conversionist attitudes and advocacy. It is of interest that Bethel Jacobs, who was especially involved in many facets of the cultural life of Hull, did not involve himself with that fifteenth-century Christian foundation, the much-esteemed Hull Grammar School.

Christian missionaries not surprisingly paid particular attention to Hull. In his *Guide to Hull* (1827), William White lists four missionary societies, including one Methodist and one Baptist. The areas of disembarkation and their environs would be visited. Conversionist literature (often in German, Yiddish or Hebrew) would naturally be among the wares which they sought to distribute. The efforts were not limited to recent immigrants. The London Society (under Anglican auspices) and the British Society for the Propagation of the Gospel among the Jews (founded under the Nonconformists) would periodically send their agents. Their journals (the *Jewish Herald* and *Jewish Messenger*, respectively) published reports on the Hull scene and the agents' work. The better-known visiting conversionist preachers addressed crowded local meetings – crowded, that is, with Christians – and their speeches were usually extensively reported in the local press. Funds were raised for the parent bodies in London.

The journals referred to the difficulty of getting a hearing once the immigrant had been made to feel as part, or prospectively so, of the local Jewish community. Among some Christians there was concern that the agents' activities seemed directed more to fund-raising than to active conversionism.

The private and public hostility towards the missionaries on the part of the local Jewish leaders was manifest. Most of the missionaries were converted Jews. In the synagogal minutes for the late 1850s, there is anxious reference to the pending conversion of the son of a member and to countervailing efforts by family and others. The outcome is not disclosed, but one has the impression that the conversion went ahead.[17] 'Most of the foreign Jews who are met with in Hull', wrote H.C. Reichardt and J. Skolkowski, missionaries, in the *Jewish Herald* in January 1850, 'have not yet been in any other part of the country, so that they have not yet assumed that unsatisfactory character which a missionary often meets with'. A telling comment.

Prominent among the popular preachers was Joseph Woolf, son of a Prussian rabbi, who, after a period as a Roman Catholic, joined the Anglican Church in 1819 and was much admired by its evangelical wing. In 1826, he raised £150 in Hull for the funds of the London Society, and later gained much fame as a missionary in the East. In the 1830s and 1840s William Ayerst, a literary figure and editor of the *Jewish Intelligence*, was among the agents in Hull for the British Society. One of his essays has an especially significant title: 'Jewish Attachment to the Sacred Literature Unabated by Poverty and Suffering'. If by 'the Sacred Literature' he meant what he called the Old Testament, his remark acknowledges the difficulties faced by the conversionists. He may by the same token have regarded the continuing attachment as offering the missionaries some groundwork for their advocacy of the 'successionist' faith. By contrast, the *Jewish Herald* in April 1852, no doubt in reference to a different layer of Jewish society, commented: 'is it not encouraging to learn that they [Jews] are losing confidence in their own traditions and consequently are the more open to instruction from the oracles of God?'

In his *High Street Hull* (1862), John Symons calculated that more than £7,500 had been contributed by citizens of Hull to the London Society. He denounced the conversionist movement and pleaded with its activists to reflect on the grievous results of any success they may have, in terms, as he put it, of the break-up of homes. In March 1873, the *Hull Advertiser* published a severe letter from a local Jew [18] attacking the Revd Joshua Kroenig, the converted Prussian-born, Yiddish-speaking talmudic scholar. He had become a Christian before his emigration to England, and between 1871, when he first assumed office in Hull as Vicar of St Barnabas', until his death in 1900, he was the senior local Christian conversionist preacher. He received an annual grant from the London Society towards conversionist work. This popular vicar was sufficiently regarded in the Anglican communion to be invited to deliver the opening address at the Church Congress assembled at Derby in 1882.

Kroenig's address, later published under the title of *The Present Religious Condition of the Jews*, surveyed current Jewish religious schisms from the point of view of how best to advance missionary work. He described Reform in Jewry as 'resting on general unitarianism leavened by a Rabbinicalistic element'. He also declared that he detected 'a large spirit of enquiry' in Jewish circles generally and not only among Reformers. 'That spirit of enquiry', he urged, 'should be utilised to bring the Jews the knowledge of the true faith'. The discussion at the Congress was coloured by the onset of the great Eastern European immigration after 1881, which led Kroenig to expand his efforts in Hull with the foundation of a Mission House.[19]

A prominent convert in Hull was Samuel Samuelson (1789–1869). He was born in Virginia, son of Henry Samuelson (formerly Hyman Samuels), a London-born trader and member of a German-Jewish family connected mainly with Hamburg. Hyman Samuels lived and traded for many years in Jamaica where he died in 1813. Samuel Henry Samuelson (originally Samuel Hermann Samuels) moved from London to Hull in the 1820s. On a date which I cannot ascertain, and either in Hull or elsewhere, he became a Christian. He died in Hull, the head of a substantial commission and shipping agency. His eldest son was Sir Bernard Samuelson (1820–1905), a prominent iron master, Liberal MP, and a promoter of technical education. The latter's eldest daughter married Henry Blundell, mayor of Hull, in 1852. His brother, Martin Samuelson, mayor of Hull in 1858, founded in 1849 an engineering business which he expanded into shipbuilding. In 1864, his firm became the Humber Iron Works and Shipbuilding Co. Ltd. It was while working in association with the company's business in Hull that the engineer (and later railway building contractor) Elim d'Avigdor met the family of Bethel Jacobs, whose daughter, Henrietta, he married in India in 1866. D'Avigdor, later prominent in the *Hovevei Zion* movement, was Sir Isaac Lyon Goldsmid's grandson and father of (Sir) Osmond d'Avigdor Goldsmid. It is not surprising that the Committee of the Western Synagogue in Hull chose the latter to lay the foundation stone of their building in 1902. He was a grandson of Bethel Jacobs, close kinsman of leading figures in the congregation, and great-grandson of Israel Jacobs, who had performed the like ceremony in respect of the Hull Synagogue in 1826 and the newly constructed synagogue in 1852.

Let us take a closer look at Bethel Jacobs' public career, and his outlook and that of his circle. In his combination of intense and self-conscious civic earnestness and attachment to Jewish tradition and practice, he was the archetype of the educated, well-read and self-reliant element among middle-class English Jews of the emancipation era. His 'commanding presence'[20] and somewhat imperious demeanour were allied to a strong will and immense energy. He had a high sense of hierarchy and a firm belief in the value of authority in public life. He shared the Victorian interest in technical inventions, including gadgetry and skilled ornamentation.

Jacobs was elected a governor of the Hull Workhouse (then called Charity Hall) at the age of 27, and was twice re-elected. These elections were characteristically commented on by the Whig journal of radical disposition, the *Hull Rockingham*, on 11 December 1841, as demonstrating that 'the profession of Judaism is perfectly accordant with the discharge of the duties of a citizen'. The editor went on to urge the opening to Jews of all public offices. Jacobs' speech at a public dinner, given by leading citizens on his retirement in 1842 (in which he made the same points), was reported in the Jewish and local press. It was at this stage that Jacobs, already well known in business, emerged as a significant figure in the public life of the city. He was an assiduous member of the Town Council from 1849 to 1852. But his main efforts lay beyond the Town Hall.

Following some degree of private tuition in Jewish studies under Samuel Simon, Jacobs lived in Leipzig as a student at the private academy of Dr Julius Fürst, the Jewish historian and bibliographer, where Jewish education and secular study, including modern languages, formed the curriculum. When, later in life, Fürst would often advertise the merits of his academy in the Anglo-Jewish press, Bethel Jacobs acted as his 'agent' in Britain and allowed his name to be used in support of his *alma mater*. At least one of his sons, the eldest, was a pupil at Fürst's academy. Jacobs fashionably believed in the general educational value of the cultivation of arts and crafts, a belief encouraged by his own artistic bent and talent. He founded the Hull College of Art, of which he was president for its first eight years, as well as serving as president of the Hull Mechanics' Institute and as a leading member of the committee of the Hull Subscription Library.[21]

The Hull Literary and Philosophical Society was founded in 1822. It was eventually housed in the extensive premises of the

Royal Institution, which was part museum, part library, and mainly a major social and literary centre, incorporating a large assembly hall. That institution, in Albion Street, was opened in 1853. Jacobs had been a member of the building committee, the scheme being much encouraged by the spirit of innovation, by the desire for an expansion of local opportunities for the study of the arts and sciences engendered by the Great Exhibition in London in 1851 and by the local related exhibition. In 1860 Jacobs, who had held each office in turn, became the Society's president, as did his eldest son, Joseph Lyon Jacobs,[22] in 1882. Bethel Jacobs served the council for 20 years. The premises in Albion Street were destroyed in air-raids during the Second World War.

The Society was the principal intellectual and literary forum in Hull and a large surrounding area north of the Humber. By 1853, its membership reached 300. Its proceedings were widely reported in the local and regional press. The professions, the Churches and the municipal leadership were well represented at its meetings. In April 1845, Jacobs lectured to the Society on 'The Customs and Ceremonies of the Hebrews, Historically Considered'. This and his other lectures to the Society attracted wide press attention, including the Jewish press. They were typical of the efforts made by comparable personalities in many cities, including London, to demonstrate their perception of the enlightened nature of Judaism and the Jewish people. The 'apologetics' inherent in the effort cannot be gainsaid, yet nor can the genuine interest it aroused in the Christian audiences. For many reasons (including the publicity given to the detractors of Jews and sometimes of Judaism) the public curiosity in the Jews and their history was a growing phenomenon. Jacobs made no pretence to original scholarship, but it is clear that he was a serious reader, possessed of a fine intellect, and a lecturer who took pains over his 'research' and his presentation. Laudatory comments in the newspapers, respectful by standard practice as no doubt they were, seemed to exceed the normal effusion. Perhaps this was a self-conscious public response among Christian readers to the young gifted Jew of local birth who, as a professing Jew and despite his self-evident attachment to the land and city of his birth, was subject to limitations on his civil rights. Support for the Jewish emancipatory cause was widespread in Hull among the commercial classes.

At the April 1845 meeting, Jacobs was faced by a series of questions on the Jewish calendar, the dietary laws and other matters. The *Hull Packet* reported that the information given in his address and his replies 'tended to remove prejudices from the minds of Christians as to the rationale of certain Jewish observances and the principles inculcated by the Synagogue'. The president of the Society, a prominent local doctor (R.F. Horner), was reported as saying that these subjects 'must be ... of deep interest to all well-constituted minds'. His meetings were described as attracting unusually large audiences. In one of his lectures, Jacobs illustrated some point by exhibiting a letter by the newly appointed Chief Rabbi. It aroused considerable notice as 'a beautiful specimen of Hebrew writing'. In his address on 'The Hebrew Language' in April 1847, he demonstrated the 'distinctive qualities' of that tongue and, in the words of the *Eastern Morning Herald*, aimed 'to prove its divine origin' by reference to 'the sacred records'.

In December 1851, Jacobs read a paper on 'the nature and characteristics of animals mentioned in the Old Testament'. The local press described the event as 'one of the most crowded meetings we have ever seen', at which chairs filled the aisles. The paper was a study in philology as well as natural history. Accounts suggest that much interest was evinced, particularly on the part of the local Christian clergy. In March 1864, in an address on 'Heraldry', Jacobs made much use of 'heraldic' references in the Hebrew Bible. He had long come to be regarded as the representative Jew in his part of the country, and one of the half-dozen leading citizens in the region. His versatility was given added edge by his services, much in demand, as vocalist in many local charity concerts.

No one was surprised by his appointment as honorary secretary of the Hull area committee for preparations for the Great Exhibition of 1851. He and his colleagues organized the assembly of exhibits for display at the Crystal Palace to illustrate the history and contemporary life and commerce of Hull. Of greater local interest was the local exhibition, organized by that committee, of artistic and industrial items related to the city.

In September 1853, the twenty-third annual meeting of the British Association for the Advancement of Science was held in Hull. That this coveted honour fell to Hull was, as was acknowledged, due, in part, to the initiative and labours of Jacobs. Early in 1852, he urged the Literary and Philosophical Society, and other bodies and persons, to press vigorously Hull's invitation to the British Association, which had on several previous years been refused. He was a member of a local deputation from Hull to Belfast, where that year the Association was holding its current meeting. Hull was one of five cities which applied to be the host for 1853, including Glasgow and Liverpool, which were considered to be especially strong candidates. The initial preparations in Hull, in which Jacobs had played a major role, and the level of local enthusiasm, persuaded the committee of the Association to opt for Hull. Jacobs had become engaged in 1852 in organizing a fund to meet the local expense and, by speech and letter, in persuading local business houses of the commercial benefits, as well as the honour and the educational advancement, which would accrue to Hull and district from the event. The Association appointed him and his friend, Dr Cooper (President of the Literary and Philosophical Society, which was the centre of the organized effort), to be the local honorary secretaries in preparing the Association's meeting in Hull for September 1853.

Over many years, Jacobs, whose Hebrew name was appropriately Bezalel, had designed *objets d'art* for use as testimonials on ceremonial occasions in Hull. The most notable was probably the 'very beautiful massive allegorical piece of plate' in the form of a candelabrum weighing 28 lbs which was presented to Dr James Alderson in December 1845. When Queen Victoria visited Hull in October 1854, she and Prince Albert stayed at the Station Hotel, which was especially fitted out for the occasion, Jacobs and his business partner, Edward Lucas, providing the gold plate with which the dining-room sideboard was decorated. For the laying of the foundation stone of the fourth Hull dock (West Dock) in 1864, Jacobs provided what was widely described as a 'magnificent' ornamental trowel. His characteristic scientific interest was displayed by his construction in July 1863, high outside his shop, of an electric time ball which was linked by electric telegraph to the Greenwich Observatory, which, it was said, enabled seamen from a distance of 10 miles to tell the exact Greenwich time and thus be assisted in their compass calculations.

Among the many laudatory obituary notices on Jacobs, that of the *Hull Morning Telegraph* on 27 December 1869 has a special nuance. He was, observed the editor, 'one of the most active townsmen in everything that could promote the instruction or amusement of the middle and upper classes of the town ... He was ever ready as lecturer or singer ... for either charitable purpose or for the instruction of the rising generation.' The first sentence reflected the deceased's public image, which might well have greatly commended itself to his Gentile peers, but in his lifetime might not necessarily have aroused unqualified approval within the highly variegated local Jewish community. The reality of the second sentence may not have alleviated the sense of distance on the part of some sections of the latter, notwithstanding the widespread respect in which he was held. The editor had hit upon perhaps a more significant matter then he appreciated.

The Jews were anxious for recognition as full citizens, but were conscious that they constituted a distinct minority not entirely at one, despite their loyalty and service, with the homogeneous life of the townsfolk. The *Hull News* on 29 January 1870 quoted Jacobs' successor as president of the Hull School of Art, the Revd H.W. Kemp, in his tribute to Jacobs, as adding, in reference to his public services, 'separated though he was in some degree from the community in which he lived by his religious persuasion'. That observation by the Christian cleric was not meant in any hostile or derogatory sense, but was a recognition of an element of inward-lookingness on the part of the Jews, however integrated. Jacobs well knew that his inhibitions, habits, interests and hopes, connected with his faith and his people's history, could arouse misunder-standing and worse.

In March 1864, John Symons was elected, after what the *Jewish Chronicle* called a 'sharp contest', to the post of deputy governor of the Hull Board of Guardians. 'Great efforts', wrote the news-paper, were made to prejudice the Board against Symons because of his religion. In 1866, when Symons stood for re-election to the Town Council, it was held against him that his now retiring colleague (a Liberal and a well-known Nonconformist) had opposed the imposition of a Church rate. This and the fact that Symons was a Jew were advanced against his candidature in a keenly fought election – in which in the event Symons headed the poll by a large margin.

Such periodic overt manifestations of anti-Jewish sentiment did not curtail the inclination on the part of local communal leaders to engage in public work. In November 1858, Bender was requested by the synagogue committee to deliver an appeal in an address to the congregation for support for the extension of the Hull Infirmary – to which members of the community sometimes had need to resort – and many congregants responded. In 1859, when famously a French invasion of England was for a short time regarded in some quarters of London as a possibility not to be discounted, prominent Jews (like other citizens generally) in a number of coastal areas, including London, entered with some verve into the volunteer movement. Jacobs became a lieutenant and the paymaster of the Hull Volunteer Rifle Corps. His partner, Edward Lucas,[23] became captain. To advance proficiency they and others engaged in musketry practice, and Messrs Jacobs and Lucas gave the corps a silver challenge cup to encourage practice. Some synagogal leaders in Hull rose high also in the masonic movement. Jacobs became master of the Humber Lodge. Solomon Cohen was a member of that Lodge for 50 years. Mosely (who had ranked as captain in the volunteers) was master of the Kingston Lodge, as later was Joseph Lyon Jacobs. Among other prominent local Jewish masons was Abraham Elzas.

In 1869, a marble bust of Bethel Jacobs was commissioned by the Literary and Philosophical Society and installed in its headquarters, the extensive Royal Institution, to whose planning he had contributed. I recall seeing that impressive marble work. It was destroyed in the demolition of the building by the war-time bombing. The bust was the work of William Day Keyworth of Hull, whose namesake father was the architect of the reconstruction of the synagogue in 1852. A fund for the work was raised by public subscription.

Writing in 1851, Moses Margoliouth, the converted Jewish conversionist, noted in his *History of the Jews in Great Britain* that some Hull Jews 'have distinguished themselves as savants and as expert civilians [sic]'. He cited Jacobs as exemplar and made particular reference to his public lectures. On Jacobs' death on 26 December 1869 at his home, 40 George Street, there was a sense of shock because of his apparently robust health and numerous activities. The *Hull News* remembered him as 'true to his faith' and added that 'he was not a bigoted slave to Judaism', whatever may have been the intended meaning of that description, which says something about its author's perceptions as well as about Jacobs.

Lewis Hansell Bergman, a dentist, was a founder-member of the Western Synagogue and its first honorary secretary. In 1902, in a brochure, published to mark the fashionable bazaar in support of the new synagogue's building fund, he wrote a memoir of the trend of events and movements of opinion which led to the withdrawal of many members of the old congregation and the creation of the new. He remembered Bethel Jacobs, whose family was to head the operation and for which Henry Feldman, who lived in Linneaus Street, played a vital role in finding a suitable site. In October 1874, the *Jewish Chronicle* estimated that there were 400 Jewish families in Hull. Pressure of numbers played a part in compelling the move – the new building in Linneaus Street had seating for over 600 people. The emergence of new areas of residence was likewise an effective encouragement to seek a new centre. The key sentence in Bergman's account is that there had been 'an era of English government' in local Jewish life. For Bergman that was in the 1860s; it was at the end of that decade that such an era began to feel under threat.

The differences were not necessarily related to levels of Orthodoxy, even though in some instances they may have been reflected. It was more a matter of style, mood, and perhaps language, in connection with which the immigration was a major factor. In addition to these differences there was a sharp consciousness of difference in social standing, perhaps related principally to economic or professional status. Western acculturation was both instinctive and self-conscious. One cannot sensibly generalize, since the old and the new congregations each partook of something inherent in the other. Each regarded itself as heir to the Hebrew Congregation of 1826.

Robinson Row had had its day. On a newly acquired site in Osborne Street, midway between Robinson Row and Linneaus Street, the Hull Hebrew Congregation, renamed the Hull Old Hebrew Congregation, erected a large new synagogue. The Jewish population of Hull at that time approached 2,000.

After 90 years of separation, and much history and change, the two congregations have now merged to form the 'reunited' Hull Hebrew Congregation. It is housed in an attractive new synagogue in the suburb of Anlaby, where many of the Jews of Hull now live, in a community of declining numbers since World War II. In the years relevant to this paper, that area was well into the countryside.

Attached to the synagogue is the Talmud Torah, formerly attached to the premises of the Western Synagogue. It is a continuation of the old synagogue school. In the neighbouring Willerby is the Reform Synagogue. The successor to the old School Street Synagogue (known as the Central) in Cogan Street was destroyed in an air-raid, as was the Osborne Street Synagogue. The former was not rebuilt. The latter was replaced by a synagogue on the Osborne Road site. Those premises, and the site of the Western Synagogue, have been sold.

NOTES

1. Charles Duschinsky, *Rabbinate of the Great Synagogue* (Oxford, 1921), pp. 264–73, presents a list of *shochetim* licensed 1822–42. Duschinsky notes on p. 269 the licensing of a *shochet* in 1831 in Scarborough 'to Israel Jacobs', in the person of Ephraim Moses who referred to Jacobs as his uncle. This may be connected with Hebrew, in which the words for uncle and friend are the same.

2. Geoffrey Green, 'Anglo-Jewish Trading Connections with Officers and Seamen of the Royal Navy, 1740–1820', *Transactions of the Jewish Historical Society of England*, Vol. 29 (1988), pp. 117–32.

3. For his rise, character and achievement, see William Massil, *Immigrant Furniture Workers in London (1881–1939) and the Jewish Contribution to the Furniture Trade* (London, 1998).

4. On 2 October 1852, the *Hull News* reported that 1,000 'arrivals' had passed through Hull from Germany per month in that year. Registrations at the port fell well short of that number. The reason for the disparity may be that some arrivals were in groups with no names registered save for the spokesmen of the respective groups. I counted 610 individual certificates of arrival at Hull for 1851; of these arrivals, at least 110 would appear to be Jews. Registration gave no indication of religion. For most of that decade there seem to have been at least 300 Jewish arrivals on an average each year at Hull, most of whom moved on, but nearly all required support, short term or otherwise. See Cecil Roth, *The Rise of Provincial Jewry* (London, 1950), pp. 70–1; V.D. Lipman, 'Survey of Anglo-Jewry in 1851', *Transactions of the Jewish Historical Society of England*, Vol. 17 (1953), pp. 184, 187; and *Social History of the Jews in England 1850–1950* (London, 1954), pp. 21–2, and *passim*; and author's paper on the Jewish community in Hull in A.N. Newman (ed.), *Provincial Jewry in Victorian Britain* (London, 1975).

5. J.J. Sheahan, *History of Kingston-upon-Hull* (Beverley, 1864; 2nd edn, 1899), pp. 567.

6. In Manchester a comparable society was set up later that year by 'a group of German merchants, most of them non-Jewish', with a view to curbing

mendicancy and petty theft: Bill Williams, *The Making of Manchester Jewry 1740–1875* (Manchester, 1976), p. 156.

7. Lewis Wolff, who died in September 1889 at the age of 62, was the secretary of these two societies for 20 and ten years, respectively. He had settled in Hull from Prussia in about 1848: *Jewish Chronicle*, 20 September 1889. His role signified a degree of professionalism which the new problems required. The earlier system of informal management of charity or distribution of aid was not well attuned to the new era, although it long survived parallel with the growth of new administrative machinery, which in Hull was much advanced with the creation of the Board of Guardians.

8. Bender (1831–1901), recently arrived in England from Germany, was appointed in Hull in 1850. To his multi-purpose duties in Hull there was later added the requirement that he give regular sermons in English, in return for extra pay. By an agreement in June 1859 that he should stay in Hull for three years in return for the five shillings increase in his pay, it was further laid down that he should in addition receive a special fee for each marriage service and that he was free to give six months notice within that period. He gave such notice and left Hull in February 1861 for Dublin. He did not relish the pressures of his duties, or the pressures on him and the congregation arising from the local fractiousness. At the end of a 21-year notable tenure in Dublin as 'Lecturer and Minister', Bender was for 15 years headmaster of Beaufort College, a boarding school near Hastings, at which Albert Hyamson, a former president of this Society, was a pupil. His son, Alfred Philipp Bender, achieved distinction as Minister of the Capetown Hebrew Congregation and Professor of Hebrew, and was a powerful advocate of Zionism in South Africa.

9. Cohen, later of Newcastle and Dalston, retired from the ministry in 1883, at the age of 53, through ill-health. He died in 1889 aged 60. His son, Lawrence Cowan (1865–1942), who was born in Hull, was journalist, playwright and West End impresario.

10. This 'right' may not have been exercised for long. From some date which is not clear – it may have been in the 1860s – non-privileged members could stand for election to the committee.

11. At that time only three provincial communities were represented on the Board, namely those of Liverpool, Manchester and Hull. For this reason, and because Meyer was a prominent figure in the London Jewish community (among his philanthropic offices was his treasurership of the Jewish Soup Kitchen), his vote on this contentious issue was likely in any event to arouse communal interest. In 1867, Meyer's eldest daughter, Emily, married Bethel Jacobs' son, Joseph Lyon Jacobs. The Hull congregation was generally represented on the Board by a London resident. Meyer was succeeded as Deputy in 1856 by Lewin Mosely, Simeon Mosely's brother (and, later, partner), then of Berners Street, W1. The Moselys were a family of dentists, one of whom, Ephraim, also in the family business, was a warden of London's Western Synagogue in the 1850s. These brothers were descendants of Moses Hamburger of the Great Synagogue in London in the eighteenth century. The family business had branches in London, Hull, Leeds, Scarborough, Sheffield

and York. Simeon advertised himself as 'surgeon dentist by appointment to the King of Hanover and Prince George of Cumberland'. The firm proffered some 'new' and 'patent' treatments.

12. For the events in London and beyond in relation to the four, see the author's 'The Anglo-Jewish Revolt', in his *Jewish Society in Victorian England* (London, 1993), pp. 104–29.

13. In 1852, the local representation fee was £7, which was one-seventh of that paid by the Great Synagogue. It was not treated locally as a negligible sum. Representation on the Board of Hull was fitful. But regardless of representation, the Hull congregation sent the Board regular statistical returns as requested. Bethel Jacobs was the first in Hull to be certified by the President of the Board to the Registrar General as Secretary for Marriages, under the Marriage Registration Act of 1836, in respect of each *chuppah* celebrated in the synagogue. He was succeeded by Mosely in 1855, who was followed by Ephraim Cohen and later by Isaac Hart who was also synagogue secretary and, for a time, acting minister. In 1869, it was reported to the Board that certain irregular marriages had taken place in Hull and Grimsby. The Board informed the Registrar General and requested the local communities to take steps to reduce the likelihood of a recurrence. Such unions were not likely to have been knowingly countenanced by the local Jewish leadership, but would not necessarily have troubled some members of the immigrant sectors who would deem rabbinic law concerning capacity to marry as governing on them.

14. For a full account of this strange affair, with its mixed motives (especially as far as Schiller-Szinessy was concerned), see Bill Williams (see n. 4) chap. 10. See also Raphael Loewe, 'Solomon Schiller-Szinessy', *Transactions of the Jewish Historical Society of England*, Vol. 21 (1968), pp. 148–9. I am grateful to the office of the Manchester Reform Congregation for copies of some relevant correspondence bearing on the Hull side of this dispute.

15. The local Courts were familiar with Jewish parties to proceedings. In March 1860, the Hull Stipendiary Magistrate presented the then regular multiple interpreter (mostly in Yiddish and German), Jacobsen, with a gift of books (three volumes of 'foreign linguistic works') in appreciation of his services. The short ceremony in Court was reported in the local and Jewish press. The scholarly, Danish-born Jacobsen served in this role from 1859 to 1882 and was often and interestingly commended for his 'fairness'. His *Revelations of a Police Court Interpreter* was published in Hull in 1886.

16. The poll-book for the election of 1835 in Hull records Bethel Jacobs' vote for Thompson. In that election he was the only Jew to vote. In that year, Jews were for the first time permitted by statute to vote without Christian oath or declaration. Jews may have voted before that legislation with the connivance of the returning officer. There is no indication that this was done in Hull.

17. In the middle decades of the nineteenth century I found reference at most to what seem to be four cases of conversion. How far they were conversions or temporary conversions of convenience I know not. In an earlier affair of the heart, one Levi, 'a Jewish silversmith of Hull', was married on 9 August 1784 to a Miss Brown of Rawby, near Brigg, in Lincolnshire. The marriage at Rawby

was recorded in the diary of one Strother, a tradesman of Hull and York, which was edited by the Revd C. Caine. The diarist, wrote the editor, showed an acquaintance 'even with Hebrew'. Possibly it was the diarist's own Hebrew interest which led him to note the marriage of Mr Levi, whom he also may have known from Hull.

18. The *Jewish Chronicle*, a consistent and sharp critic of the efforts and methods of the conversionists, publicly warned that correspondent to take care in his language lest he fell foul of the libel laws.

19. For that Congress and the 'Zionistic' tone of conversionist redemptionism, see this author's 'Early and Middle Nineteenth-century British Opinion on the Restoration of the Jews', in M. Davis (ed.), *With Eyes Towards Zion* III (New York, 1986), pp. 72–101, and 95–6 (concerning Hull), and chap. 5 of his *Changing Times in Anglo-Jewry: Studies in Diversity, 1840–1914* (1999).

20. Per L.H. Bergman in his memoir (1902), referred to on p. 158, on the founding families of the Western Synagogue, Hull.

21. Bethel Jacobs 'was a very versatile man, an excellent flautist, a good violin-cello player. He also had a fine taste in music, and an intimate knowledge of the old English school of madrigal composers': in G.H. Smith, *A History of Hull Organs and Organists* (Hull, *c.* 1910), p. 58. In February 1852, in a typically widely reported lecture, Jacobs addressed the regional Anglican Religious and Literary Society on 'The Theory of Sound as applied to Music', which appears to have met with the approval of the local *cognoscenti*. As for Dr Smith's said assessment, while allowing for the possibility of an element of *de mortuis* pietism, I have no reason to doubt his judgement. Also A.G. Credland, *Artists and Craftsmen in Hull and East Yorkshire* (Hull City Council, 2000), pp. 74–9.

22. Bethel and Esther Jacobs had 13 children, of whom two died young. They were a gifted family and received a wide education. The eldest, Joseph Lyon Jacobs, was a notable local solicitor of high intellect who contributed much to the cultural life of Hull and played an active role in local Jewish welfare. He was a popular lecturer on Jewish and other themes, and in November 1857 lectured at Sussex Hall in London on national proverbs from many languages, an address which was appreciatively reported in the *City Press* of London. In 1881, he founded the Hull branch of the Anglo-Jewish Association. He died in 1883, aged 47, following a fall from an upper window at his home in Beverley Road. In 1884, his widow, through Simeon Singer's good offices, presented to Jews' College his 'valuable collection of Hebrew and theological works'. It was characteristic of Bethel and Esther Jacobs that their especially talented daughter, Rosa, should have had an extended education in France and Germany over four years. She was a linguist and cultured in the arts. She was described on her death as of 'high culture and powerful intellect'. Another son, Benjamin Septimus, an architect, was a senior member of the team assisting his brother, Charles, an engineer of great distinction, in the design of the Hudson River tunnel in New York in 1892–94. B.S. Jacobs was the honorary architect of the Hull Western Synagogue and the principal founder and first president of that congregation: John Lewenstein, *The Story of the*

Hull Western Synagogue (Hull, 1953), and Dr Lionel Rosen, *Short History of the Jewish Community in Hull* (Hull, 1956). He married Isabel, daughter of Moses Kisch of Norwich, granddaughter of Daniel de Pass of Kensington. Rosa Jacobs, in 1875, married Maurice Solomons, an optician and public figure in Dublin. They were among the principal founders of the Adelaide Road Synagogue in that city. Their son, Bethel Solomons, a noted obstetrician and a leading personality in the cultural life of Dublin, was the first president of that city's Liberal Synagogue. Another of Jacobs' daughters, Maria, married Frederick Halford, then of Manchester, a member of the extensive family wholesale clothing business of Hyams. Though an Ashkenazi, he became a leading personality in the London Sephardi community. His great-grandfather was Moses Lazarus of eighteenth-century Rochford, formerly of Worms. A granddaughter of Maria and Frederick Halford married Sir Alan Mocatta. In 1950, she was elected an Elder of the Spanish and Portuguese Congregation in London, an event which pioneered the opening in London of Orthodox synagogal management to ladies. Four of Bethel Jacobs' children married out of the Jewish faith. Charles's wife was a member of the Plymouth Brethren, of which movement he became an adherent.

I have not discovered whether Israel Jacobs was born in England, or where he came from before coming to Hull. It had been surmised that he was the son of Isaac ben Jacob of Totnes, formerly of Furth. Israel Jacobs was Yisroel ben Bezalel. The supposed filial link with Isaac of Totnes was, I believe rightly, rejected in a letter to me by the late Alex Jacob, who had a family and historical interest in the Jewish communities of the West Country. I share Jacob's rejection of such surmise. Israel Jacobs may well have spent some time in that region before settling in Hull. Nor have I been able to discover the provenance or lineage of his wife. Jacob, apparently basing himself on family tradition, thought she was a widow. The late Sir Alan Green, grandson of Maria and Frederick Halford, wrote to me of a family tree then in his possession showing her to have been Sarah Barnett and giving her years as 1770–1853. I have accepted that identification. On 27 May 1853, the *Jewish Chronicle* reported that 'Sarah, wife of Israel Jacobs' died in Hull on 21 May 1853 aged 83, and noted 'her active charity and extensive benevolence'. The *Sheffield Mercury*, on 9 January 1830, notes the marriage on 30 December 1829 'by special licence at her home of the only daughter of I. Jacobs jeweller of Hull' to L. Lazarus of Bath. This refers to Israel Jacobs, and his daughter, Deborah.

23. Edward Lucas ceased to be partner in 1862. In 1857, the stock, fixtures and utensils in the shops [*sic*], workshops and showroom of Messrs Jacobs and Lucas ('all communicating' in Whitefriargate) were insured for £4000. At that time the household goods in Jacobs' house in George Street were insured for £500, and the china, glass and pictures separately insured for a further £100. I am grateful to Dr Ann Bennett for this information.

5

Sir Moses Montefiore: A Modern Appreciation[*]

When Montefiore was born, Catherine the Great was Empress of Russia and Dr Johnson still held court in London. When he died, Albert Einstein was alive, Leo Pinsker had written *Auto-Emancipation*, and the great westward Jewish migrations were well under way. This combination of distance and proximity gives Montefiore a prismatic quality. He lived through a series of divers epochs, outliving each, and was sometimes at odds with the successively new.

His strenuous attention to congregational and charitable responsibilities was part of the *noblesse oblige* way of life common to the governing circles of the Jewish community, Sephardi and Ashkenazi. It was a highly personalized family commitment. As reflected in his strikingly long tenures of communal office,[1] he was one of the most assiduous exponents of that way of life. The course of conduct which for many years was epitomized by his communal activity was a continuation of long-standing responses connected not only with traditional Jewish norms and religious duty, but also with Jewish public relations within the wider society. The leadership wanted to be seen caring for the Jewish needy, engaging in the education and westernization of 'foreigners' and their families, and sustaining the familiar religious patterns and institutions of Jewish life. More attention was paid to the Jewish education of the poor than to that of the middle classes, whose wants in that direction were often greater.

---

*Published in *Transactions of the Jewish Historical Society of England,* Vol. 29 (1988); being the major part of the author's lecture to the Society on 11 July 1984, in connection with the bicentennial Montefiore celebrations.

Sir Moses embodied a philosophy which equated leadership with the philanthropic impulse. In his case there was the additional fact of his sheer energy. That quality steps out of the pages of his published diaries.[2]

During the last 20 years of his life the adulation of him became universal and endemic. Inherited assumptions about him and the veneration of his memory inhibited frank study of his role as a communal leader. The 'heroic element' obtruded. Furthermore, his career reinforced the idea – which ran deep in Anglo-Jewry in any event – that personal influence in public relations mattered more than representational capacity. It strengthened the then current belief in the legitimacy of the power of the notables.

His career illustrates the public and private success of the Anglo-Jewish pluto-aristocracy. The various echelons of the Jewish middle classes followed their fashion. People at the large base of the Jewish social and economic pyramid were more concerned with subsistence, or with their own efforts to move higher in the social and economic scale. Everyone was conscious to some degree of British power. It was widely remembered that Montefiore had acted in overseas matters with the encouragement of Her Majesty's Government. His purposes abroad appeared related to a liberalism which it had become the boast of that Government to promote. These circumstances underlay not only Montefiore's position as a Jewish spokesman, but also his image as a decidedly British public figure.

He was not a man of ideas. He did not have an original turn of mind. His cautious pragmatism was allied to the pursuit of ideals as well as immediate practical causes. This combination gave the substance and style of his leadership a distinctive quality which endowed his marked Victorianism with features which even in his own time were both old and new.

On a wide range of issues which he faced, one detects the impact of dilemmas created by the beckoning world which was opened to the Jews of the West in the eighteenth century. At the height of his career, between the 1830s and the 1860s inclusive, many issues were brought into sharp focus which in one way or another have continued to be debated ever since. They are questions concerning the proper degree of assimilation, the criteria for judging the matter, the nature of Jewish distinctiveness in modern society, and the relation between integration and practical 'messianism'.[3]

The conventional picture of his era long tended to be roseate, somewhat reverentially portrayed, with its historiography tilted towards the lives of a comparatively small number of families. The conflicting philosophies within the Jewish community, the deeper divisions within the leadership, and the nuts and bolts of communal machinery, were little written about. It was as though it was felt that the setting out, episode by episode, of the stages of the emancipation campaign and of the Reform secession, said enough. Whether he liked it or not, Montefiore was at the centre of the scene in a variety of capacities in regard to many of the deeper issues, as well as the more immediate outward or institutional questions.

He was instinctively sympathetic to causes and assumptions which by the mid-nineteenth century had become old-fashioned. Events have made many in our own generation much more attuned to a sense of urgency, in the need for and the naturalness of consciously seeking to put bounds to assimilation, than was once the case.[4] Between Montefiore and many of the leading Jewish emancipationists there were differences of policy and of nuance on that score. He was conservative by temperament, conviction and habit.

We today may regard his approach on some topics as simplistic and sometimes even untenable; yet his retentive grasping on to a dissolving age strikes in us chords of recognition. He had about him something of a *reluctant* Victorian, which, for example, Sir David Salomons in no sense was. Salomons' robust modernity in his epoch has for us today an element of touching confidence. Montefiore shared in that confidence, but with reservations which the twentieth century could understand better than the nineteenth.

At the same time, he was the quintessential Victorian in other ways. He was at his most English in his visible piety, his pride in the public acclaim of his domesticity, and his especially high view of public service. He emerged into prominence when the Evangelical Revival was at its height. Victorian thrift and economic individualism mingled with social conscience and the developing notions of social welfare. The Anglican Evangelicals and the Nonconformists had made conventional among the middle classes those external qualities which were in practice evinced in any event by Sir Moses. They were qualities which largely belonged to his own self-consciously demonstrative Judaism. The Englishman and the Jew blended in him with a naturalness which had great appeal, even among those Jews who failed to share his pietism. That appeal outlived him.

One of the sharpest conflicts of his career centred round his efforts in 1853 to exclude from the Board of Deputies four members of the Reform congregation in London who had been elected as Deputies by provincial Orthodox synagogues. The dispute extended beyond the instant issue. Broad questions were raised concerning not only the relations between provincial communities and the London leadership, but also the system of communal government generally.

The four had considerable support in the Provinces, including that of recognized heads of the respective local congregations. For example, Elias Davis, Common Councillor in the City of London and an Aldgate wholesale clothier, had in Norwich the backing of that celebrated East Anglian personality, Joel Fox. Davis was the true leader of the four, and in the 1840s and 1850s championed a series of efforts to curb the power of the old established system. In Chatham, Samuel Ellis of Euston Square, London, had the vigorous support of the well-known Kent figure, Simon Magnus. Men such as Fox and Magnus were not only local congregational leaders, but were also in the van of provincial emancipationist endeavour.

There were frequent calls from such leaders, and from vocal London communal activists such as Henry Keeling (a prominent City jeweller) and Lewis Braham (a notable solicitor), for changes which would have involved a restructure of the pattern of communal leadership; they would have included a greater use of committees, wider consultation, and greater professionalism. The four aspiring Deputies were excluded by Montefiore's casting vote. His private and public roles in this protracted affair were severely attacked in wide segments of leading communal opinion. This reaction indicated the strength of feeling on the religious and administrative questions inherent in the arguments. It also gave notice of the rising influence and the growing *esprit de corps* of the new businessmen and professional men from outside the ruling families, who were now edging their way forward in the communal hierarchy. Montefiore was slow to perceive that his long retention of high office could in practice operate as a fetter on their emergence, with their talents and imagination lost to the succession.

There were also sharp and persistent differences of opinion over what should be the relationship between the English law of marriage and divorce on the one hand, and Jewish religious law on the other hand. The differences reflected a deep diversity of attitude over the status of the Jew in society in a changing world. I do not thereby refer to the status of the Reform congregation in this sphere: that was itself an issue of acute controversy within the Board and within the Jewish community, in the course of which Montefiore's tradition-rooted policy was hotly challenged by Salomons and others prominent in the Orthodox community as well as by the leaders of Reform.

Montefiore would have preferred English Jews to be allowed by law to marry in accordance with the permitted *halachic* degrees, regardless of the general rules of prohibition applicable under the law of the land. However, the prevailing opinion came to be that this distinctiveness should not be pressed for. The issue was angrily argued within the first years of his presidency of the Board.

In 1838, Salomons retired from the Board, partly because of these and related divisions of opinion, and partly because of what he deemed to be the Board's dilatoriness and inadequate support in the emancipation campaign. Samuel Ellis, later one of the four of 1853, and at that time Deputy for the Western Synagogue in London, resigned with him. It was essentially because of disappointment with Montefiore's leadership.

These differences caused Montefiore great anxiety. Even as early as 1838, barely three years after his accession as President of the Board of Deputies, he had qualms about continuing in office. In the 1840s, the differences were vividly illustrated by the embarrassing divergences in representations made to the Government by committees headed respectively by Montefiore and the Goldsmids. The former expressed readiness to accept a stage-by-stage programme for civic and political emancipation. The latter urged immediate total abolition of the disabilities. In the event, the Prime Minister, Sir Robert Peel, adopted the former approach.

The debates of 1853–54 became absorbed in even keener discussion over the efforts of the West London Synagogue of British Jews to procure by statute their own marriage registration arrangements outside the Registration Act 1836. That statute had given sole recognition to the Board in this field. The question whether to oppose those efforts was probably the most acrimoniously contested subject in Montefiore's career. The dispute ceased at a late stage when it became clear that for Parliamentary reasons the relevant Bill would in any case not complete its passage. When the Bill was revived in 1856, the Board's leaders decided neither to support nor oppose it, and it became law. Had Montefiore pursued a course hostile to the measure, there can be no reasonable doubt that at that time he would have been most unlikely to attract a majority of Deputies.

Such bruising debates severely tested his stamina. He was afflicted by periodic bouts of ill-health. He was now in his seventies. But the conflicts were not at an end. He and the Chief Rabbi, Nathan Marcus Adler, wanted the law to recognize rabbinic divorce, and thus permit the remarriage of English Jews without first meeting the considerable requirements of the civil law of divorce. Salomons and his school of thought considered that Jews, as Englishmen, should be bound by the law of the land in addition, as he certainly hoped, to their own religious rules. In this dispute, which was much publicized, Salomons' view prevailed and ultimately gained the crucial support of the Government – to Montefiore's personal chagrin and the Board's public discomfiture.

For Montefiore, considerations of creed, tradition and public policy converged. In the 1830s, it was still common for the Jewish community to be referred to in ordinary course by Christian friends as 'the Jewish nation'. This caused him none of the concern, then or later, which it gave to other prominent Jews, especially of the younger generation. He was President of the Board of Deputies for a total of 28 years, spread over a period of 39 years. In spite of his personal and instinctive courtesy and his readiness to accept change when it proved in his eyes inescapable, he expected in that office, and generally, that those whom he sought to serve and those who aspired to leadership would share his inherited approaches.

Montefiore repeatedly expressed private and public misgivings over his re-elections to the presidency. The press was first admitted to the Board in 1853, at the height of that year's controversies. Not until 1854 was any standing committee created. When it was formed, it was part of the healing process after the verbal battles of those years. Both reforms had long been called for by Jacob Franklin, Abraham Benisch, Henry Faudel and others. If Montefiore came to perceive the need for a broader-based system of communal government and for some regular consultative machinery, he hardly regarded any new procedures as a restraint on his personal authority. A certain arbitrariness on his part persisted, and this was increasingly criticized. He was not one to acclimatize himself easily to new constraints or to the politics of accountability.

One of the most remarkable facts about his communal career was his consistent readiness to retain office and submit himself unsparingly to public debate and critical scrutiny for so long. For a man of his *hauteur*, this reveals a remarkable strength of attachment to public duty as he saw it. This phenomenon goes far to explain the extraordinary acclaim which he enjoyed unbrokenly from the mid-1860s. He had stayed the course, and it was never a sinecure. Like the Queen, there were fewer and fewer who could remember when he was not 'monarch'. As he approached his eighties, astonishment turned to adulation, marked by a widespread sense of indebtedness for unprecedented and strenuous service at home and abroad. He took on a larger-than-life image. The quarrels of the 1840s and the differences of the 1850s were, after all, now quiescent, if not resolved. And emancipation had by this time been securely achieved.

His failure over the Mortara Affair in the late 1850s was accompanied by greater personal sympathy for his considerable and much publicized personal efforts. The episode aroused resentful criticism of what was considered to be an unreasonably unbending Vatican. It encouraged the creation of the *Alliance Israélite Universelle* in 1860, an event pointing to a different – though not necessarily mutually exclusive – kind of Jewish diplomacy from that associated with the highly personalized intercessions of Montefiore. He never truly reconciled himself to any such predetermined coordinating machinery. By habit and choice he reserved his position. His attitude was consistent with his belief in his influence at home. Given the stability of British public life and Britain's commercial, naval and political power, his belief in the goodwill and support of the British Government in proper cases strongly reinforced his sense of independence. To his fellow-Jews, and many others, he acquired a uniqueness for which there was neither precedent nor any likelihood, as posterity soon perceived, of any comparable successor.

When it was announced in 1863 that he had offered to visit Morocco on the Jewish behalf, there was communal consternation that at his age he should be prepared to undertake that onerous, even dangerous, journey. All his travels abroad were long and arduous. With some misgivings, he was allowed his lordly way by his colleagues in 1863. His wife's death in 1862 had evoked widespread sympathy. His Moroccan mission set the seal, so to speak, upon his canonization.

In politics he was more interested in personality than in party.[5] He respected establishments and protocol. Montefiore saw public duty as a function of station. He was not a politician's politician. Nor did he have much interest in political slogans. Montefiore had the altruism of a public-spirited Whig aristocrat and the paternalistic impulse of the compassionate Tory. These were not thought-out positions. Indeed, their formulation is misleading unless this is recognized as the reflex of temperament and the reactions of instinct.

Montefiore's political associates, personal friends and business colleagues were from all parties and included prominent Tories and High Churchmen as well as many Nonconformist figures, lay and religious. He could have had no illusions about the strong and deep-rooted reserve towards the Jews in Tory and some Anglican quarters. The promotion of the Act of 1845 – which opened the municipalities to Jews – by the Tory administration of Peel and Lyndhurst encouraged him against regarding the Whigs as having any monopoly of party goodwill to the Jewish claims. Whatever inhibitions Montefiore retained against giving political effect to a preference for a party whose outlook on society he undoubtedly shared, the opening of the House of Commons to Jews in 1858 (under a Tory administration) disposed of them. In his closing decades, he was regarded by his contemporaries as an unequivocal political Conservative; his natural stance. He retained his genuine personal respect and admiration for Gladstone, who by the 1860s had completed, via the Peelites, his odyssey out of the Conservative ranks.

The attempts to democratize (comparatively) and rationalize the system of communal government in Anglo-Jewry continued into the 1860s and beyond, but in a more subdued tone. Montefiore was no longer the target. His presence was to some extent a becalming, though not an obviating, factor. There was still vocal discontent over the limited sources, not to say the oligarchic nature, of communal government. A typical proposal for expansion was made by the *Jewish Chronicle* on 17 June 1869. Let there be added to the Board, wrote the editor (Abraham Benisch) all Jewish MPs, Queen's Counsel, Royal Academicians and other specifically nominated persons.

Some part of the criticism was met by the creation of the Anglo-Jewish Association in 1871, which incorporated leading Reformers (including prominent MPs), and other notable public figures to whom the novelty, independence and apparent capacity for speedy action of the new body had a strong appeal. Benisch, who was the principal initiator of the Association, had also long urged the establishment of an international Jewish body in pursuit of Jewish causes. The Association was created with that object in Benisch's mind, an aim which the leaders of the Board viewed with some caution and in some instances distinct disapproval.

With the great immigration after 1881, and the rise of political Zionism in the 1890s, the communal debate concerning the system of communal government became merged with new kinds of communal stress and contention. Many who were formerly in disagreement were now united in their distaste for the new modes and ideas which gathered momentum. In their different ways the new groupings, each with some justification, appealed to the record and impulses of Montefiore.

I now turn to an estimate of the spirit and motivation of Montefiore's European missions and his visits to Palestine. In both sets of journeys there was a common element which goes to the root of Victorian Jewish opinion. It was the element of optimism, namely the belief that prejudice would give way to reason in the advancing technological age, and that such movements were part of a providential pattern. With this belief there came a reliance on the openness of kings and captains to enlightened argument. The whole of Montefiore's public career rested on the assumption that improved education, social amelioration and the rational presentation of a case would assuage bigotry.

While he imbibed the Victorian belief in the inevitability of progress and in the ultimate triumph of reason, much of his public life was spent in encounters with the opposite realities. I do not think the contrast occurred to him as carrying any implications which need cast doubt upon the worth of his efforts.

His belief in the ultimate messianic redemption of the Jews was accompanied by his strongly held opinion concerning the piety and virtue involved in giving succour to Jews resident in the Holy Land. In these sentiments he was in tune with high social fashion and imperial interest. There was a wide acknowledgement by Christians and Jews of the place of Jerusalem in the providence of Jewish history. Christian conversionists were busy in the advocacy of some link between Jewish restorationism and Jewish conversion. British interests, intellectual speculation and religious enthusiasms gave attraction to the idea of the Jewish return to Jerusalem.

However disparate the motivations, there remained a common residue of providentiality which gave respectability and social acceptance to Jewish ideas about the Return. Much was left unspoken, but the central eschatological idea endured, of a pending grand design, however inscrutable as to time, manner or agency, which would radically affect the status of Jews everywhere and alter the frequently discussed, depressed condition of the Holy Land. Some Christians who nurtured their own beliefs and expectations were, meanwhile, intellectually and emotionally sympathetic to Jewish efforts to relieve that condition and improve the lot of the Jews wherever they might be. They were allies, at times, of Jewish effort and aspiration.

If that relief and improvement could arise under British auspices or, better still, if Great Britain were seen to be engaged in practical deeds to those ends, then the interests of compassion, liberalism, commercial opportunity and British influence in the East would all be served, as well as divine purposes of a longer-term nature.

From the Jewish point of view, all such efforts reinforced the hoped-for beneficent consequences of the international Jewish kinship and Jewish religious duties. There was thus a convergence of aspirations which endowed Montefiore's missions overseas, including his visits to Palestine, with a highly Victorian flavour. His involvement with the development of Jewish life in the Holy Land, for all its emphasis on self-help, was essentially a matter of philanthropy, patronage and welfare. He did not think in political terms. But his insistence on frequent public demonstration of the Jewish hope and expectation of national redemption, and his declared perception of that hope as an encouragement to his own work in Palestine, went far beyond the polite, drawing-room-style

173

acknowledgment of messianic belief adopted by most of his Anglo-Jewish contemporaries. He is nearer to us than they are in his emphasis, and in his responses to his own convictions.

With regard to Russian Jewry, Montefiore wrote in July 1878 as follows to Gerson von Bleichröder, the banker and Bismarck's financial adviser:[6]

> The best way to obtain the cooperation of the Emperor ... and his Ministers is to show our confidence in their desire to ameliorate the condition of the Jews ... Nor need I impress on your mind the lesson which history so clearly teaches us that the social and political condition of a large religious community can only be gradually raised ... It also appears to me most important that every effort should be made to induce our wealthier coreligionists in the East to do all that lies in their power to educate and raise their less fortunate brethren.

Virtually every phrase of that classic passage represents a vital strand in Montefiore's assumptions, outlook and policy in all fields of Jewish public relations at home and abroad. Two years later, he gave yet more explicit expression to his hopeful thoughts, in response to Bleichröder's report on the growth of anti-Semitic movements in Germany and elsewhere:[7]

> I entertain the hope that by prudence and discretion on our part, and increased enlightenment based on principles of humanity among non-Israelites, an improvement in the condition of our brethren will ultimately by effected. In the meanwhile we must not relax our earnest activity and when occasion requires it hold up high the banner of our religion, for we must always bear in mind that 'it is not by might nor power that Israel prevails but by the Spirit of ... the Lord of Hosts'.

When Montefiore visited Russia in 1872, he took pride and pleasure in what he deemed to be improvements in the style of Russian Jewish life by comparison with his observations on his visit in 1846. He felt that his earlier advice to Russian Jewish leaders had been taken to heart in the encouragement of agriculture, manual skills and a certain degree of westernization, and that ministerial assurances on behalf of the Czarist Government had not wholly proved dead letters. In the fateful month of May 1881, he wrote to the President of the Board of Deputies (Arthur Cohen, his nephew) expressing confidence in assurances of protection given to him on those visits.[8] He supported the Board's decision not to press for official representations to be made to the Russian Government in connection with the anti-Jewish outbreaks. 'I am fully convinced', he added, 'that it is only by mild and judicious representation – relying in advance as it were on their kindness and humanity – that you have a chance of your application reaching the throne of the Emperor.'

Popular violence, ministerial hostility or chicanery, and the apparent unassimilability of the massive Jewish numbers in Eastern Europe did not deflect Montefiore's confidence. It was part of an ideology which one was to hear again from Oswald John Simon, Laurie Magnus and others in their debates with the Zionists. They rested their own hopes upon the ultimate rationality of governments and peoples, and prayed in aid of the patience, philanthropy and respect-attracting interventions or attempts of their now irreproachable senior exemplar.[9]

But let not the significance of his missions be too far underrated. In 1840, in the later stages of the Damascus Affair, the French Government felt obliged to submit to the wishes of the Powers whom the British Government, in a Jewish cause in which Britain had her own interest, had brought into concert. The resurgence of the ritual-murder charge in Damascus, and the readiness of intelligent Christians in high places in Paris and even public figures in London to believe it or to treat it as though true, had been in stark contrast to the rationality which it was thought the earlier century had bequeathed. The Affair led to the marshalling by Jews and their supporters of sympathetic Gentile opinion in the capitals of the West. The public meetings convened in 1840, and the international Jewish cooperation, were precursors of a familiar style of agitation and public relations.

At the time of the Queen's Jubilee in 1887, the *Jewish Chronicle* justly called the Jewish response to the events in Damascus and Paris 'the first great expression of Jewish solidarity'. The role of Montefiore's intervention with Mehemet Ali in Egypt, and with the Sultan in Constantinople, in giving practical effect to that solidarity and to the public opinion which it influenced, was considerable. The potential influence of Jewish representations was often commented upon; sometimes, as in the French Chamber of Deputies in 1840, in terms of grudging admiration. These events were not lost upon Jewish opinion.

By their declared purposes, his missions abroad helped to set standards by which governmental acts of omission or commission were, or could be, tested. They helped to set precedents for Jewish effort and possible governmental intervention in suitable cases.

Montefiore was an important bridge between the age of Jewish powerlessness which preceded him and the age of aspiration to statehood which followed him. His career was rooted in the concept of Jewish peoplehood. If he was never jolted towards the notion of statehood, his activities formed a developing part of the ground scene, especially his initiatives and practical support for settlement, industry and agriculture in Palestine. His activities were conducive, with many other factors, to the day-to-day growth of the Zionist enterprise and thus to the pre-history of the Balfour Declaration.

NOTES

1. He held office as President of the London Board for Shechita, with short interludes, from 1842 to 1880.
2. The *Diaries of Sir Moses and Lady Montefiore* were edited by Louis Loewe and first appeared in 1890. They were handsomely republished by the Jewish Historical Society and the Jewish Museum in 1983.
3. Concerning particular issues in Victorian Anglo-Jewry, see the author's 'Post-Emancipation Jewry: The Anglo-Jewish Experience' and 'The Uneasy Victorian: Montefiore as Communal Leader', both in his *Jewish Society in Victorian England* (Vallentine Mitchell, 1993).
4. Absorption connotes the loss of transmissible distinctiveness. The process of assimilation, which was engaged in and encouraged within their community by Jewish emancipationists, was in some respects consciously limited to stem absorption. The author's paper on 'Self-imposed Limits on Assimilation by Victorian Jewish Emancipationsts', delivered to the London conference convened by the Institute of Jewish Studies in June 1985, was published in Jonathan Frankel and S.J. Zipperstein, *Assimilation and Community* (1992) and in Israel Finestein, *Anglo-Jewry in Changing Times* (1999). The differences which remained between the leading Jewish emancipationists and Montefiore's school of thought were, as seen from our historical vantage point, but not necessarily in Montefiore's day, often related more to questions of pace than principle. Pace and principle are frequently indistinguishable issues.
5. On an unstated date in October 1831, the *Diaries* record that friends reported to Montefiore the Lords' rejection of the Reform Bill of that year. 'Mr Montefiore', wrote Loewe, 'on hearing that Lord Chancellor Brougham had

spoken in a very illiberal spirit of the Jews, observed "So much for Whig friends".' This relates to a passage in Brougham's immensely long and often fiery speech on 7 October, the fifth and final day of a frequently heated debate. Among other grounds, critics of the Bill had attacked it as seeking to base the franchise on population as distinct from property rights and public responsibility. 'What say you', declared the Lord Chancellor,

> to close boroughs coming by barter or sale into the hands of Jew jobbers, gambling loan-contractors and scheming attorneys ... ? That a peer or a speculating attorney or a jobbing Jew or a gambler from the Stock Exchange by vesting in his own person the old walls of Sarum ... or a summer house at Gatton and making fictitious ... and monetary transfers of them to an agent or two for the purpose of enabling them to vote as if they had the property ... is itself a monstrous abuse ... and becomes the most disgusting hypocrisy when it is seriously treated as a franchise by virtue of property. (*Parl. Debs*, Vol. VIII, 3rd Series, Cls. 240–2).

This notable reformer thus incidentally expressed fashionably held views about the proclivities of Jewish finance, so persistently purveyed by William Cobbett. Brougham, who would have repudiated Cobbett's general anti-Jewish sentiments, supported the Jewish cause in Parliament during the emancipation debates, as was common among the Whigs.

6. Fritz Stern, *Gold and Iron: Bismarck, Bleichröder and the German Empire* (1977), p. 378.
7. *Diaries*, II (see n. 2), p. 294 (13 June 1880).
8. *Ibid.*, p.300.
9. In December 1879, there appeared in *The Times* a long and unprecedented correspondence in which many prominent Jews took part. This public exchange may be said to mark the onset of modern Jewish history in the Anglo-Jewish context. The debate turned on the issue as to whether Jews voted as Englishmen and whether there was a Jewish vote. Gladstone's Midlothian campaign was at its height. Disraeli's policy for the containment of Russia involved amicable Anglo-Turkish relations. Gladstone's concern for the Christian communities in the Ottoman Empire inclined him towards a pro-Russian stance. It was easier for the Tories to contemplate official representations to Russia over the Jewish position in the Czarist Empire than it was for the Liberals, who looked to the Czar as an ally in support of a policy directed to clearing the Ottoman forces out of Europe. Some Liberal politicians who were Jews, while sharing their leader's anxiety for the protection of the Christian subjects of the Sultan, publicly disavowed his apparent reluctance to press the Jewish case in southeast Europe. Prominent among them was Sir John Simon, QC, MP. Questions were raised in this new phase of Jewish history which, in Montefiore's heyday, had not emerged in practical form. The nature and direction of the influence of the emancipated Jewish leaders in the West came under closer scrutiny, in proportion to the diversity of options open to British policy in the new combinations of power politics, nationalist aspirations in southeast Europe, and the growing European xenophobia which coloured the closing decades of the old century.

177

6

The Lay Leadership of the United Synagogue from Lionel Cohen to Sir Robert Waley Cohen*

The three main figures in this story are Lionel Louis Cohen (1832–87), who was the principal founder of the United Synagogue; the first Lord Rothschild (1840–1915); and Sir Robert Waley Cohen (1877–1952). They were all descendants of Levi Barent Cohen (1740–1808), the merchant immigrant from Holland who settled in London around 1770. He became prominent in the City as a financier; in the Jewish community, as a founder and the first president of the Bread, Meat and Coal Charity and warden of the Great Synagogue; and in Jewish history as a great ancestor.[1]

He was the father-in-law of Nathan Mayer Rothschild, who founded a dynasty of his own in England, and of Sir Moses Montefiore. Sir Anthony de Rothschild (1810–76), the first president of the United Synagogue, was Levi Barent Cohen's grandson. The first two vice-presidents, namely Lionel Louis Cohen and Sampson Lucas (1821–79), were grandsons of his eldest son, Joseph.

These facts remind us how much the lay leadership of the United Synagogue was a family affair. It was an English institution, founded by recently emancipated Jews, accustomed by family tradition and

---

*Based on author's address on the occasion of the Centenary of the United Synagogue and first published in S.S. Levin (ed.), *A Century of Jewish Life, 1870–1970* (1970).

historical circumstances to lead. They were a small group within the privileged membership of the uniting congregations. The rank of privileged member was not abolished until 1880, and even then without prejudice to the rights of existing privileged members.[2] The impetus towards union came from a few leading men, largely connected with the Great Synagogue and living in the West End, who controlled, or could vitally influence, the levers of communal power.

In the 1850s, communal leadership was still deeply engaged in the struggle for political emancipation. The admission of a professing Jew to the House of Commons in 1858, in the person of Sir Anthony's brother, Lionel de Rothschild, marked the successful conclusion of that long campaign, and freed the way towards further constructive thinking within the communal scene. By the onset of the great immigration from 1881, the United Synagogue had taken root. Eventually its membership consisted largely of that immigrant stock. The leadership remained in the hands of the old families.

The immediate object of the founders was limited. It had two aspects. They wanted to rationalise the London Ashkenazi synagogal system, and to provide for future growth. The two parts of their plan were interrelated. That is to say that the saving of money, effort and goodwill through rationalization of the system would be of direct practical value in meeting future needs, including essential non-synagogal needs. Central control and planning were of the essence of the union. Against the background of the long-standing, voluntary nature of Anglo-Jewish communal life, the fact that the founders were able to secure the union on these terms is a mark of their capacity for leadership and their sheer practical ability.

Lionel Cohen was a man of astonishing industry and great intellect. He was a prominent banker, a trustee of the London Stock Exchange, and for many years a highly regarded member of the Conservative Party. For the last two years of his life, he represented Paddington North in the Conservative interest in the House of Commons, and was an acknowledged expert in the House on trade and finance. Anthony de Rothschild, like Cohen, was a warden of the Great Synagogue until 1870. In his manner, he represented, wrote the *Jewish Chronicle* on his death, 'a plain old fashioned English squire'.

Sampson Lucas, who succeeded to the presidency of the union

on Rothschild's death, was a fellow-director with Rothschild of the Alliance Insurance Company. He died after only three years as president. The *Jewish Chronicle* described him as having 'a cautious and calculating mind' and added that 'his chief characteristic' was his 'thorough English nature'. In those self-conscious days, references to the ideal of the English gentleman were frequent in Jewish obituary notices.

Lucas' family had a long association with the New Synagogue. He was for many years a warden of the Bayswater Synagogue, the recruiting ground of many honorary officers of the United Synagogue. He had not been uncritical of the idea of union. He was anxious to retain some degree of autonomy for the local boards. It was he who saw to it that each synagogue in the union should have its own budget. This was followed in 1866 by an arrangement whereby, instead of all expenditure being under the Council's control, a 'final surplus' was declared for expenditure by each respective synagogue.

Lucas was succeeded by Lionel de Rothschild's son, Sir Nathaniel de Rothschild, MP, who in 1885 became Lord Rothschild. The new president was a prominent Liberal in politics, who in 1886 became a Unionist in opposition to Gladstone's policy of Irish Home Rule. His departure from the Liberal Party increased the fashionability of Conservatism and Unionism in the politics of leading Jews. In 1870, all eight Jewish MPs were Liberals. Five of them, including three Rothschilds, were members of the Central Synagogue. The remainder, including Sir Francis Goldsmid and Julian Goldsmid, were members of the Reform Synagogue.

The old allegiance among Jews to the Liberal Party became less marked as the years of struggle for emancipation receded. The tendency towards Conservatism[3] reflected the social outlook of what might be termed the upper strata of Anglo-Jewish society.

Among the members of the first Council were Jacob Waley (1819–73) and Algernon E. Sydney (1836–1916). They were important allies of Cohen in formulating and presenting the terms of union to the Jewish community and to the Charity Commissioners. Waley was a notable conveyancer, formerly Professor of Political Economy at University College, London, and the first president of the Anglo-Jewish Association. Sydney was appointed honorary solicitor to the United Synagogue at the first Council meeting. The following editorial reference in the *Jewish Chronicle* on Waley's death captures the spirit of the first post-emancipation generation of English Jews:

> He showed that it was possible for an English Jew, while actively working for and identifying himself with the interests of the community, to exhibit broad sympathies; to take his place in the ranks of those who promote the culture of the age; to do service ... to the country of his birth and the profession of his adoption; to be in every way a high minded refined English gentleman.[4]

Prominent among the first honorary officers was the Exeter-born Henry Solomon (1814–91). Among his titles to fame was that, with other commercial positions, he was chairman of the Ocean and Guarantee Corporation. Solomon was the Chief Rabbi's son-in-law and for 36 years, from its inception to his death, treasurer of Jews' College. A colleague of his on the first Council was Arthur Cohen (1829–1914), a cousin of Sir Anthony de Rothschild, and later the leader of the Commercial Bar, a notable Liberal MP and president of the Board of Deputies.

The men most actively associated in the venture of the United Synagogue were largely busy men in commerce or the professions. In the elections to the first Council, there were 'nomination lists' from the wardens of the respective synagogues in favour of selected candidates. This procedure presumably deterred some would-be candidates, and was strongly disapproved of by the *Jewish Chronicle*. Heavy canvassing was reported during the actual elections, especially at the Great Synagogue. On 9 December 1870, after the elections, the editor expressed surprise that 'more preliminary excitement was not evinced in the election'. The calibre of those who initiated the United Synagogue, and of many of their associates in the undertaking, had already been shown by their success outside the Jewish community. For those of them who belonged to the great ruling families, the added layer of traditional *noblesse oblige* further reinforced their position.

It was Lionel Cohen's idea that, from the start, all Council meetings should be open to the press. He was a frequent contributor to the *Jewish Chronicle*, often in unsigned articles or under a pseudonym. He sought the editor's aid in many communal issues, and his handling of publicity was masterly. From its inception, the

United Synagogue and its growth struck the imagination of the Jewish community. For long, the leaders of the United Synagogue were treated by many as the repository of ultimate wisdom in the management of communal affairs.

'We regard the event', wrote the *Jewish Chronicle* on 16 December 1870, with reference to the first meeting of the Council, 'as of the greatest communal importance and the commencement of a new era in our history.' The point was that here was a new instrument in the hands of profoundly respected and highly self-conscious men, who were anxious to give to what was called English Judaism a distinctive character. It was not established merely to put an end to the recurring 'demarcation' disputes between the uniting congregations. The leaders were concerned with future communal expansion, in numbers and geography, and wanted to prepare to meet it. They took for granted that a unitary system was good. Such a system facilitated forward planning. It also restricted the influence of self-centred or short-sighted local interests in favour of wider needs, synagogal, charitable or organizational.

There was in any event in the leadership of the United Synagogue an instinct for control. The founders created an 'established' synagogue. To some extent it was a conscious device to protect English Judaism against inroads from Reform. The provisions in the Deed of Foundation and Trust relating to the powers of the Chief Rabbi were crucial to the entire scheme. It is a paradox that men who were so imbued with the soundness of all things English, and who were so alive to English and Anglo-Jewish traditions, should have enshrined in the scheme the reference to 'the Polish or German ritual'. Perhaps this is in part explained by a conscious or unconscious analogy with the time-hallowed 'Spanish and Portuguese' forms of what was still, in some respects, the senior branch of Anglo-Jewry. However, a more significant object of the provisions was to provide constitutional safeguards against the intrusion of any practices from the reformed prayer book of David Woolf Marks or his congregation.

A further and powerful influence working in favour of an established synagogue was England. Words like 'vestry', 'board', 'overseer', 'ecclesiastical' and even perhaps 'minister', were typically English and Anglican terms. Lionel Cohen from time to time in political speeches would point out the merits of an established church and warned against disestablishment. In these speeches he was loyal to the ideas of his party. He was criticized by his brother-in-law, the Liberal politician, Samuel Montagu, who thought it was improper and impolitic for a Jew to enter into this particular argument.[5] So keenly was Cohen affected by the virtues of establishment that he included the kernel of establishment, namely the Chief Rabbinate provisions, into the draft scheme of the Act. It is not surprising that the Charity Commissioners, like Sir David Salomons, demurred. 'The tendency of opinion', wrote Salomons at the time, 'is against state interference in religious matters ... The omitted clauses are mainly provisions that so far as I know are neither granted nor desired by any great religious denominations of this country. In this respect the Established Church stands by itself.'[6]

The provisions gave the Chief Rabbi the sole supervision and control of the form of worship and all matters connected with the religious administration of the United Synagogue. In conformity with the original agreement between the synagogues, those provisions were incorporated by the Deed, in default of being given legislative sanction. They helped to create a remarkable degree of uniformity, to which in any event the development of the Chief Rabbinate was conducive. Uniformity was later further encouraged by Singer's Prayer Book, whose title, 'The Authorised Daily Prayer Book', is Anglican and sounded mistakenly as though it had been issued under the sanction of Parliament.

This was the spirit of the early leaders of the United Synagogue; orderly, authoritative and defined. The good sense and practicality of English government appealed to them as virtues, which in many respects they were. The machinery for financial control induced habits of economy. It was a case of good accountancy in the service of the Jewish community.

The size and growth of the United Synagogue appeared to justify the great amount of time devoted by its leaders to the details of its administration. The phrase 'a United Synagogue man' meant something. Among the leaders, a community of outlook and interest developed and was bequeathed. The tone and style which they gave to the United Synagogue persisted, and indeed may prove to some extent indelible. Benevolent despotism became the order of the day, tempered by democratic forms and a patrician sense of obligation. Admiring critics called it paternalism. In the fields of its choice, it gave constructive leadership.

The election of Sir Nathaniel de Rothschild to the presidency in 1879 was one of a series of events which ushered in a new epoch in the history of the institution. Lionel Cohen had been the driving force throughout and he continued to be so until his death at the age of 55. He had encouraged and assisted the establishment of new synagogues in the outlying areas, created effective working arrangements with the Board of Guardians, of which he had been a founder, set precedents of conduct between local synagogal boards and the central organs of administration and enhanced the impact of the United Synagogue upon the communal scene as a whole. He remained a vice-president until his death, a position which has often, in the United Synagogue, been the effective office of power. To work 'in the spirit of Lionel Cohen' became an ambition and a commendation.

Among his notable colleagues as vice-president was Sir Barrow Helbert Ellis (1823–87), a former member of the Viceroy's Council, and for the last eight years of his life chairman of the Council of Jews' College. Ellis predeceased Cohen by a few days. They were close friends, and Cohen was deeply affected by his death. Less than two years later, there died Asher Asher (1837–89), Cohen's principal lieutenant in the creation and development of the United Synagogue. Asher had been secretary of the Great Synagogue since 1866, and was the first secretary of the United Synagogue. He was a doctor of medicine of Glasgow University, a Jewish scholar and fluent Hebraist, whose special field of study was *minhagim*, and a gifted administrator with vision.[7]

In the 1880s, there opened what may fairly be described as the age of Lord Rothschild. He was president for 36 years until his death in 1915. It was an age marked by increasing deference inside the United Synagogue to its lay head. In its earlier phase, the age coincided with the high point of Victorian England. The Queen's Jubilees somehow gave added prestige and influence within the Jewish community to the Jewish peer, who managed large segments of its life from his office in the City. Unlike Waley Cohen, who ruled from Woburn House, and often ate there, Rothschild preferred his own desk at New Court. By temperament and conviction, he favoured the widening scope and influence of the United Synagogue.

He was personally committed to the socially ameliorative East

End Scheme, to whose preparation and partial implementation he gave much labour. He did not bridge the religious and ideological gulf which, in spite of himself, divided him from the mass of the immigrants and from the *chevroth*. He also became much taken up with the transfer of the New Synagogue to Stamford Hill and the sale of the old site in Great St Helens. That event classically illustrates the objects and performances of the United Synagogue. In spite of some local opposition, it was evident that the movement of population rendered the transfer most desirable, quite apart from the fact that in the City the synagogue was in constant and growing deficit. The transfer was delayed when a number of members in 1909 managed to raise funds to discharge certain pressing liabilities. However, the change was pressed by the United Synagogue. In addition to meeting the growing need for a large synagogue in the new areas, the transaction released considerable funds towards later synagogal development in London.

In these and other undertakings, Rothschild was greatly assisted by Albert Henry Jessel (1864–1917), a nephew of Lionel Cohen and of the famous Master of the Rolls, and himself a prominent leader at the Chancery Bar. Jessel was a particularly active vice-president, a tough negotiator, and an effective advocate at the Council and elsewhere of the policies of the honorary officers and sometimes of his own, where they might differ. He was a prominent figure in the Jewish Voluntary Schools Association, which he largely initiated.

Rothschild and Jessel were the main advocates of the election of Dr Hertz as chief rabbi in 1913. Rothschild's support settled the issue, but Jessel's part in the controversies surrounding the search and selection greatly assisted the passage. The opinions and personality of the new incumbent belonged to yet a new age. There is some irony in the fact that his appointment was sponsored by the old guard. Rothschild's son, the second Lord Rothschild (1868–1937), was a Zionist and the recipient of the Balfour Declaration.

The first Lord Rothschild's deep interest in the Jewish schools, especially the Jews' Free School, was more than a family tradition. He considered them to be a vital agency for assimilating the children of foreign parents into the Anglo-Jewish community and into English society. His antipathy to Yiddish sprang from the same source.

He was succeeded as president of the United Synagogue by his brother, Leopold (1845–1917), who died two years later. Leopold had been a close friend of Edward VII, who attended his wedding while Prince of Wales. He twice won the Derby. The new president was his son, Major Lionel de Rothschild (1882–1942), Unionist MP, later treasurer of the Board of Deputies, and an avowed and vocal opponent of Zionism. Leopold de Rothschild and his successor maintained the family tradition of devotion to a large number of practical good causes within and beyond the Jewish community.

The passing of Lord Rothschild provides a convenient occasion to examine a number of features of the United Synagogue which by that time had become deeply characteristic. There was an emphasis on forms, and a concern for the decorous. The men who wielded power in the United Synagogue were essentially practical men, sometimes with limited inclination or aptitude for thinking on issues broader than prudent administration in their allotted spheres. The status and burdens of the United Synagogue attracted their expertise. Thereby might they fulfil their Jewish duty, as well as possibly endow the institution with something of their own prestige. In particular, they did not necessarily feel that any obligation attached to them to promote Jewish learning.

A number of them were dedicated to the Jewish voluntary schools. Some of them had themselves been educated at one of the more fashionable Jewish academies. An increasing number had attended public schools. Lionel Cohen had been one of the initiators of the Jewish House at Clifton College. The horizons of the United Synagogue did not extend far into the fields of Jewish education, although a growing number of its synagogues had Jewish religion classes on their premises. Wise and sincere men, many of whom were prominent in educational and charitable efforts in Anglo-Jewry as well as in the administration of the United Synagogue, failed to give full weight to the proposition that Judaism was and must be much wider than the synagogue.

A fair illustration of their attitude to Jewish learning might be found in the relationship in the early years between the United Synagogue and Jews College. In 1878, the Council of the former debated a proposed increase of its annual grant to the College from £50 to £200. The advocates of increase urged that:

> the necessity for English Jews to have a number of efficiently trained and cultured ministers is everyday becoming more urgent … with

the general change of the times, the social status, resources and wants of the Jews have likewise changed, and it is our duty to provide worthily for a new position and new requirements.

The increase was approved by a majority, in the face of the vigorous opposition of Noah Davis (1823–1913), an honorary officer of the United Synagogue.

Davis was a member of the London Stock Exchange whose father, Mark Davis, had fought at Waterloo. Noah now strove against the communal tide. 'Jews College', he declared, 'is a luxury in which the Council cannot indulge'. Among his supporters on that occasion were Sampson Lucas and Nathaniel de Rothschild, respectively president and vice-president. The issue was undoubtedly complicated by the then apparently serious financial position of the United Synagogue. It is fair to add that the opponents did not say that Jews' College should not be supported. They stated that its support should be general and that the United Synagogue should not adopt a special responsibility. The Rothschilds contributed.

However, one cannot escape the feeling, as one reads the reports of such debates, that the importance of making adequate provision for the training of ministers and teachers for the Jewish community was not adequately appreciated, and not given its true priority. In 1881, the College moved from Finsbury Square to Tavistock House, Tavistock Square. It applied to the United Synagogue, the premier religious organization in the Jewish community, for a contribution of £100 towards the building fund of £3,000, in addition to its annual vote of £200 to the College. The Council voted the grant by a majority of 23 to17. Among those who voted against the grant were Nathaniel de Rothschild, now the president, and Noah Davis.

In February 1911, the Finance Committee recommended that the Council should terminate its annual grant to the College, which then stood at £200. The Council voted against the recommendation. The ground on which the recommendation was presented was the pressure on the financial resources of the United Synagogue.

Among the foremost advocates of the College at the Council were Charles Samuel (1821–1903), a wholesale clothier who was for many years from its inception an honorary officer of the United Synagogue and for 24 years a treasurer of Jews College, of which he was a substantial benefactor; and Sir Adolph Tuck (1854–1926), the noted art publisher and philanthropist, who succeeded Samuel as treasurer of the Jews' College in 1902, which post he held until his death. On Tuck's death, the *Jewish Chronicle* commented that 'no budget night of the olden days would have been complete without an amendment by Sir Adolph to the proposed meagre grant to the College'.

Another, and related, topic is the conception of the Jewish minister in the minds of the leaders of the United Synagogue. The United Synagogue was content that the incumbents in its synagogues should be non-rabbinic pastoral preachers. That category of Jewish cleric had many virtues, particularly in the post-emancipation period. The idea of the Jewish minister, in the sense in which the term came to be used, was a product of the United Synagogue. It contrasted with the foreign-trained, or untrained, factotum. It also contrasted with the rabbinically learned and somewhat remote, and usually foreign-trained, scholar-minister. The distinctive Anglo-Jewish clergymen came into being, of whom a number were men of high quality and considerable influence.

The lay leadership feared that rabbinic training might involve the introduction of the outlook found among the immigrants from Eastern Europe, which was alien to them. In 1911, the *Jewish Year Book* made the point in telling fashion. 'We appear', wrote the editor, 'to be on the eve of an upheaval which may cause a distinct cleavage between English Judaism and the religious system represented by a number of rabbis who are practically independent of and manifestly hostile to the English rabbinate'. Albert Jessel was in this connection, perhaps, the leading protagonist of what might be called the West, as well as the West End. He was described as 'essentially occidental' in his upbringing and sympathies, and as being 'not in accord with the administrators of Jews College in their design to produce a high standard of rabbinical learning at the expense, as he thought, of English culture'.[8]

Well before the end of the first half-century, the question of recruiting lay leaders for the United Synagogue became acute. The original novelty and challenge had gone. Wider opportunities outside the Jewish community presented themselves, especially to the old families. There was also a falling off in Jewish enthusiasm and religious attachment. Furthermore, the preoccupations of World War I, and the heavy loss of life within the strata from which the leaders had formerly come, depleted the ranks. Another factor which intensified the problem of recruitment was that a number of prospective office-holders had made their way into the Reform and Liberal Synagogues.

In commenting on the death of Sir Benjamin Cohen (1844–1909), younger brother of Lionel, and like him president of the Board of Guardians, vice-president of the United Synagogue and Conservative MP, the *Jewish Chronicle* described him as 'a member of an able generation which has now almost gone'. The editor continued: 'The work those men have done will endure but needs supplementing and adopting to the necessities of the new day. Yet we do not hear on the threshold the tread of the feet of the young men who will take up the great burden'. 'I maintain', said the chief rabbi, in reference to Sir Benjamin at the Bayswater Synagogue where he had been warden, 'that the languid and half-hearted support given by our younger brethren to the cause of Judaism, its synagogue and charities, constitutes even a greater menace to Anglo-Jewry' than the then projected Liberal schism.[9]

In the years immediately following, the death of hardly any prominent figure in the Jewish community occurred without the same point being made, with increasing force. When Felix Davis (1863–1916), a notable and particularly popular vice-president died, *Mentor* in the *Jewish Chronicle* wrote that the event 'compels the question ... will the United Synagogue find the needed recruits, ... the same earnest, fine-hearted, whole-souled men who will continue the work'. In a memorable phrase, he asked whether the United Synagogue did in the past or did in the present encourage young talent 'to see the greatness of the little work and the importance of the pettiness it has to compass'. His answer was that it had not done so in the past, he doubted whether it did in the present and he urged the need to begin to do so now.

Within the old families the leaders did, in fact, strive to encourage the younger generation to accept the burdens. In 1913, there was appointed as treasurer a younger member of the Cohen family, who later became the dominant influence in the United Synagogue and the most influential layman in the Jewish community. It is of some interest that it was Jessel who invited Waley Cohen to take office. 'The Council', he wrote to Cohen, 'is not easily led (or driven) by the Honorary Officers as was the case when I was first elected on it 24 years ago ... but the influence of the present lot (of Honorary Officers) is higher than it has been for some years'.[10]

Waley Cohen was a nephew of Lionel Louis Cohen and a grandson of Jacob Waley. He filled the vacancy left by the death of Carl Stettauer (1859–1913), the Bavarian-born leather merchant and a leading figure in the Hampstead Synagogue. Stettauer was a prominent member of the London County Council and an energetic chairman of the Russo-Jewish Committee at a critical period in the history of that Committee.

Before turning to the age of Waley Cohen, it is necessary to recall the changing composition of the United Synagogue. By 1920, most of the members of the United Synagogue were Eastern European immigrants or their children. This preponderance was reflected in the Council. The attitude of the leaders of the United Synagogue was that the immigrants and their families should be made to approximate in style and thought, as far as possible, to those of the English Jew. This is not the place for an examination of the interrelations between the United Synagogue and the Federation of Synagogues, or of the special character or impact of the Machzike Hadath Synagogue and community.

In 1890, Lord Rothschild invited the Sephardim and the West London Synagogue of British Jews to send delegates to the conference convened by the United Synagogue, to consider the appointment to the chief rabbinate. It would not have been possible or thought proper in any later or earlier period for any such invitation to have been extended to the latter congregation. Neither invitation was accepted.

A similar latitudinarianism was shown over Claude Montefiore's membership of the Jewish Religious Education Board. His sister's husband, Henry Lucas (1842–1910), was president of the Board, which was founded under Lucas' aegis in 1895. Lucas, brother of Sampson Lucas, and a member of the Chancery Bar, succeeded Lionel Cohen as vice-president of the United Synagogue. He had been president of the Jewish Association for the Diffusion of Religious Knowledge, the precursor of the Jewish Religious Education Board, to whose progress he contributed much.

Montefiore was a member of the newly created Board, and Henry Lucas defended his brother-in-law's membership in the face of mounting criticism, arising from Montefiore's published 'left' religious views Montefiore's retirement from the Board prevented a crisis. In 1903, Jessel and Felix Davis, after much agitation at the Council of the United Synagogue, retired from Montefiore's Jewish Religious Union, the precursor of the Liberal Synagogue.

Henry Lucas' son, Dr Nathaniel S. Lucas (1884–1968), was likewise for many years an honorary officer of the United Synagogue and president of the Jewish Religious Education Board. He followed in his father's tradition in these and other respects.

Sir Robert Waley Cohen applied his mind to an understanding of the conflicting ideologies within the community. He became vice-president in 1918 and president in 1942. The leadership of the United Synagogue was little touched by the revolution which took place at the Board of Deputies in 1917.[11] The non-Zionism, or anti-Zionism, of its leaders contrasted with the growing mood of the Council and of the membership, and of local synagogues and boards. Lionel de Rothschild's chairmanship of the League of British Jews after the First World War was indicative, and inevitably provocative. During World War II, Waley Cohen, who was a vice-president of the Board, retired from the Board, together with a number of like-minded members of the old school.

They believed that under the new Zionist dispensation at the Board there was nothing useful they could do there. They contended that the Board had been finally captured by the Zionists and had lost its independence. They continued to express their reservations over the idea of a Jewish state, and in particular their alarm at the strains between Zionist policy and the British Mandatory Government and their fears over what was called 'dual loyalties'. The Anglo-Jewish Association became at that time the principal forum for these sentiments.

For 30 years, until his death in 1952, Sir Robert's was the main personal influence in the affairs of the United Synagogue. He was a man of many contrasts. Accustomed to big decisions on broad issues in commerce and industry, he was ever ready to study with meticulous care the detail of United Synagogue affairs. Always attentive to the mood of the Council, he would not be shaken out of his resolve by it. He was a strong man, with a great capacity to lead. To him, democracy in the United Synagogue was a method for more conveniently getting his own way. He was a man of action with imagination. He was not an observant Jew or much of a synagogue-goer, but he regarded the maintenance of traditional Judaism in Anglo-Jewry as desirable, even necessary. He was not a Zionist in the accepted sense, but his practical involvement in the building up of Palestine and the development of the Yishuv was substantial.

The membership of the United Synagogue, and especially its Council and local boards, were less prone than previously to accept policies formulated by the inner circle of leaders. The autonomy of local synagogues remained highly restricted. There was an ever-recurring conflict, of varying degrees of intensity, between the old style leadership and the new membership of the United Synagogue. Waley Cohen was able, with only few exceptions, to contain the conflicts within such limited compass that they tended to become rather personal issues, in which by his prestige, power and persuasion he was able to succeed without upheaval.

The most celebrated exception was with regard to the chief rabbi and his contradictory public messages to the synagogues over Zionism in the closing months of Hertz's life. It was a clash between personalities as well as policies, and was a kind of culmination of more than 20 years of intermittent conflict. This particular manifestation of the conflict was echoed in tumultuous consequential debates at the Council. The lay leaders wanted to keep politics out of the synagogues; the chief rabbi wanted to bring the influence of the synagogue to bear upon the strengthening of Zionism at a crucial time in Zionist history. It was his conviction that Judaism was broader than religion in the sense to which they were accustomed.

Waley Cohen's communal career is in many ways the history of the metropolitan Jewish community. A number of his hopes remained unfulfilled, but his achievements were considerable, not least in meeting the special problems caused by evacuation and otherwise during World War II. As to what might be called his disappointments, perhaps the most noteworthy concerned the proposal, which he urged before and after World War I, to remove Jews' College to Oxford or Cambridge. With the support, among other notable figures, of the president of the United Synagogue, he incorporated this plan in the initial scheme for the Jewish War Memorial, of which he was the principal founder, and which became the Jewish Memorial Council.

He was a graduate of Cambridge, as was the president. They

believed that there was no better link between Judaism and the English spirit than to have the religious leaders of the community trained at a Jewish college in the atmosphere of one of the ancient Universities.

In the language of his biographer, Robert Henriques, Waley Cohen 'always held that in the British and Jewish traditions there were elements peculiarly suited to each other'.[12] His plan met with strenuous opposition, not least from the Principal of the College, Adolph Buchler, and came to nought.

Waley Cohen also believed in regional rabbinates, especially for London. Pilot schemes to that end were devised and lapsed. But for the outbreak of war in 1939, the plan might have prospered. He also mooted in vain the idea of a United Synagogue for the country as a whole. He deeply regretted the falling away among young people of Jewish religious loyalty and the increasing indifference to Judaism. It is not easy to determine his own personal particular religious standpoint, or to discover the rationale in his own mind of his institutional attachment to Orthodoxy. He regarded the future of the Jewish community as bound up with adherence to Judaism, and if one may hazard a guess, he regarded Orthodoxy as more readily transmissible. He was clearly impressed and moved by the antiquity of the Jewish tradition, and had a reverence for the wisdom and the heritage of his predecessors in the leadership of the United Synagogue, with so many of whom he had family connections.

He presided over a vast expansion of the United Synagogue and played a decisive role in the inception and growth of the District Synagogue Scheme. He extended the influence of the United Synagogue into wider areas of communal life, developed the Jewish Memorial Council to the limit of prudence in the light of its resources, was co-founder, with Nathan Morris, of the London Board of Jewish Religious Education, created Woburn House, and appointed to the Beth Din and earned the respect of Dayan Y. Abramsky.[13]

Waley Cohen was aided by a succession of able colleagues, from Albert Morris Woolf (1856–1925) of St John's Wood and Samuel Moses (1866–1934) of Hampstead, to Frank Samuel (1889–1954), who succeeded him as president, and Isaac W. Goldberg (1894–1969).

He was called and acknowledged himself to be 'the last of the Grand Dukes'. He was irascible and self-willed, but he understood human nature. In particular, he was prepared to be venturesome in communal planning, and somehow found time for new thinking. In these respects, he was much in the pattern of his uncle, Lionel Louis Cohen. Between them, they seem to me to personify the history of the United Synagogue. When Sir Robert died, it was universally acknowledged that his like would not again be seen. If the dominance of the old leadership became a thing of the past, the tradition of service, which was at its core, remained as an example, even to a leadership of a wholly different stamp.

NOTES

1. See Lord Justice Cohen, 'Levi Barent Cohen and Some of his Descendants', *Transactions of the Jewish Historical Society of England*, Vol. 16 (1952); Lucien Wolf, *Essays in Jewish History* (ed. Cecil Roth) (1934), pp. 233–40; the genealogical tables in (and generally) Hannah F. Cohen, *Changing Faces* (1937), and Chaim Bermant, *The Cousinhood* (1971); and the author's 'Lionel L. Cohen' in *Hampstead Synagogue Review*, December 1954.
2. See Vivian D. Lipman, 'Synagogal Organisation in Anglo-Jewry', *Jewish Journal of Sociology*, Vol. 1 (1959), p. 80, etc., for a study of the gradual liberalization of the system. Originally, while all members could vote, candidature for the Council was restricted to privileged members.
3. Perhaps the most notable Conservative political figures among the honorary officers have been Henry de Worms (1840–1903), later Lord Pirbright; and Sir Isidore Salmon MP, L.C.C. (1876–1941), chairman of J. Lyons & Co., Sir Leonard Franklin (1862–1944), banker and for some years treasurer of the Burial Society of the United Synagogue, was a well-known Liberal figure.
4. See generally Howard Brotz, 'Position of the Jews in English Society', *Jewish Journal of Sociology*, Vol. 1 (1959), pp. 94–113.
5. See in particular *Jewish Chronicle*, 30 October and 6 November 1885.
6. *Jewish Chronicle*, 30 December 1870. The immediate object of his letter was to support the proposal that the clauses should be accepted by the synagogues, in spite of their deletion from the statutory scheme. This was striking support, as Salomons had long been the principal Jewish protagonist of the voluntary principle. However, abandonment now would have meant a serious departure from the agreed terms of the union.
7. *Some Notes and Articles by the late Asher Asher M.D.*, with a biographical sketch (in Hebrew) by David Kohn-Zedek and collected obituaries (1916). In its obituary, the *Jewish Chronicle* commented that Asher 'always placed religion above theology'. This was also true of the organization which he

nurtured and of the habit of mind of its lay leadership. Dr Kenneth Collins'
lecture on Asher to the Jewish Historical Society of England on 24 May 2001
was published in *Transactions of the Jewish Historical Society of England*,
Vol. 37 (2002), pp. 163–79.

8. *Jewish Chronicle*, 5 January 1917. For an extreme critique of 'an "official"
religion attached to the Synagogue' towards the end of the century, see
Maurice Simon, *Jewish Review*, Vol. 2 (1911), pp. 305–6. Israel Zangwill's
article entitled 'English Judaism' in the first volume of the *Jewish Quarterly
Review* (1889) is a satirical but no less pungent commentary on the low place
of Jewish study in what appeared to be the scale of values of Anglo-Jewish
society. Solomon Schechter was a noteworthy and more balanced, though far
from reticent, commentator on this topic.

9. *Jewish Chronicle*, 19 November 1909.

10. Robert Henriques, *Sir Robert Waley Cohen 1877–1952* (1966), p. 179. See
also G.J. Webber, *A Tribute to the late Sir Robert Waley Cohen* (1953), and
A.N. Newman, *The United Synagogue 1870–1970* (1977).

11. When officers of the Board, including the president, D.L. Alexander, resigned
over the Zionist issue, the event was described by the *Jewish Chronicle* on 14
September 1917 as 'the overthrow of the old system'. It went on:

> (the event) responded to the well-defined feeling among the Jewish masses
> … At a time when almost every hour shows the mischief and futility of
> entrusting the affairs of whole peoples to a few independent autocrats, there
> can be no revival of those discredited methods in English Jewry … English
> Jewry has been launched on the democratic flood.

These exaggerated sentiments expressed the views of the redoubtable editor,
Leopold Greenberg. This famous communal episode undoubtedly affected the
power structure inside Anglo-Jewry, sharpened lines of division, and was a
herald of further change. The United Synagogue could hardly in the long run
remain unaffected.

12. Henriques, *Sir Waley Cohen*, p. 17.

13. 'Regret was expressed in several quarters that the opportunity of the vacancy
had not been seized for the purpose of appointing an English-speaking Dayan
able to minister to the needs of the younger generation in East London' –
Jewish Chronicle, 27 September 1935. The vacancy was caused by the retirement of Dayan I. Hillman to Palestine. The appointment of Rabbi Abramsky,
then at the Machzike Adath, was an act of statesmanship and courage.

7

Israel Zangwill in His Day, 1864–1926[*]

Zangwill would have rejoiced at this handsome new edition of his masterpiece,[1] which first appeared in 1892. The occasion was his fiftieth anniversary. The Introduction is by a well-known Jewish historian, who is a highly-placed British civil servant, a devout Jew and an Oxonian. Zangwill would have been impressed by each attribute, not least the last-mentioned. He would have been intrigued, if not puzzled, at the combination, which might even have suggested to him a sequel or two.

But what would have struck him most forcibly is that the grandchildren of his ghetto have become the grandparents and great-grandparents in a latter-day ghetto, strangely dissimilar from the old one but unmistakably in line. Old echoes ring and are responded to. We are in the midst of one of the periodic bouts of Zangwill's popularity. Only this time it is flavoured with the invaluable curiosity of critical research. Zangwill is at last paid the compliment of being treated as a classic without panegyric.[2]

Dr Lipman's Introduction is written with charm and zest, and reflects his own brand of lightly carried but deep-layered erudition. He sketches the historical background, and the persons, places and periods which Zangwill's sharp observation and deft pen imported from life. From Zangwill's living models he moves to the Jewish life of London in and around the 1880s, including internal hopes and sometimes hostility outside. Many readers will be grateful for the light he throws on Zangwill's raw material.

Zangwill's style has tended to conceal his essential detachment

---

*Published in the *Jewish Quarterly*, London (Spring, 1977).

from his theme. This is not a great novel. It is discursive, episodic and, in part, a collection of impressions, humorous anecdote and social comment. It all hangs together through an interconnecting realism achieved from close quarters. His irony and jolting paradox are there. So too his characteristic mischievous phrases. His acerbic asides gleam along the pages. And throughout there is his tenderness for the Jewish plight, allied to a suppressed resentment at the historical processes which produced it.

'A dead and gone wag called the street Fashion Street', he writes in the chapter headed 'The Bread of Affliction', and 'most of the people who live in it do not even see the joke'. It is the opening sentence of the book, and what a prologue is therein contained. The limitation in the words 'most of the people' is equally relevant to what he had to say. He was one of those who had won a way out. If he detected the exact nuances of the old East End's varied assumptions and aspirations and managed to convey the local shapes and sounds with sharp accuracy, it was, partly, precisely because he was at least one stage removed and knew it. This fact gave him the artist's freedom. Whatever utility the book might have had in Jewish public relations at a time of ceaseless polemics about Jewish immigration and Jewish character, he was not to be confused with the sitter.

There is quoted in the Introduction Zangwill's famous reply to Mayer Sulzberger's invitation to write a novel such as this. He agreed that 'there is (a Jewish novel) inside me and it must come out one day'. He went on: 'only I could not undertake ... to write a novel which ... would appeal exclusively to a section ... Behind all the Jewish details there must be the human interest which will raise it into that cosmopolitan thing, a work of art.' Here is the true setting for the book. It is not still-life, but life in motion.

That is the special quality of *Children of the Ghetto*, in spite of being a period piece. Its characters are largely out-moded. Even much of the old style of pride is lost. But the work tells of a changing society. It is against the background of its many-sided, changing nature that the despair, hopes and foibles of the actors take on their added dimension. Zangwill in his own life embodied many of the most important changes.

The key to much of Zangwill's thought and indeed to a full understanding of this work is, I believe, to be found in the following passage concerning the 'Ghetto', which appears in his 'Proem' to the novel. 'And they', he wrote,

> who have won their way beyond its boundaries, must still play their parts in tragedies and comedies – tragedies of spiritual struggle, comedies of material ambition – which are the aftermath of its centuries of dominance, the sequel of that long cruel night in Jewry which coincides with the Christian Era.

Virtually every phrase in this passage is brimful with comment and implication about the Jews and about himself.

He was well aware of the already increasingly discussed distinctions between 'racial Jew' and 'religious Jew'. He refers to the topic in this book. The Jews around the 1840s, he comments, 'would have looked upon the modern distinctions between racial and religious Jews as the sophistries of the convert or the missionary'.

On the appearance of Holbrook Jackson's celebrated *The Eighteen Nineties* in 1913, Bernard Shaw asked the famous question whether it all really happened. It was not asked with incredulity, but from knowledge that it was indeed true. Experiment and change were everywhere. The slow upheaval of society, towards which the Reform Act of 1867 and the Education Act of 1870 had contributed, was for everyone to see. In the wake of the success of Gladstonian Liberalism emerged new kinds of social questions, attracting solutions to which the old individualism was not geared. Mid-century confidence had somewhat ebbed. The letter of the Bible was dethroned. No one could be sure whether anxiety or exhilaration was the more appropriate sentiment with which to scan the future. 'The modern world', writes Zangwill in the twelfth chapter, is 'where the ends of the ages meet.' It is a striking phrase, both in its Jewish context and, generally, as regards the interaction of the end of one age with the onset of another.

It is probably only now that it is possible realistically to assess the 1880s and 1890s. There is today an intuitive sense that it was in those years that our own age took its distinctive beginnings, nurtured though they were throughout the nineteenth century. The movements in thought and action during those decades have, to a significant extent, worked themselves out. We, at this remoteness of time, for better and for worse, are the heirs, and feel entitled to judge. Two world wars and much else have reinforced our right to sit in judgement on the old *fin de siècle*, which was so like and so grossly unlike our own time, which is even more adventurous and more perilous.

It is not in the least surprising that we should be in the midst of a boom in Victorian studies. The unashamed confidence of the Victorian age is enviable. Nor is it surprising that our interest should be deeply tinged by a strange fellow-feeling for its closing years, with their alienation, disenchantment, resignation, and, with it all, then as now, new ideals and fresh social adjustments.

The modern Jewish world began in those years. The last ten or 20 years of the nineteenth century were mightily full of consequence for the Jews. It is a large and continuing topic. As far as Great Britain was concerned, there arose therein, in the midst of all the changes, a large, restless, intelligent and acutely self-conscious 'alien' Jewish community. The Jews could not be expected to remain immune to all the diverse forces playing upon public life and private *mores*. No doubt, with Jews, the transformations would be comparatively muted, for they sensed strong cohesive factors from within and without, and there was considerable, and to a great extent, consequential inertia. But transformations there were, and of a remarkably analagous kind to those in the wider community.

After all, there was no true ghetto. All the novelties and stresses of the day prevailed in one degree or another in the Jewish fold. There were comparable fissures and revolts between what was established and the more independent-minded, both in the 'ecclesiastical' and secular fields. Personal, doctrinal, philosophical and social issues were intermingled. Nor were dissensions always on the 'left'. In every sphere, there were eruptions, whether of greater or less severity, against any semblance of presumed or privilege-bound authority. There was a new self-confidence on the part of the hitherto quiescent. New enthusiasms captured even sceptical minds.

Zangwill was aware of it all. Much of it was reflected in his own experience, and he incorporated the elements in one guise or another in *Children of the Ghetto*. In Esther Ansell's conversations with Raphael Leon, one feels that it is Zangwill thinking aloud in his novel. As a liberal humanist, he could intellectually afford to look benignly on all facets of the passing show. Having achieved his own freedom, he could pick and choose what to look upon gravely and what to smile at openly. In a strange kind of way, one feels as one reads the book that it constitutes an epitaph on a place and on an age, as much as being an indulgent encomium. There are indications in the work that Zangwill knew it, and perhaps so intended. After all, impermanence is the only common factor through history.

Zangwill scorned respectability, but did not, could not, shun all aspects of it. His important article on 'English Judaism' in the *Jewish Quarterly Review* in 1889, was in large part directed to disclosing the deadening hand of that bourgeois ailment. Many passages in the novel are reminiscent of the article. He meant many things by respectability. They included, I think, the philistinism of unimaginative businessmen, the fear of the unconventional, and the decay of intellectual honesty. These aspects he abhorred, especially when they were accompanied by the sort of self-abnegation which sometimes springs from an unreflecting, self-justifying conformity. All this he held up to public scrutiny, with varying degrees of charitableness. It is this touch – the touch of the well-informed critic of established *shibboleths* – that transforms him into something more than an entertaining feuilletonist.

'Judaea', writes Zangwill in *Children of the Ghetto*, with regard to the old anglicization,

> prostrated itself before the Dagon of its hereditary foe, the Philistine, and respectability crept on to freeze the blood of the Orient with its frigid finger, and to blur the vivid tints of the East into the uniform grey of English middle-class life.

Yet, one of the great attractions to Zangwill of that life, and of the major trends in English public life at large, was its comparative placidity and its libertarianism. He admired England and her ways. For a Jew conscious of the volatile pressures on Jewish life elsewhere, this was at times a heady appeal. In describing Josef Strelitski's reaction to it, Zangwill writes, in relation to this figure in his novel, that 'the voluptuousness of the sensation cannot be known to born freemen'. That recent arrival from Czardom found the 'atmosphere' here 'untainted by spies, venal officials and jeering soldiery ... the ground was stable ... no arbitrary ukase ... hung over the head ... faith was free and action untrammelled'.

For all his detachment and his talk of the 'next religion', Zangwill was a proud Jew in an old school. He was among the first English novelists to present Jews in recognisable forms, civic and unstereotyped. He was a great precursor of that circle of Jewish social critics in the arts, whose arrows are sharpened by their first-hand knowledge.

Further, he raised questions born of the modern Jewish age, and did so at a time when, so to speak, their presentation was more malleable than was later possible. Putting aside traditional dogma, could there be a distinctively Jewish culture? If so, what were its ingredients and essential character? What is the Jew? In later life, as Zionist, Territorialist and a leading exponent of Jewish opinion, such subjects engaged Zangwill's constant attention. It is clear from *Children of the Ghetto* that in his 20s, they were already a major preoccupation. In one way or another they are alluded to, directly or by implication. Such implication is found at times in his descriptions and comments – often in themselves highly amusing but no less pointed – concerning those Jews and Jewish groups for whom there were no conscious problems of Jewish identity but only questions of technique for a changeless continuity.

Although they did not realise it, these issues were latent in much of the polemics of the early emancipationists, long before Zangwill was born. He was aware of the virtual inescapability of these questions. He was alert to them all the more, and not the less, by reason of the fact that he would probably have agreed in many respects with Lord Curzon that Great Britain was 'the greatest element for good which the world has ever seen'.

And yet it was from Judaism and the Jewish experience that Zangwill derived his humanism, and even his rationalism. His progressive outlook on so many causes was conditioned and stimulated by his Jewish instincts for compassion, justice and the inviolable worth of the human personality. Could so vast and constantly productive a heritage be about to see its expiry? Or are its recurring fruits eloquent of its immortality?

Esther Ansell's style of thinking, and especially the development of her thought, are the nearest in the book to that of its author. She describes herself as 'a curious mixture'. She asks herself whether 'one can worship the gods of the Greeks without believing in them'. 'Our tiny race', she observes, 'may well be proud of having given humanity its greatest ... books. Why can't Judaism [she adds] take a natural view of things and an honest pride in its genuine history, instead of building its synagogues on shifting sand?' Perhaps part of an answer is proffered by the author in his earlier reference to the praying in what the novelist called the Congregation of the Sons of the Covenant; 'if they did not always know what they were saying, they always meant it'.

Elsewhere in these pages, Zangwill speaks of 'the steady silent drift of the new generation away from the old landmarks'. He adds: 'The finer spirits ... were groping for a purpose and a destiny, doubtful even if the racial isolation they perpetuated were not an anachronism.' He described the 'Asmonean Society' – obviously the Maccabeans – as a body 'where for the first time in history, Jews gathered with nothing in common save blood ... artists, lawyers, writers, doctors ... each thinking himself a solitary exception to a race of bigots who met one another (at the Asmonean) in mutual astonishment'. Behind the poetic licence, Zangwill makes his serious point.

Ultimately, however, Esther Ansell's 'dead ancestors that would not be shaken off lived and moved in her ... Had the Jew come so far only to break down at last ...?' Whatever may be said about the Victorian melodramatics of the closing pages, who can doubt the author's ineradicable outlook? Running through all the factors which make for dissolution, he felt a unifying element, born of antiquity, sustained by improbable providence, conscious of a hope, unsurprised by adversity, and cognisant of achievement. That its purpose was beneficent and universal, Zangwill could not doubt, not that the children and grandchildren of the ghetto were its witting and unwitting instruments. In the end, as at the beginning, he was a Hebrew, with all his contrariness.

NOTES

1. Israel Zangwill, *Children of the Ghetto*, with introduction by Vivian D. Lipman (The Victorian Library: Leicester University Press, 1977).
2. This was written in 1977. A further period of special interest in Zangwill, around the turn of the century, centred principally on a long public exhibition at the Jewish Museum in London, accompanied by public lectures on the lives, world, and influence, of Zangwill and his major Anglo-Jewish literary contemporaries.

8

Lucien Wolf (1857–1930): A Study in Ambivalence[*]

Consistency is not necessarily a virtue. And there may be some inner consistency within the ambivalence. In any case, Wolf could have made a reasonable plea in mitigation via the proposition that changing times, with their new perils and opportunities, may call for new-style solutions to old-new problems.

This is neither an historical narrative nor a biographical study. It is an impressionist portrayal of a prominent public figure who was also a particularly private man, the object being to explore Wolf's inner contrasts and examine any threads of consistency. He wrote much. In later years, with failing eyesight, he wrote less, but his memory was sharp, his acolytes many and his commitment to his public tasks unabated.

The late Dr A.S. Diamond, one-time president of the Jewish Historical Society, told me of his visits to Wolf in his latter years in rooms in Grays Inn, where, over cups of tea, Wolf would comment on the current scene and reminisce within a private coterie. Yet the *Jewish Chronicle* recorded that shortly before he died he was preparing for his normal visit to Geneva during the session of the League of Nations Assembly on the Minority Treaties, a report amply confirmed in the records of the Board of Deputies.

He was a robust defender of Jewish interests, as he saw them. He was not only a journalist, historian and communal civil servant,

---

*An extended version of the Presidential Address given to the Jewish Historical Society of England on 11 November 1993 as part of the commemoration of its centenary. The author is grateful to Professor Abramsky for his observations. This paper was first published in *Transactions of the Jewish Historical Society of England*, Vol. 35 (2000).

but a pragmatic politician with his own personal influence in political circles. This was connected with his power of articulating a case, his mastery of European languages, his vast knowledge related to issues with which he had to deal, and his standing and contacts through his journalism.[1] He had a deep and characteristically self-conscious loyalty to Britain. This was combined with an intense desire to save Jews, protect and advance their civil rights, and encourage the development of a recognizable Jewish culture. He saw the Jewish cause as part of the wider human cause.

He could not bring himself to regard the expansion of liberalism in the West as having been a flash in the pan. Had he thought that this was all it was, history would have lost meaning for him. There was nothing 'antiquarian' about him.

To examine the impact of the wider opening of society on the contemporary Jewish community in Britain remained for him a continuing and significant interest. He was as much concerned to measure the intellectual capacities of modern Jews as he was, as a historian, to study the old history of the Jews in the Canary Islands. He remained a moralist in his estimate of the ends which he sought to serve – peace, individual freedom, cultural integrity and intellectual advancement.

It would not have occurred to Wolf that his emphasis on the growth of 'toleration' and 'liberalism' as hallmarks of English history was demeaning to the 'beneficiaries'. He was a Liberal in politics, of the kind which admired Macaulay. He adhered to the view that Britain was in the van of 'civilization'. As a child of his times he would have had difficulty in understanding the notion of any kind of anti-Jewish implication in 'toleration'. 'Emancipation as a Jewish aspiration', wrote the late Professor Natan Rotenstreich, 'was never conceived as an attempt to destroy the collective Jewish entity. It implied in many cases a reinterpretation of the nature of Jewish collectivity – for instance a shift from an ethnic to a religious orientation ... Assimilation ... is an adjustment, an acculturation, a *modus vivendi* ...'[2] While Wolf was acutely aware of the challenge presented to Jews by the emancipation, he would have fully understood those observations. He seemed to regard political Zionists as despairingly avoiding facing that challenge.

Wolf knew only too well that since the emancipation, Jews had found that neither their own 'enlightenment' nor the degree of the world's 'enlightenment' offered any antidote against the continuing, virtually universal need for the Jew to justify himself and to explain what and who he was. He also knew that with the new freedoms had come an inner Jewish erosion or an aggravation thereof. If anything, the anti-Jewish malaise had gained some momentum in the wake of the emancipation, whose success had at the same time encouraged and facilitated the tide of 'radical assimilation'.

Wolf was regarded as the arch secular opponent of political Zionism. He was especially critical of the movement in the immediate prehistory of the Balfour Declaration. But he did not take as seriously as some of his associates the notion that there ought to be read into the civic and political emancipation an understanding, or quasi-contract, between British political society and the Jewish emancipationist leadership, whereby in his day an attachment to political Zionism should by definition properly be proscribed. He had a genuine understanding of the antiquity of the Zionist aspiration, including the political dimension. He always had difficulty in accepting Hermann Adler's contention that the Jewish nation had ended with the fall of the Temple. He would have wondered, like Zangwill, what, on such a basis, could remain of the liturgy, even allowing for the eschatological expositions presented from time to time.

In 1878, in response to pejorative public references to the international interests of the Jews, such as over Romanian Jewry and their wish for British Governmental intervention, Adler publicly declared that the Jewish interest is 'wholly a matter of sympathy which nature establishes between those who think alike, behave alike, and hope alike'. Wolf realized that any attempted analogies with Christian protests over outrages against Christians in Turkish-controlled areas in Southeast Europe left questions unanswered. What was the relationship between the Jewish cause and British policy in given instances? The humanitarian base of the Jewish concern was not regarded by anyone as the only facet of interest. There was an international Jewish kinship rooted in Jewish history. It was somehow related to Jewish peoplehood, and both found expression in the Jewish national idea as mutual cause and effect. Wolf did not regard these pressing sentiments as inconsistent with Jewish integration into Western society or with the loyalty of Jews as citizens.

The Conjoint Committee of the Board of Deputies and the Anglo-Jewish Association was the direct successor to the joint foreign-affairs committee set up by the two bodies in 1878. The latter was instituted amid the then well-known reservations on the Board's side. The personal standing of leading members of the AJA made it desirable to combine forces in the field of 'foreign affairs' at a time of rising anxiety over the assault on the civic rights and status of the Jews in Romania. It is difficult today to detect any democratic impulse in the creation of the committee. Yet at the time it seemed to represent a significant broadening and a welcome rationalization of the communal system, and a breaking of the old centralized oligarchic hold on communal power.

The Board did not admit Reform members into its ranks until 1886. The exclusion was ever more widely recognized as an anomaly, in that the main spokesmen in the House of Commons on the 'foreign' Jewish issues were members of Reform. On the death of Sir Francis Goldsmid in 1878, he was in effect succeeded as the principal Jewish spokesman in that sphere in Parliament by his fellow-Reformer, Sir John Simon. Further, the Board had by some been perceived as excessively insular, little interested in joint action with Jewish representatives abroad, relying on its own standing with the British Government, and unduly precedent-bound. The founder of the AJA was Abraham Benisch, whose proto-Zionism was one of the impulsions in his seeking to create firm machinery for international Jewish cooperation, in connection with which he envisaged the AJA as a likely progenitor. By the time Wolf became Secretary of the committee in 1888, that vision had not been wholly lost, but the 'Zionistic' element of the late founder's thinking was no longer to the fore in any political sense.

It is said that Wolf enjoyed the company of the 'notables' then and later. No doubt he did. His association with them was part of his *métier*. But he was not, and did not become, a subordinate. He became their mentor and pursued his own initiatives. He had his own access to the world of diplomacy. The immigrant's son came to dominate the thinking of the committee of 'cousins' and their friends in the formulation of policy. When in 1917 he became director of the successor joint committee, on the dissolution of the old Conjoint Committee, Sir Anthony de Rothschild and (later Sir) Robert Waley Cohen were among its principal members.

From his earliest days in journalism, Wolf's articles attracted special attention. This was more particularly the case with his articles (mainly unsigned) in the *Jewish World*, from 1880, on the modern role of the Jew. This was partly because the subject was under wide public scrutiny and partly because of their literary quality. In particular, the interest was also related to the campaigning character of the journal under its founder, George Lyon, since its inception in 1873. Lyon was a forceful polemicist of independent mind, and a regular critic both of the British Government and of the Jewish communal leadership for what he saw as their inadequate response to the Jewish cause abroad, especially in Russia and Romania. Lyon was also a persistent advocate of liturgical reform. Wolf long supported the editor's stands on these issues.

There was an inherent irony in the quality of his personality as well as in the versatility of his expertise. The motive for his involvement in nurturing the movement for the foundation of the Jewish Historical Society was directly connected with his concern to preserve and strengthen among Jews the sense of the Jewish historical legacy. This purpose was not predominantly 'apologetical', nor was it related to any desire to enhance the picture or authority of the old families. His attitude was similar to that which led him to take a leading role in the development of the Jewish Literary Society movement and of the Union of Jewish Literary Societies, of which he became an active president. The annual reports of the Union carried, under its English name on the outer cover, its Hebrew name in Hebrew script – *Agudat Dorshei Da'at* 'Union of Teachers [or Seekers] of Knowledge'. Its constituent societies in London and beyond were more than social. Lecturers included the leading Jewish scholars in Britain. To Wolf, the societies were necessary agents in adult Jewish education. The lectures were often reported at length in the Jewish press, and many appeared in the *Anglo-Jewish Annual,* published by the Union.

In January 1896, in a public address to an assembly of Jewish youth in London, Wolf defined 'the chief duty of the rising generation of Jews'. It was, he said, 'to cultivate the Jewish historic spirit'. He added: 'There will be no future for Judaism or rehabilitation of the race without it. I earnestly appeal to you for the study of our inspiring traditions, for the loving care of our great heritage.' Wolf never wavered in that stance, or in his view of the importance of such admonition, which went beyond communal polemics. The lecture, extensively reported, was in line with his life-long special interest in the objects and proceedings of this Society. His expressions go beyond putting on a brave show against the detractors of the Jews.

Making allowances for any resort to rhetoric engendered by the occasion, one notes with particular interest his hopes for the Society as set out in his inaugural lecture in 1893. 'I hope', he said,

> that we shall do something ... to study the social, political and intellectual life of the [Jewish] community, not the biographies of leading but not always representative men but ... the complex ramifications of the entire organism, to conceive of our own past not as a shallow village tale but as an integral part of that greatest epic of human strivings which is the history of Israel.

There is no reason to think that Wolf was not expressing his genuine sentiment and aspiration. It was a consistent theme with him.

He was concerned that Jews should know their history and that it should also be read by others. This was directed not only to telling the world about 'the Jewish contribution' to Britain or the world (in order, as many felt was desirable, to demonstrate the value and the justice of Jewish emancipation), but also because of his own inborn attachment to the task of cultivating interest and pride in the distinctive elements of the Jewish past. In his own way, he was an active Jewish educationist. He would certainly have agreed with Burke that 'a people will not look forward to posterity who never look back to their ancestors'. I imagine that he would also have agreed with Rabbi Simeon Singer's dictum, in a different context, that 'divines are so human'. His Jewishness was less theological than historical.

In the *Jewish World*, Wolf also carried the old theme of Jewish mission beyond the traditional ambit of furthering human moral enlightenment, into the realm of practical social service for the wider society and not only within his own community. This was in line with Lyon's undogmatic and undenominational principles of social progress – as well as with what became a central feature of Hermann Adler's publicly proclaimed, practical Jewish philosophy. Wolf also welcomed what he conceived to be the 'purifying' effect

208

of the progressive modernization of the Jewish faith, which, he considered, would facilitate the Jewish task in the world. While Wolf's expressions coincided with Lyon's concern for practical and equitable devices for social organization and improving the lot of mankind, they also related to Wolf's own understanding of a Jewish purpose and duty. For him it was part of the business of preserving a Jewish particularity within integration.

If his form of modernism detached him from the rabbinic tradition, his historical sense detached him no less from some of those with whom Adler had his own philosophic and theological differences. From the early 1880s, Wolf was engaged in a series of public disputations with Claude Montefiore. Their exchanges concerned the nature of Jewishness and the Jewish role in society. In the *Contemporary Review,* in September 1882, Montefiore cited with approval Adler's statement that 'the great bond which unites Israel is not one of race but the bond of a common religion'. This was part of Adler's response to allegations that Judaism was a 'tribal religion'. Wolf dissociated himself from Adler's dictum, which he called 'very dangerous', and was no less opposed to Montefiore's conclusions. Montefiore envisaged at the time an 'extension' of Judaism 'beyond the Jewish race'.

Montefiore considered, at that period, that out of a 'denationalized [his word] Judaism', working in association with a reformed Christianity, there might emerge a unified and widely acceptable creed of ethical humanism. In an editorial in the *Jewish World* in September 1882, Wolf wrote that 'to denationalize' Judaism would be 'to lose it and with it the work of 50 centuries'. In Judaism, he declared, 'the religion' and 'the race' are 'almost indistinguishable'. He seemed unable to divest himself of the conviction that the historicity of Judaism was an essential ingredient of its essence.

Wolf charged Adler with retaining, through his form of rabbinic Judaism, some elements of faith and practice which he thought gave colour to what Gentile critics regarded or described as tending to excessive Jewish isolation and detachment. When Montefiore seized hold of Adler's contention that Judaism was not synonymous with race or nation, Wolf chided him for, in effect, exploiting Adler's theme and subverting it. He rebuked Montefiore for implying a concession to those who spoke of the alleged 'Jewish tribalism', which it was Montefiore's wish to exorcise.

What precipitated the Wolf–Montefiore exchanges was the public invitation in 1880 by a prominent Christian conversionist cleric to the Archbishop of Canterbury and the chief rabbi to meet, in order to examine the present and future connection between the restoration of the Jews to Jerusalem and their conversion. Wolf scoffed at the suggestion. Montefiore was less hostile to the idea of a meeting. Wolf's sense of, and regard for, Jewish particularity, however it might be defined and explained, detached him from Montefiore's standpoint. Whether that particularity was providential or historical or, in some light, both, may not in practice have seemed as important to him as to other Jews on the 'right' or 'left' of the religious spectrum. This for him was probably a question on which he treasured a private agnosticism. He seemed to retain it as an open question, which he may have preferred not to strive to resolve.

While guarding against seeking to encase his career into an unchanging philosophic framework, one may be permitted to enquire whether early principles, or remnants of his early thinking, might be detected in his later outlooks and policies. There is a line of similarity. He retained his stress on the ethnic element in Jewish history, old and new. This did not mean that he adopted any sort of 'purist' view of 'Jewish race'. He saw in Jewish observance a positivist factor making for Jewish survival, and for a sense of superiority, without arrogance, over the civilizations within which they have lived.

Wolf's article in the *Fortnightly Review* in August 1884, entitled 'What is Judaism? A Question for Today', lengthily presents his then answer to that query. It was in that year that he had published his pietistic biography of Sir Moses Montefiore. Earlier articles by him, including his exchanges with Claude Montefiore and his own responses to allegations of 'Jewish tribalism', were now exceeded in scope and depth of argument. Describing himself as 'Orthodox', and without rejecting contentions relating to the 'legalism' of Judaism, he asserted that it was the observances which had ensured Jewish 'separation'. Judaism is 'a positivistic system differing only from the latter-day Positivism of Auguste Comte in that it has operated during some thousands of years with results which raise it altogether out of the region of empirical philosophy'. He adds:

The proper method of ascertaining the nature of Judaism must be not by a collation of biblical texts but by an induction from the phenomena of fact that in Judaism, the religion and the race are almost interchangeable terms. The rigid observance, during long centuries, by a peculiarly exclusive people has necessarily resulted in the people becoming the manifestation of its laws ... the most striking phenomenon in Jewish life is the survival of the race.

In reply to criticism that he had underplayed the role of 'theological doctrine' in Judaism, Wolf wrote in the *Jewish Chronicle,* on 15 August 1884, that he differs from Orthodoxy in its 'more speculative teachings'. To practise a distinctive legalism from moral considerations of purity and holiness, he went on, 'is arrogance which directly invites the attacks of our enemies'.

In his essay entitled 'The Queen's Jewry', written on the occasion of Victoria's jubilee in 1897 and reprinted in Cecil Roth's edition of Wolf's writings, Wolf stated:

The best characteristics of the foreign Jew have been cultivated; the worst has been got rid of ... So far from the foreign Jew degrading the English community he has been raised very nearly to its level ... in the next generation no trace will remain of the foreign Jew which caused so much anxiety between 1880 and 1890 ...

Such passages reflected Wolf's desire to present the Jewish community as part of England, rejoicing with fellow-subjects on the royal occasion. In some respects, as he must have known, the article was out of date. The community was ever more divided, the tensions between old and new were increasing in intensity and political Zionism was already one of the major issues.

However, there was more to his objective in 1897 than his desire to present a calm 'English' exterior in his image of the Jewish community. He felt that schools (Jewish day schools in the immigrant areas as well as municipal schools everywhere), the growing force of fashion and the tide of social aspiration would assure some merging, to a sufficient extent, to create a cohesive English Jewish community. There was an ethnic bond which was part of and also went beyond the then current patronizing air. He harboured no illusions about the leaders of the emancipation campaigns. 'The agitation against the Jewish disabilities', he wrote in 1891, 'was ... a struggle for the privileges of the rich men, and the disabilities which were contested did not weigh on the daily rank and file.'³ Like Lionel Louis Cohen and others, he had no doubt that the old and new would profoundly influence one another's thinking and forms of Jewishness, whatever sharp differences would remain in some quarters.

Typical of the background occasioning anxieties on the part of the established Jewish leadership was the attack on Jews in the Liberal *Daily Graphic* in October 1897, and the issue of their inward-lookingness and separate interests. In the *Contemporary Review* later that year, Herzl commented that 'the Gentile has never yet disputed our nationality. That role has been reserved for the Jews.' What gave added significance to the controversies was Arnold White's later proposals in the *Contemporary Review* for the sponsoring by the Powers, especially Britain, of a Jewish state in or near Palestine. This critic of unrestricted Jewish immigration into Britain commented that Adler defends 'the patriotic idea for English Jews as though this were incompatible with the creation of a home secured by public rights for those Jews who either cannot or will not be assimilated in the country of their adoption'. Wolf might silently have shared in that criticism of Adler, but was also aware of an issue which had been raised in some quarters, notably by the historian and Liberal, Goldwin Smith, as to whether a Jew can be a patriot. It had long been the task of Hermann Adler to rebut that insinuation, for which charge vocal opponents of the immigration were ready to find support in what Wolf regarded as the implication of the homelessness of the Jews in Zionist declarations and polemics. On the issue of Jewish immigration, Wolf's attitude was a mixture of humanitarian sympathy, Jewish fellow-feeling and concern over the reactions to the social and economic effects of a large influx. He seems to have remained in a state of embarrassed ambivalence on the question. It sharpened his hope for the liberalization of the Russian system of government.

Both of Wolf's articles in the *Encyclopaedia Britannica* in 1911, on 'Anti-Semitism' and 'Zionism' respectively, demonstrate the pull of his strong Jewish historical consciousness. In substance and tone they are in line with his role in his public exchanges of earlier years. He wrote in the latter article:

> Zionism is the lineal heir of the attachment to Zion which led the Babylonian exiles under Zerubavel to rebuild the Temple and which

flamed up the heroic struggle of the Maccabeans. The idea that it is a setback for Jewish history is a controversial fiction.[4] The great bulk of the Jewish people have throughout their history remained faithful to the dream of restoration of their national life in Judea. The Zionist movement is today the greatest popular movement that Jewish history has ever known.

No one in Wolf's lifetime had a sharper awareness of Wolf's ambivalence than Leopold Greenberg. Whatever their differences, they had a high mutual regard personally for one another as journalists and as practical men of affairs. Greenberg formed the impression that Wolf's dissent from Herzlian Zionism reflected at least in part a 'personal predilection', and was 'quasi-religious'. Greenberg wrote in the *Jewish Chronicle*, on 29 August 1930, that he had asked Wolf a number of times to explain inconsistencies between his opposition and his article in the *Encyclopaedia*. He added: 'He never seemed to be disposed to do so at all freely'. He had 'a strong religious bias'.

In his article in the *Encyclopaedia* on 'Anti-Semitism' he declared that that movement 'so far from injuring the Jews, has really given Jewish racial separatism a new lease of life'. The agitation had coincided 'with the revival of interest in Jewish history' and 'has helped to transfer Jewish solidarity from a religious to a racial basis'. He added:

> The bond of a common race, vitalised by a new pride in Hebrew history and spurred on to resistance by the insults of the anti-Semites, has given a new spirit and a new source of strength to Judaism at a moment when the approximation of ethical systems and the revolt against dogma were sapping its essentially religious foundations.

'The great bulk of the Jewish people', observed Wolf on Zionism, 'have throughout their history remained faithful to the dream of a restoration of their national life in Judea'. But the 'growth of toleration' and the development of emancipation provided 'alternatives' to nationalism; and 'the narrow nationalist spirit everywhere yielded before the hope or the progress of local emancipation'. It was at this point that his close readers might have detected some element of ambiguity in the author's own position. 'Mendelssohnian culture', he went on, by its promotion of the study of Jewish history, 'gave a fresh impulse to the racial consciousness of the Jews'. What he termed the 'new Judaism' had 'only reconstructed [the Jewish nationalist tradition] on a wider and more sober foundation'. This 'new race consciousness was fed by a glorious martyr history which ran side by side with the histories of the newly adopted nationalities of the Jews and was not unworthy of the companionship'. It was from this 'race consciousness' that there came 'a fresh interest in the Holy Land – an ideal rather than a politico-nationalist interest'.

Wolf's subsequent language might have seemed to some to translate the historical nature of Zionism into a movement of modern legitimacy. The 'spread of anti-Semitic doctrines throughout Europe' raised doubts as to whether 'the Mendelssohnian denationalization of Judaism possessed elements of permanency', and thereupon 'the Jewish nationalist spirit reasserted itself in a practical form'. Wolf dwells on what he sees as the 'impracticability' of political Zionism, in the light of the attitude of Turkey, the rivalry of the Powers, and the heightened tension between 'Orthodox' and 'secular'. But in 1911, regardless of his continuing repute as an opponent of political Zionism, his article must have struck some as setting out a case for the naturalness and legitimacy of the Zionist movement. Impracticability would, for Zionists, be a future matter for politics, awaiting opportunity and Jewish effort.

Wolf no doubt appreciated the possible implications of his argument, for he adds that 'with the passing away of anti-Semitism, Jewish nationalism will disappear'. Surveying the European scene, he expressed the belief that 'nationalities are daily losing more of their racial character' under the influence of 'religious toleration' and their naturalization laws. 'The coming nationality', he comfortingly asserts, 'will be essentially a matter of education and economics, and this will not exclude Jews as such'. Thus it was that he was able to conclude that 'modern Zionism is vitiated by its erroneous premises ... [namely] that anti-Semitism is unconquerable'.

It is clear that Wolf did not regard the Jewish national idea or the Jewish nation as at an end. The national ethos and history pervaded the lives of Jewish communities and individual Jews, but he averred that in the active practical form of political Zionism it was otiose and need not be the only outlet. His presentation was consistent with the proposition that (despite Wolf's liberal optimistic prophecy – part of the Victorian inheritance) hostile contingencies might well render an active Jewish nationalist spirit natural and necessary. Herzl had thought that such time had arrived. Later, Wolf might well have shared that conviction, but for the feared implication which he read into Zionism; that is the implication of the homelessness of the Jews of the West, which he deemed ran counter to and even threatened the policy and philosophy of integration which he considered to be the unalterable central theme of all Jewish public relations in the West.

Wolf's pre-war opposition to a British alliance with the Tzarist regime had been connected with his belief that the Jewish plight in Russia was part of the plight of the Russian people. He saw the regime as an effete but entrenched autocracy, to bolster which would in no way encourage or facilitate any liberal solution. The overthrow of the Tzar was seen by him as the prelude to the liberalization of the whole governmental system, in which the relief of the Jews from special pressures and discriminatory legislation would form a natural part.

The contrast between the integrationist Wolf advocating civil rights, and the later quasi-autonomist Wolf advocating links with the philosophy of Dubnow and with elements of Bundist ideology, is no less striking for being explainable on the grounds of imperative expediency. It is sufficiently striking to render it legitimate to ask whether this 'radical shift', as it has been called, does not reflect to some degree Wolf's inner and early expressed attitudes. The ideas behind his later attitude did not represent lines of thinking unnatural to him. His readiness to change tack was tantamount to a readiness to identify himself with a scheme of things which was reconcilable with significant facets of his own earlier, if theoretical, analysis of Jewishness and its development.

In his paper, tellingly entitled 'Lucien Wolf's efforts for the Jewish Communities of Central and Eastern Europe', Professor Abramsky comments that Wolf 'held contradictory points of view on the issue' of whether the 'notion of nationality as an ethnic and cultural status' could be combined with the search for the civil rights of Jews as citizens.[5] Not surprisingly, Wolf's advocacy was opposed both by Zionists and by the various brands of assimilationists. Yet there was some consistency between, on the one hand, Wolf's role in the formulation of the post-war minority clauses (a role now famously explored and presented by Dr Mark Levene) and, on the other hand, Wolf's much-cited article in the *Edinburgh Review* in April 1917, and much of what he wrote before World War I.

What Professor Abramsky describes as his 'extraordinary elasticity of mind' can perhaps reasonably be qualified by attributing to Wolf a certain inner consistency. As Professor Abramsky observes, Wolf did indeed remain an anti-Zionist. Be that as it may, he did not abandon at any time his attachment to the reality of the Jewish national idea, whatever language he adopted in anti-Zionist polemics at given moments. His span of years saw rapid and fundamental changes in the fortunes and prospects of the Jewish people. He was the product of the unique combination of his own cultivated intellectual interests, his own historical instincts and assessments, his perception of the different Jewish needs in the West and in the East, and his encounters with political opportunities and challenges which improbably presented themselves to this communal civil servant and international politician. He can only be judged as classically *sui generis*.

Wolf traced two important results to 'the anti-Semitic agitation'. One was the 'strong revival of the national spirit among the Jews in a political form'. The other was 'the recent movement which seeks to unite the Jewish people in an effort to raise the Jewish character and to promote the higher consciousness of the dignity of the Jewish people'. Both movements, he commented, are 'elements of fresh vitality to Judaism and they are probably destined to produce important fruit in future years'.

There is an apparent inconsistency between, on the one hand, Wolf's expressed belief that in the new age 'racial' prejudice and national xenophobia were on the wane and that, with their going, Zionism would lose its impetus and would likewise wane, and, on the other hand, his statement that Zionism (like the intellectual and 'literary' Jewish responses to anti-Semitism) was 'probably destined to produce important fruit in future years'. He may have meant that while political Zionism might wane, Zionism as a movement for Hebraic revival would persist and achieve significant cultural results for the Jewish people. Whatever view one may form as to his meaning, it is difficult to avoid the conclusion that for him the Jewish national ethos – reflecting a common history, an enduring kinship (international yet bonded), common religious and cultural sources and common aspirations – was a distinctive feature of recognizable Jewish existence. It was an ethos which for Wolf, no less than for avowed Zionists, rendered unreal the contention that the sole bond was the religious one. To him the complex nature of the reality would somehow have turned such a proposition, in the sense in which it was presented by anti-Zionist polemicists, into one that was palpably misleading.

There was some possible ambiguity of perhaps deeper import in his attributed motivation or source for the literary revival. He was aware of the growth in Anglo-Jewish society of an interest in Jewish history and literature, including Hebrew study. It was partly of immigrant origin and to some extent 'natively' Anglo-Jewish. He was conscious of the value of his own role in this degree of 'renaissance'. He considered the creation of the Maccabaeans Society in 1891 as a prime illustration of the emergence of a new Jewish intellectual level in Anglo-Jewry.[6] He saw it all as an element in the Jewish intellectual fervour springing from the European Mendelssohnian revolution and a wider interest in the nature of Jewishness in the face of modern science and philosophic speculation. How far was it a reaction to anti-Semitism? How far was it self-generated, especially in the wake of the increasing number of university-trained Jewish professional men and women? How far was it the result of the instinctive as well as the considered efforts to westernize the Jewish community? Such, after all, had been a major part of the leadership's programme since the early Victorian years.

While these reasons are not mutually exclusive, there may be some special significance in the statement in Wolf's article on Zionism, that without the ancient 'national spirit', Zionism 'could never have assumed its present formidable proportions'. He was at pains to emphasize the continuing impact of the national spirit, independent of this or that political or any Zionistic form. He had no difficulty in recognizing it in the contemporary intellectual scene, independent of political form. He gives the impression that this spirit, as an inherent product and quality of Jewish experience, was for him a proper source of pride in its own right, a creative ingredient in Jewish life, a part of what was the distinguishable character of the Jewish people. How far he related it to Jewish religious belief, how far he perceived the Jewish religion, in whatever form, as being cause and/or consequence of it, only he (if indeed he) could have made clear, if that were possible. When Greenberg referred to his attitude to Zionism as being 'quasi-religious', that close observer of Wolf was giving some expression to that imponderable.

In 1917, the Zionist Organization published a 24-page *Reply to the Case of the Anti-Zionists* by (later Sir) Leon Simon. That select group comprised Sir Philip Magnus, Laurie Magnus, Claude Montefiore and Lucien Wolf. Simon was dismissive of what he called Wolf's 'parade of learning and objectivity' and pronounced him 'ignorant of the considerable body of modern Hebrew literature in which the ideas of Jewish nationalism were developed and crystallized'. Simon refers to Wolf's 'sympathetic article on Zionism' in the *Encyclopaedia Britannica*. He charged Wolf with later 'representing the Bundists as being the true Jewish nationalists'. In his trenchant criticisms of all four protagonists, Simon's critique of Wolf is, by reason of Wolf's changing nuances and standpoints, somewhat different from that of each of the others, equally sharp though it is. Simon contrasted Wolf's apparent contention (which Simon rejected) that 'the Jews were always primarily a religious community' with his later apparent attachment to the idea of a secular Jewish 'nationality' of the Bundist type. In fact there was always in Wolf's conception of the Jews as a religious community an inextricable element of nationality. Simon was not alone in finding Wolf's duality of thought perplexing. At the bottom of it all, one may wonder whether Wolf ever wholly lost the impression made on him by his father's tales of the latter's boyhood when, as Wolf wrote, his father 'had felt the heart-ache of the Jewish people'; his father's 'recollections of home ... made me love the symbols and spirit of Judaism'.[3]

While one must pay attention to the tactical political context of Wolf's statements to British Ministers in 1916–17, one notes the concession which he, in the name of the Conjoint Committee, was ready to make in order to ward off a governmental declaration in a form sought by the Zionists – which in his view would reflect on the status of the Jews in Britain, both those who deemed themselves integrated and those whom it was sought to integrate.[7] He advised Balfour in January 1917 that there was no objection to the Jewish community in Palestine developing into a 'local Jewish nation and a Jewish state', the latter not claiming 'the allegiance of the Jews of Western Europe, who are satisfied with their local nationalities'.[8]

In his much-discussed article in the *Edinburgh Review* in April 1917 on 'The Jewish National Movement', Wolf observed that the Jews in Russia 'constituted a nationality only third in rank among the peoples which will claim emancipation after the war'. Their 'national consciousness' was 'intense'. He added:

> Nor is their ... national aim less definite than that of any other race in Eastern or South East Europe. Two thousand years of European history [had] made of the Jews a European people with new ideas, new relationships, a new culture and a new language and literature of their own. To sweep all this away and forget it was impossible.

While Wolf was attributing this approach to Jewish leaders in the East, it is clear that he was also reflecting his own thoughts on the reality. Nor was the language of the philosophy which he thus enunciated necessarily limited to 'secular' Jews. 'This Jewish secular nationality' in the East, he wrote, 'admirable though it be in many ways, is a new and utterly revolutionary departure in Jewish life. It is not necessarily bound up with Judaism.'

Wolf could not exclude the religious impulse from the nationalist sentiment, whether old or new. The secularist character of Dubnow's aspiration for national autonomy, or the socialism of the Bundist forms of proposed autonomy, did not exhaust in his view the categories of Jewish nationality. Nor did that phenomenon, in old or new forms, hold for him the instinctive terrors which beset some of those Anglo-Jewish communal figures whom he 'served' in London. His interpolation – 'admirable though it be in many ways' – is redolent of some degree of regret that 'Jewish secular nationality' is 'not necessarily bound up with Judaism'. And when he wrote of the effects of 2,000 years of European history, he could not have failed to be conscious that those effects had no less impressed themselves on Jewish immigrants to the West. Those effects had their role in strengthening (perhaps, more accurately, reviving) the inner Jewish life of his own Jewish community.

On 24 May 1917, there was published in *The Times* the well-known letter from the Conjoint Committee as a riposte to the Zionist efforts to influence the expected governmental declaration.

The letter expressed readiness to cooperate in 'making Palestine a Jewish spiritual centre by securing for the local Jews, and the colonists who might join them, such conditions of life as would best enable them to develop the Jewish genius on lines of its own'. The Committee, while crucially repudiating any implication that the Jews of the world constituted 'one homeless nationality, incapable of complete social and political identification with the nations among whom they dwell', declared that it had no objection against 'a local Jewish nationality establishing itself' in that land. The letter, drafted by Wolf, thereby made a kind of acknowledgement of Jewish nationality, in the hope of pre-empting official acceptance of the fuller Zionist case.

For Wolf, such acknowledgement, albeit in a local context, was not new. For some of his colleagues, it might have seemed a desperate compromise in the face of the mounting Zionist pressure on the Government and the Government's own reasons for viewing with favour a declaration which, within limits, went significantly far to meet the Zionists' demands.

Wolf's opposition to the Zionists differed in nature from that of other critics. For example, the school of Judah Magnes perceived any notion of a Jewish nationality, local or otherwise, as a plain threat to Judaism. Among his own Jewish associates with whom he discussed issues posed by the rise of political Zionism, Wolf took a path of his own. However much he shared some of their conclusions, he did not necessarily share their outlook, nor always the policy implications which they drew therefrom. He could not accept as a basis for policy or guidance any idea of some Jewish duty or need to endure affliction pending better times at the end of days. And in his own way, he was as concerned as Ahad Ha'am about the content of Jewishness, as distinct from political striving for statehood, as a solution for the ills of the Jews of the West.

When the vision of a new liberalized Russia faded, he did not see in that disappointment any reason for dismissing the vision of integration as merely a mirage elsewhere, nor for ceasing to search for a system of rights in quasi-autonomous Jewish regions where numbers and circumstances required and permitted it. His double or multiple policies did not constitute or reflect any conscious inner contradiction on his part. No inhibitions were aroused in him. It represented a realistic programme in the Jewish world as he found it. To the non-ideological pragmatist, the image or argument suggestive of Jewish homelessness was far more disturbing. He saw such imputation as plainly contrary to reality for large communities of Jews, and as going to the root of emancipation, injurious to integration, and a marked weakening of Jewish counter-arguments against the charges of 'international', 'cosmopolitan' and 'irretrievably alien'. Such a prospective (as was thought) image was considered to put at risk the achievement of the nineteenth century. For all his understanding and sophistication, Wolf retained the optimism and anxiety whose combination was a feature of Victorian Jewish public relations. His ambivalence was part of the ambivalence of 'the Jew'.

When Greenberg wrote, in his 1930 obituary notice, of Wolf's 'strong religious bias', he had in mind his assessment of the later Wolf whom he knew. It is also an assessment consistent with Wolf's early approach to the nature of Jewishness. He did not emulate Lyon's close interest in theism, the creed of the Judeophile, Charles Voysey, who founded the Theistic Church in the 1870s. He also publicly distanced himself from Montefiore's theology on the grounds that it was an avenue to theism.

Wolf, the pragmatist, well read in current literature on the scientific and philosophical revolutions, might not have resolved the problem of reconciling his thinking with any kind of dogmatic system. He remained drawn to the belief in the worthwhileness of sustaining a recognizable form of undogmatic Judaism, a topic related to his conception of a Jewish particularity born of historical experience. In his declarations of the 1880s and 1890s and his support for movements for the racial, religious and linguistic rights of Jewish communities in the successor states in the East (together with their civil rights), there is detectable an intellectual (and to some degree emotional) line of consistency. Requirements in the West and remedies in the East, reflecting the different contexts and opportunities, were not mutually incompatible in an overall Jewish policy. He saw the Jewish people as living at different levels of experience.

Where Zionists such as Greenberg were 'political', Wolf would have considered himself 'cultural', a concept which Greenberg might from his standpoint have deemed an off-shoot of 'religious'. To Adler, it would have seemed the product of the 'secular'. To Montefiore, it would have seemed gratuitously 'particularist'. Wolf was content to perplex them all.

1. In addition to his regular articles in the *Jewish Chronicle*, Wolf wrote extensively in the *Jewish World* from 1874, becoming its senior leader writer; and was, from 1905, until its incorporation into the *Jewish Chronicle* in 1908, its editor. For 20 years, from 1890, he was the foreign editor of the *Daily Graphic,* and then and later a frequent contributor to the national political and literary journals, notably as Diplomaticus in the *Fortnightly Review.* His presentation of the Jewish plight in Russia attracted wide attention, as did his exposure of the myths of 'Jewish menace' fostered by the so-called Protocols of the Elders of Zion. Among journalists he was a scholar of immense erudition. Among politicians he was a well-equipped man of affairs. He had a prismatic quality.

2. 'Emancipation and its Aftermath', in David Sidorsky (ed.), *The Future of the Jewish Community in America* (1973), p. 53.

3. Cecil Roth (ed.), *Essays in Jewish History by Lucien Wolf* (London, 1934), pp. 51–4.

4. He referred to Adler as one of the 'modern rabbis' who have made this 'false analogy'. He explained that 'all Hebrew politics were theocratic', but this did not mean that 'on that account [they] were less practical or less disposed to express themselves in active political form'. At the same time he opposed any implication that the Jews were everywhere a homeless people, since huge numbers had established their homes in free societies and were not minded to uproot themselves or put their status at risk.

5. Chimen Abramsky, 'Lucien Wolf's Efforts for the Jewish Communities of Eastern and Central Europe', *Transactions of the Jewish Historical Society of England,* Vol. 29 (1988), pp. 281–96; Mark Levene, 'Anglo-Jewish Foreign Policy in Crisis: Lucien Wolf, the Conjoint Committee and the War 1914–18', *Transactions of the Jewish Historical Society of England,* Vol. 30 (1989), pp. 179–98, and *War, Jews and the New Europe: The Diplomacy of Lucien Wolf 1914–19* (London, 1992). See also Max (Lord) Beloff, 'Lucien Wolf and the Anglo-Russian Entente 1907–14', in *The Intellectual in Politics and Other Essays* (1970), pp. 111–42, S.A. Cohen, *English Zionists and British Jews* (Princeton, NJ, 1982) and 'Ideological Components in Anglo-Jewish Opposition to Zionism Before and During the First World War: a Restatement', *Transactions of the Jewish Historical Society of England,* Vol. 30 (1989), pp. 149–62; Israel Finestein, *Jewish Society in Victorian England* (1993), and *Changing Times in Anglo-Jewry: Studies in Diversity 1840–1914* (1999); Josef Fraenkel, 'Lucien Wolf and Theodor Herzl', *Transactions of the Jewish Historical Society of England,* Vol. 20 (1964), pp. 161–88; Isaiah Friedman, *The Question of Palestine 1914–18* (London, 1973); Sharman Kadish, *Bolsheviks and British Jews* (London, 1992); S. Massil, 'The Foundation of the Jewish Historical Society', *Transactions of the Jewish Historical Society of England,* Vol. 33 (1995), pp. 225–38; Roth, *Essays in Jewish History by Lucien Wolf;* and L. Stein, *The Balfour Declaration* (London, 1961).

6. On 24 February 1911, the *Jewish Chronicle* described the Society as 'a voluntary association, in the main of professional men, for the purpose of putting forward our best side from the intellectual point of view to the world and showing the

Jews are not entirely a commercial community but have another aspect to their existence'. This represented a long-standing feature of Victorian Jewish public relations. I am not sure Wolf would have adopted that language, though there was some ambiguity in his grounds for his particular welcome at that time for the Society. He was at least as much concerned with the desirable impact on the level of Jewish life culturally as on outside image. In the 1890s, to draw a distinction between the two motivations would have had a curious air.

7. In 1916, Wolf publicly warned the Jewish community of the 'danger' which he thought would accrue to the community if the Jews of the East End (and comparable areas) achieved weight in determining communal policy commensurate with their numbers. What he had in mind was the degree of support from those quarters to the political Zionist movement. This concern reinforced the desire of the Conjoint Committee and himself to expand the 'representative' base of the Committee. The plan was to co-opt nominated 'representatives' from other communal bodies. The plan was considered at the AJA Council in January 1916. Moses Gaster was the sole critic. The immediate question arose from the invitation extended to the important Jewish Friendly Society movement to send representatives for co-option. It was made clear in the general plan that those co-opted were to be in a minority on the Committee and were to be in agreement with the Committee's policy. The AJA had received a letter of protest from the National Council for Jewish Rights, a largely East End association, of which Wolf had agreed to be president on its formation in 1915. The National Council, of which Gaster was now president, objected to the acceptance of the 'representatives' nominated to the Committee by the United Council of the Jewish Friendly Societies, on the ground that the latter had accepted the invitation on condition, not fulfilled, that the Committee would be enlarged on a democratic basis. The Committee remained no more representative than it was before the abortive plan, being no more than an unreformed extension of the old system. Wolf cultivated the friendship of Jewish figures and institutions in the East End. He was a kind of bridge, notwithstanding his strong affiliations. He knew that the East End was divided – with many gradations within the spectrum – between those who regarded the leadership of the Board of Deputies and the AJA (and indeed, the leadership of the United Synagogue) as constituting a wholly unacceptable elitist oligarchy whose hold they wished to break, and those who, through fashion, social aspiration, personal interest or conviction, sought to ally themselves with, or take their cue from, the upper echelons. Although he was seen as a loyal and indispensable coadjutor by his immediate associates, and as a fixed opponent by the leading political Zionists, this son of the Bohemian-born liberal who fled to England in the wake of the 1848 revolutions and reactions thereto, was, on many divers sides of communal debate, perceived as an ambiguous personality. From the report of the AJA Council meeting in the *Jewish Chronicle* of 12 January 1917, it appears that Wolf had some difficulty in justifying the attendance of the two 'representatives' from the United Council on the Conjoint Committee in the light of the clearly unfulfilled condition.

8. Stein, *Balfour Declarations*, p. 444.

9

Selig Brodetsky (1888–1954): The Prodigy from Fashion Street[*]

In 1893, the president of the Board of Deputies of British Jews was Arthur Cohen, QC, nephew of the late Sir Moses Montefiore, kinsman of the Rothschilds. In that year Brodetsky, aged five, arrived in England from his native Olviopol in the Ukraine, with his mother and her other children. They took up residence in a room off Brick Lane, Whitechapel. His father had preceded them. They all soon moved to somewhat more 'spacious' accommodation in Fashion Street, and later lived in Dunk Street and Cecil Street. It was at No. 6 in the latter road, near Mile End, that the family lived in 1908, when there burst upon East London the news that this young man – already something of a wonder because of winning his way to Cambridge – headed the year's mathematics list, namely becoming Senior Wrangler.

Arthur Cohen's family preceded the Brodetskys to England by 125 years. Cohen preceded Brodetsky to Cambridge by 57 years. Among the celebrations over Brodetsky's Senior Wranglership was a public dinner held in his honour by the Maccabaeans Club at the Trocadero, near Piccadilly Circus, at which the aged Cohen presided. They had both studied mathematics at Cambridge. Cohen's degree had been deferred for some years because under the old law, amended in 1856 for Cambridge, receipt of the degree required subscription to the Anglican creed. The Maccabaeans had

---

*First published (in part) in A.N. Newman (ed.), *The Jewish East End 1840–1939* (1981).

224

been hosts to Herzl in 1895. Their then principal member, Israel Zangwill, was enthusiastic over Herzl's Zionist plan, but the general body of scholars, writers and professional men who composed the Club were not all equally stirred.

Whether or not Brodetsky's father knew of that gathering or of the mixed response, he certainly knew of the fervour aroused by the mass meeting addressed by Herzl the next year at the Jewish Working Men's Club in Great Alie Street. Akiva Brodetsky shared the excitement, attended the meeting, and was a convinced advocate of the new cause. He had long been a member of the Choveve Zion, and in due course became a Mizrachist. The 4th Zionist Congress, held in London in 1900, stimulated Zionist debate. Selig Brodetsky remembered the sight and sound of the Kamenetser Maggid, the noted East End 'preacher', whose religious Zionism was at odds with Herzlian Zionism.

The elder Brodetsky held a succession of humble posts in synagogues in Whitechapel – Princelet Street, Fashion Street, Philpot Street. Selig painted the scene in his *Memoirs*, published in 1960 under the direction of his son Paul, who died at an early age in 1979. If Akiva Brodetsky remained poor, he retained a distinctive pride, long recalled by people who knew him. It was connected at least in part with a variety of intellectual concerns. He had a wide curiosity, untrained and unsystematic though he was. He was interested in mathematics and astronomy, well versed in Talmud and Midrash, and was a notable Hebraist. By all accounts, Selig Brodetsky's mother was a woman of intellect and good looks, which the son inherited.

The young Brodetsky successively attended the Hanbury Street Board School, the Jews' Free School and the Central Foundation School. At the same time he was in receipt of intensive Jewish education, mainly through the medium of Yiddish at the Brick Lane Talmud Torah. He showed great Talmudic talent, read widely, followed public affairs closely and was familiar with Zionist polemics from an early age.

His Senior Wranglership was a mixed blessing. No Jewish student had attained such distinction or acclaim in England since the short-lived Numa Hartog – likewise of Trinity College, Cambridge – 40 years earlier. Here was a foreign-born Jew reaching a coveted intellectual position against a background of political discussion on alien immigration. The Aliens Act of 1905 had not stemmed immigration. Brodetsky's achievement brought home to interested parties the talent latent in the immigration, and the varied contributions to public life which might be expected.

Brodetsky became an instant public figure, as had Hartog. In the latter's day, it was the recent emancipation which heightened the impact of the success of that Senior Wrangler of 1869. But the present circumstances were more dramatic. The number of Jews at the universities, especially at the ancient universities, before World War I fell vastly short of later proportions. It was inevitable that this kind of success on the part of an East End Jew should prove a major public event.

The *éclat* was remembered for decades. In no time, the young man was giving interviews, addressing public meetings, lionized. He did not cease to regard himself as in a special sense a communal hero, entitled to attention and even admiration. He was not bombastic or immodest. The effect was subtler. The experience reinforced his sensitivity, as did also the sharp contrast between his home circumstances and the University. As he himself made clear, he suffered at the University from an inferiority complex. In 1892, in *Children of the Ghetto*, Zangwill had written thus of Fashion Street:

> A dead and gone wag called the street Fashion Street, and most of the people who live there do not even see the joke. If it could exchange names with Rotten Row, both places would be more appropriately designated. It is a dull, squalid, narrow thoroughfare – connecting Spitalfields with Whitechapel, and branching off in blind alleys.

Brodetsky saw the joke only too well, and did not unreservedly relish it.

Among the public offices held by Brodetsky at Cambridge was that of Honorary Secretary of the University Zionist Society. The president of that newly formed association was the Sephardi, Cyril Picciotto, son of a well-known Victorian historian of Anglo-Jewry. The elder Picciotto shared the equanimity of the Victorian Jewish leadership and did not experience the full force of the unreason and hostility which beset the Jews in later times, even in the West. The relationship between Brodetsky and the younger Picciotto was a kind of forerunner of his later relationships with the heirs of the emancipation. Without any prejudice to his Zionism, Brodetsky had a personal admiration for the *noblesse oblige* character of the communal service of the old families. His public disputes with them on the Zionist issue did not destroy his respect for the Jewish commitment of the successors of the 'grand dukes'. He also had an instinct for practical cooperation. He believed that it was in the communal interest that personal relationships should not lightly be broken, least of all in the higher ranks of leadership.

For 20 and more years from 1928, he was a member of the Executive of the World Zionist Organization, and in the 1930s and 1940s he was head of the Political Department of the Jewish Agency in London. He became the most prominent Zionist in England, next to Weizmann. He travelled widely, at home and abroad, in connection with these duties. By the time he retired as President of the Board and assumed the office of President of the Hebrew University in 1949, the strain of public life had already begun to tell.

Brodetsky was a born teacher and a popular lecturer. In particular, he had a flair for teaching mathematics, especially in the small groups to which its advanced study lent itself. He was incapable of speaking down to his pupils. He was also an effective popularizer. His book on the meaning of mathematics was translated into many languages, including Hebrew.

His career was marked by an extraordinary capacity to arouse enthusiasm on the part of young people in causes adopted by himself. He took his work for Maccabi seriously. There was in his encounters, perhaps especially with students, an infectious good humour, accompanied by sharp questioning about their studies and their Jewish interests. He had a life-long concern lest the wider opportunities open to emancipated Jews would erode their Jewish identity. He was conscious of the fact that his public life, from its inception in the East End, was a demonstration that this need not be the case.[1]

Brodetsky was a General Zionist who had little patience with the party politics of the movement. A lengthy article by him in the *Jewish Chronicle*, on 7 September 1934, set out his approach, and now is, in its detail, of much historical interest. His views on the philosophy and aims of Zionism were further expounded in his Lucien Wolf Memorial Lecture in 1942, entitled 'The Jews in the Post-War Settlement', published by the Jewish Historical Society.

His article on the political significance of the Balfour Declaration in the volume entitled *The Jewish National Home* (edited by Paul Goodman, 1943) also merits attention for a study of Brodetsky's standpoint. In 1916, he contributed an essay on 'A Hebrew University in Jerusalem' in *Zionism: Problems and Views* (edited by Paul Goodman and A.D. Lewis) which presented his views on the Jewish role in the world, as well as the potential role of such a University.[2] These four papers may be said to reveal his Zionist creed.

Weizmann's effort to obtain for Brodetsky a teaching post at the Hebrew University or at the Haifa Technion came to nought. In 1914, he exchanged his lectureship in Applied Mathematics at Bristol University for a comparable post at Leeds, where, in 1924, he became Professor in the subject. In addition to his full participation in the administrative work of the University, he was the leading figure for many years in the Association of University Teachers. He also became engaged in many special projects, including a widely noted biography of Isaac Newton and a much discussed study, in conjunction with Herbert Loewe, in 1928, on the intellectual level of Anglo-Jewish life. He was an acknowledged authority on aerodynamics, and assisted the Ministry of Defence in peace and war in that field. The University of Leeds was generous in allowing him time to engage in his multifarious public activities, Zionist, Jewish and general. Supported by his Bialystok-born wife and a devoted family circle, as well as by a robust physique, he sustained a formidable workload. He came to realize that his Zionist work had limited his scientific and academic achievement.

He was a consistent advocate of the opinions and policies of his fellow-scientist, Chaim Weizmann, whose attachment to England he shared. Weizmann's undogmatic and practical approach appealed to his scientific and liberal mind. He wrote his recollections of a sometimes turbulent life, at a time when illness was upon him. The book was written in some adversity, after his deeply unsettling years as President of the Hebrew University. His old vigour had gone. There was an element of bitterness and disillusion.

He felt the slings and arrows of public life personally and acutely. It was a serious weakness in a public figure. Sometimes his judgement was affected by his reactions to what he saw as slights. It was easier for him to give a qualified 'yes' than an outright 'no', to pressure groups or individual representations. It was a response which he might later regret, and which could plunge him unwillingly into apparently contrasting positions. He had neither the ruthlessness of a politician nor any talent or inclination for political infighting. He was an idealist and an optimist.

He belongs in many respects to an age gone beyond retrieve – the pre-1948 age and, indeed, the pre-1939 age. It included a time when most Jews in England of middle age remembered the pre-1914 immigration, when Yiddish was still an everyday language, when the Balfour Declaration was a recent event, and British power was the governing influence in the Middle East. Few foresaw the catastrophe that was to come. None could foretell its magnitude. Few could tell that Jewish statehood was so close.

In many respects, Brodetsky epitomized the whole first generation of post-1880 immigrant Jews. He was a kind of model for the committed or potentially committed Jewish intellectuals of that era. Lucien Wolf had declared to the Council of the Anglo-Jewish Association in October 1916, that should the members of Jews in the East End be given voice in communal counsels commensurate with their communal proportion, the community would be transformed. Wolf was no supporter of that transfer of power. However much the newcomers and their children would, with remarkable speed, become integrated into English and Anglo-Jewish life and inherit the institutions and the stability of the earlier Anglo-Jewry, there were bound to be changes of emphasis, less insularity, a wider democracy, less respect for the say-so of lay authority. Brodetsky's election to the presidency of the Board in 1940 was universally acknowledged as the symbol of such a new era in Anglo-Jewish affairs. He was the first academician to hold that office, as well as the first Eastern European Jew and the first Jew of the East End.

It is difficult today to recapture the special relationship that sprang up between Brodetsky and Jewish audiences from the mid-1920s. We have become more sophisticated. The media, especially television, have somewhat blunted our receptivity. Even in the 1930s, the platform was still of great importance in public education. Brodetsky was not a polished orator. He had neither the elegant style of his predecessor at the Board, Neville Laski, nor the balanced cadences of his fellow-East End graduate of Cambridge, Dr Abraham Cohen, who succeeded him at the Board. His distinctive presence, with his expressive face, was familiar to Jewish audiences up and down Britain.

Brodetsky was ebullient and expansive. His style was direct, conversational, full of quip and irony, interspersed with banter and Yiddish. At his best, he surely had no equal in Britain. The East End in a way came into its own with Zangwill and Brodetsky. He was in great demand. It was for him a kind of self-appointed, Jewish educational task. In the 1930s, he was the most prolific Jewish platform speaker in the country. His impact upon provincial communities, many of them of like mind on many issues with the East End of London, was immense, and contributed much to Jewish public opinion.

It is not easy to describe Brodetsky's attitudes towards traditional Judaism. He knew the system well. He was ill at ease with it, but remained a formal adherent. He was an increasingly secular Jew, but was unable to divest himself of the belief that there was a higher power than science could ever scale. Nor did he care to overthrow tradition, lest by such a course Jews might lose much of the secret of their survival capacity, as well as much of the strength and spirit which had moulded the Jewish contribution to Western civilization.

He was an enlightened humanist, with a passion for social justice. He supported the great reformist Liberal Ministry of 1906. He later supported the Labour Party. His politics were always undoctrinaire and progressive. He was the classical social democrat of the non-Marxist left, in which compassion played at least as great a role as political dogma. His humanism was of a universal nature, which brought him into contact with many movements of thought and action beyond Jewry.

He was of the view that a national home for the Jews was an historical necessity, and plain justice. He also saw the movement towards it as a form of Hebrew revivalism. He was convinced that out of its achievement would emerge improved standards of living and social amelioration in the Middle East. He further believed that out of Zion would come new lessons in social order which would reinforce what he regarded as the long-standing, beneficent Jewish influence in the world, springing from the Bible and the prophets. If he was a liberal humanist, he was also a Jewish humanist, imbued with the idea that through their unique history and their literature and traditions, the Jews had acquired a positive feel for social justice.

His training and associations gave him a profound respect for English institutions and for Jewish institutions founded on English models. His birth and upbringing disinclined him to seek entry into any of the magic circles from which communal leaders had tended to emerge. In his combination of qualities and instincts, he was a man apart from many of the principal protagonists in the communal scene in both the Zionist and non-Zionist camps.

He had a high conception of the status and independence of the Board of Deputies. It was an unruly assembly. The presidency at such a time was an unaccustomed role for him.[3] His combination of the presidency with his post at the Jewish Agency was deeply controversial. His retention of both made him all the more anxious to maintain the visible independence of the Board and its broad representative character. He sought to keep the large 'Zionist Progressive Group' (managed at the Board by Lavy Bakstansky, general secretary of the English Zionist Federation and a highly skilled debater) within what Brodetsky regarded as proper bounds.

Brodetsky viewed the suggestion, persistently advocated by Laski, that he should cease to hold one office or the other, as implying that a British Jew could not properly be a political Zionist, a notion which he rejected. He was at one with the 'Group' on the Zionist issue, but at odds with its leaders over the price which he thought the Board might pay for their methods which might encourage the image of outside influences. In public speeches he usually took care to state in which capacity he spoke, but the critics of the 'Group's' politics held such caution to be ineffective. Those critics tended to relegate him to the rank of a malleable president and an ambivalent politician. He was under considerable strain as chairman, and at times was lack-lustre. His platform talents, largely instinctive and elsewhere so impressive, proved less effective at the Board. If he and Laski were often in a state of mutual exasperation, so too were Brodetsky and Bakstansky.

Brodetsky was an unprecedented figure in the community's history, a kind of folk personality among wide sections of Anglo-Jewry, with a natural approachability. He was the first genuinely popular hero on a national scale in that community. He gave to popular enthusiasms the respectability of academic standing, his special status arising from shared elemental sources ultimately springing from Eastern European Jewish life.

In 1976, the then President of the Board, Lord Fisher of Camden, delivered the Seventeenth Brodetsky Memorial Lecture. His subject was Brodetsky. Despite widely different careers, the two men had much in common, associated with their East London background and the Eastern European origins of their families. Fisher referred to the pressures of communal office, especially in an epoch of great stress, such as Brodetsky's. This gifted and sensitive man bore a heavy brunt. He was surely among the most colourful of the children of the English 'ghetto', as well as one of the most distinguished.

NOTES

1. Israel Finestein, 'Cambridge Contrasts', in William Frankel and Harvey Miller (eds), *Town & Tallith* (1989), pp. 47–51. In a telling phrase in his Brodetsky Memorial Lecture in Leeds (1963), Professor Louis Rosenhead, Brodetsky's former student, described him as 'in himself a social education to us'. He supported the scheme, in which Sir Robert Waley Cohen was a prime mover, to erect adequate premises for an independent synagogue in Cambridge for the Cambridge Jewish Student Society, to be managed by the students, and be 'non-sectarian' and open to all, including town residents. Brodetsky did not limit his encouragement of Jewish self-identification to students and the academic community. He often warned of the central importance for the future of a sufficiently endowed and professionalized Jewish educational service, including a Jewish day-school network.

2. His short, controversy-ridden tenure in Jerusalem saddened him. His experience in university administration was not readily applicable to Israel, nor was his idea of a National University. There was personal discord, tinged with party politics. He returned to London shaken and ill.

3. Brodetsky strenuously familiarized himself with the work of all the Board's committees. His advice and active support were eagerly sought and not in vain. He had little stomach for the sharp adversarial conduct of affairs on the floor of the Board. Seemingly on the defensive in more than one direction at once, he, at times, gave the impression of indecision. Constitutional argument wearied him, and 'points of order' were his special bane.

SELECT BIBLIOGRAPHY

Aldermann, Geoffrey, *Modern British Jewry* (1992).

Bolchover, Richard, *British Jewry and the Holocaust* (1993).

Brodetsky, Selig, *Memoirs* (1960).

Cohen, Stuart A., 'Another View of Brodetsky's Role and Achievement', *Jewish Journal of Sociology*, 24, 2 (1982).

Shatzkes, Pamela, *Holocaust and Rescue: Impotent or Indifferent? Anglo-Jewry, 1938–1945* (2002).

Shimoni, Gideon, 'Selig Brodetsky and the Ascendancy of Zionism in Anglo-Jewry', *Jewish Journal of Sociology*, 22, 2 (1980).

10

Sir Arthur Goodhart, QC (1891–1978): Jewish Lawyer of the Common Law[*]

Arthur Lehman Goodhart was born in New York, son of a wealthy stockbroking family whose traits of high intellect, public-spiritedness and philanthropic impulse he inherited. His maternal uncles were Governor of New York State and Chief Judge of the New York Court of Appeals. After graduating at Yale, he studied law at Trinity College, Cambridge, between 1912 and 1914. He gained distinction at both universities. On returning to New York, he practised law until the American entry into World War I, when he joined the army. After the war, he served as the legal member of the American mission to the newly reconstituted Poland, and in 1920 published his *Poland and the Minority Races*.

He was called to the English Bar in 1919. Between 1921 and 1931, he lectured in law at Cambridge, where he was part founder of the *Cambridge Law Journal*, which he edited. He was appointed Professor of Jurisprudence at Oxford (1931–51) and Master of University College, Oxford (1951–63). Perhaps no position outside his university posts was more welcomed by Goodhart than that of editor of the *Law Quarterly Review* (1923–71), later described by *The Times* as the 'leading legal journal in the English-speaking

---

[*]An expansion of part of the author's address, on 17 March 1999, to the then British Section of the International Association of Jewish Lawyers, originally entitled 'Blackstone, Bentham and Deuteronomy'.

world'. He was appointed on the advice of Sir Frederick Pollock, the distinguished legal historian and jurist. Goodhart's legal works, notably his decades of celebrated notes on contemporary cases in the *Review*, and his many articles therein, amply bore out *The Times*' comment that 'he was essentially a modernist, though with a deep consciousness of and regard for the traditional common law spirit'.

Goodhart retained throughout his American citizenship. Many public honours came his way. In 1948, he was made an honorary knight in recognition of his 'outstanding services to the common interests' of Britain and the United States in war and peace.

Whence have the judges derived their right of judicial review? When they seek to intervene to remedy breaches of 'natural justice'; who defines that? A glimpse of possible answers is given by Tom Paine in his *Rights of Man* (1791). In reference to the statement in Genesis that human kind was made in the divine image, that revolutionary observed that if this does not have divine authority, 'it is at least historical authority', showing 'that the equality of man, so far from being a modern doctrine, is the oldest upon record'.

Those and related issues have been abundantly written about, most prolifically in the English-speaking world and Israel. Likewise, upon what belief or ideas does the notion of rights ultimately turn; or is it all a matter solely of expediency, power, mutual convenience, or the indolence or fear of those who are expected to obey the laws by whomsoever made? They have all had their respective advocates.

It has often been noted that had the historical Hebraic element not entered Western society, the world's history over two millennia would have been radically different in every aspect. That element was principally projected by the Hebrew Bible. The kernel of its influence was the moral nature of law – the notion that the rules governing individual and public conduct were not to be arbitrary or capricious, but were to be gathered from and given intrinsic authority by a conscious morality of ultimately transcendental origin and inspiration. Even when the metaphysical overtones were eroded, the practical consequences of the old outlook remained.

England came to occupy a particular place within the spread of the Bible's influence. This occurred for reasons of history, geography and perhaps temperament, which itself was no doubt influenced by history and geography.

The nearest definition of the common law of England is the ever-expanding corpus of cases decided over the centuries by the Judges. In due course, it extended and in varying degrees extends – subject to statute and other reservations – to America, the Commonwealth, and Israel. It was described in the thirteenth century by Henry de Bracton, Judge and common law codifier, as right reason written down.

When James I, in the seventeenth century, seemed to contend that the judges were appointed to do the royal bidding, Sir Edward Coke, Chief Justice, rebutted that suggestion, citing (as he thought) Bracton in support of the principle that the King was subject to the Almighty and to the law; the judges, though appointed by him, were not his agents to perform his will. Those propositions are enunciated in the Hebrew Bible.

Scholars and practitioners in the common law had ever been ready to justify the principles of that law and applaud its continuity by reference to biblical texts and biblical analogies or presumed analogies. Perhaps the most striking analogies related to parliamentary assemblies. In their contests with the Stuart monarchy, some lawyers and parliamentarians – more passionate than scientific – prayed in aid of the consultative *ad hoc* 'assemblies' – the 'elders' – convened by the kings of ancient Israel. They drew support from such narratives to demonstrate the virtue of royal respect for the law, the moral evil of any royal flouting of it, and the vice of royal failure to summon and heed Parliament.

The wisdom of the common law came to be seen as the following of judicial precedent and its application by the Judges in successive cases, while allowing for changed circumstances. That wisdom was deemed synonymous with judicial probity and moral awareness. Thus it was, for example, that the requirement in Exodus 23 that the judge shall not be overawed by the multitude (or by a majority considered by him to be wrong) was a reinforcement in England of judicial independence. Likewise, the injunction in Deuteronomy 16 that the judge shall be no respecter of persons was given a contemporary ring. The point was driven home by Solomon's prayer (1 Kings: 3) that as a judge he might be given 'an understanding heart – that I may discern between good and evil'.

Perhaps no more affirmative, or in his day authoritative, exposition of the moral nature of law and its administration could be found than in the classic books of commentary on the laws of

England by Sir William Blackstone, the first Vinerian Professor of English Law at Oxford and prominent judge, which were published in the 1760s. 'When the Supreme Being', he wrote, 'formed the universe and created matter out of nothing, he impressed certain principles upon that matter – [these are] eternal – laws of good and evil, which the Creator has enabled human reason to discern'. There is also a 'revealed law', found only in Scripture, which is not necessarily attainable by reason. The latter law 'is of infinitely more authority than the moral system which is framed by ethical writers'. Both sets of law are the 'law of nature', one set of which has evolved by the divinely 'implanted' powers of reasoning. No law, he declared, could be valid which was not consistent with either set.

What the proper principles were in a given instance, especially those of natural law as defined by reason, were matters of judgement. In that sphere the moral training, rationality, independence and character of the judges were vital.

In the wake of the philosophical and political revolutions in Europe and the emergence of new types of need and aspiration, a far more positivist approach to the nature and purpose of law emerged. Yet the consequent onslaught on Blackstone and on the traditions associated with him, which was launched in the nineteenth century by utilitarians, philosophic radicals, and secularists, did not wholly undo the operation of the older spirit of the law and constitution; it had become enshrined in many features of the constitutional system and English life. The common law had long become irretrievably infused with that spirit.

The Bible says nothing about equality except by the strong implication of equality of access to righteous judgement. It says nothing about democracy except in its emphasis on the value of the human personality. It says nothing about rights except as may be inferred from its adumbration of duties.[1] Blackstone had written at the outset of his *Commentaries* that 'the principal aim of society is to protect individuals in the enjoyment of those absolute rights which were vested in them by the immutable laws of nature'. Later generations shared neither Blackstone's nuances nor his inspiration. Jeremy Bentham was prominent among those who treated them with some derision. That did not mean that they fled from the search for a moral basis for law. The issue as to what constitutes good law, and as to why it is to be observed, remained moral issues, even if they were tested on practical grounds. Why should might not be right if it is thought to be directed to good ends, and why should not those who wield that might be allowed to determine what constitutes good ends?

Goodhart resonantly entitled the first of his Hamlyn Lectures (1953) 'English Law and the Moral Law'. 'England', he therein stated, 'has been a nation founded on law for a longer period than any other nation in the history of the world'. He had no illusion about human frailty, the fragility of all human systems, and the imperative of eternal vigilance to preserve the rule of law. He had no illusions about the tensions between liberty and equality. He significantly cited the observation of the eminent Congregational churchman, Dr Nathaniel Micklem, in the latter's *The Law and the Laws* (1952): 'We cannot reject the religion of the Bible and permanently retain law and justice.' One need not detect in Goodhart any particular theology or metaphysical system of thought in order to be able to discern his attachment to the belief in an inner morality of the common law.

'The type of moral law', he observed, 'based on reason, divorced from other authority, seems to be the one which has had the most influence in English law.' He regarded the common law, in spite of and because of the regular need and facility for necessary reform, as a civilized and civilizing force.

How far would he have agreed with the formulation of Lord MacMillan, philosopher and Scottish Law Lord? In his paper on 'Law and Religion', MacMillan observed:

> While our legislators no longer claim divine sanction for their enactments and our judges no longer claim that their decisions are divinely inspired, the law, I make bold to say, is still something more than a merely secular code of conduct.[2]

MacMillan accepted Professor Jenks' description of the law as something 'which may be defined, at least provisionally, as that force or tendency which makes for righteousness': Edward Jenks, *The New Jurisprudence* (1933).

In so far as Goodhart subscribed to the idea of an objective moral law, I suggest that it would be difficult to dissociate him from the view that its content cannot be determined solely by pragmatic reference. His lack of any dogma in his legal analyses does not invalidate this suggestion. In his Hamlyn Lectures, he saw the law as reflecting some superior will, which he illustrated by his naming two possible sources, namely 'some of the Ten Commandments' or the 'implied commands discoverable through reason'. He was not thereby preaching nor expressing any deist or theistic position. Yet one senses that he would have been slow to reject outright the whole of MacMillan's language.

Writing in 1947,[3] Lord Simonds, later Lord Chancellor, commented that when Edward I's judges issued writs called *habeas corpus* to produce and protect the King's subjects from arbitrary imprisonment, they did not do so by virtue of any statutory authority but 'because that freedom was an inherent right – what Thomas Jefferson would have called a self-evident truth'. That perceived right was accompanied by the principle that some limits are to be set to governmental power. If Coke was wishfully thinking about notions which he read into old law reports and tended to over-idealize them, he was nevertheless right in his conception that in the earlier era legal proprieties were somehow connected, as in his day and for much later, with what was seen as springing from divine prescription.

Goodhart adopted the much-cited view of Pollock that 'law is enforced because it is law; it is not law because the State enforces it'. 'There is in England', wrote Goodhart, 'a close bond between law and morals'. To the question 'where does the sense of obligation come from?', Goodhart posits a state of mind which includes the sentiment of reverence, 'conscious or otherwise'. 'Even though some people can be controlled only by sanctions, the rules are not obligatory because there are sanctions.' Coercion may procure obedience, 'but that does not make the law obligatory'.

This was an underlying theme in Goodhart's address in Middle Temple Hall in 1959, under the aegis of the Council of Christians and Jews. It was that year's Sir Robert Waley Cohen Memorial Lecture, and was entitled 'Tolerance and The Law'. The interconnection between law and opinion involves a degree of interdependence between the two. Law has an educational effect, as well as itself and its acceptance being conditioned by the culture and habits of society.

Goodhart may have gone too far in his venerational language on the common law. He may have had an over-rosy view of the depth and extent of law-abidingness. But his probe into the instinctive acceptability of the rule of law and its provisions points to the nature of law-abidingness. His view was that when an act is a duty – seen and acknowledged to be such – the duty cannot be explained in terms of 'command'. Otherwise it is an imposition. In considering why people accept the obligation of the law, why they tend to abide by the conventions and rules of society, he placed his special emphasis on a kind of 'reverence'; a response which is 'intuitive' and connected with the acquired habits of society and traditions of behaviour.

The law-abidingness may not be as firm in one generation as in its predecessor or perhaps never as strong or pervasive as one might prefer to think. But Goodhart was indicating a vital source for the instinct. He was concerned to delineate the contrast which arises from Thomas Hobbes' dictum in the seventeenth century that unless force establishes law, people would not know the difference between any right and any wrong. That is the antitheses of Goodhart's idea of the acceptance of law arising from the way of life of a people, or most of them. Such does not preclude protest, but it does preclude unaccountability. If the instinct to obey springs from English history, by the same token it springs from the 'self-existent' era in English legal history, as defined by Sir John Salmond (see below).

Since his day, new issues have arisen, old questions have become sharper, and pending issues have emerged in practical form. In particular there is the ever-growing mass of legislation, primary and secondary, including European law. None of this would, I think, have undermined Goodhart's reliance on the Judges to sustain the development of the principles of the common law in ever-changing circumstances.

Lord Morris of Borth-y-Gest, a great authority on the common law, delivered an address (later published) to the Bentham Club in 1973 on 'Natural Justice'.[4] He proffered the following definition of justice. 'It would seem to be', he declared, 'the product of what we are pleased to call civilized man or the man who believes in a superior being.' He does not suggest that these two categories are necessarily identical. Nor would Goodhart have so suggested. Morris stated that when the judges invoke natural justice, they avail themselves of experience and rely 'essentially' on 'principles which they consider could be upheld as ethical, right and reasonable'.

Goodhart would have emphasized the test of 'reasonableness'

239

and would have measured that very test not by arbitrary personal decision, but by the principles of the common law itself, subjecting it to necessary change upon its own canons of interpretation and its ceaseless evolution (however prolonged the individual stages) in accordance with the notions of the 'reasonable man'.[5] The utility of precedent can over time be assessed by the 'reasonable man' as having worn itself out. Goodhart would have included in his test of 'reasonableness' the ingredient described by Morris as the regard for 'the mutual need of neighbours'.

The former Lord Chancellor, Lord Hailsham, went further. He was uneasy at the thought of leaving solely to reason the definition of justice, or allowing utility to determine the issue. While seeking to avoid any taint of dogmatism, he proffered his own subjective response to the question as to what is the distinctive quality of the approach of the common law. In his *Values: Collapse and Cure* (1994), he challenged the idea that law is 'the command of the ruler', as promulgated by John Austin in the nineteenth century, or 'what the Courts will decide', as advanced by Professor Herbert Hart in the twentieth century, or the long-term outcome of some notional ancient compact, as was fashionably argued by revolutionaries and authoritarians from their conflicting points of view in the seventeenth and eighteenth centuries. Lord Hailsham could not disconnect the question of 'what constitutes a good law' from what he terms 'values'.

He found his own answer in the source literature of the Judaeo-Christian tradition, the Hebrew Bible. It is evoked by the spirit of regard for the individual personality and of mutual duties, which is perceived by him as being inculcated in Scripture. The sanction for the said regard is ultimately not pragmatic but 'spiritual'. It is translated in practice into fairness as understood by a mature, reasonable person.

Goodhart was not minded to limit the use of the term 'moral' to principles and procedures of law whose authority and acceptability rested on tenets of religious faith. While not excluding the idea that such faith was, or may well have been, the historical and original ideological source of such principles and procedures, he was content to invest a degree of his own personal moral fervour in his jurisprudential examination and elucidation of the common law. He would no doubt have agreed with Lord Woolf's characteristic observation that 'one of the strengths of the common law' is that 'it enables the Courts to vary the extent of their intervention to reflect current needs'.

'All rules of law', wrote Sir John Salmond in 1902,[6] 'have historical sources ... There can be found in every legal system certain ultimate principles from which all others are derived but which are themselves self-existent.' English lawyers are the heirs of the seventeenth century, which had its own long pre-history. Goodhart seemed to treat that pre-history as, in Salmond's sense, the 'self-existent' part in the development of English common law. He recognized the biblical role in that pre-history, but saw in English common law a system which in its style of development was *sui generis*. It was his self-imposed task to illumine its principles by sharp jurisprudential scrutiny of the cases. By so doing he helped to clarify and mould the common law. His analytical tradition endures.

There is much testimony to the style and substance of Goodhart's influence on the development of the law. Typical were the observations of Mr Justice Megarry, who had long worked closely with him on the *Law Quarterly Review*, in the volume of that journal for 1975 (p. 2). Goodhart 'always went straight to the heart of the matter and put his point so simply, directly and reasonably'. On the Law Reform Committee, his contributions were 'so sane, so practical and yet so firmly rooted in principle (and) put in a way which would disarm even the most zealous practitioner suspicious of academic pretensions'. His dry humour and his instinct for friendship were often commented on. The hospitality of Goodhart and his English wife was a distinctive feature of their public life.

It was widely noted that Goodhart's authority in legal thinking, aided by his exceptionally felicitous language and unfailing clarity, was a major factor in the decline in the second half of the twentieth century of the long, firmly held tradition whereby the citation in Court of a passage from the work of a living author was excluded. His opinions came to be cited with a welcoming judicial leave. His influence in the dissolving of barriers between the academic lawyer and the practitioner was considerable, advantageous both to university law faculties and the legal profession. He was not afraid to criticize a judge's reasoning or conclusion, when appropriate. His courtesy was not prejudicial to the force of his constructive expressions of dissent. His celebrated notes on cases in the *Review* made him everyone's tutor.

In 1953, he delivered at the Hebrew University of Jerusalem the first in the continuing series of Lionel Cohen Lectures. The series had been instituted by the 'legal group' of the Friends of the Hebrew University in Britain. The invitation was a tribute to Goodhart as Jew and as lawyer. He admired the independence of the judiciary of Israel, and the extent of the reception in Israel of common law principles. His acceptance of the invitation reinforced the acknowledgement, by many Judges and practitioners in Britain, of Israel as a member of what is sometimes called the common law family. After the Six-Day War of 1967, Goodhart gave significant public support to the case for Israel's presence on the West Bank pending assured security.

As to his general estimate of Jewish lawyers and of their motivation, significant guidance is found in his published version (1949) of his Lucien Wolf Memorial Lecture to the Jewish Historical Society of England in 1947, under the title of *Five Jewish Lawyers of the Common Law*. The chosen five were Judah Benjamin, Sir George Jessel, Lord Reading, Justice Louis Brandeis and Justice Benjamin Cardozo.

'The Jewish people', he wrote in his Introduction, 'have always been known as the People of the Law ... It is therefore not surprising that the Jews have made important contributions to legal thought in most of the countries of the modern world.' He added:

> At a time when the Jews have been criticized and attacked in many countries, I do not think it is improper to point out how great a contribution they have made to one of the major forces in civilization, the English common law.

While expressly disowning any kind of chauvinism, Goodhart observed with Cardozo that 'the passion to shape the forms of justice has been one of the dominant forces in the life of the Jewish people from the time of the mighty tablets to the days in which we live'. Accordingly, he went on, 'it is not surprising' to find that the five played their part in (what Cardozo called) the 'enobling tradition' of the law.

In his Conclusion (pp. 63–6) to this widely read book, Goodhart set out certain common features among the five, namely: clarity of thought, with an insistence on the primary need to establish the facts; their interest in scholarship, devotion to which 'has been recognised as a Jewish attitude'; and 'intellectual courage'. The last-mentioned feature is linked to their 'fundamental liberalism'.

He elaborated on that 'liberalism' in language which surely reflects his own inclination. None of the five, he states, 'was prepared to accept the established rules merely because they have long been established'. They felt free to criticize those parts of the law:

> which were no longer consonant with the needs of contemporary society ... I have always felt that the Jews, belonging as they do to a minority group, can best fulfil the function of the constructive critic; they are less conditioned ... to accept things as they are.

These thoughts represented no sudden adoption by Goodhart of the approach which he had found so magisterially embodied in the reasoning of Jewish lawyers of the common law. The attitude was part of his own life-long liberalism and moral valour. In his address on 'Recent Tendencies in English Jurisprudence' (*Essays in Jurisprudence and the Common Law* (1931), p. 43), he declared: 'It is the part of the lawyer to see that the legal system does not become bound by fixed categories which will make adjustment to modern needs difficult'. History may justifiably enrol Sir Arthur Goodhart in his own eminent, chosen gallery of Jewish lawyers of the common law.

NOTES

1. Sol Roth, *Halakhah and Politics: The Jewish Idea of the State* (1988), and 'Judaism and Democracy', *Torah U-Madda Journal*, Vol. 2 (1999), p. 67. In 1892, the famous scientist sceptic, Thomas Huxley, pungently referred to the Bible's 'insistence' upon 'the equality of duties, the liberty to bring about the righteousness which is somewhat different from struggling for "rights", and the fraternity of taking thought for one's neighbour as for oneself': *Essays upon Some Controversial Questions*, pp. 52–3, cited by Professor W.E. Barnes, 'The Permanent Value of the Old Testament', in H.B. Swete (ed.), *Cambridge Theological Essays* (1905), p. 368.
2. Lord MacMillan, *Law and Other Things* (1937).
3. Ernest Barker (ed.), 'The Law', *The Character of England* (1947), pp. 112–35.
4. Lord Lloyd of Hampstead *et al.* (eds), *Current Legal Problems* (1973), pp. 1–16.
5. In a different context, Lord Devlin, in his published Maccabean Lecture (1959) entitled 'The Enforcement of Morals', declared 'a sense of public morality' to be an 'essential element in the bonding which keeps society together'. He related that public sense of morality to 'common sense'.
6. Salmond's *Jurisprudence*, 12th edn, P.J. Fitzgerald (ed.) (1966), p. 111.

11

Dr Vivian David Lipman CVO, FSA, FRHistS 1921–90*

Vivian Lipman was a civil servant of great distinction, an historian of the front rank in his chosen fields, and a pious Jew. His piety and faith are essential ingredients in understanding his character and outlook.

He was a family man and a private man. He was rarely at ease in the public glare. Lipman was deeply attached to his Jewish heritage, and to the study both of its sources and of the media, through which over the ages that religious, cultural and literary inheritance has been channelled, moulded and perceived. He also had a high degree of public spiritedness for British society as a whole, especially for the efficacy of its institutions and its developing social relations. His instinctive interest in history reflected an interest in people, and was not confined to the Jewish sector. His extensive reading of British history was in part a reflection of his patriotism. His pleasure in his Fellowship of the Royal Historical Society was a considered and not a trite reaction.

I have no doubt that these were among the qualities which infused his work as a public administrator, in which sphere his talents and achievements won such wide acclaim. Added to these gifts were a sharp mind, a remarkably capacious intellect, an unfailing ability to detect and formulate with pellucid clarity the issues that mattered, and a flair for the labour of detailed research and for the marshalling and analysis of the results.

---

*Memorial address on Dr Lipman to Jewish Historical Society of England in *Transactions of the Jewish Historical Society of England*, Vol. 31 (1990).

Such factors caused him to shine brightly in his capacity as Jewish historian. He had a life-long and profound curiosity about the ever-changing contemporary Jewish scene, and a kind of personal commitment to the elucidation of its beginnings in the eighteenth and nineteenth centuries, particularly so far as the Jews in the United Kingdom were concerned. His devotion to the Jewish Historical Society of England became part of the pattern of his life, in which pattern Sonia, his wife who predeceased him, shared. This was for both of them an extension of their domesticity, to the great benefit of the Society and of Jewish scholarship.

He was well aware of his intellectual gifts. He would not hesitate in conversation to illustrate the range of his multi-faceted knowledge. It would be done by way of a distinctly playful presentation of a piece of recondite information. While others would be impressed, he would take boyish amusement in the apparent ease with which he carried his immense learning. Nobody could define this as immodesty. It was more a form of gamesmanship in which all had their parts. In demeanour and personal relations he had an unaffected modesty, which sometimes concealed a considerable inner confidence. That confidence, which became manifest when required, was, again in a wholly distinctive way, often accompanied by a constitutional shyness which in no way lessened the impact of his confidence, but, for his audience, reinforced its effect. His wit and humour took time to reveal themselves, except in the company of intimates.

The combination of such characteristics might have led the unwary to think of him as remote and likely to be impractical. He was neither remote nor impractical. He was a superb committee member, full of wise ideas and prolific in devices for handling practical situations. Down-to-earth and endowed with insight into people's thinking and reactions, he was an invaluable colleague. He always gave of his best. His ready helpfulness to students became proverbial.

His felicity of expression in writing and in speech delighted scholar and layman alike. It was an important element in his large contribution to Anglo-Jewish historiography. His polymathic versatility, as well as his sheer industry, is illustrated in his undoubted feel for medieval studies. His monumental *The Jews of Medieval Norwich* (1967) vividly demonstrates it.

Lipman held many offices in the Jewish Historical Society, adding prestige to each of them. He attended closely to detail as well as to policy. As Chairman of the Programme Committee, he extended the bounds of the Society's conventional interests, encouraging young scholars and newer themes. As Editor of its Publications, his exactitude never became pedantry, but added quality and effectiveness to our publications. As president, he brought lustre to the Society by his addresses and his personality. The *Transactions* bear extensive witness to his success in all those fields, as do his editing of *Three Centuries of Anglo-Jewish History* (1961), and his joint editing with Sonia of *Jewish Life in Modern Britain*, which contains the proceedings of the conference on that subject convened in London by the Board of Deputies in 1977.

The latter volume was a follow-up to the work of like title published in 1964 in consequence of the conference held in London in 1962, under the auspices of the Board and of the Hebrew University's Institute of Contemporary Jewry. At that conference he delivered an address, included in the volume of 1964 on 'Topics and Methods of Future Research in Contemporary Anglo-Jewish History'. It proved to be a highly influential and prophetic paper, typical of his style in substance and form. Its influence may be detected in the proceedings of the conference of 1977, to which he made his own characteristic contributions.

As we approach the centenary of the Society [1993], three figures may fairly be said to stand out. They are Lucien Wolf, Cecil Roth and Vivian Lipman. Each undoubtedly reflected the priorities and aspirations of their respective successive ages, yet each significantly expanded the scope of Jewish historical writing. His *Social History of the Jews in England, 1850–1950* (1954) was a pioneer work, of enduring value to researchers in, and teachers of, Anglo-Jewish history. The social and economic subjects with which it dealt, the statistical studies which it included, its examination of demographic changes and the changing occupational structures, and its close study of the 'non-establishment' segments of the Jewish community, render that work a landmark in Anglo-Jewish scholarship and literature.

Lipman's numerous papers on demographic history between the mid-Victorian period and the present day continued this genre of study. They form a striking department of original and analytical production within his considerable output. He was also concerned with the interrelations between the divers layers of the communal structure; with the reality of the mode of life and work of the broad mass of the evolving community; and with the impact of immigrations on the existing community, on the immigrants themselves, and on the old and new communal institutions. It was no accident that he had a long personal interest in the writings of the Webbs, not least the attitudes to Jewish issues on the part of Beatrice Webb. They were forerunners of the new ethos of social awareness and new approaches to social studies.

His impressive paper entitled 'The Age of Emancipation, 1815–1880' in *Three Centuries* – which was probably (with the notes thereto) his best single piece in literary terms – again demonstrated his concern to study layers of life and thought outside the governing groups. His role in this kind of research will be increasingly appreciated. His articles on these and related subjects appeared in *Transactions*, the *Jewish Journal of Sociology*, the *Jewish Chronicle*, *L'Eylah*, and elsewhere. His 'The Structure of London Jewry in the Mid-Nineteenth Century' in the *Festschrift* for Sir Israel Brodie (1967) is especially noteworthy in the wide range of his unfailingly original and stimulating studies.

I would also make special reference to Vol. 21 of *Transactions* (1968). It was a *tour de force* on his part that there appear in that volume two rich papers by himself on subjects as diverse as 'The Rise of Anglo-Jewish Suburbia' and 'Anatomy of Medieval Anglo-Jewry' (which was his presidential address in 1965). The former paper was an expanded version of his presidential address in 1966. It was, in a sense, a sequel to his memorable study in volume XVIII on 'A Survey of Anglo-Jewry, 1851', which was largely based on the census of that year. The 'Suburbia' study was concerned with demographic, occupational and residential movements among the Jews in England during and since the Emancipation. Whatever differences there were between the themes of the two papers in Vol. 21, there was the undoubted connecting link through the study of how and where people lived and what work they did, all based on research into often untapped sources and replete with original conclusions and fresh interpretations.

Vivian Lipman greatly welcomed his association with the Littman Library of Jewish Civilization. It served to broaden his opportunities to advance the cause of Jewish studies, especially in the historical field. He was especially pleased, as was his wife, Sonia, with their notable collection of studies on *The Century of Moses Montefiore* (1985), which they edited with great zeal and skill, and in which Sonia's own study, entitled 'The Making of a Victorian Gentleman', was a significant feature.

The last work which he lived to see was his *Americans and the Holy Land* (1989). His study therein of British records, throwing light on American involvement in Palestine during the hundred years prior to the Balfour Declaration, adds new material to and provides fresh insights into the subject. Vivian had already contributed a major paper to the colloquium in Washington in 1983, convened by the America–Holy Land Studies Project, on America–Holy Land material in British Archives between 1820 and 1930. That paper was published in *With Eyes Towards Zion* (1986), edited by Professor Moshe Davis, the academic chairman of the International Centre for the University Teaching of Jewish Civilization. Lipman acknowledged the help and encouragement given to him by that Centre and the Palestine Exploration Fund (with which he was closely associated) in connection with these new branches of his scholarly enterprise. He was devoted to the welfare and honour of the State of Israel, and saw in these works a significant contribution to the history both of the evolution of Israel and the study of the Jewish people within the family of peoples.

As we pay tribute to this scholar and friend, we may properly regard ourselves as blessed by the memory of him, enriched and fortified by his example and achievements, and fortunate to have had him among us. In this is to be found his legacy to us all. We say to his son, Anthony, and all the family, that we are proud to have known him, and that he and Sonia will not be forgotten.[1]

NOTES

1. A moving and well-informed tribute to Dr Lipman by his former pupil Dr Ada Rapaport-Albert appears in the *Transactions of the Jewish Historical Society of England*, Vol. 31 (1990), pp. xx–xxii.

12

Professor Sir Isaiah Berlin, OM 1909–97*

Dr Hardy, Fellow of Wolfson College, Oxford, is the past editor of a well-known collection of Berlin's lectures and essays. He brought some of them out of the comparative obscurity into which Berlin had seemed not to mind consigning them. He was strangely careless about the fate of his works, as though he meant it when he said that he was overrated. Dr Hardy's present co-editor is Lecturer in German Studies at Bradford University. They have perceptively assembled 15 of what they deem Berlin's most representative essays. For good measure, they have added his lively assessments of Churchill and Roosevelt, perhaps to ease the reader's task.

A.L. Rowse describes Berlin as 'unintelligible in several languages'. An unfair remark which makes a point. To read Berlin seriously calls for stamina. You wind your way through thickets of long, involved sentences. You brave his protracted, unbracketed parentheses and their interwoven complex analogies and contrasts. You finally emerge into the dim sunlight of conclusions of which you were warned at the outset, and which generally do one of two things. They demonstrate the contradictions and self-delusions of those whom Berlin has closely examined on the couch of his penetrating intellect. Or they reveal the world's misconceptions about the significance of those personalities. You are left somehow enriched by the strenuous intellectual adventure which each essay involves. But you also marvel at the author's own paradoxes and ironies. He

---

*Published in *Jewish Review* (April, 1999), as a review of Henry Hardy and Roger Hausheer (eds), *The Proper Study of Mankind: An Anthology of Essays by Isaiah Berlin* (Pimlico Press, 1998).

seems to know everything while sure of nothing. For him, very rarely is anything or anyone as good or as bad as appears.

Berlin concludes his powerful 65-page study of Tolstoy – surely his masterpiece in relentless analysis – by a description of the old man as he lay dying. He was 'oppressed by the burden of his intellectual infallibility and his sense of perpetual error'. He was 'the greatest of those who can neither reconcile nor leave unreconciled the conflict of what there is with what there ought to be'. No wonder that (as Lord Annan notes in his Foreword) one of Berlin's 'favourite quotations' was Kant's comment: 'Out of the crooked timber of humanity no straight thing was ever made.'

Machiavelli, Herder, Herzen and others are here submitted to Berlin's investigative scalpels in a series of surgical explorations of mind, motive and circumstance. His accounts of his meetings with Boris Pasternak and the poet, Anna Akhamatova, in Russia after World War II are deeply moving. They disclose that his famous intellectuality was a façade which shaded his strong and instinctive compassion, his hatred of all cruelty, and his conviction as to the all-importance of human relationships. The historian and philosopher was a man first, and never ceased to be so, in that order.

This historian of ideas was obsessed with the notion that good ends tend to conflict. No amount of elegant conversational sparkle or veneer could conceal his passionate concern for justice. The trouble was that justice has many definitions. If liberty and equality are crucial elements in justice, they are often incompatible with one another. His essay 'The Pursuit of the Ideal', given pride of place in this book, contains the quintessence of his public thinking. 'The goals and motives', he declares therein, 'that guide human action must be looked at in the light of all that we know and understand; their roots and growth, and above all their validity, must be critically examined with every intellectual resource we have.' He added that the social and political collisions to which conflicts of values are conducive can 'be minimised by promoting and preserving an uneasy equilibrium – which is in constant need of repair'. Such promotion is a 'pre-condition for decent societies and morally acceptable behaviour'. In the humaneness and the necessary imprecision of these passages is to be found the core of Berlin's contribution to modern society.

He smiles disapprovingly on all self-righteousness, puncturing with scant mercy comfortable, self-induced rationalizations and preconceptions. He warns against the turning of good into something much less good by the application of the blinding bandages of 'unerring' presuppositions. The Professor was not hostile to ideals, nor was he an enemy of faith. He was a friend of enquiry and an admirer of that respect for diversity without which, in his perception, the republic of letters faces the peril of being transformed into a congerie of learned yet unenlightened tyrannies.

Berlin's Zionism was more utilitarian than ideological. The Jews needed a national home. They had suffered too long from its absence. This was justification enough for him. The events of the twentieth century gave the need an imperative quality. There could be no other place for the National Home than the ancestral home. He believed that a prerequisite of peace for Israel was the recognition of the national aspiration of the Palestinian Arabs and territorial compromise.

He had a natural pride in being a Jew, but he had no illusions. He was a sensitive Jew. He shared the widespread Jewish sense of being an outsider. I doubt whether he saw the here-and-now as being the be-all and end-all of existence, but he was not much interested in such enquiry. He could not define the relevant questions nor even any provisional workaday answers. His Judaism was his moral sense, and his moral sense was his Judaism. He was prepared to attribute this state of mind to the influence upon him of birth and upbringing. He respected those who, while believing, sought to impose nothing on him. He did not mind if they hopefully tried to find common ground with him. He had a filial pleasure in and a curiosity about his chassidic connections. Talk of the divine left him politely speechless. If there was a mystery in life he was content to limit his study of it to the examination of man in society.

He was less interested in dogma than in the effect dogmatism might have on persons and societies. What mattered to him more was to discover 'the springs of (human) action' – Jeremy Bentham's phrase. He did not preach, but by his works he advanced the idea of the practical value – and he would not, I think, have been shy to say the moral worth – of the difficult art (it is also a science) of cultivating mutual respect amid intense differences. He might well have joined Hillel in making a philosophy out of not being quick to play the judge.

13

The Board and the Jewish Community*

The Board of Deputies is the representative body of Anglo-Jewry. While this is a truism to most, to some it is a grudgingly conceded fact, and there are even a few who persist in refusing to recognize the claim.

Anglo-Jewry is a Zionist community, by which is meant a community which welcomes and gives practical assistance to the State of Israel, and sees in the movement represented by the Zionist Organisation a great educational and moral force which can strengthen Jewish pride and self-respect the world over. The Jewish community is also aware that Anglo-Jewry is part of the larger congregation of Jews in the Diaspora, with whom it has ties of deep emotion and common interest. At the same time, Jews in this country, as citizens and denizens, are loyal to Great Britain, much as many of them might express strong disagreement with the Government's policy from time to time, and are proud of their citizenship of and loyalty to a country which has had so long a tradition of friendship with the Jewish people. The community is more than eager to see the old cordiality and mutual respect return between Great Britain and Jewish endeavour in Palestine. In all these attitudes the Board accurately represents the community, and has given it a lead in articulation.

In the sphere of combating anti-Semitism, the community is under no illusion that there is an easy remedy for this disease. It feels that it is of too long a growth in European history to be eliminated entirely in any length of time that can be planned ahead.

---

*Published in *Zionist Review* (London: English Zionist Federation, 1948).

In the long run, education and the amelioration of social conditions might reduce its incidence. In the meantime, anti-Semitism is a threat to British social and political life as well as to Jews, and it falls to the Jewish community to impress that danger on the general public and on the Government, to rally support from all sections of political opinion, and to call for additional legislation to curb the menace. The community wants the fight to be carried, in a united fashion and by all legal means, at the street corners and wherever else the enemy extends his work. In this approach to the problem, the community generally is at one with the Board, though much remains to be done by the Board in educating some elements of the community to responsible thinking in this sphere, as is shown by the poor response so far to the Defence Appeal.

There are in the Board, as outside, non-Zionists or former non-Zionists. There are one or two, speaking for a small number outside, who emphasize their natural allegiance to this country in such a way as to appear, perhaps unfairly to themselves, to deprive themselves of the capacity for ever taking a deeply felt Jewish view. Some Deputies untiringly press for ever greater activism, whether in the field of enlightening public opinion on Palestine affairs, or in the field of combating anti-Semitism. This policy has the vocal support at the Board of the handful of Communists there. Though the Board as a whole retains its confidence in its Defence Committee, which it regards as doing its job as well as its funds allow, the feeling that the Defence Committee should declare its policy more openly and be more active in its pressure on public opinion is not confined to the Communists. Nor should it be forgotten that, over Palestine, the Communists, by their support for current Russian policies, happen at the moment to be nearer in step with the Zionists than was ever possible in the past. This is hardly an alliance. Just as the spokesmen for the 'Ultra-Orthodox' view sometimes find themselves in the same lobby as the Liberal and Reform Jews in opposition to what is looked upon as the secular nationalism of the Zionist majority, so too the Zionists, at times, find some support from the far Left. The Board is representative and alive. There is hardly an attitude in the Jewish community which cannot find a spokesman at the Board.

Those who doubt or deny that the Board represents the community do so either because they disagree with its views, or because they have not accustomed themselves to the new leadership. Some also believe that those in charge of the affairs of the Board have attachments elsewhere to which they subordinate its interests. Some sincerely take the view that the voting at the Board is not the result of independent thinking on the part of Deputies, but is inspired by a few skilful party managers. It is noteworthy that, so far, the claim has not been put forward with any show of conviction that the Board, on large issues, has been out of step with the community.

The disinclination to recognize the representative character of the Board on account of disagreement with its views is both illogical and undemocratic.

The new leadership of the Board is Zionist. The Jewish disaster in Europe, coupled with the British Government's Palestine policy, as set out in the White Paper of 1939, produced an indignation which made a non-Zionist President of the Board an anomaly. Professor Brodetsky's accession to office eight years ago indicated the change. A deeply moved and often noisy Zionist majority was returned, which, since 1943, has shown itself in the composition of most of the Committees which the Board has elected, and has determined the policies of the Board. A silent revolution (or not so silent, its critics would say!) was brought about in the administration of the community. The former leaders were reduced to an influential minority; influential both because of their experience and ability, and because of their points of contact inside the community and outside. No thanks are due to those members of the minority who have stayed in the fight, for its was their duty. The debates at the Board have certainly been richer by their presence.

The charges relating to the attachments which certain prominent Deputies have outside the Board arises from an over-simplified view of Jewish life. It has been alleged that some members of the Board put their allegiance to the World Jewish Congress before their duty to the Board. It has also been a constant refrain of the critics that the policies of the Board are often dictated by a caucus with its headquarters in the offices of the Zionist Federation. Allegations of this kind overlook the fact that every citizen has a multiplicity of personal, social and political attachments.

A citizen who is a Jew has, among others, a series of Jewish attachments, which need in no way conflict either with his duties as a citizen or with his obligations as a member of this or that Jewish body. A member of the Board of Deputies may be a Zionist or a non-Zionist. He may be a supporter or even a member of the World Jewish Congress, or he may be indifferent or even hostile to that organization. The final arbiter in loyalties, in a free country, is the conscience, unless the law is infringed. No one has suggested that the law has been infringed by the maligned multiplicity of Jewish attachments. It is sometimes suggested that discretion and tactics should dictate a more cautious attitude. What are discretion and wise tactics are matters of opinion, and whatever our views on them, they in themselves provide no grounds for a denial of the representative character or authority of the Board.

The charge that voting at the Board is not free is usually related, by those who make it, to the charge of dictation from the office of the English Zionist Federation in Great Russell Street. It is certainly true that there has come into being at the Board a system of groups. There is the Zionist Progressive Group, as the majority group is called, and there is the Independent Group, which is the principal minority group. There is also the Orthodox Group, and there is the tiny group of Communists. The leadership of the majority group is in the hands of persons who are closely associated with the Zionist Federation or with the British Section of the World Jewish Congress. The leadership of the Independent Group is largely in the hands of persons closely associated with the Anglo-Jewish Association. While there is some overlapping in the membership of the Groups, the system reflects the divisions in the Board. Like minds produce like voting. If inspired voting means voting inspired by likemindedness, no one should complain. If it means an unthinking acceptance by the many of the dictation of the few, that would be highly regrettable, and the Board should be constantly on the alert to prevent that happening.

The Board is a deliberative assembly, without sanctions. It depends for its effectiveness on the confidence reposed in it by the community, and it strives to earn the highest. The attention and intelligent interest of the community make its task easier.

255

14

The Group System at the Board of Deputies*

The group system at the Board of Deputies of British Jews has not been formally adopted or recognized. It is none the less a markedly operative arrangement, whereby the main basic divisions of thought and outlook inside the membership of the Board are represented by distinctive groups, and sometimes stimulated by them. Each group has its leaders and committee, its principal orators and its own internal differences. There are Deputies who belong to no group, and there are some who belong to more than one group. The president, on occasion, 'has had conversations' with group leaders on different sides of the Board.

The system is as near to a party system as the procedure, functions and history of the Board allow. The Board meets once a month, and lacks the debating time in which the forms of party politics might develop as in a Parliamentary chamber; nor have the affairs of the Board the extensive publicity which is essential to the formation of nationally based party followings. There is neither the discipline nor the wherewithal for the establishment of the party structure that we take for granted in national politics. The Board has no sanctions, and it exists on the voluntary principle.

A further feature which works against the creation of a party system is that the president of the Board is also the chairman of debates. He combines the duties of a Speaker with those of a maker of policy. Should these two functions be separated at the Board, the president would be either the chairman of debates alone, or would

*Published in *Concord*, journal of Jewish Defence Committee of the Board (June 1949).

come into the body of the hall as some kind of 'Leader of the House' or leader of the majority group. The way would be open for the growth of 'Government' and 'Opposition', with all the consequences of party life in the Board and in the community. The present position of the president is an important safeguard against the intensification of differences inside the Board.

The history of the Board has not, until recently, required a group system, still less a party system. For most of its existence its members, in the main, thought alike on large issues, nor were those issues as heart-searching or as harsh as those of our day. It was when the more recently arrived elements of Anglo-Jewry found representation in the expanding Board in substantial numbers that differences assumed important proportions, and the possibility of a group system came into being. The existence of the group system is testimony to the inevitable differences that arose, when the community had had time to undergo the full impact of immigration from Eastern Europe, the great surge of emotion at the contemporary Jewish Holocaust, and the feelings aroused by events in Palestine. The foundation of the State of Israel has reduced the tension but the differences, which have acquired traditions of their own, persist. Their expression is related today, among other matters, to a discussion on the correct emphasis on the community's attachment to Israel. The rancour of this discussion is the aftermath of a long section of communal history. These are problems which have made the Board not only a forum for discussion, but an arena.

The emergence of the 'Zionist Progressive Group' as an effective combination in 1943 had been heralded in the preceding session of the Board. The significance of the disbandment in that year of the Joint Foreign Committee of the Board and the Anglo-Jewish Association was not only political, but also, in the context of this article, 'constitutional'. It was a triumph for the group system, as well as for the Zionist Progressive Group. The extent of control of the Board by the Group produced, in turn, the 'Independent Group', on the other side of the Board, consisting of Deputies who disliked the policies of the majority group, or its methods, or both. The Independent Group was hampered by the absence from the Board of several prominent communal figures who decided to stand aloof from its affairs rather than tilt at the majority windmills. This attitude was a forerunner of some of the more recent secessions.

The absentees and the spokesmen of the Independent Group were men who had frequently led the Board until 1939. The assertion made on behalf of that Group, that it would dissolve itself if only the Zionist Progressive Group would dissolve itself first, was of no avail. By the end of the 1943–46 session the group system had become a familiar part of the life of the Board. It was not the existence of the system that was resented so much as the massiveness of the Zionist group and the uses to which it was put. Those who differed from it felt powerless against its efforts. The 'caucus', as it was called by its detractors, made its full weight felt in the election to committees, in debates at the Board and in the Board's decisions. The formation of the 'Orthodox Group', in the session 1946–49, might be regarded as a further demonstration of the hold which the idea of the group system had exercised over Deputies. The tiny Communist group of Deputies could not be excluded from the list of groups at the Board.

The Zionist Progressive Group consists of all shades of Zionist opinion, though not all Zionists at the Board have joined it or attend its deliberations, where its policy is fashioned. At its head are leading figures in the English Zionist Federation or in the British Section of the World Jewish Congress. Since 1943, their followers in the Board have been in a substantial majority. The *raison d'être* of the Group was to range the Board unequivocally on the side of the Jewish Agency for Palestine and in support of what came to be known as the Biltmore Programme for a Jewish state. To that end, the Group sought to eliminate from influence at the Board those elements which were opposed to, or were doubtful supporters of, that Programme. While the Group sincerely denounced the activities of the Irgun and the Sternists, it condemned at the same time the restrictive policy of the British Government in Palestine, which, it felt, could have destroyed the ground from which those activities were said to spring, by meeting its obligations to the Jewish National Home.

Since the establishment of the State of Israel, the Group has sought to instil into the Board and into the Jewish community not only pride at the event (which is shared by the whole Board), but also enthusiasm for cultural relations between Anglo-Jewry and Israel. It sees in the desire to define, and thereby delimit, the community's attachment to Israel, an effort to erect psychological barriers, at a time when the emphasis should be on mutual attraction and on the affirmation of the existence of *one* Jewish people. The Group asserts the allegiance of Anglo-Jewry to Great Britain, and sees no conflict between that and its attitude to Israel. It cherishes the hope of an early and intimate *rapprochement* between the two countries. It is claimed that in all this, the Group is the reflection in the Board of the bulk of the Jewish community. It should be added that the leaders of the Group are mainly left-wing politically. There are differences in political opinion and religious practice among the leaders, as among the rank and file.

The Independent Group consists of many shades of political and religious opinion, though not all Deputies who claim to be independent identify themselves with it. Its leaders are mainly men associated with the Anglo-Jewish Association. They see in the Zionist Progressive Group an attempt to make the Board serve the ends of outside bodies, whether the Jewish Agency or the English Zionist Federation, or the World Jewish Congress. The principal members of the Group are mostly right-wing politically. The Group believes that the Board has lost weight with the British Government, on account of its allegedly unreflecting Zionism and the appearance it has given of accepting uncritically the anti-British attitude of vocal leaders of American Jewry. It emphasizes the exclusive allegiance of British Jews to this country, and most of its members considered Professor Brodetsky's dual position as President of the Board and Executive member of the Jewish Agency, at a time when relations between the Agency and the British Government were highly strained, as an embarrassment both to the Board and the community.

Some of its members have long been opposed to the idea of a Jewish state. Others have been non-Zionists and some are Zionists. All its members deplore what they regard as the regimentation of the Board by the majority. They claim that the policies of the majority, and therefore of the Board, are determined by one or two individuals who are identified with the English Zionist Federation, and that one or two men alone are able to engineer the policies of the Board as they please. It is alleged that this domination over the Board is secured by their influence on elections to, and elections at, the Board. The methods of the 'caucus' are described as the methods of the whip system. Amendments to the constitution of the Board, which were designed to put these methods out of court, were sponsored in debate by members of the Independent Group (though it should be noted that they had been recommended by a committee appointed by the Board), but were defeated by those very methods, it is claimed, which the amendments sought to render illegal. The proposed amendments were later adopted.

The group system cannot exist without some degree of group discipline, however weakly imposed. It lacks the ruthlessness of party discipline, but must exceed in severity the etiquette of the drawing room! To deplore the fact that the methods exist is to deny the right of the group system to exist. To deny that right seems to fly in the face of reality. In any case, such discipline as is found at the Board is the voluntary discipline of those who think alike. Of course, no group has ever supported a candidate for office who subscribes to views which are unacceptable to its own main tenets. The packing of committees is a term of abuse for a well-known concomitant of any system of groups. The danger inherent in the group system is that it might encourage apathy among the members of large groups, or might place a premium on thoughtless acceptance of advice. A healthy system requires an alert Board, and an alert Board can afford the system. The acceptance of guidance from group leaders is not an evil. It has advantages, but the price is too high if guidance is allowed to become dictation or electoral threat. That depends on the good sense and the courage of Deputies, both within the groups and in the proceedings of the Board.

15

The Board of Deputies of British Jews[*]

The new Board of Deputies, whose triennial session began in June 1949, inherits a series of problems which will severely tax its wisdom and courage. It would be unfortunate if current controversies, however dramatic and significant they might be, were to conceal from the Board some of the less stirring issues which concern its own future as a working institution. In recent years, the Board has been so deeply occupied with affairs vitally affecting the Jewish people that, as the Treasurer declared at the end of the last session, the Board has had neither the time nor the freedom of mind to undertake necessary long-term schemes.

FINANCE

One of the grave if prosaic weaknesses of the Board is its financial insolvency. At current rates, the Board is spending about twice as much as its income, and this deficit will probably be progressively

---

*This article was written before the first meeting of the new Board and was published in *Chayenu (Our Life)*, the journal of 'Jewish Religious Labour', in July 1949. The secession referred to in the text followed the refusal by the outgoing president, Professor Brodetsky, in accordance with the constitution, to certify for statutory purposes the marriage secretaries of the Liberal Synagogue, having regard to the refusal by the then Chief Rabbinate in Commission (there being an interregnum) to certify that Synagogue as a congregation of 'persons professing the Jewish religion'. In 1959, Parliament empowered an officer of that Synagogue to perform their own certification, as the Reform Synagogue had been authorized to do by statute in 1856. The Board did not oppose either measure.

increased. Its income, which is almost entirely derived from dues payable by constituencies, remains static, while, with the expansion of its activities, the budget becomes larger each year.

The state of its finances is not only an indignity to the representative body of Anglo-Jewry, but a serious inconvenience. The Board must have an assured and regular income, which should not be dependent on the success of a popular appeal. In any case, the Defence Appeal is generally understood by the community to be directed towards raising money for the restricted field of activity defined by its title. The administration of the Board, and all the activities summed up in the term 'foreign affairs', cannot be allowed to suffer. The Board will have to find additional basic income, even if it means increasing substantially the dues from the constituencies.

THE BOARD AND THE COMMUNITY

The problem of finance cannot be divorced from that of securing effective 'public relations' within the community. The Board is greatly concerned with public relations in regard to the Gentile community, but it has not always realized that it has important duties in the field of public relations as far as the Jewish community is concerned. Accompanying the justifiable pride with which Zionists acclaim the representative attitude of the Board in recent years over Palestine, there is a feeling that the Board's voice has not penetrated into the community itself.

Far too few Deputies report to their constituencies, and not enough constituencies examine and discuss such reports as are presented to them. The notable exceptions which are reported in the Jewish Press hide the general apathy. There have been spectacular occasions when the Board was given comparative prominence by the BBC or the national Press, and no doubt the community at such times took note. But such occasions are rare, and the Board is not a spectacular body. It has had neither the staff nor the funds to undertake a serious attempt to put itself across to the community. Its defence work is its best-known activity. Much less is known about its associations with Jewish communities overseas. Its work in connection with the Social and Economic Council and other agencies of the United Nations is a growing sphere of interest in which the

Board has been, and can continue to be, of great help to Jews in many lands. Its services deserve wider recognition.

EDUCATION COMMITTEE

It might be appropriate to refer here to the Education Committee of the Board, whose existence sometimes causes wonder. At an early date, the Education Committee must indicate its programme and demonstrate its intention to pursue it. In the past session, it was obliged to strive to steer clear of the shoals of controversy, and it did so with such a zeal that it found extreme difficulty in adopting and executing a positive educational programme. The functions of the Committee must be such as lie outside the competence of the various executive educational bodies in the community. Cooperation in Jewish education among bodies with different religious outlooks is rarely easy. The Committee must cooperate with whom it can. But it is bound to take into account the diversity of opinion in the Board on religion and other matters, and if that diversity makes it impossible for the Board to have a working educational programme of its own, then the Committee should say so. It would then become a watching Committee, on the look-out for those legal or personal problems in the educational life of the community which might more easily be dealt with by a representative committee than by any one of the educational organizations directly engaged in denominational instruction.

WORLD JEWISH CONGRESS

It is too early to say whether in the coming session the Board will again be asked to affiliate to the World Jewish Congress, but the relations between the two bodies will probably be one of the main topics for debate. There are several forms of relationship, short of affiliation, which the Board might consider. Even those who favour outright affiliation have felt it would be premature to press for it until the community had been 'educated' into appreciating the need. The recent secessionists from the Board were the keenest opponents,, and their departure might seem to have strengthened the hands of those who have long wanted affiliation. It would nevertheless be the opposite of statesmanship if the present position were to be used to push ahead with this highly controversial proposal. Opposition to affiliation is not confined to the secession-ists. It is true that the vote, in 1936, against affiliation was a very narrow one, and that events since then have brought many Jews into sympathy with the idea of a World Jewish Congress. It should be realized, however, that among the opponents would be persons who have been in sympathy with the policies and methods of the Board throughout the last eventful two sessions.

There can be effective cooperation with the Congress, without affiliation. The Board welcomes international action where it is useful. Its relations with the Jewish Agency for Palestine and its membership of the Co-ordinating Board of Jewish Organizations are proof of that. Such technical matters as restitution of property in ex-enemy countries, and such political matters as measures against the infringement of the rights of Jews abroad, can be pursued by the Board and the Congress working in consultation. Machinery for consultation should exist not between these two bodies alone, but between *all* the principal Jewish organizations concerned in this kind of work.

Such cooperation was achieved in connection with the peace treaties with the ex-enemy satellite countries, and in connection with the discussions at the United Nations on the Declaration of Human Rights and the Genocide Convention. Not all these organizations had the same outlook on all matters, but then differences made consultation all the more necessary. Where the differences are too great to be overridden, an independent memorandum to the authorities concerned is unavoidable.

The abrupt posing of constitutional problems at a time of high feelings is a crude procedure. The new Board will have to consider its external relations at an early date, and much will depend on the qualities of the newly elected president (Dr Abraham Cohen).[1]

THE LEADERSHIP OF THE BOARD

Much will depend on the leadership of the Board in other directions also. The community cannot take the recent secessions lightly. The secession, however indirectly, gave practical expression to divisions which have perturbed the community at least since the Biltmore Programme,[2] and in some ways since the Balfour Declaration. It will be for the new president to examine at once how far he can go in seeking their return, without infringing the right of the majority of the Board to exert its full weight in the debates and decisions of the Board.

The question of the Liberal Marriage Secretaries is but one of the acute problems with which he will be faced. The fundamental factor leading to the decision of the AJA, the Liberals, the West London Synagogue and the Spanish and Portuguese Congregation not to elect deputies, was the massive Zionist majority and its methods. Can the new leadership of the Board bestride the community and save the Board from the dreary prospect of debates unenlivened by dissension?

RELATIONS WITH ISRAEL

About a year ago, there was some discussion in the Board about the extent to which it would be appropriate for the Board to declare its view on affairs relating to Israel. It was wisely agreed that the Board, like any other legal organization in this country, might speak its mind on any matter of public interest, and that, while the sovereignty of the State of Israel was undisputed, the Board might exercise its freedom of speech even on such matters as were of direct interest to the Israeli Government. It was not supposed that the Board would wish to speak on the domestic affairs of Israel. The decision of the Board was concerned with those 'external' matters in which other Powers are likely to be interested. There was nothing exceptional in this attitude, but it did not touch upon the question of relations between Anglo-Jewry and Israel outside the now comparatively obscure sphere of resolutions. The Board rejoiced in the establishment of the new State, but, like so many members of the community, gropes for an acceptable and effective relationship with it. No question of political allegiance is involved here. The Board prizes with great possessiveness the rights and duties encumbent upon it and its members as citizens and denizens of this country, but it cannot be indifferent to the task of establishing a new orientation towards Anglo-Jewry in the light of the momentous fact of the State of Israel. It has been formally suggested that the Palestine Committee of the Board be renamed the Eretz Israel Committee. Deputies will look to the new Committee not for the truisms which accompany all great events, but for wise leadership in a most significant issue.

NOTES

1. Dr Cohen's opponent, whom he defeated by a comparatively limited majority of votes, was Dr Israel Feldman, a medical practitioner, a former Chairman of the Board's Palestine Committee (as it was then called) and a leading figure in the United Synagogue. During the campaign he was wrongly accused of not being 'a Zionist'. He had long-standing ties with prominent members of the Independent Group at the Board. Had the secessionists (mentioned in the text) not withdrawn from the Board for a period which in the event covered the presidential election, there can be little doubt that their votes would have secured victory for Dr Feldman. Dr Cohen, former Minister of the Singer's Hill Synagogue, Birmingham, was a notable member of the British Section of the World Jewish Congress and was associated with the Zionist Progressive Group since its inception at the Board in 1942–43.
2. Statement of policy declared by the Extraordinary Zionist Conference, convened at the Biltmore Hotel in New York in May 1942, in favour of the creation of a 'Jewish Commonwealth' within the then Mandatory Palestine.

16

I.L. Goldsmid and the Beverley Election of 1847*

The autumn of 1857 was a decisive moment in the struggle which, for nearly 30 years, had absorbed so much of the energy of the Anglo-Jewish leadership. Jewish emancipation at that time had come to mean the legal admission of professing Jews into Parliament. Social emancipation had long been largely achieved. In the previous decade, municipal disabilities and certain other historical discriminations in law had been abolished. Westminster was now a promised land: that is, 'promised' in the mind of the emancipationists by the strength of opinion in their favour in the House of Commons and by a growing acknowledgement of the patriotism and visible service of its seekers.

What was regarded as a stubborn rearguard delay was fostered by significant sections of the Tory Party and sustained by influential Anglican clerics in the House of Lords and in the country. It was felt that their efforts should not and could not indefinitely thwart the repeated intentions of a majority in the Commons. Between 1847 and 1857, Lionel de Rothschild was to be repeatedly elected to Parliament by the City of London and on each occasion was famously repulsed by the Speaker for refusing to subscribe to the Christological oath imposed by ancient statute.

Rothschild's election in 1847 was followed by yet another Bill, introduced by Lord John Russell, to exempt Jews from that requirement. That Bill led to the final series of collisions between the Houses on the issue, from which there ultimately emerged – mainly through

---

*Published in the *Jewish Chronicle* on 19 November 1957, under the title 'Forcing the Pace of the Law'.

the assiduous efforts of Sir David Salomons – a compromise whereby each House was empowered to decide for itself the form of admission oaths. Under that compromise, enshrined in the Jewish Relief Act of 1858, Rothschild took his seat in the House of Commons.

The books which have recounted these episodes have tended to concentrate on London and the Home Counties. Contests in more distant centres merit assessment in the overall narrative. In particular, Sir Isaac Lyon Goldsmid's candidature at Beverley throws its own light on public sentiment and on the motives of the Jewish emancipationists. In that year, Jews stood for Parliament for the first time. It was a deliberate attempt to force the pace of the law. Should any be elected and refuse to take the full oath in the House on account of being a Jew, the effect might well be to fortify opinion in favour of the abolition of the restriction. It was this kind of direct action which, in the person of Salomons, had brought success on the municipal front in the 1840s.

In 1847, in addition to Goldsmid standing at Beverley and Rothschild in the City, Salomons was a candidate at Greenwich, Meyer de Rothschild at Hythe and Goldsmid's son, Francis, at Yarmouth. Lionel de Rothschild was probably the least militant of the five by temperament. His somewhat quiescent disposition in the matter was no doubt associated with an ingrained belief that the legislators' fairness and wisdom would, in the end, be conducive to the desired result.

Salomons did not share such complacency. On being elected at Greenwich he refused to withdraw from the chamber of the House until a gesture of force had been used, and after he had taken his seat, spoken and voted in practical defiance of the law. It is likely that, had Goldsmid been returned at Beverley, he would have acted in a similar manner and faced the consequent criminal proceedings which befell Salomons. The Court adjudged Salomons to be technically guilty but expressed some sympathetic support for his cause and expressly encouraged the reform of the rules which in due course came about.

The ancient market town of Beverley, dominated by its great Minster, was a flourishing Anglican stronghold with about 1,200 voters. Despite the marked Tory influence of local landowners, the town took much of its political colour from the great port of Hull, eight miles away. In Hull, religious Nonconformity was strong, and the Liberal Party generally predominated. The main issue in the General Election of 1847 was the tariff question. In 1846, the Tory Prime Minister, Sir Robert Peel, had broken his Party by adopting the Whig (later Liberal) policy of free trade and repealing the Corn Laws. His measure was viewed as being contrary to the commercial interests of the landed agricultural producers.

Beverley, which returned two members to Parliament, was represented by two free-traders, J. W. Hogg, a Peelite, and John Towneley, a liberal-minded Whig. Since Hogg was now standing elsewhere, and Goldsmid, a liberal Whig, was a natural free-trader, Goldsmid's chances were bright. *The Times* reported that the disarray among the local Tories was greater than ever. Indeed, so late was the nomination of a Tory candidate that on 30 July, two days after the election, the *Jewish Chronicle* proudly announced the election unopposed of Goldsmid and Towneley.

The Tory candidate was Sackville Lane Fox, hitherto MP for Ipswich and a vigorous protectionist. He was also a vocal Protestant champion, ironically described by the *Hull Advertiser* as 'the Lord George Gordon of the nineteenth century'. The incursion of Fox, whose local standing was heightened by his Yorkshire birth, shifted the principal issue from the tariff to religious disabilities.

The Beverley election was extensively reported in the Hull press. There was general tribute to the Jewish financier's munificence regardless of creed and for his identification with causes, such as penal reform and university education, which had no sectarian impulse. But, commented the Tory newspaper, the *Hull Packet*, he is a 'Radical Jew' and his candidature 'an anti-Christian movement'. The editor added, a few days after the election, that 'it is the sacred duty of every Christian elector to resist all attempts to place the despisers of Christ in Parliament' and 'to prevent those who believe Christianity to be a delusion' from engaging in the legislative process.

During the election, Fox exuberantly denounced what he called 'the many direct and indirect efforts to undermine the principles of the Church of England'. Ranged against Fox was the *Hull Advertiser*, the organ of the Nonconformists. It viewed Goldsmid's candidature as the test of Whig (Liberal) opinion strength in East Yorkshire. The editor denied that there was any 'hot-bed of anti-Jewish bigotry in Yorkshire'.

It proved to be an unhappy campaign for Goldsmid. He was

unversed in electioneering tactics, still less in the corruption which was then not uncommon in the electoral system. He publicly declared his intention of conducting the campaign on 'principles of purity', but he lacked the machinery to ensure that his local supporters would, in practice, follow his ideal. Electoral corruption, commented the *Hull Advertiser*, 'would be inconsistent with the antecedents of the Hebrew emancipation question'.

But Goldsmid's friends were his worst enemies, and he was saddled with some of their guilt. Some of Fox's agents also bought votes. Goldsmid and Towneley had originally planned a joint campaign, but Goldsmid's dismissal of his colleague's request that the finances of the contest should be managed by their local committee broke their partnership. With what the *Hull Packet* called 'the characteristic caution of his race', Goldsmid insisted on knowing how the money was to be spent and preferred to retain control over disbursements. The result was that the local committee lost its enthusiasm for Goldsmid and most of its members canvassed solely for Towneley. Goldsmid had influential support, including that of some prominent Tories and a few Churchmen. The Peelites favoured him. George Liddell, a powerful Hull banker and a Tory, canvassed for him. But he did not recover from the Liberal rift.

Goldsmid's published election address was given extensive local publicity. Dated from his home, St John's Lodge, Regent's Park, this statement put the abolition of religious disabilities at the centre of his purpose: 'I seek to be returned as your MP', he declared in his first public speech in Beverley,

> in order to give full effect to the principle and have an opportunity of showing that as a people we Jews are worthy citizens ... Should you send me to Parliament you will confer a favour not on me alone ... You would favour and make grateful 25,000 human beings living in this country like myself of the Jewish persuasion ... I take my stand on this honourable footing, so that having tried me, you may say, 'This Jew has performed his duty.' Such a character would be my pride. I will strive to discharge my office with credit, that the country may say, 'This Jew has performed his part well; why may not every other?'

Here we have the authentic spring of the emancipationist impulse on the Jewish side. Goldsmid, who initiated the movement

20 years earlier, sought to rectify a jarring anomaly. It was not so much an injustice as an illogicality that Englishmen, albeit Jews, should be excluded from Parliament. The Englishman of the Jewish persuasion was born.

It was this idea that lay behind Salomon's dissociation in 1852 from the Chief Rabbi's scheme for a Jewish school for the Jewish middle classes. He preferred the City of London School or some such establishment. This dominant idea also gave added zest to his successful opposition in 1857 to the doctrine that a rabbinic divorce should suffice in English law to dissolve the marriage of English Jews. Towards the end of his life, Salomons even doubted the wisdom of having a Jewish representative assembly to approach the Government on behalf of Anglo-Jewry. At no time did Goldsmid recognize the Board of Deputies as the sole official channel of Jewish communication to the Government.

One feels that the emancipationist idea was also partly productive of the Anglo-Jewish disinclination in the 1840s to seek a Jewish political concession in the Holy Land, which might have implied that the Jews of England were in exile awaiting redemption. In the stress of the emancipation campaign, such possible consequential inhibitions were only dimly perceived or not at all contemplated.

17

The Jewish National Idea: Polemics in Britain, 1847–97*

In the summer of 1847, 50 years before the First Zionist Congress, the Prime Minister, Lord John Russell, announced his Government's intention to introduce a Bill to allow professing Jews into Parliament. The prospect was hailed with delight by leaders of the Jewish community as a long-awaited act of justice and a millennial-type event. It would be an example to the world, a deed of delayed fairness, a crucially significant indication of the new age. This was their perception. In 1845, after much contention, municipal office had been opened to the Jews. That development sharpened the expectations of the emancipationists for the success of Russell's Bill, and at the same time enhanced the efforts of their opponents to secure its rejection.

'Are the truths of Christianity to be an open question in Parliament?' cried one critic. 'Are members of the Jewish nation, with their own national aspirations for Jerusalem, to be involved in the highest counsels of State?', enquired another. The Jews in London have more in common with those of Vienna than with their Christian neighbours here, warned a third. Russell's Bill was accepted by a majority in the Commons but was thrown out by the Lords. The necessary legislation was not enacted until 1858. The Lords had finally given way under the ironic influence of the then Tory Prime Minister, Lord Derby, weary over what had been a politically troublesome bone of contention between the two Houses since 1833.

Russell's proposal was intensely debated over many days in that

---

*Published in *Le'ela* (London: Jews' College, 1998).

original session of 1847–48. The issues were comprehensively examined on all sides of the argument, in particular in William Gladstone's mammoth and carefully reasoned speech on 12 December 1847. This long-standing opponent of such a measure had now changed his mind. He was a pious Anglican, a notable theologian, and a consummate economist and politician. Gladstone had moved from the ranks of unbending Toryism into a form of liberal Conservatism and, in the 1860s, was to found the Liberal Party. His status and his chiselled oratory ensured the closest attention to his address.

Its liberal content well illustrates the double-edge (not always conscious but nonetheless real) found in many advocates of the Jewish cause. Civil emancipation was accorded to the Jews as much in spite of their characteristics (genuine or attributed) as because of their commended qualities. No Gentile exponent of their case was oblivious of their separateness, their international kinship, their common and distinctive history, and their own special aspirations. Disraeli, the baptized Jew, publicly (and contrary to his party's outlook) supported the Jewish claim. His party leader, Lord Derby, was not personally hostile to Jews, but he gravely pondered the question as to whether Jews, while Jews, could be Englishmen. At best he had reservations. Conversion did not necessarily make the difference.

'From an outcast', wrote Gladstone in the preface to his published speech of 1847,

> the Jew came to be only an alien among us; from an alien, he came to be a citizen; from a citizen having rights of person and property only, he has obtained by fresh stages access to the franchise, to the magistracy, and to municipal government. Political prudence – and justice – may require us now to concede a demand which, in an earlier age of social development or in times of different doctrine and practice as to national religion, it might have required us to resist.

While Jewish spokesmen welcomed Gladstone's support, there was significantly no reliance placed by him on the principle of their entitlement as citizens. Their request was for him a matter of bestowal, to be judged on prudential and pragmatic grounds. This was a widely held approach.

Gladstone shared the view of Lord Ashley (later Lord Shaftesbury) that the Jews 'had discarded many of their extravagant and anti-social doctrines and had become much more fit to be incorporated in the framework of general society'. Not everyone accepted those propositions. As for Ashley himself – and despite what he regarded as their 'improvement' – he opposed Jewish entry into the 'Christian' Parliament. Gladstone did not think that the 'few' Jews who were likely to seek entry would imply the religious indifference of Parliament or be a religious threat to stability.

In his own typically cautious language, Gladstone noted with approval that Ashley had at least 'discarded the argument drawn from the supposition that the Jews are a separate nation in such a sense as to be disqualified from the performance of civic duties'. Whether they in fact constituted a 'separate nation' was not expressly determined in Gladstone's speech, but the implication was that this indeed was what they were. Many non-Jews deemed the Jews' national character as a self-evident impediment to their full emancipation since they had their own 'national' interests.

Gladstone was much taken up with such concerns in the 1870s. His main political rival was Disraeli. The latter had rejuvenated the old stricken Tory party (which Disraeli had long before helped to break). Gladstone disliked the man whom he regarded as a flamboyant political 'conjurer'. When Disraeli was Prime Minister in the second half of the 1870s, Gladstone accused him of pursuing 'Judaic aims' in his foreign policy. He also suggested that Jews tended to vote as Jews in the Jewish interest as a kind of bloc. He thought they were indifferent to the plight of the Christian subjects of the Turks who controlled lands in the Balkans. In the then Russo-Turkish tensions, he considered that Disraeli's pro-Turkish outlook and his undoubted reserve towards Russia were dictated by his response to the condition of the Jews under Czarist rule. Gladstone wanted to see the Ottomans ousted from Europe 'bag and baggage', for which aim he saw Christian Russia as a natural ally.

In turn, some leading Liberals were dismayed over what they perceived as their leader's inadequate response to the outbreaks of violence against Jews in Russia in and from 1881, when he was again Prime Minister. In particular, he was severely upbraided in public by one of his own prominent MPs, Sir John Simon, QC, a founder member of the West London Synagogue of British Jews. 'Is all sympathy', Simon asked, 'reserved for the Christians, and none to spare for the Jews?' He warned of the danger of Jewish departures from the Liberal Party. Gladstone countered such strictures by contending that Britain had no *locus standi* for formal intervention, that such public representations could do more harm than good, and that in any case, more information was needed both about the groups engaged in the violence, and the nature and effect of the Russian Government's reactions, and their own regulations concerning the Jews.

Arthur Cohen, a prominent lawyer, a Liberal MP and President of the Board of Deputies, shared his leader's opinion. The question, however, was raised – what was the Jewish interest in politics, especially in foreign affairs? As Englishmen they might have concerns which differed from their concerns and anxieties as Jews. The prolific Liberal publicist and historian, Professor Goldwin Smith, famously asked whether a Jew could be a patriot. He suggested that the Jews were entitled to a state of their own – such as, he said, the Greeks and Italians had achieved in that century. Later, Arnold White, who had been Baron de Hirsch's agent in negotiating with the Russians for the emigration of Jews to South America, publicly expressed surprise over the hostile attitude of the Chief Rabbi, Dr Hermann Adler, towards political Zionism, and over Adler's widely noted assertion that since the destruction of the Temple there was no Jewish nation.

The humanitarian and creedal bases of the international interest of the Jews were not perceived as the only facet of their concern. There was an international Jewish kinship rooted in Jewish history and peoplehood, which was seen as giving an impetus towards the reality and expression of the Jewish national idea, both as cause and effect.

Jews genuinely affirmed their loyalty. There were Jews in both political parties. Jews were divided among themselves on issues raised between Gladstone and Simon. Unfriendly Gentile critics remained unmoved. Adler became the major personal protagonist of the right of the Jewish citizen to react as citizen and as Jew against oppression and injustice. Political Zionism was regarded by him, and those who thought like him, as likely to make their task the more difficult. They deemed the concept of a Jewish nation to be of no advantage to their cause.

There was an instinctive concern among many Jews and Gentiles to know and define the comparatively new place of Jews in the wider society. Few could be wholly indifferent to the question. In some quarters there was a comforting conviction that the progress of scientific studies, free trade, European peace, improved social conditions and wider educational opportunities would erode old prejudices. Jewish integration was held by many Jews in communal office to be a natural consequence of such changes, secured by industrial growth and commercial expansion. Integration was held to be an added safeguard against the old malaise of irrational dislike and hurtful prejudice. Conventional Jewish thinking was that the contribution of Jews to society – and indeed of Judaism to the world – was a desirable, even obligatory, theme for Jews to dwell upon.

Even the pragmatist and close observer, Lucien Wolf, thought that anti-Semitism would prove a temporary phenomenon; an interruption in the spread of enlightenment and its consequences. He later modified his opinion. The economic depression of the 1870s, nationalist fervour, political chicanery and religious hostility made the emancipationist summer on the European scene seem at times, indeed, only an interlude. Jewish spokesmen who referred to the purpose of the Jewish mission, in dispersion, as being to advance the moral enlightenment of mankind, carried little weight with Gentile critics. To them, such preaching reinforced their notion of Jewish separateness. It had fallen to Gentiles, wrote Herzl somewhat bitterly in a London journal, to assert the existence of the Jewish nation, and to the rabbis (they were not the only ones) to deny it.

Adler's attitude to political Zionism arose out of his attitude to biblical prophecy and rabbinic commentary thereon. The implications of that attitude coincided with what he saw as contemporary practical wisdom. Public prudence was for him further reinforced by a belief in the impracticability of the Zionist scheme. He found himself, in an important sense, allied with others whose Jewish belief took a wholly different form from his but who were no less convinced of the imprudence and unprophetic nature of the Zionist movement. Some of them gave even starker expression than Adler to their grounds of opposition. 'As a believing Jew', declared Laurie Magnus, a leading member of the West London Synagogue of British Jews, in a public address in 1903, 'I refuse to make shift with any instalment of the harvest [by which he meant the biblically promised Jewish apogee] or to accept a convenient relief from the present affliction of my people as a dividend in full for the joy which they will ultimately reap.' To the Zionists, and to Wolf, such effusions bore no relation to current needs or future prospects. There were Orthodox rabbis in London and beyond who rejected the outlook and conclusions of the non-Zionists, whether religious or otherwise.

When Sir Samuel Montagu, in May 1891, invited Gladstone to use his good offices to seek to stem the violence in Russia, he publicly replied in terms comparable to his earlier responses. He had already roundly condemned the continuing violence. In telling language he observed to Montagu: 'You have, I doubt not, effective organisations in this country on behalf of your fellow nationals abroad.' In response to further enquiry, he also commented: 'I view with warm and friendly interest any plan for the large introduction of Jews into Palestine and shall be very glad if the Sultan gives his support to such a measure.'

Adler, long before his appointment as Chief Rabbi in 1891, had robustly rejected the public claim by prominent Christian clerics that the ruins of Jerusalem would remain and that Jerusalem would not be rebuilt. He declared that it was part of the Jewish creed that the 'glory' of the city would be restored and that under divine providence a reign of peace would ensue. In 1885, he visited Palestine, toured the country, and distributed aid to immigrants from the funds of the Russo-Jewish Committee centred in London. He was in favour, both on religious and practical grounds, of Jews settling in that land.

Deeply held convictions as to the value and significance of complete civic and political emancipation, together with force of habit, personal considerations and instincts both of *noblesse oblige* and family attachments, combined to create an ideology as firm for a time as that of the Zionists. Those who were reared in the nineteenth-century climate of certainty as to the wisdom of the prevailing system of communal government retained an inbred set of preferences, tinged with fear at the prospect of any radical change. There was engendered a spirit of conflict between Zionists and their Jewish opponents which endured for half a century, with religion playing a mixed role.

In and around the 1880s, great issues were debated within the Jewish community concerning the nature and fate of the Jew, but largely within the leisure of theory. In due course, all the issues were to be thrust forward with sharp practical immediacy. The vast and many improbabilities of Jewish history have rarely matched what was later to be seen. In the generation which preceded that of the Balfour Declaration, and before Herzl appeared on the scene, the 'futuristic' topics under discussion were not very far away in their reality, only 'round the bend in the river', unbeknown.

NOTE

The author dealt more fully with Wolf's ambivalence in his presidential lecture on Wolf to the Jewish Historical Society in 1994, which appears in this volume; and with the diversity of communal opinion on these and related issues in chaps 1 and 6 in his *Anglo-Jewish Society in Victorian England* (1993). Adler's position is more amply examined in chap. 8 of the author's *Anglo-Jewry in Changing Times: Studies in Diversity, 1840–1914* (1999). See also Rav (Lord) Jakobovits, 'The Attitude to Zionism of British Chief Rabbis from Their Writings' in his *If Only My People: Zionism in My Life* (1984). For further communal politics and personalities, see S.A. Cohen, *English Zionists and British Jews* (1982); E.C. Black, *The Social Politics of Anglo-Jewry, 1880–1920* (1988); V.D. Lipman, *A History of the Jews in Britain since 1858* (1990); and Geoffrey Alderman, *Modern British Jewry* (1992). For Samuel Montagu and Zionism, see Cecil Bloom thereon, *Transactions of the Jewish Historical Society of England*, Vol. 34 (1996), pp. 17–41. For characteristic respective presentations, see Hermann Adler's published address to the North London Synagogue entitled *Religious Zionism versus Political Zionism* (1898); Claude Montefiore, 'Nation or Religious Community', *Transactions of the Jewish Historical Society of England*, Vol. 4 (1903); Wolf's long and widely noted article on Zionism in the eleventh issue of *Encyclopedia Britannica* (1911); and Haham Moses Gaster, 'Judaism a National Religion', in Harry Sacher (ed.), *Zionism and the Jewish Future* (1916). Dr Mark Levene's works on Wolf are an important contribution to the historical study of this period.

18

Adler and Salomons: Two Ages[*]

In April 1857, the prospect of reform in the divorce law aroused anxiety in certain sections of Anglo-Jewry lest the community's presumed rights be interfered with. Before 1857, only Parliament could dissolve a valid marriage. The cost of such private legislation limited this remedy to the rich. At most, the Courts could order judicial separation, and the sole Courts in the field were the ancient ecclesiastical tribunals applying mainly canon law. The Matrimonial Causes Act of 1857 created a comparatively cheap Divorce Court staffed by lay judges with power to dissolve marriages on grounds specified in the Act. The Ecclesiastical Courts were deprived of their matrimonial jurisdiction.

Until these changes, there was some reason to think that the law recognized the *Get*. So believed the Chief Rabbi, Nathan Marcus Adler, who relied on judicial dicta in *Lindo* v. *Belisario* (1795) and *Moss* v. *Smith* (1840), and on the possible implications of the statutory recognition of Jewish marriages since 1753. H.S.Q. Henriques, addressing the Royal Commission on Divorce in 1910, denied that the Jewish divorce of parties domiciled in England had been valid in English law before 1857. The practical question in 1857 was whether to seek to include in the Act a clause protecting the assumed legal validity of the *Get*. By according a monopoly of jurisdiction to the new Divorce Court, the measure could well be deemed to terminate such presumed validity.

The Bill began its career through Parliament on 11 May 1857,

---

[*]First published in the *Jewish Chronicle*, 19 April 1957, under the title 'Anglo-Jewry and the Law of Divorce'.

in the Lords. The Attorney-General, Sir Richard Bethell, assured Adler and Montefiore in conference that it did not affect existing Jewish rights, and the Home Secretary, Sir George Grey, spoke to them in like terms. But if Jews could resort to the proposed new tribunal, the children of a remarriage following its decree would, in the absence of a *Get*, be illegitimate in Jewish law. This crucial and unspoken reservation pressed Adler into urging the Board of Deputies to petition for an amendment to the Bill which would exclude Jews from its operation. Following the Board's intervention, the Lord Chancellor, Lord Cranworth, moved an additional clause on the report stage, which was accepted by the Lords without opposition on 12 June. It was drafted by the Board's eminent solicitor and Secretary, Sampson Samuel, and approved by the Chief Rabbi. 'Nothing herein contained', ran the clause, 'shall give the Court hereby established jurisdiction in relation to any marriage of persons both professing the Jewish religion contracted or solemnized according to their own usages.'

PERSONAL INFLUENCE

But when the Bill was presented for its third reading in the Lords, this far-reaching amendment was omitted. The Government had dropped it because of private approaches by Sir David Salomons and Lionel de Rothschild to the Ministers in charge of the Bill. Their personal influence effectively countered the previous official representations of the chief rabbi and the Board. An extraordinary meeting of the Deputies was thereupon held on 22 June. The most prominent advocate of deletion of the clause at this meeting was Simon Magnus, the wealthy coal-factor of Chatham, who represented the Sheerness Synagogue and was shortly to be elected mayor of Queenborough. An influential exponent of Adler's views was Henry Harris, a City solicitor and president of the Maiden Lane Congregation. The debate was inconclusive, the Board deciding to await the Bill's return to the Commons before resolving whether to attempt the reinsertion of the clause. Montefiore was abroad, and the president was the ailing and irresolute Isaac Foligno.

To Salomons and Rothschild, who absented themselves from this Board meeting, the clause was peculiarly inopportune. The campaign for emancipation was entering its decisive phase. On 15 May, the Prime Minister, Palmerston, had himself introduced an Oaths Bill aimed at opening Parliament to Jews. Significant opponents of emancipation, such as Sir John Pakington, had veered in favour. Some hostile Peers wavered. The architects of emancipation knew the kind of argument likely to be adduced in opposition. Sir Frederick Thesiger, a former Attorney-General, declared in the Commons on 15 June: 'There is something in the habits of the Jews, in their exclusive character, in the nature of their institutions, which appears to me to incapacitate them from taking a complete part in the councils of a Christian country.' On 10 July, when Palmerston's Bill was before the Lords – where it was defeated – Lord Derby said:

> I am not prepared to deny to the Jews that which I am sure they themselves would be the last to abjure, namely their nationality and their character as a nation. No doubt they submit to the laws and discharge the duties of citizens ... They retain their laws and their peculiar customs. Though among us, they are not of us. They do not generally associate freely with their fellow-subjects; they have interests wholly apart.

To avoid supplying further ammunition for these contentions was an overwhelming anxiety to Salomons.

Under pressure from Adler, the Board of Deputies, presided over by Nathan Lindo, decided on 29 June to ask the Government to restore the clause in the Bill which was now in the Commons. At this meeting the main antagonist to this course was Alderman Benjamin Phillips, later Sir Benjamin and the second Jewish Lord Mayor of London. The Government refused the Board's request, and the Bill became law without Cranworth's amendment.

The *Jewish Chronicle* of the day deplored the action of 'eminent Jews' who 'snatched from the hands of their coreligionists a boon transmitted to them by their fathers.' 'We have yet to learn', wrote the editor, Abraham Benisch, 'that a knowledge of commercial law necessarily imparts theological lore or that station and wealth, which give claim to representation, also confer it without previous commission.' Salomons and Rothschild had set 'a most dangerous precedent' by 'substituting individual will for that of the community'. It is somewhat ironical that in 1871, Benisch was a prime mover, in company with Salomons and others, in instituting the Anglo-Jewish Association in the face of the Board's known disapproval.

'I believe', wrote Salomons in the *Jewish Chronicle*, on 10 July 1857, 'that the power of divorce by the Jewish ecclesiastical authorities ought to be entirely abrogated. There can be no reason now why the Jews should not be brought within the pale of a general measure.' He quoted approvingly the remark of a French Jew that 'when we marry in France we marry as Frenchmen and are subject to all the laws which apply to Frenchmen'. The new Act would not oblige the Jewish clergy to officiate at any marriage which offended their conscience.

But Adler did not easily admit defeat. He prevailed upon the Board of Deputies to seek Counsel's opinion on the bearing of the Act. Among those consulted was Travers Twiss, Regius Professor in Civil Law at Oxford. Their joint opinion, given in February 1858, was that 'the Jewish Ecclesiastical Board of London' was still entitled to grant divorces and that it was 'lawful' for the parties so divorced to remarry in English law.

Adler was gratified by this authoritative confirmation. But in 1866, he encountered the superior opinion of the Registrar-General, Sir George Graham, sustained by the Law Officers. In May 1866, Graham drew the Board's attention to the case of one Nathan Rosenfeld, then living in Cardiff. He had married according to Jewish law in 1845 in his native Austria, and the marriage was terminated by the *Get* through the London Beth Din in 1862. Rosenfeld, whose wife was still alive, now wished to marry again. Graham invited the Board's opinion on the *Get*. The Board submitted this delicate question to Adler, whose reply was transmitted to Graham. Adler cited Twiss' opinion and added: 'I have not objected to grant divorces in rare instances on grounds established on the Jewish marriage law, such power having been possessed and exercised by the Jewish ecclesiastical authorities from time immemorial.' The Registrar-General's reply was conclusive:

> Guided by the best legal advice to which I have access, I cannot coincide in the opinion that a marriage contracted between two persons of the Jewish persuasion can be dissolved in England by a Jewish tribunal. I cannot recognise (such a divorce) as valid.

Since 1866, the Beth Din has never sanctioned a divorce of

parties domiciled in England without the prior decree of the Court. At the end of the century there was an increase in 'irregular divorces' by 'foreign rabbis' in which no prior decree was obtained. The parties would regard themselves as free to remarry, and issue of the second marriage would be illegitimate in English law. The woman could have had no claim for maintenance against her second 'husband', and her first husband was not likely to give her a home. In 1910, the President of the Board, David Alexander, and the Chief Rabbi, Hermann Adler, invited the recently appointed Royal Commission on matrimonial law to recommend the imposition of severe penalties on all who participated in 'irregular divorces'. The Commission made the suggested recommendation, but it was not given statutory effect. Nor was this official Jewish request allowed to go unscathed in the Jewish community, least of all in the Yiddish press.

The difference between Salomons and Nathan Marcus Adler was between an Englishman of the Jewish persuasion and a Jew of British citizenship. Salomons thought in terms of a religious minority enjoying equality in the law. Adler, also intent on emancipation, was yet affected by the conception of the Jewish 'nation'. Salomons treated both the terminology and its implications as archaic. Fifty years later, the then Chief Rabbi evinced those qualities of communal thought which Salomons had nurtured. Especially among the recent immigrants there was a loud echo of the first Adler and of battles long ago.

19

Jewish Emancipation and Nationality Debated*

The year 1958 sees the tenth anniversary of the State of Israel and the hundredth of the entry of professing Jews into Parliament. The idea of Jewish national restoration and the emancipationist movement sometimes aroused tension in the minds of both Jews and Christians. By the side of the legal debates over Jewish emancipation was the ancient belief and hope that in some way there would eventually be a Jewish national 'redemption'. Such an outlook had to be reconciled with the here-and-now claims of the leading Jewish spokesmen for the civic and political rights of citizens.

Their task was rendered the more difficult, or at least more complicated, by the very idea of a Jewish nation and by manifestations of nationhood. The Jews were unique. During the debate in the House of Lords in August 1833 on Sir Robert Grant's second Bill to repeal Jewish civil disabilities, the Archbishop of Canterbury, William Howley, opposing the measure (which was rejected in the Lords) declared: 'I look upon the Jews as the most remarkable people on earth ... They bear a testimony, irrefutable because it is involuntary, to the faith of the Gospel, attesting the truth of the prophecies ... by their own misfortunes.' He saw in the Jewish plight divine punishment for their rejection of Jesus. He added: 'In this light I cannot but view them with admiration for the constancy with which ... under every vicissitude they have adhered to their faith.' While believing in their ultimate conversion, he regarded their civil

---

*Published in the *Jewish Chronicle*, 14 February 1958, under the title 'Emancipationist Apologetics'.

emancipation meanwhile as contrary to the divine plan for their dispersion and rightlessness.

This doctrine was not confined to critics of Grant's Bill. For example, the Archbishop of Dublin, Richard Whateley, a prominent advocate of the Jewish claims, observed in the House of Lords that:

> nationally the Jews are under a judgment. Look upon that nation as paying the penalty of their rejection of the Messiah ... But we must be very careful how we without an express commission, take upon ourselves to be the executioners of divine judgment, lest we bring a portion of those judgments on ourselves.

He did not regard religious differences as proper grounds for civil exclusion.

In such an age, it is not surprising that Jewish 'messianism' should be to the fore in public discussion on the successive Bills which came before Parliament. In May 1848, in the debate on Lord John Russell's proposals, which revived Grant's measure, Lord Winchilsea said he was ready 'to grant the Jews every toleration that was consistent with the maintenance of Christianity', but he would not admit them to Parliament. They were 'a distinct and peculiar people, bearing their nationality of character in whatever part of the world they were dispersed'.

In the House of Commons the speech of Spencer Walpole, an eminent Tory barrister, attracted special attention. 'The Jew', he said, 'is of a separate creed and interest. He is not a citizen of this country but of the world: he has no land which he can call his own, save the Land of Promise.'

One of the best-known and most outspoken of the foes of Jewish admission into Parliament was Sir Robert Inglis, a Tory MP for Oxford University. 'No Christian', he told the House of Commons in February 1853,

> who knows anything of Jewish literature or of their history can fail to know that it is their distinguishing boast and characteristic that they are a separate nation ... reserved for a great purpose as a peculiar people, which human eyes cannot penetrate and that their highest aspiration is a return to their own land.

The first published Jewish statement of objection to these lines of argument was by Barnard Van Oven, Fellow of the Royal College of Surgeons and a notable communal leader, entitled *Appeal to the British Nation on behalf of the Jews* (1829). Some Jews detected an incompatibility between the emancipationist movement and the messianic belief. On 21 February 1845, the *Jewish Chronicle* described them as 'a narrow-minded' and 'very small minority ... who consider our desire of our being emancipated incompatible with our prayers for the coming of the Messiah'.

At that time, on the eve of the enactment of the Act of 1845 which opened municipal office to professing Jews, the *Jewish Chronicle*, on 7 February 1845, had shown some agitation over persistent allegations that 'the truly pious Jew considers himself an alien, though by birth a British Jew, as he looks upon Palestine as his native land'. The editor urged the emancipationists to embark on an educational programme to disabuse the minds not only of Christians but also of those Jews who implied this consequence into Jewish messianism.

The replies of the emancipationists to the charges and fears are of considerable historical interest. They form part of the Jewish reaction to the age which followed the French Revolution. They represent some attenuation of Jewish cohesion in the new era. In a later generation, the impulse to divest Judaism of its 'redemptionist' and national features carried the heirs of the early emancipationists into stern anti-Zionism.

The immediate Jewish reaction was to deny that the belief in the 'Return' had affected the allegiance of Jews to the Sovereign and to assert that the precepts of Judaism required that it should not. 'The restoration of Israel', commented Van Oven, 'has been delayed 1,800 years and may be delayed many more, and it would be absurd to allow the anticipation of such an event to influence our political conduct or feelings.' 'It is undoubtedly true', wrote Francis Goldsmid, the most influential of the Jewish publicists, in his 'Reply to the Arguments, etc.' (1848),

> that the Jews regard the coming of the Messiah and their restoration to the Promised Land as certain events. The inference that [this] renders them incapable of love for their native land or unfit to serve it is disproved by the experience of every age and country ... where they have been treated like citizens.

They were not alone in anticipating a far-off universal divine event. 'Many Christians', wrote Goldsmid, look forward to a second advent of the Messiah, as to an event on the happening of which all distinctions of states and nations will be forgotten throughout the globe ... And yet it has not been found in practice that the predictions of religion ... have made the inhabitants of this or any other land culpably inattentive to their public or private welfare.

In his Commons speech in April 1833, Macauley had put it yet more forcefully. 'Surely', he contended,

it would be the grossest ignorance of human nature to imagine that the anticipation of an event which has been vainly expected during many centuries, of an event which even those who confidently expect that it will happen do not confidently expect that they or their children or grandchildren will see, can ever occupy the minds of men to such a degree as to make them regardless of what is near, present and certain.

There must have appeared in these emancipationist rejoinders a certain inconclusiveness within the context of the debate. The critics were less concerned with the nearness or farness of the talked-of Jewish national restoration than with the present and continuing state of belief, which was seen as a reflection of their present and continuing 'nationality'. Had it been contended that, upon the granting of full citizenship and with the passage of time, the Jewish messianic notion would wither away and that with it would dissolve its concomitant idea of a Jewish nation, the critics might have deemed the argument more logical. Whether that would have made a difference to their own response to the Jewish claims is at best a moot point. The Jews had not been the only non-Anglicans to suffer legal discrimination.

Goldsmid felt unable to free himself from the attachment to what he deemed a central tenet of Judaism. He sought to propel messianism, in any form, out of the contemporary scene into an unknowable future. 'When the term [separate nation or separate people]', he wrote, 'is applied to the past or the future, its signification is obvious ... But has the phrase, which it is justly said the Jews employ, any *present* meaning?'

With a view to avoiding or attenuating the suggested implications of the restorationist creed, some supportive publicists queried the actuality of the 'return' in any literal sense. One such was Charles Egan, lawyer and Christian theologian. In his *The Status of the Jews in England* (1848), Egan, who believed in the ultimate conversion of the Jews, argued at length that 'the idea alleged to be entertained by the Jews respecting their eventual return to Jerusalem' is 'far too doubtful for any Christian to advance as an argument against' their civil emancipation. Egan insisted that they 'merely form a separate race', as distinct from 'nationality'. It was not an argument likely to appeal at that time to any of the parties to the protracted debate.

The doctrine that the Jews did not constitute a 'nation' was often allied to the suggestion that any 'national' characteristics would be eroded or be much mitigated through the bestowal of full citizenship through the process of civil emancipation. Eloquent expression was given to this conviction by R.L. Sheil, an Irish Roman Catholic, in the Commons in February 1848. 'I know', he said,

> the notion is entertained by some that there is no such thing as an English, or a Spanish, or an Italian Jew, that a Jew is a Jew and nothing else, that his nationality is engrossed by the country of his hopes and recollections. When his name and race were branded and oppressed … it is not wonderful that on the banks of the Seine or the Thames, as with his fathers by the rivers of Babylon, the psalm of exile should speak comfort to his heart. But in proportion as you have mitigated the law against the Jew, his devotion to the land of his birth has been revived.

There were also increasing signs of a radical Jewish opinion which tried to oust the national idea from Jewish doctrine. In Germany, the influence of Moses Mendelssohn and the French Revolution acted sharply on Jewish communities which had not enjoyed the social emancipation which had long been the lot of Anglo-Jewry. In 1812, David Friedlander, an advanced reformer of Judaism and a leader in the movement for Jewish emancipation in Prussia, called for the deletion of all prayers which envisaged a Return to Zion or which carried a nationalist implication. The far-reaching reforms urged in the next generation by Samuel Holdheim and Abraham Geiger reflected emancipationist sentiment as well as the 'Science of Judaism'. Geiger went so far as to avow that Hebrew should be excised from Jewish ritual.

The messianic idea was deprived of its national content and the messianic age was interpreted as a future era of universal peace and good will. The Conference of American Reform in Philadelphia (1869) and Pittsburgh (1885), largely under the impact of the German-Jewish immigration, explicitly abandoned the expectation of a Return to Palestine. 'We consider ourselves no longer a nation', ran the 'platform' of 1885, 'but a religious community'. It is significant that Samson Raphael Hirsch, the principal protagonist of the Orthodox reaction against Reform in Germany and a firm believer in the divine election of the Jewish people and its ultimate national Restoration, disavowed practical efforts to achieve the 'Return'.

In the second and third generations of emancipated Anglo-Jewry, especially in the socially advanced and religiously reformed sections, these polemics could not fail to evoke a response. A self-conscious patriotism and a heightened rationalism tended to outmode the messianism of an earlier epoch. The onset of political Zionism and the transformation of the Return from a theological proposition into a contemporary activist programme sharpened the old conflict. Claude Montefiore, the founder of Liberal Judaism in England and the most effective English exponent of the mission of Jewish dispersion, was in the van of anti-Zionism. Oswald John Simon, who declined to follow Montefiore out of Reform into Liberalism because of his 'reverence' for 'certain aspects of the historic presentation of our faith', nevertheless subscribed to Montefiore's thesis that, while the Jews were once a nation, they were now a 'church'. Dissociating himself from the ideals of Zionism, Simon, in a much-canvassed letter to *The Times*, on 30 August 1897, while the First Zionist Congress was in session, declared that Judaism could have a wider appeal than 'the artificial limits of race' and could be the means of 'establishing a common worship' among Jews and Gentiles.

In a widely reported address to a Jewish meeting in January 1903, Laurie Magnus found himself enmeshed in old equivocations. 'We may continue to pray', he said, 'that the Restoration may be brought about in our time; indeed, I should consider no public service complete which did not include that prayer. But for purposes of practical citizenship, we must take our fate as we find it.' The Chief Rabbi, Hermann Adler, while not sharing Montefiore's idea of mission and while not discarding the traditional belief in the ultimate (but vaguely and ambiguously explained) fulfilment of

Prophecy, had no doubts about his own anti-Zionism. 'Since the destruction of the Temple', he told the *Manchester Dispatch* in a hotly discussed interview in April 1909, 'we no longer constitute a nation; we are a religious communion. We are bound together with our brethren throughout the world primarily by the ties of a common faith. But in regard to all other matters we consider ourselves Englishmen.'

These questions were not initiated by Zionism. They were at the core of prolonged debate in the days of emancipation more than a century ago.

20

Jewish National Identity: The Ubiquity of Jewish Assimilation and the Permanence of Jewish Peoplehood*

Jewish national consciousness and identity are no less real, even though they may sometimes appear submerged. So it was during the emancipation, so it sometimes is today. There is a touch of historical analogy, perhaps in a somewhat unexpected way. The emancipationists were not considering the question of providing a home for the Jewish people. They applied their minds, as best as they could in their generation, to a new social order and to what they believed was the dawning of a new world outlook

Responsible Jewish leaders in Herzl's day solemnly declared that the Jewish nation had ceased to exist, yet they could not easily reconcile those pronouncements with their own prayer books, with their own kinds of publicly announced messianism, or with their brand of kinship with Jewries abroad. Even the doctrine of Jewish mission, about which his critics on the religious right as on the left said a great deal, rested on nothing less than the proposition that the Jews were invested as a people with a particular character or responsibility. Whether such was by divine providence

*Based on the author's articles in *Forum* Vols 46 (1982) and 47 (1983), prepared in connection with the fifth and seventh Presidential international seminars in Jerusalem on relations between Israel and the Jewish world.

or through historical forces or by some sense of *noblesse oblige* mattered little. What it meant to many of them was that their history, customs, language, historical recollections and literature, even their notion of their ultimate home, had to be retained and transmitted.

Acute-minded Gentiles saw the particularism which all this involved. In the end it was an unassimilable particularism.

There is a form of instinctive self-preservation in many Diaspora communities. Whatever may be the current demographic and other prophecies it by no means follows that this state of communal mind is without Jewish national consciousness and identity. Indeed, I believe that it is a Jewish national consciousness and identity which sustained, sustains, and even promotes, the instinct for distinctive Jewish self-preservation.

The Jewish position has special features, by reason of the special history, indeed the highly improbable history, of our people. The Jewish Diaspora condition gives clear evidence of special kinds of national consciousness. There is a Jewish self-consciousness, an awareness of a distinct self, and the sharing of a common history. There is the self-justifying wish to preserve and explain Jewish survival and the various forms of undoubted Jewish identity. The sentiments are combined with the acknowledgement of some degree of interdependence with the State of Israel. There is also the deeply significant recognition by the wider society of the fact and the naturalness of these phenomena.

Nationality, except where it impinges upon consideration of law and is related to citizenship, is an ethnic, cultural and historical matter. It is not necessarily the same as nationhood. The latter may connote the sense of exile for those of its members 'outside'. Let it be acknowledged, as a fact, that there are many Jews who have taken pride in their membership of the Jewish nation who have not considered themselves in exile.

Despite assimilation, and out-marriage, and a low birth rate, the size and influence of the Diaspora will remain considerable. Many Jewish communities show Jewishly creative and preservative powers. One major reason for this has been the establishment and survival of the State of Israel. Communal effort becomes more and more concerned with planning to preserve and intensify a recognizable and transmissible Jewish identity. Israel has inspired and inspires in innumerable ways the perpetuation of Jewish communal life. The point is that the impact of Israel has not broken the mould of emancipation. In many ways it has strengthened it.

There is also a new spirit in international Jewish consultations. One example will do; there were many disputes before, and even for some time following, 1948, over the propriety and wisdom of any international coordination of Jewish efforts in defence of Jewish interests. We have now moved into a different world.

The events in Jewish history since 1933 have sharpened an inescapable sense of the common fate of the Jewish people. It is heightened in many influential quarters by an unease that the success of the emancipation has, in practice, also made huge inroads into Jewish identity, and by the growing perception of the limitations of secularity as a transmissible medium for Jewish life in the Diaspora. There is also the realization that the creation of the State of Israel has not settled the questions of Jewish purpose in the Diaspora. It has, in some ways, more acutely defined them. All this against the background of an increasing number of anti-Semitic incidents, a mingling of anti-Semitism with anti-Zionism and a growing concern, on the part of the Jews, to sustain the position in society gained for them by emancipation. That concern now exists in the new epoch of a Jewish state, to whose honour, welfare and safety Jews are attached by strong historical, religious and emotional bonds.

Assimilation is the process of becoming like others. It is also the term used for the process or the act of being absorbed. Between these stages or phases, there is an infinity of gradations. Not every form of assimilation is willed, even if it be the natural consequence or concomitant of behaviour. Modes of life are not always calculated. In the flux of migration, or under the impact of inheritance and environment, or by way of education and temperament, people's characters, preferences, habits, assumptions and outlook are often determined, or at least crucially influenced, without reference to such questions as, 'Is this assimilationist?'

Emancipation was assimilationist. So was religious reformism. So too, in its own way, was neo-Orthodoxy. Political Zionism likewise had its own kind of assimilationist content ideologically and in practice. At the heart of any form of assimilation is the degree of departure from, or the extent of emendation of, the idea and the consciousness of the 'chosenness' of the Jews. After all, Jewish history came into being upon that notion. In a passing but significant comment many years ago, Jacob Talmon observed:

> Nowadays the Jew is afflicted by a *malaise*; he looks over his shoulder, he is no longer convinced of the chosenness of the Jewish people. He resents the whole suggestion as arrogance and *hubris*. In this respect we have all imbued not a little of Toynbee.[1]

In no manner are the Jews more distinctive as a people than in their highly improbable history. It has no analogy. Their survival in dispersion has in itself been a remarkable historical phenomenon. There are those who say that given their ostracism and persecution, their survival is in reality unsurprising. I do not pause to consider that view. The fact is that the survival was accompanied by two features of far-reaching significance. One was the retention of faith in an earthly redemption – a physical, this-world redemption and restoration. The other feature was the retention of belief – not limited to Jews – in the relevance of that redemption to a universal readjustment of values and style of life.

Of no other people was it said that 'the stone which the builders despised is become the head-stone of the corner'. This statement was at one and the same time accepted history and a believed-in prophecy. The important point is that the longer the prophecy tarried in fulfilment and the greater the contrast between the actuality and the hope, the more riveted became the attachment to the hope and to the belief. A people of aspiration acquired attributes of a nation, the most distinctive of which was the 'meta-historical' dimension by which it defined its identity and that of its members and by which it described the purpose of its dispersion and the nature of what might follow thereafter.

This kind of hope, belief and conviction formed, until barely two centuries ago, the staple nourishment of the intellectual and emotional life of the dispersed Jewish communities. It continued to play a notable and quasi-compulsive role in the thought and the assumptions of those who had not rejected the notion of providential design in Jewish history, and of many others. Secular Zionists did not easily free themselves from the old language and the old categories of thinking. One may legitimately inquire whether there truly is such a type as a 'secular Jew'.[2] The Jewish national idea and prospect could not, without artificiality, be divorced from the ideas and ideals which had long given meaning to Jewish identity and substance to Jewish purpose.

Morris Ginsberg once referred to 'the objective interdependence of the different (Jewish) communities'.[3] It was 'objective' because it 'does not depend entirely on their own volition'. This is hardly a recipe for the transmission of distinctive Jewishness, nor can mutual awareness safely be deemed a sufficiently sustaining ingredient. Exit from the ghetto was a form of assimilation. When efforts are made to halt a developing assimilation, the 'mischief' which it is sought to stem relates to the erosion of the particular identity of the Jew; an identity fashioned by history.

There is much contemporary wisdom in the observation of Jacob Katz that 'the foundations of the traditional Jewish society were undermined precisely by the *Maskilim* who retained their connection with the Jewish community as such and wished only to modernize its system of values'.[4] To proceed upon the basis that the core of the tradition matters little but that the character and identity which sprang from it matter much may have an intellectual appeal, but may prove self-defeating. Upon such basis, one may erect a social structure and a system of education and call them Jewish, when in truth they may be more accurately defined as, so to speak, 'post-Jewish'. The legitimacy of such procedure may be said to be grounded in the inscrutable forces of history and in the unyielding demands of realism. But it is open to question whether such systems do not compound the irretrievable loss of Jewish identity that was the ultimate scourge within assimilation. It would be an historical irony of massive proportions if 'Zionism', with all its saving qualities, was to have emerged as an avenue to unwitting assimilation.

Such a prospective irony would be all the greater on recollecting the far-reaching critique regarding all forms of assimilation made by many Herzlian Zionists and post-Herzlian Zionists of various schools of thought. It was by no means limited to Ahad Ha'Amists, though members of that circle were often in the forefront. One of them was Sir Leon Simon, the leading expounder in English of Ahad Ha'Am's moral and political philosophy. In a widely noted pamphlet in 1915 entitled *Zionism and the Jewish Problem*, Simon defined the problem in dark colours and in a different direction from what Herzl had seen as the pre-eminent Jewish problem. 'The tragedy of assimilation', wrote Simon, 'is not that the Jew ceases to be a Jew, but that he remains a Jew and becomes something else at the same time. He becomes an anomaly; Jew and non-Jew in one.' The use of the word 'tragedy' indicates the extent to which urbane Westerners might feel disillusioned when looking at emancipation and its full range of consequences.

If the outer gift of emancipation was legal equality, the essence of the new state of affairs for the life of the Jew was the sense of choice, the presence of options. There were unavoidable risks. As is always the case with an ever-widening freedom, the new opportunities involved new-style responsibilities. To some degree or other, the latter could be faced or ignored. The emancipation was an historical necessity. It was also a postulate of justice. It accorded with all the major philosophies which, in the eighteenth and nineteenth centuries, seemed set fair to shape the future. History does not tease. Great movements of people and great waves of opinion are facts, which are themselves the effects and causes of other historical events and processes in a ceaseless and by no means predictable chain of actions and reactions. If emancipation was a necessary and just cause, it was also full of challenge to the Jews as individuals and as a people.

It is a mistake to set against one another the motivation of emancipation and the inspiration of Zionism. There is much truth, largely self-evident, in the statement that emancipation was a necessary precursor to Zionism, or rather that the two *motifs* were each inherent in the other, in terms of the moral entitlement of the Jews, and in the self-esteem of liberalism and of the nations. Emancipation and Zionism, writes Professor Salo Baron, 'rather than being antagonistic principles as then generally believed (in 1848) ... really complemented one another'.[5]

The strains and stresses between the heirs of emancipation and the advocates of political Zionism reflected an inherent tension between two world-outlooks within Jewry. Yet many Jews who welcomed some forms of post-emancipationist assimilation were no less ardently attached to all efforts for the upbuilding of the Yishuv and to the hope of Jewish statehood. They regarded those forms of assimilation as part and parcel of modern Jewish life. The tensions were often as much within the individual as within the group. In a perceptive comment, Charles Liebman observes:

Pluralism, in societies such as the United States, has often implied a general society formed by sub-communities of a religious or ethnic-cultural nature. The facts of life are such that, at least in countries of the Diaspora which resemble the United States, it is not simply that the society is pluralistic but rather that the individual himself is defined by his pluralistic affiliations in cross-cutting groups.[6]

A substantial segment of modern Jewish history has been taken up by the intertwining of 'Americanism' and Zionism, as well as by the distinctions between them. Justice Brandeis, for example, first came to Zionism 'wholly as an American'. He described assimilation as 'national suicide', and saw in political Zionism the means for regeneration. He affirmed the Diaspora. It was part of the Jewish people. The struggle against 'national suicide' would not be assisted by the denial of its legitimacy.[7]

The major risk inherent in emancipation was that the emphasis upon the Jew as citizen and man could, and often did, militate against the sense of need on his part to sustain his character as a Jew. The risk was all the greater since he was called upon to readjust himself in society at a time when 'enlightenment' meant to increasing numbers of advanced minds freedom from the authority of tradition. With that freedom came the assumption that greater scientific knowledge and improved education would overthrow prejudice and facilitate in due course the arrival of an era of universal rationalism. The shock of that beguiling prospect was almost as great, though far less catastrophic, as the eventual realization of the groundlessness of the optimism.

'To maintain Jewish existence within emancipation', wrote Professor Nathan Rotenstreich instructively, 'calls for a parallel principle related to the Jews themselves, to their self-reflection, and to the problems engendered by emancipation.'[8] 'Emancipation', he observed, 'as a Jewish aspiration was never conceived as an attempt to destroy the collective Jewish entity.' Assimilation was 'an adjustment' to the surrounding world; but 'on a basic issue, emancipation failed – Jewish existence *per se* is ... not safeguarded.' Without disputing the central ground of that approach, reality dictates the need for antidotes rather than last rites. Professor Rotenstreich did not for a moment decry the aims or achievements of emancipation. Jews have often, by instinct and conviction, tended to pursue social and universalist amelioration. It is within the tradition of Judaism.

The tendency may also be connected with the inclination to emphasize their conscious membership of the wider society. In some cases these tendencies have become a kind of sublimated or substitute Jewishness, consciously or otherwise. For the mass of Jews, this slide away from the main streams of Jewish life may give as much concern as any excessively inward-looking Jewish reactions to the Jewish encounter with the wider society.

Those who plead the case for Judaism as a cohesive force in Jewish life are well aware that dogmatism has had its day; that, for most, a reasoning approach in matters of faith is a prerequisite for serious study. Nationality has its own inspirational power. Ethnicity has, for many in the Diaspora, its own attractions. Those who today plead the cause of Judaism as a cohesive and transmissible force do not do so by way of admonition. They but ask the question as to what gave the Jews their distinctiveness and their sense of purpose. They raise with anxiety the issue as to whether continuity, recognizable identity, and national self-esteem can be secured on other grounds. Whatever promotes those values and conditions stems assimilation. Whatever may undermine them partakes of undesirable assimilation.

The nub of the unacceptable forms of assimilation – wherever they have occurred – is detachment from the Jewish people. The detachment may be by way of undermining any distinctive Jewish identity on the part of Jews in the Diaspora, or by way of a sort of self-sufficient territorialism within the State of Israel. The unacceptability arises in part from the inconsistency between such detachment and a subjective preference for recognizable continuity. And when that continuity is thought of as having long been, in a sense, the butt of neighbours' derision or barely concealed hostility, it becomes for some a matter of pride and self-esteem – on an extended family scale – to preserve the insignia of survival and bolster devices for assuring recognizable and distinctive continuity.

When, furthermore, the distinctive elements which fashioned the character of the group are thought of as being among the decisive factors which have shaped the character of Western civilization, the subjective and *a priori* reasoning set out in the foregoing paragraph becomes involved with two other notions. One is that the ill-requited response to the Jewish contribution to the spirit and progress of the human family should put the Jews on

298

guard against allowing the submergence, through tedium or apathy, of the distinctiveness of the Jew. The second notion is that there is no ground for any assumption that the distinctiveness has played itself out or that its inner sources cannot, in the modern world, usefully be sought and re-sought.

In one form or another, these considerations embody the ratio – so far as one is called for – for at all being concerned over the impact of assimilation and the ceaseless quest for distinctive and recognizable survival.

These thoughts go beyond the gut reaction of self-conscious ethnicity. They have to be assessed against an historical background. Behind the intense preoccupation of the emancipationists with being like others, there was the belief or the assumption that for practical purposes they were indeed like others once the ghetto, physical or otherwise, was breached. Emancipation was achieved either in a context of religiosity, as in England, or in a spirit of utopianism, as in America or France, or in connection with new forms of political liberalism and national reorganization, as elsewhere in Europe. In England, the Jewish emancipationists presented themselves as a section of English Nonconformity, seeking to share status with the great Christian bodies who were in a state of dissent from the Church of England. In the other contexts, Jews could, as indeed in England, pursue their creedal differentia as a private matter, untouched by the new dispensations in society and clothed in theories of civic responsibility and/or natural rights.

The reappraisal of the nature and source of authority in society coincided with a critical review of the virtues and practices of political liberalism. These assessments came at a time when the hold of religion in society was also weakening. Emancipated Jewish communities and their heirs continued to be imbued with the enthusiasms which on all sides had ushered in the emancipation, but which were under renewed scrutiny and even attack. The Jews became the touchstone of a liberal era on the wane. Their interests, even their safety, appeared to be bound up with the retention of the essential principles of an older age. Political Zionism responded to the predicament and its consequences. It saw the *pathology* of emancipation, which movement it often treated as based upon an illusory hope.

Yet the antithesis was not between Emancipation and Zionism.

Both were responses to historical situations. In Israel, as in the Diaspora, there is a dichotomy between, on the one hand, content-ment with ethnicity by default of anything else and, on the other hand, a willed and conscious attachment to the sources of our character. Ethnicity by default of anything else cannot long be sustained in the Diaspora, save under the influence of anti-Semitism. A willed and conscious attachment to sources is consistent with a considerable degree of integration in the Diaspora. The moral, cultural and educational impact of Israel has undoubtedly been, and is, immense. Ethnicity can be highly assimilationist, not only in its own longer-term effects but also in its inner core.

Emancipation and Zionism, each in its own way, sought to relieve the Jews of outer oppression and inner inhibition. Jews were to be enabled to accommodate themselves in the world free from their ancient status of abnormality. Both movements have had to contend with the fact that there is an inherent anomaly within the very idea of Jewishness. The Jews have been at one and the same time particularist and universalist. Their brand of particularism was invested with the broadest universalist aspirations – the pith of their distinctiveness – which were bound up with their peoplehood and their ideals and duties as individuals and as members of that people. To infringe in principle upon the syllogism is instantly to transform the essential character of Jewish life. No one would sensibly under-rate the intellectual and practical problems which are inherent in efforts to secure a mutual accommodation between that essential character of Jewish life and the modern world. At least, let the momentous nature of these questions be understood. Knowingly or not, they are at the root of many an agitation in the Jewish mind – an agitation which is often expressed in terms which sound remote from those questions but which in fact are closely interwoven with or spring from them.

'The Jews once settled in their own State', Herzl wrote in *The Jewish State*, 'would probably have no more enemies ... The Diaspora cannot take place again unless the whole civilization of the earth collapsed; and such a consummation could be feared by none but foolish men.' Such optimism had many common origins with that which moved the emancipationists. It rested upon faith in the ultimate triumph of reason. Science and the advance of tech-nology had introduced their own age of faith. At a deeper level,

300

Herzl's confidence arose also from his conception of 'the Jewish problem' as being the unwelcome presence of Jews, beyond a certain proportion, in Gentile society. To remove the problem, so defined, was the object in his mind of his programme.

The object of these remarks is not to imply an adverse criticism of Herzl. He was the child of his age and environment. I am not treating that subject here. The point is that to Herzlian Zionism, the entire collision of ideas between the Judaism out of which the Zionist ideal grew, and statism which could evoke quite different enthusiasms, remained undiscerned. This potential duality of the definition and purpose of the Jew is at the centre of the inner tensions in modern Jewish life. In 1918, Israel Zangwill, in his published lecture entitled *Chosen Peoples*, referred to 'the recurring clash of centripetal and centrifugal forces'. The essentiality of political Zionism can all too easily conceal the no less essential need to retain and nourish the uniqueness of Jewish identity.

The study of that uniqueness and identity may take many forms. It can be part of an historical study without having any bearing upon contemporary behaviour or involving any attachment to any of the categories under study. It can be part of the study of the human spirit. Alexander Altmann has pointedly observed that in the modern world, Jewish thought is:

> concerned with the significance of the Jewish religion as a manifestation of the human spirit, and its place within the larger framework of thought, be it conceived as universal reason, dialectic of the mind, the system of culture, or the human existence as such.[9]

These inevitable encounters with the world do not exhaust the utility or the *Jewish* significance of Jewish study. They belong to the assimilationist consequence of the Jewish entry into the modern scientific world. They do not negate the inner Jewish need to examine and sustain the influences which have determined the nature and the role of Jewish life.

Jewish peoplehood encompasses Israel and the Diaspora. What that people has stood for, and stands for, is one of the factors making for the conscious and worthwhile separateness of Jewish peoplehood in the Diaspora. In words full of mixed hope and anxiety, and giving expression to deeply moving sentiments, Gershom Scholem declared:

There is something preliminary, something provisional about Jewish history; hence its inability to give of itself entirely. There is something grand about living in hope, but at the same time there is something profoundly unreal about it ... the blazing landscape of redemption (as if it were a point of focus) has concentrated in itself the historical outlook of Judaism. Little wonder that overtones of Messianism have accompanied the modern Jewish readiness for irrevocable action in the concrete realm, when it is set out on the utopian return to Zion ... Whether or not Jewish history will be able to endure this entry into the concrete realm without perishing in the crisis of the Messianic claim which has virtually been conjured up – that is the question which out of his great and dangerous past the Jew of this age poses to his present and to his future.[10]

In that connection, politics are not enough; secularity offers no remedy. I echo the intimation of Jacob Neusner:

The issue is not belief or unbelief. It is for those who say they believe, how to contemplate the reality in which they believe. Those who say they do not believe need also to reflect upon their unbelief, unless they hold, as do some, that all we are, and all we shall ever be, is here and now.[11]

NOTES

1. *The Identity of the Jewish Intellectual*, Proceedings of the Conference in London (10 November 1963) under the auspices of the World Jewish Congress, British Section, pp. 48–9.
2. Israel Finestein, 'The Secular Jew: Does He Exist and Why?', *Jewish Journal of Sociology*, Vol. 19 (1977).
3. 'European Jewish Communities Today and Some Questions for Tomorrow', *Jewish Journal of Sociology*, Vol. 6 (1964).
4. *Tradition and Crisis* (New York, 1971), pp. 265–6.
5. 'The Impact of the Revolution of 1848 on Jewish Emancipation', *Jewish Social Studies*, Vol. 11 (1949).
6. 'Dimensions of Authority on the Contemporary Jewish Community', *Jewish Journal of Sociology*, Vol. 12 (1970).
7. *Menorah Journal*, Vol. 1 (1915); Leonard Stein in *The Balfour Declaration* (1961), pp. 193–4, commented critically on the cautionary nature of Brandeis' Zionism generally.
8. 'Emancipation and its Aftermath', in David Sidorsky (ed.), *The Future of the Jewish Community in America* (Philadelphia, 1973).

9. 'Judaism and World Philosophy', in Louis Finkelstein (ed.), *The Jews*, Vol. 2 (Philadelphia, 1949), p. 662.
10. *The Messianic Idea in Judaism* (1971), pp. 35–6.
11. *The Condition of Jewish Belief*, compiled by the editors of *Community* magazine (New York, 1966), p. 157.

21

Special Features of Jewish History*

One of the most radical and shaping ideas of Judaism was that there is religious meaning in history. The dialogue between God and the Jewish people is traced in the contours of that people's destiny through time. The God of Abraham, Judah Halevi observed, is not the God of Aristotle, for He is found not in metaphysics but in history. How does a historian relate to this claim?

The study of history is the exploration of cause and effect. It is a difficult business since causes and effects are never single. And effects are always in themselves causes. There are always cross-currents, contradictions and ceaseless flux.

In these circumstances, it is bold to claim to detect a pattern. Yet to contend unreservedly that there is no pattern is presumptious. To speak of pattern in the sense of design or plan goes beyond history into faith or theology. To repudiate all notion of design is no less an entry into speculation. As is well known, history is the arch-subject for arriving at pre-determined conclusions.

The historian who believes in divine providence is no less committed than the complete secularist to the search both for the truth of what happened and for the chains of interconnected events in all their elusive order. Such a historian will bring to this study that sense of mystery which, for him, pervades life. He will approach his task with the reverence which he deems called for by his acknowledgement of the unknowability of the ultimate 'Why?' and 'Whence?' He will at times have intense difficulty in detecting any design. He will find abundant evidence of man's wilfulness and waywardness.

---

*Published in *L'Eylah* (June 1988).

MEANINGS IN HISTORY

In 1893, Lord Acton delivered a famous inaugural lecture as Regius Professor of Modern History at Cambridge. 'History', he declared, 'compels us to fasten on abiding issues, and rescues us from the temporary and transient.' It is a profound observation. History is a form of judgement. It requires us to exercise perspective, proportion and understanding. A wise generation examines and recounts the deeds and ideas of another in order the better to fathom the nature of society, the impact of the human personality, and the reasons for and the character of trends in thought and behaviour. With a modest optimism one may hope to derive guidance and hope for the present and future.

The historian's researches are, like every scientific enquiry honestly pursued, an investigation into the earthly operation of that mystery which runs through all things. There is a sense in which true scholarship partakes of an act of worship. Historical study is no exception.

Jewish history raises special issues. It poses questions unique to itself. What is Jewish history? Has it specifically to do with sets of ideas and practices so that without them there can be no Jewish history? Can there truly be a secularist Jew? Or is that a contradiction in terms? These are utterly distinctive Jewish-type questions.

JUDAISM: RELIGIOUS OR NATIONAL DESTINY?

In his notable survey of the Anglo-Jewish community, published in 1853, John Mills, a Christian pastor, had this to say about his subject: 'In the Jew's estimation, his faith and his nation are synonymous. To profess one is to belong to the other, and to change the former is to deny the latter.' Jewish spokesmen did not demur. When in the next generation similar thoughts about the Jews were expressed by Professor Goldwin Smith, historian and Liberal politician, he was severely rebuked on behalf of the Jewish community, which preferred to divest its Judaism of any contemporary national content.

What were the differences between the two publicists and between the two generations? Mills, who supported the Jewish campaign to abolish Jewish civil disabilities, was a conversionist, as were many of the leading Christian advocates of the Jewish cause. Smith did not believe that the mass of the Jews were a fruitful ground for conversionism. He regarded the Jews as largely unassimilable, and propounded a Zionistic plan for Jewish settlement in the Holy Land. He was and is classified as an anti-Semite. Such ironies are the stuff of Jewish history. They regularly recur in diverse forms and contexts.

To the Gentile world, the emancipation of the Jews was a rational ingredient in the general liberalization of society. In the eyes of their friends it was a benign development consistent with the new age of scientific growth, commercial expansion and social amelioration. For the Jews the development was climactic. It presented new types of problem. How to safeguard Jewish cohesion? How to ensure the transmissibility of Jewish faith and observance? How to explain Jewish inward-lookingness in a modern and open society?

We continue to grapple with the rush of consequences which flowed from the emancipation. The viability of the Jew's recognizable Jewishness is closely entwined with qualities so easily under threat in such a society. The challenge of the open society is distinctive of Jewish history. The modern era of Jewish history opened in the eighteenth century with that challenge.

IRONIES OF EMANCIPATION

Professor Peter Medding of the Hebrew University presented the matter with commendable graphic effect ten years ago in a notable article entitled 'Equality and the Shrinkage of Jewish Identity' (in Professor M. Davis (ed.), *World Jewry and the State of Israel*). 'Jewish religious definition', he wrote,

> affected all levels of existence … It encompassed the ethnic ties of blood … people and territory; the psychological aspects of man's identity and place in the greater universe; the cultural values by which a man gave expression to his ideals, goals, aspirations, and the meanings attached to them and to the universe at large … All these levels were bound together in an inextricable set of roles and loyalties which constituted Jewish identity … Emancipation by permitting Jews to participate in the larger society afforded choices where none existed before … Where demands were made for the development

306

of an exclusive national identity that was coterminous with citizenship, the Jew was caught in a state of conflict, which called for resolution ...' (pp. 120–1)

In addition to probing the mutual responses to that new and ever-changing scene, Jewish historical study has also to come to terms with the organized attempt by the regime of that country which was the epicentre of the emancipation and one of the most advanced states of the West, to abolish the Jews by extermination. The people who gave the Western world its monotheism, the idea of righteousness and the concept of a moral world order, was picked upon as the personification of evil and fit only to be rooted out. To which conclusions, if any, do these considerations drive one?

The Jewish historian can rarely limit himself, even if he wishes, to setting out the facts. At every turn he encounters the great imponderables encased in words like 'progress', 'destiny' and 'nature'. He alights again and again, with special sharpness, upon questions which go to the essence of man's character and purpose.

EUROPE AND AMERICA

When the first President of Israel was a boy most Jews – between seven and eight million – lived in the empires of the Romanoffs and the Hapsburgs. Of that number, about five million lived in the Pale of Settlement under the Czar. The great streams of migration from the two empires and Romania began in the 1880s. Jewish life and world history were to be dramatically changed by that emigration. Out of this massive shift of people arose a new Jewish civilization, principally that of modern American Jewry, with its millions of population and its levers of power within the Jewish world and its many-faceted influence on American and Western life.

It is temptingly easy to describe American Jewry as the new Babylon. One major difference is that Babylonian Jewry never ceased to regard itself as in exile. The American Jewish civilization rejects any such idea. The utopian, egalitarian, 'new world' image of America, with no history of a State Church and without any of the old European entanglements with inquisitions or expulsions, is not readily compatible with thoughts of exile. Ethnic plurality is part of Americanism. Thus there arose in Jewish history a great new fact, which became and remains as challenging to the Jewish historian as it is to the sociologist, educator, communal planner and politician.

The issues posed by the emancipation were sharpened in content and extended in area by the rapid and irretrievable transformations in the wake of the colossal and unprecedented upheaval and resettlement. Its causes, courses and consequences have long been the subjects of research, analysis and interpretation. It is a Jewish phenomenon. Even now the effects of the migrations upon our lives and upon the future nature of Jewish existence cannot be fully assessed or with any great confidence foreshadowed.

At the height of the emigration there were many acute scholars and observers who held the great mass of Jews in Eastern Europe to be a fit collective candidate for autonomy. A careful historian like Simon Dubnow saw in the Jewry of the Pale of Settlement a nationality in some respects analogous to the impressive array of nationalities seeking forms of recognition, independence or autonomy inside or outside the two empires. Of course in the Jewish case there were differences – the Jewish messianic belief, a strange history of persecution, a lively sense of international Jewish kinship, the religious definition of Jew. But to Dubnow the Jews were such a deeply rooted and 'permanent' feature of the European scene, and stoutly exhibited so many indices of an entire and distinct Yiddish-based civilization, that it seemed natural and prudent to look askance upon the new-fangled and speculative movement called Zionism. After all, here in Eastern Europe was reality, with a sure guaranty derived from land, numbers, culture and almost a thousand years of continuity. The Germans killed the aged Dubnow during their eastward advance in 1941.

Again and again Jews have figured prominently in the hidden agenda of providence. They and mankind have marvelled at the consequences, when they have not been appalled by them.

INTEGRATION AND DISTINCTIVENESS

The contrasts in Jewish history are many and great. The intense international kinship involved and involves a deep family-like concern extending far beyond the immediate environment. At the same time there has been, and remains, a widespread wish, even a yearning, for acceptance into the normality of that local environment. This contrast or combination is the key to much of the special flavour which envelops Jewish history. It is part of the substance of Jewish life.

This contrast is linked with another contrast: namely a marked sense of otherness combined with a highly sensitive and prickly response to any emphasis upon that otherness by the wider society. The more integrated the Jews became, the greater the effort in public relations. The great industry of extolling the Jewish contribution to mankind began in the age of Jewish emancipation.

Heinrich Graetz's many-volumed *History of the Jews* appeared between 1853 and 1876. This monumental work was the first Jewish history of the Jewish people in the modern style. It was based upon the latest research and was a companion volume to the emancipation. In his Preface to the well-known English translation from the German in 1891, Graetz defined his objective in terms which belong instantly to his own era.

'It is the heartfelt aspiration of the author', he wrote,

> that this historical work in its English garb may attain its object of putting an end to the hostile bearing against the Jewish race, so that it may no longer be begrudged the peculiar sphere whereto it has been predestined through the events and sorrows of thousands of years, and it may be permitted to fulfil its appointed mission without molestation.

Every word of this passage reveals the age, with its new Jewish dawn, the rising new anti-Semitism, the continuing conscious sense of Jewish mission, the optimistic belief in the healing power of time, and the importance attached to the example of the English-speaking world.

Graetz's emphasis upon the Jewish strands in Western civilization and upon the purposes of Jewish separateness aroused long and vocal opposition in Germany from those elements in society (notably the influential historian and right-wing German nationalist, Von Treitschke) who objected both to the nature and extent of Jewish influence (past and present) and to the cultivation of Jewish separateness.

How different was the approach to Jewish history of what came to be called the Jerusalem school of Jewish history.[1] It centred on the Hebrew University. Its main founder was Professor Benzion Dinur (Dinaburg). Whatever may have been the diverse nuances within that circle, its strong national consciousness inclined its adherents to look into all stages of Jewish history for movements towards national revival. They tested the strength and significance of an epoch by reference to that feature. Other streams of life and thought tended to be treated as less truly creative and as somewhat artificial.

Some historians expressly repudiated any notion of the inauthenticity of the Diaspora. There continue to be, both in the realms of scholarship and in the sphere of internal Jewish politics, divergencies of outlook on this score. Interpretations concerning the character and direction of Jewish history merge in the public forum with assumptions and conclusions concerning the survival capacity of Diaspora communities, the ultimate worthwhileness of Diaspora goals, and the nature of the Israel–Diaspora partnership.

In the course of one short generation, ending around the 1920s, there were presented to the Jewish people, with comparative historical suddenness, a galaxy of options as to what the Jews were, what their history signified, and whither they should go, physically, socially and intellectually. The Orthodox emancipationists, the Reform emancipationists, the political Zionists, the Achad Ha'amists, the cultural Yiddishists and the socialists all had their respective ideals, remedies and heroes.

The Jewish historian probes these conflicting and at times overlapping cadres of response to the Jewish predicament, and seeks their sources and effects. He finds himself, as the protagonists of these various ideologies found themselves, engaged in the study of elemental questions – as to what the Jew is, what (if any) is his particular role, and what is the rationale for his distinctive survival.

The poignancy and relevance of such questions are accentuated by other contrasts in Jewish history. They include the contrasts between the influence of Judaism and the millennial Jewish powerlessness; between the long inner belief in ancient covenants and the external reality of enmity and oppression; and between the pariah-like quality attached to the Jews over the centuries of Christian power and the continued Jewish sense of chosenness for high purposes for all mankind. The effects of these contrasts upon

310

the Jewish mind and upon Jewish–Gentile relations belong to the pith of Jewish historical study. There are no parallels.

Some Jewish historians decry any emphasis upon the martyrology of our history. Sir Lewis Namier, the Lithuanian-born political Zionist, chose not to study Jewish history. That eminent British historian declared that this was because there seemed to him to be no Jewish history except martyrology. It was an incautious observation, reflecting his deep resentment over the Jew's historical inferior status and his own conviction as to the irremediability of anti-Semitism. He could not bear to get to close quarters with the Jewish past, during which others had lorded it over the Jews who seemed to him either to justify that situation and/or await its replacements from outer space.

SUFFERING AND SURVIVAL

When the Jewish historian turns to the tragedies of Jewish history he meets the core of Jewish experience and enters into the mystery of Jewish survival. It is difficult for him not to become poet and philosopher as well. Writing in Berlin in 1855 in a famous history of the Jewish liturgy, Leopold Zunz referred in deeply moving terms to this aspect of the Jewish record. Some national literatures, he commented, are deemed rich because they possess some great classical tragedies. 'What place', he enquired, 'should be assigned to a tragedy extending over 15 centuries and composed and enacted by the heroes themselves?'

When the crusading armies travelled across Europe to try to wrest the Holy Land from the Turk, their enthusiasm, hate and avarice were first wreaked upon individual Jewish communities *en route*. The huge total of Jewish deaths can only be surmised. The 'crusading' process pushed Jews eastwards and contributed much to the creation of large Jewish settlements in Poland, most of which, in the eighteenth century, came under Czarist rule.

The impact of the deeds of the crusaders upon the whole range of Jewish history is incalculable. Many later historical events which had immediate and dire results for Jews added to and complicated the far-reaching effects of the earlier episodes.

The Cossack pogroms of the seventeenth century played a vital part in the reception and expansion of the false messianic movement of Shabbatai Zevi. The collapse of that movement was an important factor in the inception and growth of the Chassidic movement in the eighteenth century, with considerable and continuing results.

The ritual murder charges in Damascus in 1840, and the cruelties which followed, shook the Western Jewish emancipationists. The charges appeared to gain credence in prominent quarters in Paris. London was not immune. Montefiore's success in obtaining a public disclaimer from the Sultan did not obscure the meaning of what had happened. The modern age was not free of the shadows from which Jews believed they were finally emerging. It was Ben Gurion's view that the Damascus Affair precipitated the movements of opinion which ultimately found expression in political Zionism.

AN ENDLESS TALE OF THE UNEXPECTED

Is it all merely historical change? To those for whom the here and now is not the whole story of life, the idea that there is an underlying purpose in history has a natural appeal. Our history is in conflict with every norm and general rule ever thought of by the interpreters of history. There is nowhere the remotest kind of comparison. It is an endless tale of the unexpected.

Jewish history has been the story of a condition: the Jewish condition. It has consisted of living in two worlds, one the everyday world, the other the meta-historical world. If history is indeed the visible part of a divine plan (for want of a better phrase), then we are all partners in the inscrutable process; that is to say all mankind. The belief that in the divine–human encounter the Jews have found themselves occupying a special role has run deep. The effect of this astounding, yet not implausible, idea has been substantial even upon many of those who were unable to adopt any such belief and who preferred, if they could, to free themselves from any sense of role. Jewish secularists (whatever that may connote) have remarkably often been creative visionaries, moralists or radical reformers. Their enthusiasms have a Jewish ring in content and style. Their certainty has sometimes been positively Chassidic, or should one say *mitnagdic*?

There has been another level on which Jews have lived in two worlds. It is closely related to the first. Jews have settled, mingled and become integrated. Yet there was always an awaiting. That has been the central feature of the Jewish condition. There has always been in the story of our people an incompleteness, a looking forward. It is an important element in the thinking of those Jews – and Christians – who have regarded the Jews as endowed with the task of bringing mankind nearer to righteousness.

That element is reflected in the profound regard attached to the biblical account of the divine covenant with Abraham. In that account, the whole world was to be blessed through his seed, whose ultimate inheritance in the 'Promised Land' was to be great and glorious. The promise was several times repeated in the biblical narrative to successors of Abraham. The Temple was seen as a promise, so too the messianic era. Even the various exiles were promises, as were the redemptions.

Even many of the Jewish emancipationist spokesmen found themselves unable to disown the restorationist idea. They felt that to do so would utterly transform Judaism. In no country was the connection between the Jewish present and the prayed-for Jewish restoration discussed more lengthily in public than in England. In reply to Gentile critics of the retention of the Jewish national idea, Jewish publicists in these debates – Reformers as well as Orthodox – declared that prayers for the Return related to a distant future and in no respect affected their patriotism, which was a moral duty for the Jew.

Some anti-Zionist successors to those mid-Victorian emancipationists, like their counterparts in other lands, based their opposition in part upon the belief that there was a divine promise that the latest exile, *Galut Edom*, would be brought to an end providentially. They regarded the Zionist enterprise as a blasphemous forcing of the divine hand. As for the Dispersion, that too had a promised purpose for the Jews were to be mankind's moral educators.

AT THE CENTRE OF WORLD HISTORY

Jews have lived, and continue to live, on the raw stage of history, taking little for granted. They are individually and collectively conscious of instant history and of the ceaseless drama of events. Not surprisingly, historians are eager to enquire into their special kind of problem-laden separateness, how it came about and why the Jews have wanted and want (if they do) to retain it. They are equally eager to enquire into their no less (though differently) problem-laden assimilation, in its varied forms and degrees. What has prompted it, what has flowed from it, and what have been the Jewish and Gentile reactions thereto? How peculiarly characteristic of Jewish life and history all such enquiries are!

In his Foreword to his *History of the Contemporary Jews* (1960), Solomon Grayzel observed: 'The Jews have always lived in the very centre of world events so that their experiences in any period have reflected the state of the human spirit.' What did that distinguished historian mean by that remarkable sentence? What is even more striking than the sentence is that it expressed a widely held sentiment bordering upon the platitudinous. It contains a plain acknowledged truth with the most profound implications, on which the whole world has long pondered, on which mankind continues to ponder and wonder, and from which friends and foes have drawn diverse conclusions, sometimes at a frightening price for Jews.

What Grayzel meant includes the following. Whether in Persian times (or even earlier) or in Greek days or under the Caesars and later, the Jews were and are at the confluence of events, geographically and/or ideologically. They were in at the birth of Christianity. They were in at the birth of Islam. They contributed significantly to the growth of capitalism and to the new economic order of the seventeenth and eighteenth centuries. They contributed with equal distinctiveness and significance to the revolutions in life and thought in two following centuries. They have made, and Jews continue to make, successive, distinctive and at times crucial contributions to the mind of man and to the social order, out of all proportion to numbers. At every stage Jews have evinced a marked analytical,speculative, innovative and at times astonishingly pragmatic turn of mind – all in a way connected with the effect of their special history and their heritage.

THE MORAL IDEA

Many causes are propounded for the Jewish goad to achievement, and many are proffered for Jewish success. Many causes are suggested for their calamities. The powerlessness of the Jews, and yet their massive influence, are among the fascinations of historians, whether the friendly, the critical or the plain curious.

When we ask what is Jewish history, we are asking what is a Jew. I am not talking about who is a Jew. That is a different subject. I am talking about the question as to what Jewishness consists of. What are the qualities without which nothing distinctively Jewish would remain? In short, what needs to be sustained when we talk of sustaining Jewish survival capacity? In spite of the polarization within Jewish life in contemporary history – and in some respects because of it – that question is increasingly relevant to communal planning in the Diaspora. The question is also increasingly relevant to the Israeli scene.

Jewish history has been concerned with the cultivation of moral ideas. They have been ideas for living whose validity and sanction have been ultimately outside the human scale. Jews have been involved in the projection of those ideas to such an extent that their role in history has been adjudged, within and without, to have acquired its special character because of them.

In the last analysis, Jewish history is the history of the human condition. Even when the metaphysical framework receded, the habits of mind, the sets of values, the assumptions about priorities were perceived to endure and to merit to endure, in the social interest of the civilized world.

A REMEMBERED FUTURE

The Jews long ago became specialists in waiting. Jewish historians are entitled, perhaps obliged, to examine the connections between the old waiting and its contemporary form and degree of fulfilment. They cannot realistically escape an investigation into the relationship between Judaism as the touchstone of Jewish life and other forms of Jewish expression, including Israel-orientated activity, which for some represent other touchstones which may have no intended connection with the creed and the lifestyle of Judaism. To the Jewish historian, history and prophecy are rarely far apart.

No other people has had to present and 'defend' its *raison d'être* for public scrutiny as have the Jews. For these past two centuries, and in some respects for a far longer period, almost every decade has added fresh nuances or complications to the debates on the issues of Jewish identity and purpose. Those issues, together with the responses thereto, have been and remain at the centre of Jewish historical study.

In a radio interview in November 1969, the late Jacob Herzog discussed the various influences which had effected his way of thinking. A significant extract was published posthumously in his *Speeches and Writings* (1975): 'In the literary field', he stated, 'I have been very influenced by Marcel Proust'. In the latter's work he detected 'the dimension of the influence of events on memory'. Proust was concerned with the impact upon memory and behaviour of times long since gone. This struck echoes in Rabbi Dr Herzog's own mind of the vast moulding effect on Jewish personality, outlook and aspiration exercised by the Jewish collective and individual memory of Jewish history.

The historical experience and massive continuity of the Jewish people have endowed the Jews with an extraordinarily strong self-consciousness and a most acute sensitivity. At all stages, that experience reflected and reinforced their character as a 'people that dwells alone' yet with a wider purpose. It is in connection with that duality, enshrined in their distinctive heritage, that what is peculiarly Jewish is to be found.

NOTE

1. Prominent among modern Israeli historians who do not share that school's interpretation of Jewish history is Professor L.P. Gartner, Emeritus Professor of Modern Jewish History at Tel Aviv University: L.P. Gartner, *History of the Jews in Modern Times* (2000), p. v.

Glossary

Beth (Batei) Din	The Jewish ecclesiastical court(s)
Beth Hamedrash	House of study, often also used for prayer
Chazan(im)/Hazan(im)	Cantor(s) leading the congregational service. Sometimes called Readers, and sometimes combined with the post of preacher
Cheder/Heder	'Room': classes for Jewish study
Chasidim/Hasidim	Adherents of religious movement among Jews dating from the latter part of the eighteenth century and marked by a heightened focus on piety tinged with mysticism and opposed by *mitnagedim* (opponents)
Choveve Zion	'Lovers of Zion': mainly religious group founded before the rise of political Zionism in favour of the settling of Jews in Palestine
Chupah	'Canopy': held over the bride and groom in the Jewish marriage ceremony called by this name
Galut Edom	Literally 'the Edom exile': the old rabbinic description of Jewish dispersion and exile following the capture of Jerusalem by the Romans (Edom was a term applied to Esau and his presumed descendants), and their destruction of the Temple in 70 CE.
Genilous Chasadim	Good deeds
Halacha/Halakha	Corpus of Jewish law

Kashrut	The system or observance of Jewish dietary laws
Kehilla	Jewish community or congregation
Malbish Arumim	'Clothing the naked'
Maskil(im)	Exponent(s) of Haskalah (enlightment), the new Jewish learning among westernised Jewish scholars in the eighteenth and nineteenth centuries
Mizrachism	Movement for religious Zionism
Matzo	Unleavened bread required for Pesach (Passover)
Meshivas Nephesh	'Restoring the soul'
Minyan	Quorum of ten adult males required for congregational prayers
Mitzva/Mitzvoth	Religious obligations; a term often used to describe an honour accorded to an individual during synagogue service
Mohel	Practitioner of the operation of circumcision
Mortara Case	Jewish child abducted and baptised in Bologna in 1858; intercessions by Montefiore and others in Rome failed to secure his return
Rosh Hakohel	Head (often honorific) of congregation; bestowed as a mark of honour
Shechita	The humane slaughter of animals for food as prescribed by Jewish law and performed by the Shochet
Talmud Torah	'Study of the Law': institute for Jewish religious instruction, usually larger and more formally organised than a Cheder
Territorialist Organisation (1905–25)	Founded by Zangwill to encourage settlement of Jews in territories, not necessarily Palestine
Torah Min Hashamaim	'Law from Heaven': this description of divine source of the Pentateuch has been variously interpreted
Yeshiva	'Sitting': college for rabbinic study, usually/mainly of the Talmud

Index

INDEX